THE FATAL THREE

CW00551304

M.E. BRADDON

THE FATAL THREE

Introduction by Jan Hewitt

SUTTON PUBLISHING

First published in this edition in 1997
Sutton Publishing Limited · Phoenix Mill
Thrupp · Stroud · Gloucestershire · GL5 2BU

Copyright © in this edition
Sutton Publishing Limited, 1997

Introduction copyright © Jan Hewitt, 1997

All rights reserved. No part of this publication may be reproduced, stored in a retrieval system, or transmitted, in any form, or by any means, electronic, mechanical, photocopying, recording or otherwise, without the prior permission of the publisher and copyright holder[s].

British Library Cataloguing in Publication Data

A catalogue record for this book is available from the British Library

ISBN 0-7509-1664-8

Cover picture: detail from Tea Time *by Jacques Jourdan (1880–1916)*
(Gavin Graham Gallery, London/Bridgeman Art Library, London)

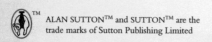 ALAN SUTTON™ and SUTTON™ are the
trade marks of Sutton Publishing Limited

Typeset in 10/11 pt Bembo Mono.
Typesetting and origination by
Sutton Publishing Limited
Printed in Great Britain by
The Guernsey Press Company Limited,
Guernsey, Channel Islands.

CONTENTS

BOOK THE FIRST
CLOTHO; OR SPINNING THE THREAD

BOOK THE SECOND

LACHESIS; OR THE METER OF DESTINY

BOOK THE THIRD

ATROPOS; OR THAT WHICH MUST BE

INTRODUCTION

Towards the end of 1888, the *Spectator* discussed *The Fatal Three* by Mary Elizabeth Braddon in a review of recent novels which also included *The Story of Charles Strange* by Mrs Henry Wood. Both women were well known as writers of sensation fiction and, after the success of Wilkie Collins' *The Woman in White* (1860), had played a major part in contributing to the emergence of the genre as a controversial literary phenomenon in the 1860s. In particular, Mary Braddon's prolific output, with fourteen three-volume novels published between 1862 and 1868 alone, came to epitomize 'sensationalism'; her life and work were focal areas for the controversy which surrounded it in that decade.

Although largely played out by the time *The Fatal Three* was written, some flavour of the earlier controversy lingers in the *Spectator*'s review, which described their work as that of 'two feminine writers who, for a quarter of a century or more, have been most successful in appealing to the tastes of the person who may be vaguely described as the average novel-reader.'[1] Its condescending tone implies a connection between 'the feminine' and certain types of popular literature which by the 1880s was becoming commonplace. Such literature was most immediately recognizable by its adherence to a specific formula:

> Both in the case of Miss Braddon and Mrs Henry Wood, this success was attained in the first instance mainly by the skilful invention and management of intricate plots and thrilling situations; and, if we remember rightly, it was in the criticism of their early novels that the word 'sensational' was first used as a critical epithet.[2]

As far as that criticism was concerned they had reason to remember rightly, for the *Spectator* had played its own part in fanning the flames of the 1860s controversy when it reviewed Braddon's *Lady Audley's Secret* in 1862 as a novel drawing on predictable forms associated with the melodramatic literature of popular tastes. Such writers, the review suggested, were in danger of pandering to the 'classes who love the horrible and the

1   *The Spectator*, vol. 61, 1888, p. 1475.
2   Ibid.

grotesque', and it feared that they might not remain content with 'their true place in literature, which is not above the basement.'[3] The *Spectator*'s later, dismissive, reference to 'the average novel reader' indicates how far, by the late 1880s, this elitism had come to be expressed in terms of a cultural, rather than the more overtly social, discourse.

In the 1860s, however, such rhetoric had been shared by other critics, and behind it lay real anxieties. The heady mixture of crime, mystery and illicit sex which provided escapism for the lower classes in many of their popular entertainments was, by mid-century, losing the largely ephemeral status by virtue of which it had escaped containment by 'polite' culture. Through the circulating libraries and railway bookstalls, sensation fiction was reaching a wider reading public, avid for its thrills. Although access to publication, heavily dominated by the requirements of the circulating libraries, demanded that its racier content be circumscribed in various ways, the resulting hybrid exacerbated rather than allayed conservative fears. Typical frameworks of conventional morality which underlay 'sensational' excesses – such as the restorative payoff of good for evil when Robert Audley ousts the transgressive Lady Audley from his uncle's family in *Lady Audley's Secret*, and himself marries the excellent but comparatively insipid Clara – tended to confirm those fears. Grafting melodramatic action onto the concerns of the bourgeois domestic novel constituted a decided affront to establishment mores.

Sensation fiction's exciting formula of sex, crime and marital intrigue, set against the apparent stability of upper middle-class life, was a combination seen by critics as particularly dangerous. It confused moral criteria by stimulating its readers' passions while simultaneously disparaging everyday life. A *Christian Remembrancer* review of 1863 notes:

> Sensation writing is an appeal to the nerves rather than to the heart. . . . We suppose that the true sensation novel feels the popular pulse with this view alone . . . and willingly and designedly draws a picture of life which shall make reality insipid and the routine of ordinary existence intolerable to the imagination.[4]

Thus the moral dictates of truth and realism central to the progressive aesthetics of mid-Victorian culture were felt to be under attack. For the greater part of the 1860s, aspects of this controversy occupied space in

---

3   *The Spectator*, 1862. Quoted by Robert Lee Wolff in *Sensational Victorian: The Life and Fiction of Mary Elizabeth Braddon* (New York and London: Garland Publishing Inc., 1979) p. 6.

4   *Christian Remembrancer*, vol. 46, 1863, p. 210.

the columns of the heavyweight quarterlies, and excited discussion in the weekly press. A large proportion was directed at the work of Mary Elizabeth Braddon.

This was partly because of the sheer number of her novels which appeared in that decade. Nor did those numbers decline as controversy faded. By the year *The Fatal Three* was published, she had over fifty novels as well as numerous articles, reviews and plays to her name. During her life, between 1835 and 1915, Braddon wrote around eighty-five novels, establishing herself as one of the country's most popular writers and attaining a comfortable lifestyle. By contemporary standards, however, her life was as unconventional as it was energetic.

Brought up by her mother after her father's disappearance when she was five, Braddon first embarked on a relatively short-lived stage career to support them both, under the name of Mary Seyton. A relish for the dramatic continued in her fiction, encouraged and promoted by her publisher, John Maxwell, whom she met around 1860. She was soon living with Maxwell, taking on the role of stepmother to his five children by his first wife, who was incarcerated in a Dublin asylum, and bearing him a further five. They were not married until after the death of the first Mrs Maxwell in 1874. Under such circumstances, it is not hard to see how the tensions between the constraints of surface respectability and the skeletons of family life might well offer obvious subject matter for scrutiny within her fiction. However, although the scenarios of Braddon's novels are invariably those of familial and marital intrigue, it would be wrong to see them as predominantly self-obsessed. The continuing demand for sensation fiction in the 1860s, and the debates surrounding it, indicate more complex connections between the genre and its reception.

A major facet of debate concerned the female protagonists of sensation novels, especially when drawn by a female author. That Lucy Audley, outwardly a perfect wife unmasked as a liar, bigamist, arsonist and would-be murderer, should be particularly cited in criticisms of sensation fiction is unsurprising. In the aftermath of the Divorce Act of 1857 (Matrimonial Causes Act), the public appetite for press coverage of scandal can be closely connected, as indeed it was at the time, to its appetite for sensation fiction. However, what is also suggested is the extent of interest in ideas about marriage and the moral absolutes of 'proper' femininity which contributed to the bourgeois ideal. In an article in the *North British Review*, for example, W. Fraser Rae was correspondingly emphatic about the incredibility of *Lady Audley's Secret* and its depiction of Lucy:

> In drawing her, the authoress may have intended to portray a female
> Mephistopheles; but, if so, she should have known that a woman
> cannot fill such a part. The nerves with which Lady Audley could

meet unmoved the friend of the man she has murdered, are the
nerves of a Lady Macbeth who is half unsexed, and not those of the
timid, gentle, innocent creature Lady Audley is represented as being.[5]

Ultimately, issues of representation were at stake as much as those of
content. However, from such 'purely literary' judgements as Rae
professed to be making, it was inevitably a short step towards more
personal allusions to the author's own background. Of particular note
was that meted out by an anonymous reviewer in an otherwise
important discussion in *Blackwood's Magazine* in 1867, later identified
(though never by Braddon herself) as the novelist Margaret Oliphant.

Oliphant had written a number of times on sensation fiction, but her
1867 article launched fresh attacks. Though she acknowledged Braddon's
considerable achievements, the credit given was decidedly double-edged,
her implication being that such fiction could only be written by someone
who knew 'the attraction of impropriety'. As discussion touched on
Braddon's latest novel, Oliphant's comments became overtly personalized:

> . . . there is something in *Rupert Godwin* which is Miss Braddon's
> own. When the poor widow's virtuous and lovely daughter earns her
> scanty living on the stage, she is made the victim of one of those
> romantic abductions which used to be so frequent in novels . . . it
> does her no harm either in reputation or anything else, . . . but it is
> purely original and not copied.[6]

Despite such insinuations Oliphant's analysis is prescient in emphasizing
the genre's crucial connections with female literary concerns.
Recognizing the extent to which Charlotte Brontë's experiments had
changed the direction of the modern novel, Oliphant deplored its effects
upon Braddon and, through her influence, on a new generation of
women writers such as Rhoda Broughton, and particularly on the
depiction of their heroines.

On a number of counts therefore, the *Spectator*'s references in 1888 to
'feminine writers' and 'average novel-readers' had more resonance than
might initially be supposed. The tripartite equation with 'sensationalism'
which would, however, have confirmed the 1860s rhetoric was, in the
case of *The Fatal Three*, largely repudiated; Braddon's more notorious
novels such as *Lady Audley's Secret* and *Aurora Floyd* were tacitly bypassed
as comparisons were drawn with her earlier work:

5   *North British Review*, vol. 43, 1865, p. 96.
6   *Blackwood's Magazine*, vol. 102, 1867, pp. 263-264.

In one of her earliest novels, *The Doctor's Wife*, Miss Braddon proved herself able to dispense almost entirely with what was called sensationalism, and yet to excite and maintain the reader's interest, — an experiment which she has since more than once repeated, and which she repeats in *The Fatal Three* . . .[7]

By the 1880s, the representation of women and marriage, though differently inflected, was as live an issue as in the 1860s. This may be why the *Spectator* lapses over-readily into the earlier rhetoric, obscuring its focus when it discusses Mildred Greswold as coming 'perilously near to wrecking her own and her husband's happiness'. It felt sympathy would be limited for

> . . . the more mature woman . . . who sacrifices the peace of a noble man and a loving, faithful husband, partly to her 'views', and partly to a fancy which might have been scattered to the winds by an hour's sensible examination of the evidence on which it rested.[8]

Mildred's character is the antithesis of what Oliphant described as the 'innocent indecency' of the sensation heroine of 1867. Her quest to uncover the truth of both her father's past and her husband's earlier marriage, amid widespread assumptions of double standards and hypocrisy, is in fact typically 'sensational' in negotiating its readers' pleasurable collusion with the resolution of its mysteries. Yet Mildred's strength of purpose also has affinities with certain feminist stances in the late Victorian purity debates and, in her, the regenerative power of purity is both extolled and offered for scrutiny. Her similarities with, yet differences from, the familiar sensation heroine uses narrative tension between close identification and the more critical distance, and develops the genre's propensity for encapsulating social debate.

This is most intriguing when seen in terms of the ban on marriage with a dead wife's sister, the focus around which the plot is constructed. Finally rescinded in 1907, the Act itself was a fitful subject of controversy throughout the nineteenth century where the sacrifice of emotional well-being took second place to issues of property.[9] As women were often felt to suffer most acutely from the law, it too became part of the context of their changing social position. Without being in any way overtly partisan

---

7   *The Spectator*, vol. 61, 1888, p. 1475.
8   Ibid.
9   See, for example, Jeffrey Weeks, *Sex, Politics and Society: The Regulation of Sexuality since 1800* (London: Longman, 1989), pp. 30–1, and Pat Jalland, *Women, Marriage and Politics 1860–1914* (Oxford: Clarendon Press, 1986), p. 112.

then, *The Fatal Three*'s popularity – particularly with a female audience – ensured its participation within a wider dynamic.

If the stigma of sensationalism remained the mark of an unacceptable standard, by the late 1880s the cultural ground was shifting to accommodate the genre – or what was defined as the best of it – on somewhat altered terms. Despite the *Spectator*'s qualifications, it too declared itself 'pleased and satisfied' by the novel:

> The author's workmanship is as careful and thorough as ever; the characters stand well upon their feet; and . . . the story is thoroughly interesting.[10]

And 'thoroughly interesting' it remains. For if, over a century later, *The Fatal Three* pleases us still with its story, by looking beyond the pleasures of its immediately 'sensational' boundaries, its later readers can also look into the wider processes of a culture reading itself.

JAN HEWITT, 1997

Further Reading

Kate Flint, *The Woman Reader 1837–1914*, Oxford: Clarendon Press, 1995.

Winifred Hughes, *The Maniac in the Cellar: The Sensation Novel of the 1860s*, Princeton N.J.: Princeton University Press, 1980.

Lyn Pykett, *The 'Improper' Feminine: The Women's Sensation Novel and the New Woman Writing*, London: Routledge, 1992.

Robert Lee Wolff, *Sensational Victorian: The Life and Fiction of Mary Elizabeth Braddon*, New York: Garland Publishing Inc., 1979.

10 *The Spectator*, vol. 61, 1888, p. 1475.

BOOK THE FIRST
CLOTHO; OR SPINNING THE THREAD

CHAPTER I

'WE HAVE BEEN SO HAPPY'

'I'm afraid she will be a terrible bore,' said the lady, with a slight pettishness in the tone of a voice that was naturally sweet.

'How can she bore us, love? She is only a child, and you can do what you like with her,' said the gentleman.

'My dear John, you have just admitted that she is between thirteen and fourteen – a great deal more than a child – a great overgrown girl, who will want to be taken about in the carriage, and to come down to the drawing-room, and who will be always in the way. Had she been a child of Mildred's age, and a playfellow for Mildred, I should not have objected half so much.'

'I'm very sorry you object; but I have no doubt she will be a playfellow for Mildred all the same, and that she will not mind spending a good deal of her life in the schoolroom.'

'Evidently, John, you don't know what girls of fourteen are. I do.'

'Naturally, Maud, since it is not so many years since you yourself were that age.'

The lady smiled, touched ever so slightly by the suggestion of youth, which was gratifying to the mother of a seven-year-old daughter.

The scene was a large old-fashioned drawing-room, in an old-fashioned street in the very best quarter of the town, bounded on the west by Park Lane and on the east by Grosvenor Square. The lady was sitting at her own particular table, in her favourite window, in the summer gloaming; the gentleman was standing with his back to the velvet-draped mantelpiece. The room was full of flowers and prettinesses of every kind, and offered unmistakable evidence of artistic taste and large means in its possessors.

The lady was young and fair, a tall slip of a woman, who afforded a Court milliner the very best possible scaffolding for expensive gowns. The gentleman was middle-aged and stout, with strongly-marked features and a resolute, straightforward expression. The lady was the daughter of an Irish peer; the gentleman was a commoner, whose fortune had been made in a great wholesale firm, which had still its mammoth warehouses near St Paul's Churchyard, and its manufactory at Lyons, but with which

John Fausset had no longer any connection. He had taken his capital out
of the business, and had cleansed himself from the stain of commercial
dealings before he married the Honourable Maud Donfrey, third
daughter of Lord Castle-Connell.

Miss Donfrey had given herself very willingly to the commoner, albeit
he was her senior by more than twenty years, and, in her own
deprecating description of him, was quite out of her set. She liked him
not a little for his own sake, and for the power his strong will exercised
over her own weaker nature; but she liked him still better for the sake of
wealth which seemed unlimited.

She was nineteen at the time of her marriage, and she had been
married nine years. Those years had brought the Honourable Mrs Fausset
only one child, the seven-year-old daughter playing about the room in
the twilight; and maternity had offered very little hindrance to the lady's
pleasures as a woman of fashion. She had been indulged to the uttermost
by a fond and admiring husband; and now for the first time in his life
John Fausset had occasion to ask his wife a favour, which was not granted
too readily. It must be owned that the favour was not a small one,
involving nothing less than the adoption of an orphan girl in whose fate
Mr Fausset was interested.

'It is very dreadful,' sighed Mrs Fausset, as if she was speaking of an
earthquake. 'We have been so happy alone together – you and I and
Mildred.'

'Yes, dearest, when we have been alone, which, you will admit, has not
been very often.'

'O, but visitors do not count. They come and go. They don't belong
to us. This dreadful girl will be one of us; or she will expect to be. I feel
as if the golden circle of home-life were going to be broken.'

'Not broken, Maud, only expanded.'

'O, but you can't expand it by letting in a stranger. Had the mother no
people of her own; no surroundings whatever; nobody but you who
could be appealed to for this wretched girl?' inquired Mrs Fausset,
fanning herself wearily, as she lolled back in her low chair.

She wore a loose cream-coloured gown, of softest silk and Indian
embroidery, and there were diamond stars trembling amongst her
feathery golden hair. The flowing garment in which she had dined alone
with her husband was to be changed presently for white satin and old
Mechlin lace, in which she was to appear at three evening parties; but in
the meantime, having for once in a way dined at home, she considered
her mode of life intensely domestic.

The seven-year-old daughter was roaming about with her doll,
sometimes in one drawing-room, sometimes in another. There were
three, opening into each other, the innermost room half conservatory,

shadowy with palms and tropical ferns. Mildred was enjoying herself in the quiet way of children accustomed to play alone, looking at the pretty things upon the various tables, peering in at the old china figures in the cabinets – the ridiculous Chelsea shepherd and shepherdess; the Chelsea lady in hawking costume, with a falcon upon her wrist; the absurd lambs, and more absurd foliage; and the Bow and Battersea ladies and gentlemen, with their blunt features and coarse complexions. Mildred was quite happy, prowling about and looking at things in silent wonder; turning over the leaves of illustrated books, and lifting the lids of gold and enamelled boxes; trying to find out the uses and meanings of things. Sometimes she came back to the front drawing-room, and seated herself on a stool at her mother's feet, solemnly listening to the conversation, following it much more earnestly, and comprehending it much better, than either her father or mother would have supposed possible.

To stop up after nine o'clock was an unwonted joy for Mildred, who went to bed ordinarily at seven. The privilege had been granted in honour of the rare occasion – a *tête-à-tête* dinner in the height of the London season.

'Is there no one else who could take her?' repeated Mrs Fausset impatiently, finding her husband slow to answer.

'There is really no one else upon whom the poor child has any claim.'

'Cannot she remain at school? You could pay for her schooling, of course. I should not mind that.'

This was generous in a lady who had brought her husband a nominal five thousand pounds, and who spent his money as freely as if it had been water.

'She cannot remain at school. She is a kind of girl who cannot get on at school. She needs home influences.'

'You mean that she is a horrid rebellious girl who has been expelled from a school, and whom I am to take because nobody else will have her.'

'You are unjust and ungenerous, Maud. The girl has not been expelled. She is a girl of peculiar temper, and very strong feelings, and she is unhappy amidst the icy formalities of an unexceptional school. Perhaps had she been sent to some struggling schoolmistress in a small way of business she might have been happier. At any rate, she is not happy, and as her people were friends of mine in the past I should like to make her girlhood happy, and to see her well married, if I can.'

'But are there not plenty of other people in the world who would do all you want if you paid them. I'm sure I should not grudge the money.'

'It is not a question of money. The girl has money of her own. She is an heiress.'

'Then she is a ward in Chancery, I suppose?'

'No, she is my ward. I am her sole trustee.'

'And you really want to have her here in our own house, and at The Hook, too, I suppose. Always with us wherever we go.'

'That is what I want – until she marries. She will be twenty in five years, and in all probability she will marry before she is twenty. It is not a life-long sacrifice that I am asking from you, Maud; and, remember, it is the first favour I have ever asked you.'

'Let the little girl come, mother,' pleaded Mildred, clambering on to her mother's knee.

She had been sitting with her head bent over her doll, and her hair falling forward over her face like golden rain, for the last ten minutes. Mrs Fausset had no suspicion that the child had been listening, and this sudden appeal was startling to the last degree.

'Wisdom has spoken from my darling's rosy lips,' said Fausset, coming over to the window and stooping to kiss his child.

'My dear John, you must know that your wish is a law to me,' replied his wife, submitting all at once to the inevitable. 'If you are really bent upon having your ward here she must come.'

'I am really bent upon it.'

'Then let her come as soon as you like.'

'I will bring her to-morrow.'

'And I shall have some one to play with,' said Mildred, in her baby voice; 'I shall give her my second best doll.'

'Not your best, Mildred?' asked the father, smiling at her.

Mildred reflected for a few moments.

'I'll wait and see what she is like,' she said, 'and if she is very nice I will give her quite my best doll. The one you brought me from Paris, father. The one that walks and talks.'

Maud Fausset sighed, and looked at the little watch dangling on her chatelaine.

'A quarter to ten! How awfully late for Mildred to be up! And it is time I dressed. I hope you are coming with me, John. Ring the bell, please. Come, Mildred.'

The child kissed her father with a hearty, clinging kiss which meant a world of love, and then she picked up her doll – not the walking-talking machine from Paris, but a friendly, old-fashioned wax and bran personage – and trotted out of the room, hanging on to her mother's gown.

'How sweet she is!' muttered the father, looking after her fondly; 'and what a happy home it has been! I hope the coming of that other one won't make any difference.'

CHAPTER II

FAY

Mrs Fausset's three parties, the last of which was a very smart ball, kept her away from home until the summer sun was rising above Grosvenor Square, and the cocks were crowing in the mews behind Upper Parchment Street. Having been so late in the morning, Mrs Fausset ignored breakfast, and only made her appearance in time for lunch, when her husband came in from his ride. He had escorted her to the first of her parties, and had left her on the way to the second, to go and finish his evening in the House, which he found much more interesting than society.

They met at luncheon, and talked of their previous night's experiences, and of indifferent matters. Not a word about the expected presence which was so soon to disturb their domestic calm. Mr Fausset affected cheerfulness, yet was evidently out of spirits. He looked round the picturesque old oak dining-room wistfully; he strolled into the inner room, with its dwarf bookcases, pictures, and bronzes, its cosy corner behind a sixfold Indian screen, a century-old screen, bought at Christie's out of a famous collection. He surveyed this temple of domestic peace, and wondered within himself whether it would be quite as peaceful when a new presence was among them.

'Surely a girl of fourteen can make no difference,' he argued, 'even if she has a peculiar temper. If she is inclined to be troublesome, she shall be made to keep herself to herself. Maud shall not be rendered unhappy by her.'

He went out soon after lunch, and came home again at afternoon tea-time in a hansom, with a girl in a black frock. A four-wheeler followed, with a large trunk and two smaller boxes. The splendid creatures in knee-breeches and powder who opened the door had been ordered to deny their mistress to everybody, so Mrs Fausset was taking tea alone in her morning-room.

The morning-room occupied the whole front of the second floor, a beautiful room with three windows, the centre a large bow jutting out over empty space. This bow-window had been added when Mr Fausset married, on a suggestion from his *fiancée*. It spoiled the external appearance of the house, but it made the room delightful. For furniture and decoration there was everything pretty, novel, eccentric, and expensive that Maud Fausset had ever been able to think of. She had only stopped her caprices and her purchases when the room would not hold another thing of beauty. There was a confusion of form and colour, but the general effect was charming; and Mrs Fausset, in a loose white muslin gown, suited the room, just as the room suited Mrs Fausset.

She was sitting in the bow-window, in a semi-circle of flowers and amidst the noises of the West End world, waiting for her husband and the new-comer, nervous and apprehensive. The scarlet Japanese tea-table stood untouched, the water bubbling in the quaint little bronze tea-kettle, swinging between a pair of rampant dragons.

She started as the door opened, but kept her seat. She did not want to spoil the new-comer by an undue appearance of interest.

John Fausset came into the room, leading a pale girl dressed in black. She was tall for her age, and very thin, and her small face had a pinched look, which made the great black eyes look larger. She was a peculiar-looking girl, with an olive tint in her complexion which hinted at a lineage not altogether English. She was badly dressed in the best materials, and had a look of never having been much cared for since she was born.

'This is Fay,' said Mr Fausset, trying to be cheerful.

His wife held out her hand, which the girl took coldly, but not shyly. She had an air of being perfectly self-possessed.

'Her name is Fay, is it? What a pretty name! By the bye, you did not tell me her surname.'

'Did I not? Her name is Fausset. She is a distant relation of my family.'

'I did not understand that last night,' said Mrs Fausset, with a puzzled air. 'You only talked of a friend.'

'Was that so? I should have said a family connection. Yes, Fay and I are namesakes, and kindred.'

He patted the girl's shoulder caressingly, and made her sit down by the little red table in front of the tea-cups, and cakes, and buns. The buns reminded him of his daughter.

'Where is Mildred?'

'She is at her music-lesson; but she will be here in a minute or two, no doubt,' answered his wife.

'Poor little mite, to have to begin lessons so soon; the chubby little fingers stuck down upon the cold hard keys. The piano is so uninviting at seven years old; such a world of labour for such a small effect. If she could turn a barrel-organ, with a monkey on the top, I'm sure she would like music ever so much better; and after a year or two of grinding it would dawn upon her that there was something wanting in that kind of music, and then she would attack the piano of her own accord, and its difficulties would not seem so hopelessly uninteresting. Are you fond of lessons, Fay?'

'I hate them,' answered the girl, with vindictive emphasis.

'And I suppose you hate books too?' said Mrs Fausset, rather scornfully.

'No, I love books.'

She looked about the spacious room, curiously, with admiring eyes. People who came from very pretty rooms of their own were lost in admiration at Mrs Fausset's morning-room, with its heterogeneous styles of art – here Louis Seize, there Japanese; Italian on one side, Indian on the other. What a dazzling effect, then, it must needs have upon this girl, who had spent the last five years of her life amidst the barren surroundings of a suburban school!

'What a pretty room!' she exclaimed at last.

'Don't you think my wife was made to live in pretty rooms?' asked Fausset, touching Maud's delicate hand as it moved among the tea-things.

'She is very pretty herself,' said Fay, bluntly.

'Yes, and all things about her should be pretty. This thing, for instance,' as Mildred came bounding into the room, and clambered on her father's knee. 'This is my daughter, Fay, and your playfellow, if you know how to play.'

'I'm afraid I don't, for they always snubbed us for anything like play,' answered the stranger, 'but Mildred shall teach me, if she will.'

She had learnt the child's name from Mr Fausset during the drive from Streatham Common to Upper Parchment Street.

Mildred stretched out her little hand to the girl in black with somewhat of a patronising air. She had lived all her little life among bright colours and beautiful objects, in a kind of butterfly world; and she concluded that this pale girl in sombre raiment must needs be poor and unhappy. She looked her prettiest, smiling down at the stranger from her father's shoulder, where she hung fondly. She looked like a cherub in a picture by Rubens, red-lipped, with eyes of azure, and flaxen hair just touched with gold, and a complexion of dazzling lily and carnation-colour suffused with light.

'I mean to give you my very best doll,' she said.

'You darling, how I shall adore you!' cried the strange girl impulsively, rising from her seat at the tea-table, and clasping Mildred in her arms.

'That is as it should be,' said Fausset, patting Fay's shoulder affectionately. 'Let there be a bond of love between you two.'

'And will you play with me, and learn your lessons with me, and sleep in my room?' asked Mildred coaxingly.

'No, darling. Fay will have a room of her own,' said Mrs Fausset, replying to the last inquiry. 'It is much nicer for girls to have rooms to themselves.'

'No, it isn't,' answered Mildred, with a touch of petulance that was pretty in so lovely a child. 'I want Fay to sleep with me. I want her to tell me stories every night.'

'You have mother to tell you stories, Mildred,' said Mrs Fausset, already inclined to be jealous.

'Not very often. Mother goes to parties almost every night.'

'Not at The Hook, love.'

'O, but at The Hook there's always company. Why can't I have Fay to tell me stories every night?' urged the child persistently.

'I don't see why they should not be together, Maud,' said Mr Fausset, always prone to indulge Mildred's lightest whim.

'It is better that Fay should have a room of her own, for a great many reasons,' replied his wife, with a look of displeasure.

'Very well, Maud, so be it,' he answered, evidently desiring to conciliate her. 'And which room is Fay to have?'

'I have given her Bell's room.'

Mr Fausset's countenance fell.

'Bell's room – a servant's room!' – he repeated blankly.

'It is very inconvenient for Bell, of course,' said Mrs Fausset. 'She will have to put up with an extra bed in the housemaid's room; and as she has always been used to a room of her own, she made herself rather disagreeable about the change.'

Mr Fausset was silent, and seemed thoughtful. Mildred had pulled Fay away from the table and led her to a distant window, where a pair of Virginian love-birds were twittering in their gilded cage, half hidden amidst the bank of feathery white spirea and yellow marguerites which filled the recess.

'I should like to see the room,' said Fausset presently, when his wife had put down her teacup.

'My dear John, why should you trouble yourself about such a detail?'

'I want to do my duty to the girl – if I can.'

'I think you might trust such a small matter to *me*, or even to my housekeeper,' Maud Fausset answered with an offended air. 'However, you are quite at liberty to make a personal inspection. Bell is very particular, and any room she occupied is sure to be nice. But you can judge for yourself. The room is on the same floor as Mildred's.'

This last remark implied that to occupy any apartment on that floor must be a privilege.

'But not with the same aspect.'

'Isn't it? No, I suppose not. The windows look the other way,' said Mrs Fausset innocently.

She was not an over-educated person. She adored Keats, Shelley, and Browning, and talked about them learnedly in a way; but she hardly knew the points of the compass.

She sauntered out of the room, a picture of languid elegance in her flowing muslin gown. There were flowers on the landing, and a scarlet Japanese screen to fence off the stairs that went downward, and a blue-and-gold Algerian curtain to hide the upward flight. This second floor was Mrs Fausset's particular domain. Her bedroom and bathroom and dressing-room were all on this floor. Mr Fausset lived there also, but seemed to be there on sufferance.

She pulled aside the Algerian curtain, and they went up to the third story. The two front rooms were Mildred's bedroom and schoolroom. The bedroom-door was open, revealing an airy room with two windows brightened by outside flower-boxes, full of gaudy red geraniums and snow-white marguerites, a gay-looking room, with a pale blue paper and a blue-and-cream-colour carpet. A little brass bed, with lace curtains, for Mildred – an iron bed, without curtains, for Mildred's maid.

The house was like many old London houses, more spacious than it looked outside. There were four or five small rooms at the back occupied by servants, and it was one of those rooms – a very small room looking into a mews – which Mr Fausset went to inspect.

It was not a delightful room. There was an outside wall at right-angles with the one window which shut off the glory of the westering sun. There was a forest of chimney-pots by way of prospect. There was not even a flower-box to redeem the dinginess of the outlook. The furniture was neat, and the room was spotlessly clean; but as much might be said of a cell in Portland Prison. A narrow iron bedstead, a couple of cane chairs, a common mahogany chest of drawers in the window, and on the chest of drawers a white toilet-cover and a small mahogany looking-glass; a deal washstand and a zinc bath. These are not luxurious surroundings; and Mr Fausset's countenance did not express approval.

'I'm sure it is quite as nice a room as she would have at any boarding-school,' said his wife, answering that disapproving look.

'Perhaps; but I want her to feel as if she were not at school, but at home.'

'She can have a prettier room at The Hook, I daresay, though we are short of bedrooms even there – if she is to go to The Hook with us.'

'Why, of course she is to go with us. She is to live with us till she marries.'

Mrs Fausset sighed, and looked profoundly melancholy.

'I don't think we shall get her married very easily,' she said.

'Why not?' asked her husband quickly, looking at her anxiously as he spoke.

'She is so remarkably plain.'

'Did she strike you so? I think her rather pretty, or at least interesting. She has magnificent eyes.'

'So has an owl in an ivy-bush,' exclaimed Mrs Fausset petulantly. 'Those great black eyes in that small pale face are positively repulsive. However, I don't want to depreciate her. She is of your kith and kin, and you are interested in her; so we must do the best we can. I only hope Mildred will get on with her.'

This conversation took place upon the stairs. Mr Fausset was at the morning-room door by this time. He opened it, and saw his daughter in the sunlit window among the flowers, with her arm round Fay's neck.

'They have begun very well,' he said.

'Children are so capricious,' answered his wife.

CHAPTER III

A SUPERIOR PERSON

Mildred and her father's ward got on remarkably well – perhaps a little too well to please Mrs Fausset, who had been jealous of the new-comer, and resentful of her intrusion from the outset. Mildred did not show herself capricious in her treatment of her playfellow. The child had never had a young companion before, and to her the advent of Fay meant the beginning of a brighter life. Until Fay came there had been no one but mother; and mother spent the greater part of her life in visiting and receiving visits. Only the briefest intervals between a ceaseless round of gaieties could be afforded to Mildred. Her mother doated on her, or thought she did; but she had allowed herself to be caught in the cogs of the great society wheel, and she was obliged to go round with the wheel. So far as brightly-furnished rooms and an expensive morning governess, ever so much too clever for the pupil's requirements, and costly toys and pretty frocks and carriage-drives, could go, Mildred was a child in an earthly paradise; but there are some children who yearn for something more than luxurious surroundings and fine clothes, and Mildred Fausset was one of those. She wanted a great deal of love – she wanted love always; not in brief snatches, as her mother gave it – hurried caresses given in the midst of dressing for a ball, hasty kisses before stepping into her carriage to be whisked off to a garden-party, or in all the pomp and splendour of ostrich feathers, diamonds, and court-train before the solemn function of a Drawing-room. Such passing glimpses of love were not enough for Mildred. She wanted warm affections interwoven with the fabric of her life; she wanted loving companionship from morning till night; and this she had from Fay. From the first moment of their clasping hands the two girls had loved each other. Each sorely in need of love, they had come together naturally, and with all the force of free undisciplined nature, meeting and mingling like two rivers.

John Fausset saw their affection, and was delighted. That loving union between the girl and the child seemed to solve all difficulties. Fay was no longer a stranger. She was a part of the family, merged in the golden circle of domestic love. Mrs Fausset looked on with jaundiced eye.

'If one could only believe it were genuine!' she sighed.

'Genuine! which of them do you suppose is pretending? Not Mildred, surely?'

'Mildred! No, indeed. *She* is truth itself.'

'Why do you suspect Fay of falsehood?'

'My dear John, I fear − I only say I fear − that your *protégée* is sly. She has a quiet self-contained air that I don't like in one so young.'

'I don't wonder she is self-contained. You do so little to draw her out.'

'Her attachment to Mildred has an exaggerated air − as if she wanted to curry favour with us by pretending to be fond of our child,' said Mrs Fausset, ignoring her husband's remark.

'Why should she curry favour? She is not here as a dependent − though she is made to wear the look of one sometimes more than I like. I have told you that her future is provided for; and as for pretending to be fond of Mildred, she is the last girl to pretend affection. She would have been better liked at school if she had been capable of pretending. There is a wild, undisciplined nature under that self-contained air you talk about.'

'There is a very bad temper, if that is what you mean. Bell has complained to me more than once on that subject.'

'I hope you have not set Bell in authority over her,' exclaimed Mr Fausset hastily.

'There must be some one to maintain order when Miss Colville is away.'

'That some one should be you or I, not Bell.'

'Bell is a conscientious person, and she would make no improper use of authority.'

'She is a very disagreeable person. That is all I know about her,' retorted Mr Fausset, as he left the room.

He was dissatisfied with Fay's position in the house, yet hardly knew how to complain or what alteration to suggest. There were no positive wrongs to resent. Fay shared Mildred's studies and amusements; they had their meals together, and took their airings together.

When Mildred went down to the morning-room or the drawing-room Fay generally went with her − generally, not always. There were times when Bell looked in at the schoolroom-door and beckoned Mildred. 'Mamma wants you alone,' she would whisper on the threshold; and Mildred ran off to be petted and paraded before some privileged visitor.

There were differences which Fay felt keenly, and inwardly resented. She was allowed to sit aloof when the drawing-room was full of fine ladies, upon Mrs Fausset's afternoon; while Mildred was brought into notice and talked about, her little graces exhibited and expatiated upon, or her childish tastes conciliated. Fay would sit looking at one of the art-books piled upon a side-table, or turning over photographs and prints in a portfolio. She never talked unless spoken to, or did anything to put herself forward.

Sometimes an officious visitor would notice her.

'What a clever-looking girl! Who is she?' asked a prosperous dowager, whose own daughters were all planted out in life, happy wives and mothers, and who could afford to interest herself in stray members of the human race.

'She is a ward of my husband's, Miss Fausset.'

'Indeed! A cousin, I suppose?'

'Hardly so near as that. A distant connection.'

Mrs Fausset's tone expressed a wish not to be bored by praise of the clever-looking girl. People soon perceived that Miss Fausset was to be taken no more notice of than a piece of furniture. She was there for some reason known to Mr and Mrs Fausset, but she was not there because she was wanted – except by Mildred. Everybody could see that Mildred wanted her. Mildred would run to her as she sat apart, and clamber on her knee, and hang upon her, and whisper and giggle with her, and warm the statue into life. Mildred would carry her tea and cakes, and make a loving fuss about her in spite of all the world.

Bell was a power in the house in Upper Parchment Street. She was that kind of old servant who is as bad as a mother-in-law, or even worse; for your mother-in-law is a lady by breeding and education, and is in somewise governed by reason, while your trustworthy old servant is apt to be a creature of impulse, influenced only by feeling. Bell was a woman of strong feelings, devotedly attached to Mrs Fausset.

Twenty-seven years ago, when Maud Donfrey was an infant, Martha Bell was the young wife of the head-gardener at Castle-Connell. The gardener and his wife lived at one of the lodges near the bank of the Shannon, and were altogether superior people for their class. Martha had been a lace-maker at Limerick, and was fairly educated. Patrick Bell was less refined, and had no ideas beyond his garden; but he was honest, sober, and thoroughly respectable. He seldom read the newspapers, and had never heard of Home Rule or the three Fs.

Their first child died within three weeks of its birth, and a wet-nurse being wanted at the great house for Lady Castle-Connell's seventh baby, Mrs Bell was chosen as altogether the best person for that confidential office. She went to live at the great white house in the beautiful gardens near the river. It was only a temporary separation, she told Patrick; and Patrick took courage at the thought that his wife would return to him as soon as Lady Castle-Connell's daughter was weaned, while in the meantime he was to enjoy the privilege of seeing her every Sunday afternoon; but somehow it happened that Martha Bell never went back to the commonly-furnished little rooms in the lodge, or to the coarse-handed husband.

Martha Bell was a woman of strong feelings. She grieved passionately for her dead baby, and she took the stranger's child reluctantly to her aching breast. But babies have a way of getting themselves loved, and one baby will creep into the place of another unawares. Before Mrs Bell had been at the great house three months she idolised her nursling. By the time she had been there a year she felt that life would be unbearable without her foster-child. Fortunately for her, she seemed as necessary to the child as the child was to her. Maud was delicate, fragile, lovely, and evanescent of aspect. Lady Castle-Connell had lost two out of her brood, partly, she feared, from carelessness in the nursery. Bell was devoted to her charge, and Bell was entreated to remain for a year or two at least.

Bell consented to remain for a year; she became accustomed to the comforts and refinements of a nobleman's house; she hated the lodge, and she cared very little for her husband. It was a relief to her when Patrick Bell sickened of his desolate home, and took it into his head to emigrate to Canada, where he had brothers and sisters settled already. He and his wife parted in the friendliest spirit, with some ideas of reunion years hence, when the Honourable Maud should have outgrown the need of a nurse; but the husband died in Canada before the wife had made up her mind to join him there. Mrs Bell lived at the great white house until Maud Donfrey left Castle-Connell as the bride of John Fausset. She went before her mistress to the house in Upper Parchment Street, and was there when the husband and wife arrived after their Continental honeymoon. From that hour she remained in possession at The Hook, Surrey, or at Upper Parchment Street, or at any temporary abode by sea or lake. Bell was always a power in Mrs Fausset's life, ruling over the other servants, dictating and fault-finding in a quiet, respectful way, discovering the weak side of everybody's character, and getting to the bottom of everybody's history. The servants hated her, and bowed down before her. Mrs Fausset was fond of her as a part of her own childhood, remembering that great love which had watched through all her infantine illnesses and delighted in all her childish joys. Yet, even despite these fond associations, there were times when Maud Fausset thought that it would be a good thing if dear old Bell would accept a liberal pension and go and live in some rose and honeysuckle cottage among the summery meadows by the Thames. Mrs Fausset had only seen that riverside region in summer, and she had hardly realised the stern fact of winter in that district. She never thought of rheumatism in connection with one of those low white-walled cottages, half-hidden

Fay neglected

Hardly— descriptive

under overhanging thatched gables, and curtained with woodbine and passion-flower, rose and myrtle. Dear old Bell was forty-eight, straight as a ramrod, very thin, with sharp features, and eager gray eyes under bushy iron-gray brows. She had thick iron-gray hair, and she never wore a cap; that was one of her privileges, and a mark of demarcation between her and the other servants – that and her afternoon gown of black silk or satin.

She had no specific duties in the house, but had something to say about everything. Mrs Fausset's French maid and Mildred's German maid were at one in their detestation of Bell; but both were eminently civil to that authority.

From the hour of Fay's advent in Upper Parchment Street, Bell had set her face against her. In the first place, she had not been taken into Mr and Mrs Fausset's confidence about the girl. She had not been consulted or appealed to in any way; and, in the second place, she had been told that her bedroom would be wanted for the new-comer, and that she must henceforward share a room with one of the housemaids, an indignity which this superior person keenly felt.

Nor did Fay do anything to conciliate this domestic power. Fay disliked Bell as heartily as Bell disliked Fay. She refused all offers of service from the confidential servant at the outset, and when Bell wanted to help in unpacking her boxes – perhaps with some idea of peering into those details of a girl's possessions which in themselves constitute a history – Fay declined her help curtly, and shut the door in her face.

Bell had sounded her mistress, but had obtained the scantiest information from that source. A distant connection of Mr Fausset's – his ward, an heiress. Not one detail beyond this could Bell extract from her mistress, who had never kept a secret from her. Evidently Mrs Fausset knew no more.

'I must say, ma'am, that for an heiress the child has been sadly neglected,' said Bell. 'Her under-linen was all at sixes and sevens till *I* took it in hand; and she came to this house with her left boot worn down at heel. Her drawers are stuffed with clothes, but many of them are out of repair; and she is such a wilful young lady that she will hardly let *me* touch her things.'

Bell had a habit of emphasising personal pronouns that referred to herself.

'You must do whatever you think proper about her clothes, whether she likes it or not,' answered Mrs Fausset, standing before her glass, and giving final touches to the feathery golden hair which her maid had arranged a few minutes before. 'If she wants new things, you can buy them for her from any of my tradespeople. Mr Fausset says she is to be looked after in every way. You had better not go to Bond Street for her under-linen.

Fay has been neglected —

Oxford Street will do; and you need not go to Stephanie for her hats. She is such a very plain girl that it would be absurd – cruel even – to dress her like Mildred.'

'Yes, indeed, it would, ma'am,' assented Bell; and then she pursued musingly: 'If it was a good school she was at, all I can say is that the wardrobe-woman was a very queer person to send any pupil away with her linen in such a neglected state. And as for her education, Miss Colville says she is shockingly backward. Miss Mildred knows more geography and more grammar than that great over-grown girl of fourteen.'

Mrs Fausset sighed.

'Yes, Bell, she has evidently been neglected; but her education matters very little. It is her disposition I am anxious about.'

'Ah, ma'am, and so am *I*,' sighed Bell.

When Bell had withdrawn, Maud Fausset sat in front of her dressing-table in a reverie. She forgot to put on her bonnet or to ring for her maid, though she had been told the carriage was waiting, and although she was due at a musical recital in ten minutes. She sat there lost in thought, while the horses jingled their bits impatiently in the street below.

'Yes, there is a mystery,' she said to herself; 'everybody sees it, even Bell.'

mystery .

CHAPTER IV

ALL SHE COULD REMEMBER

The London season was waning, and fewer carriages rolled westward to the Park gates in the low sunlight of late afternoon, and fewer riders trotted eastward towards Grosvenor Square in the brighter sunshine before luncheon. Town was gay still; but the flood-tide of pleasure was over. The river of London life was on the ebb, and people were beginning to talk about grouse-moors in Scotland and sulphur-springs in Germany.

Fay had lived in Upper Parchment Street nearly two months. It seemed to her impatient spirit as if she had lived there half a lifetime. The life would have been hateful to her without Mildred's love. That made amends for a good deal, but it could not make amends for everything; not for Bell's quiet insolence, for instance.

Bell had replenished the alien's wardrobe. Everything she had bought was of excellent quality, and expensive after its kind; but had a prize been

The Alien /Fay

offered for bad taste, Bell would have taken it by her selections of raiment on this occasion. Not once did she allow Fay to have a voice in the matter.

'Mrs Fausset deputed *me* to choose the things, miss,' she said, 'and I hope *I* know my duty.'

'I suppose I *am* very ugly,' said Fay resignedly, as she contemplated her small features in the glass, overshadowed by a mushroom hat of coarse brown straw, with a big brown bow, 'but in this hat I look positively hideous.'

The hat was an excellent hat: that good coarse Dunstable, which costs money and wears for ever, the ribbon of the best quality; but Hebe herself would have looked plain under a hat shaped like a bell-glass.

Fay's remark was recorded to Mrs Fausset as the indication of a discontented spirit.

Not being able to learn anything about Fay's history from her mistress, Bell had tried to obtain a little light from the girl herself, but without avail. Questioned about her school, Fay had replied that she hated her school, and didn't want to talk of it. Questioned about her mother, she answered that her mother's name was too sacred to be spoken about to a stranger; and on a subtle attempt to obtain information about her father, the girl flushed crimson, started up angrily from her chair, and told the highly respectable Bell that she was not in the habit of chattering to servants, or being questioned by them.

After this it was war to the knife on Martha Bell's part.

Miss Colville, the expensive morning governess, was in somewise above prejudice, and was a person of liberal mind, allowing for the fact that she had lived all her life in other people's houses, looking on at lives of fashionable frivolity in which she had no share, and had been obliged to study Debrett's annual volume as if it were her Bible, lest she should commit herself in every other speech, so intricate are the ramifications and intermarriages of the Upper Ten Thousand. Miss Colville was not unkind to Fay Fausset, and was conscientious in her instructions; but even she resented the mystery of the girl's existence, and felt that her presence blemished the respectability of the household. By and by, when she should be seeking new employment, and should have occasion to refer to Mrs Fausset, and to talk of her pupils in Upper Parchment Street, there would be a difficulty in accounting for Fay. A ward of Mr Fausset's, a distant connection: the whole thing sounded improbable. An heiress who had come to the house with torn embroidery upon her under-linen. A mystery – yes, no doubt a mystery. And in Miss Colville's ultra-particular phase of life no manner of mystery was considered respectable; except always those open secrets in the very highest circles which society agrees to ignore.

In spite of these drawbacks, Miss Colville was fairly kind to her new charge. Fay was backward in grammar and geography; she was a dullard about science; but she could chatter French, she knew a little Italian, and in music she was highly gifted. In this she resembled Mildred, who adored music, and had taken her first lessons on the piano as a water-fowl takes to a pond, joyously, as to her native element. Fay was not advanced in the *technique* of the art, but she played and sang charmingly, for the most part by ear; and she used to play and sing to Mildred in the summer twilight, till Bell came like a prison-warder and insisted upon Mildred's going to bed.

'I nursed your mamma, miss,' she would say, 'and *I* never allowed her to spoil her complexion with late hours as Miss Fay is leading you on to do.'

At seven Mildred cared neither for health nor complexion in the abstract, and she loved Fay's music and Fay's stories. Fay would tell her a fairy tale, with musical accompaniments, improvised to suit the story. This was Beauty's father groping through the dark wood. Then came the swaying of branches, the rustling of summer leaves, the long, long sigh of the night wind, the hoot of the owl, and the roll of distant thunder. Here came Fatima's brothers to the rescue, with a triumphant march, and the trampling of fiery steeds, careering up and down the piano in presto arpeggios, bursting open the gates of Bluebeard's Castle with a fortissimo volley of chords.

'*I* never heard any one make such a noise on a piano,' said Bell, bristling with indignation.

At eight o'clock Fay's day and evening were done. Mildred vanished like the setting of the sun. She would like to have had Fay to sit beside her bed and tell her stories, and talk to her, till she dropped to sleep; but this happiness was sternly interdicted by Bell.

'She would keep you awake half the night, Miss Mildred, over-exciting you with her stories; and what would your pa and the doctors say to *me*?' exclaimed Bell.

The door of the bright, pretty bedchamber closed upon Mildred, and Fay went back to the schoolroom heavy of heart, to enjoy the privilege of sitting up by herself till half-past nine, a privilege conceded to superior years. In that dismal hour and a half the girl had leisure to contemplate the solitude of her friendless life. Take Mildred from her, and she had no one – nothing. Mr Fausset had meant to be kind to her, perhaps. He had talked very kindly to her in the long drive from Streatham. He had promised her a home and the love of kindred; but evil influences had come in his way, and he had given her – Bell. Perhaps she was of a jealous, exacting disposition; for, fondly as she loved Mildred, she could not help comparing Mildred's lot with her own: Mildred's bright, airy

room and flower-decked windows, looking over the tree-tops in the
Park, with her dingy cell opening upon a forest of chimneys, and tainted
with odours of stables and kitchen; Mildred's butterfly frocks of lace and
muslin, with the substantial ugliness of her own attire; Mildred's manifold
possessions – trinkets, toys, books, games, pictures, and flowers – with
her empty dressing-table and unadorned walls.

'At your age white frocks would be ridiculous,' said Bell; yet Fay saw
other girls of her age flaunting in white muslin all that summer through.

Sometimes the footman forgot to bring her lamp, and she would sit
in the schoolroom window, looking down into the street, and watching
the carriages roll by in endless procession, with their lamps flaming in
the pale gray night, carrying their freight to balls and parties, hurrying
from pleasure to pleasure on swift-revolving wheels. A melancholy hour
this for the longing heart of youth, even when the schoolgirl's future
participation in all these pleasures is a certainty, or contingent only
upon life; but what was it for this girl, who had all girlhood's yearnings
for pleasure and excitement, and who knew not if that sparkling
draught would ever touch her lips, who felt herself an alien in this fine
house, a stranger at this fashionable end of the town? It was no new
thing for her to sit alone in the twilight, a prey to melancholy thoughts.
Ever since she could remember, her life had been solitary and loveless.
The home ties and tender associations which sweeten other lives were
unknown to her. She had never known what love meant till she felt
Mildred's warm arms clinging round her neck, and Mildred's soft cheek
pressed against hers. Her life had been a shifting scene peopled with
strangers. Dim and misty memories of childhood's earliest dawn
conjured up a cottage-garden on a windy hill; the sea stretching far
away in the distance, bright and blue, but unattainable; a patch of grass
on one side, a patch of potatoes on the other; a bed of wallflowers and
stocks and yellow marigolds in front of the parlour window; a family of
hens and an arrogant cock strutting in the foreground; and, standing
out sharply against the sky and the sea, a tall column surmounted by a
statue.

How she had longed to get nearer that vast expanse of water, to find
out what the sea was like! From some points in the view it seemed so
near, almost as if she could touch it with her outstretched hands; from
other points it looked so far away. She used to stand on a bank behind the
cottage and watch the white-sailed boats going out to sea, and the
steamers with their trailing smoke melting and vanishing on the horizon.

'Where do they go?' she asked in her baby French. 'Where do they
go?'

Those were the first words she remembered speaking, and nobody
seemed ever to have answered that eager question.

No one had cared for her in those days. She was very sure of that, looking back upon that monotonous childhood: a long series of empty hours in a cottage garden, and with no companions except the fowls, and no voice except that of the cow in the meadow hard by: a cow which sent forth meaningless bellows occasionally, and which she feared as if it had been a lion.

There was a woman in a white cap whom she called Nounou, and who seemed too busy to care about anybody; a woman who did all the housework, and dug the potato-garden, and looked after the fowls, and milked the cow and made butter, and rode to market on a donkey once or twice a week: a woman who was always in a hurry. There was a man who came home from work at sundown, and there were two boys in blouses and sabots, the youngest of whom was too old to play with the nurse-child. Long summer days in the chalky garden, long hours of listless monotony in front of the wide bright sea, had left a sense of oppression upon Fay's mind. She did not know even the name of the town she had seen far below the long ridge of chalky hill – a town of tall white houses and domes and spires, which had seemed a vast metropolis to the eyes of infancy. She had but to shut her eyes in her evening solitude, and she could conjure up the picture of roofs and spires, and hill and sea, and the tall column in its railed enclosure; yet she knew no more of town or hill than that they were on the other side of the Channel.

She remembered lying in a narrow little bed, that rocked desperately on a windy day, and looking out at the white sea-foam dashing against a curious oval window, like a giant's eye; and then she remembered her first wondering experience of railway travelling; a train flashing past green fields and hop-gardens and houses; and then darkness and the jolting of a cab; and after that being carried half-asleep into a strange house, and waking to find herself in a strange room, all very clean and neat, with a white-curtained bed and white muslin window-curtains, and on looking out of the window, behold, there was a patch of common all abloom with yellow gorse.

She remembered dimly that she had travelled in the charge of a little gray-haired man, who disappeared after the journey. She found herself now in the care of an elderly lady, very prim and strict, but not absolutely unkind; who wore a silk gown, and a gold watch at her waistband, and who talked in an unknown tongue. Everything here was prettier than in Nounou's house, and there was a better garden, a garden where there were more flowers and no potatoes, and there was the common in the front of the garden, all hillocks and hollows, where she was allowed to amuse herself in charge of a ruddy-faced girl in a lavender cotton frock.

The old lady taught her the unknown tongue, which she discovered in time to be English, and a good deal besides – reading and writing, for instance, and the rudiments of music, a little arithmetic, grammar, and geography. She took kindly to music and reading, and she liked to dabble with ink; but the other lessons were abhorrent, and she gave the orderly old lady a good deal of trouble. There was no love between them, only endurance on either side; and the long days on the common were almost as desolate as the days on the chalky hill above the sea.

At last there came a change. The dressmaker sent home three new frocks, all uncompromisingly ugly; the little old gray-haired man reappeared, looking exactly as he had looked on board the steamer, and a fly carried Fay and this guardian to the railway-station on the common, and thence the train took them to a great dark city, which the man told Fay was London; and then they went in a cab through streets that seemed endless, till at last the streets melted into a wide high-road, with trees on either side, and the cab drove into a garden of shining laurels and rhododendrons, and pulled up before a classic portico. Fay had no memory of any house so grand as this, although it was only the conventional suburban villa of sixty or seventy years ago.

Just at first the change seemed delightful. That circular carriage-sweep, those shining rhododendrons with great rose-coloured trusses of bloom, the drooping gold of the laburnums, and the masses of perfumed lilac, were beautiful in her eyes. Not so beautiful the long, bare schoolroom and the willow-pattern cups and saucers. Not so beautiful that all-pervading atmosphere of restraint which made school odious to Fay from the outset.

She stayed there for years – an eternity it seemed to her, looking back upon its hopeless monotony. Pleasure, variety, excitement, she had none. Life was an everlasting treadmill – up and down, down and up, over and over again. The same dull round of lessons; a dismal uniformity of food; Sunday penance in the shape of two long services in a badly ventilated church, and one long catechism in a dreary schoolroom. No gaol can be much duller than a well-regulated middle-class girls' school. Fay could complain of no ill-treatment. She was well fed, comfortably housed, warmly clad; but her life was a burden to her.

She had a bad temper; was irritable, impatient, quick to take offence, and prone to fits of sullenness. This was the opinion of the authorities; and her faults increased as she grew older. She was not absolutely rebellious towards the governesses; but there was always something amiss. She was idle and listless at her studies, took no interest in anything but her music-lessons, and was altogether an unsatisfactory pupil, She had no lasting friendships among her schoolfellows. She was capricious in her likings, and was prone to fancy herself slighted or ill-treated on the smallest provocation. The general verdict condemned her as the most disagreeable girl in the school. With the meaner souls among her schoolfellows it was considered an affront that she should have no antecedents worth talking about, no relatives, no home, and no hampers or presents. Even the servants neglected her as a young person without surroundings, upon whom kindness would be thrown away. The wardrobe-woman left her clothes unmended, feeling that it mattered very little in what order they were kept, since the girl never went home for the holidays, and there was no mother or aunt to investigate her trunks. She was condemned on every hand as a discreditable mystery; and when, one unlucky afternoon, a sultry afternoon at the beginning of a hot summer, she lost her temper in the middle of a class-lesson, burst into a torrent of angry speech, half defiance, half reproach, bounced up from her seat, and rushed out of the schoolroom, there were few to pity, and none to sympathise.

The proprietress of the school was elderly and lymphatic. Miss Fausset had been stigmatised as a troublesome pupil for a long time. There were continual complaints about Miss Fausset's conduct, worrying complaints, which spoilt Miss Constable's dinner and interfered with her digestion. Really, the only course open to that prosperous, over-fed personage was to get rid of Miss Fausset. There was an amiable family of three sisters – highly connected young persons, whose father was in the wine trade – waiting for vacancies in that old-established seminary.

'We will make a *tabula rasa* of a troublesome past,' said Miss Constable, who loved fine words. 'Miss Fausset must go.'

Thus it was that John Fausset had been suddenly called upon to find a new home for his ward; and thus it was that Fay had been brought to Upper Parchment Street.

No doubt Upper Parchment Street was better than school; but if it had not been for Mildred the atmosphere on the edge of Hyde Park would have been no more congenial than the atmosphere at Streatham. Fay felt herself an intruder in that splendid house, where, amidst that multitude of pretty things, she could not put her finger upon one gracious object that belonged to her – nothing that was her 'very own,' as Mildred called it; for she had refused Mildred's doll and all other proffered gifts, too proud to profit by a child's lavish generosity. Mrs Fausset made her no gifts, never talked to her, rarely looked at her.

Fay knew that Mrs Fausset disliked her. She had divined as much from the first, and she knew only too well that dislike had grown with experience. She was allowed to go down to afternoon tea with Mildred; but had she been deaf and dumb her society could not have been less cultivated by the mistress of the house. Mrs Fausset's feelings were patent to the whole household, and were common talk in the servants' hall. 'No wonder,' said the women; the men said 'What a shame!' but footmen and housemaids were at one in their treatment of Fay, which was neglectful, and occasionally insolent. It would hardly have been possible for them to behave well to the intruder and keep in favour with Bell, who was absolute – a superior power to butler or housekeeper, a person with no stated office, and the supreme right to interfere with everybody.

Bell sighed and shook her head whenever Miss Fay was mentioned. She bridled with pent-up indignation, as if the girl's existence were an injury to her, Martha Bell. 'If *I* hadn't nursed Mrs Fausset when she was the loveliest infant that ever drew breath, *I* shouldn't feel it so much,' said Bell; and then tears would spring to her eyes and chokings would convulse her throat, and the housekeeper would shake her head and sympathise mysteriously.

At the end of July the establishment migrated from Parchment Street to The Hook, Mr Fausset's riverside villa between Chertsey and Windsor. The Hook was an expanse of meadow-land bordered with willows, round which the river made a loop; and on this enchanted bit of ground – a spot loved by the river-god – Mr Fausset had built for himself the most delightful embodiment of that much-abused word villa; a long, low, white house, with spacious rooms, broad corridors, a double flight of marble stairs, meeting on a landing lit by an Italian cupola – a villa surrounded with a classic colonnade, and looking out upon peerless gardens sloping to the willow-shadowed stream.

To Fay The Hook seemed like a vision of Paradise. It was almost happiness even to her impatient spirit to sit in a corner of those lovely grounds, screened from the outer world by a dense wall of Portugal laurels and arbutus, with the blue water and the low, flat meadows of the further shore for her only prospect.

Miss Colville was left behind in London. For Fay and Mildred life was a perpetual holiday. Mrs Fausset was almost as much in society at The Hook as she had been in London. Visitors came and visitors went. She was never alone. There were parties at Henley and Marlow, and Wargrave and Goring. Two pairs of horses were kept hard at work carrying Mr and Mrs Fausset about that lovely riverside landscape to garden-parties and dinners, picnics and regattas. John Fausset went because his wife liked him to go, and because he liked to see her happy and admired. The two girls were left, for the most part, to their own devices, under the supervision of Bell. They lived in the gardens, with an occasional excursion into the unknown world along the river. There was a trustworthy under-gardener, who was a good oarsman, and in his charge Mildred was allowed to go on the water in a big wherry, which looked substantial enough to have carried a select boarding-school.

This life by the Thames was the nearest approach to absolute happiness which Fay had ever known; but for her there was to be no such thing as unbroken bliss. In the midst of the sultry August weather Mildred fell ill –

a mild attack of scarlet fever, which sounded less alarming to Mrs Fausset's ear, because the doctor spoke of it as scarlatina. It was a very mild case, the local practitioner told Mrs Fausset; there was no occasion to send for a London physician; there was no occasion for alarm. Mildred must keep her bed for a fortnight, and must be isolated from the rest of the house. Her own maid might nurse her if she had had the complaint.

'How could she have caught the fever?' Mrs Fausset asked, with an injured air; and there was a grand investigation, but no scarlet fever to be heard of nearer than Maidenhead.

'People are so artful in hiding these things,' said Mrs Fausset; and ten minutes afterwards she begged the doctor not to mention Mildred's malady to any of her neighbours.

'We have such a host of engagements, and crowds of visitors coming from London,' she said. 'People are so ridiculously nervous. Of course I shall be extremely careful.'

The doctor gave elaborate instructions about isolation. Such measures being taken, Mrs Fausset might receive all fashionable London with safety.

'And it is really such a mild case that you need not put yourself about in any way,' concluded the doctor.

'Dear, sweet pet, we must do all we can to amuse her,' sighed the fond mother.

Mild as the case might be, the patient had to suffer thirst and headache, a dry and swollen throat, and restless nights. Her most eager desire was for Fay's company, and as it was ascertained that Fay had suffered from scarlet fever some years before in a somewhat severe form, it was considered she might safely assist in the sick-room.

She was there almost all day, and very often in the night. She read to Mildred, and sang to her, and played with her, and indulged every changing fancy and caprice of sickness. Her love was inexhaustible, indefatigable, for ever on the watch. If Mildred woke from a feverish dream in the deep of night, with a little agitated sob or cry, she found a figure in a white dressing-gown bending over her, and loving arms encircling her before she had time to feel frightened. Fay slept in a little dressing-room opening out of Mildred's large, airy bedroom, so as to be near her darling. It was a mere closet, with a truckle-bed brought down from the servants' attic; but it was good enough for Fay, whose only thought was of the child who loved her as none other had ever loved within her memory.

Mrs Fausset was prettily anxious about her child. She would come to Mildred's room in her dressing-gown before her leisurely morning toilet, to hear the last report. She would sit by the bed for five minutes showering kisses on the pale cheeks, and then she would go away to her long summer-day of frivolous pleasures and society talk. Ripples of laughter and snatches of speech came floating in at the open windows; and at Mildred's behest Fay would stand at a window and report the proceedings of that happy world outside.

'They are going out in the boat. They are going to have tea on the lawn. Your mamma is walking up and down with Sir Horace Clavering. Miss Grenville and her sister are playing croquet;' and so on, and so on, all day.

Mildred tossed about on her pretty white bed impatiently.

'It is very horrid being shut up here on these fine days,' she said; 'or it would be horrid without you, Fay. Mamma does not come to see me much.'

Mamma came three or four times a day; but her visits were of the briefest. She would come into the room beaming with smiles, looking like living sunlight in her exquisite white gown, with its delicate ribbons and cloudy lace – a fleecy white cloud just touched with rose-colour, as if she were an embodiment of the summer dawn. Sometimes she brought Mildred a peach, or a bunch of hothouse grapes, or an orchid, or a new picture-book; but beautiful as these offerings were, the child did not always value them. She would push the plate of grapes or the peach aside impatiently when her mother was gone, or she would entreat Fay to eat the dainty.

'Mamma thinks I am greedy,' she said; 'but I ain't, am I, Fay?'

Those three weeks in the sick-room, those wakeful nights and long, slow summer days, strengthened the bond of love between the two girls. By the time Mildred was convalescent they seemed to have loved each other for years. Mildred could hardly remember what her life was like before she had Fay for a companion. Mrs Fausset saw this growing affection not without jealousy; but it was very convenient that there should be some one in the house whose companionship kept Mildred happy, and she even went so far as to admit that Fay was 'useful.'

'I cannot be with the dear child half so much as I should like to be,' she said; 'visitors are so exacting.'

Fay had slept very little during Mildred's illness, and now that the child was nearly well the elder girl began to flag somewhat, and was tired early in the evening, and glad to go to bed at the same hour as the patient, who, under Bell's supervision, was made to retire before eight. She was now well enough to sit up all day, and to drive out in a pony-carriage in the sunny hours after early dinner. Fay went with her, of course. Pony and landscape would have been wanting in charm without Fay's company. Both girls had gone to bed one sultry evening in the faint gray twilight. Fay was sleeping profoundly; but Mildred, after dozing a little, was lying half-awake, with closed eyelids, in the flower-scented room.

The day had been exceptionally warm. The windows were all open, and a door between Mildred's bedroom and sitting-room had been left ajar.

Bell was in the sitting-room at her favourite task of clearing up the scattered toys and books, and reducing all things to mathematical precision. Meta, Mildred's German maid, was sitting at needlework near the window by the light of a shaded lamp. The light shone in the twilight through the partly-open door, and gave Mildred a sense of company. They began to talk presently, and Mildred listened, idly at first, and soothed by the sound of their voices, but afterwards with keen curiosity.

'I know I shouldn't like to be treated so,' said Meta.

'*I* don't see that she has anything to complain of,' answered Bell. 'She has a good home, and everything provided for her. What more can she want?'

'I should want a good deal more if I was a heiress.'

'*An* heiress,' corrected Bell, who prided herself on having cultivated her mind, and was somewhat pedantic of speech. 'That's all nonsense, Meta. She's no more an heiress than I am. Mr Fausset told my poor young mistress that just to throw dust in her eyes. Heiress, indeed! An heiress without a relative in the world that she can speak of – an heiress that has dropped from the moon. Don't tell *me*.'

Nobody was telling Mrs Bell anything; but she had a resentful air, as if combating the arguments of an invisible adversary.

There was a silence during which Mildred nearly fell asleep; and then the voices began again.

'It's impossible for sisters to be fonder of each other than those two are,' said Meta.

'There's nothing strange in that, considering they *are* sisters,' answered Bell angrily.

'O, but you've no right to say that, Mrs Bell; it's going too far.'

'Haven't I a right to use my eyes and ears? Can't I see the family look in those two faces, though Miss Mildred is pretty and Miss Fay is plain? Can't I hear the same tones in the two voices, and haven't I seen his way of bringing that girl into the house, and his guilty look before my poor injured mistress? Of course they're sisters. Who could ever doubt it? *She* doesn't, I know, poor dear.'

She, in this connection, meant Mrs Fausset.

There was only one point in this speech which the innocent child seized upon. She and Fay were said to be sisters. O, how she had longed for a sister in the last year or so of her life, since she had found out the meaning of solitude among fairest surroundings! How all the brightest things she possessed had palled upon her for want of sisterly companionship! How she had longed for a baby-sister even, and had envied the children in households where a new baby was an annual

institution! She had wondered why her mother did not treat herself to a
new baby occasionally, as so many of her mother's friends did. And now
Fay had been given to her, ever so much better than a baby, which would
have taken such a long time to grow up. Mildred had never calculated
how long, but she concluded that it would be some months before the
most forward baby would be of a companionable age. Fay had been given
to her – a ready-made companion, versed in fairy tales, able to conjure
up an enchanted world out of the schoolroom piano, skilful with pencil
and colour-box, able to draw the faces and figures and palaces and
woodlands of that fairy world, able to amuse and entertain her in a
hundred ways. And Fay was her sister after all. She dropped asleep in a
flutter of pleasurable excitement. She would ask her mother all about it
to-morrow; and in the meantime she would say nothing to Fay. It was
fun to have a secret from Fay.

A batch of visitors left next day after lunch. Mr and Mrs Fausset were
to be alone for forty-eight hours, a rare oasis of domesticity in the society
desert. Mildred had been promised that the first day there was no
company she was to have tea with mamma in the tent on the lawn. She
claimed the fulfilment of that promise to-day.

It was a lovely day after the sultry, thundery night. Mrs Fausset reclined
in her basket-chair in the shelter of the tent. Fay and Mildred sat side by
side on a low bamboo bench on the grass: the little girl, fairy-like, in her
white muslin and flowing flaxen hair, the big girl in olive-coloured
alpaca, with dark hair clustering in short curls about the small intelligent
head. There could hardly have been a stronger contrast than that between
the two girls; and yet Bell was right. There was a family look, an
undefinable resemblance of contour and expression which would have
struck a very attentive observer – something in the line of the delicate
eyebrow, something in the angle of the forehead.

'Mamma,' said Mildred suddenly, clambering into her mother's lap,
'why mayn't I call Fay sister?'

Mrs Fausset started, and flushed crimson.

'What nonsense, child! Why, because it would be most ridiculous.'

'But she *is* my sister,' urged Mildred, looking full into her mother's
eyes, with tremendous resolution in her own. 'I love her like a sister, and
she is my sister. Bell says so.'

'Bell is an impertinent person,' cried Mrs Fausset angrily. 'When did
she say so?'

'Last night, when she thought I was asleep. Mayn't I call Fay sister?'
persisted Mildred coaxingly.

'On no account. I never heard anything so shameful. To think that Bell
should gossip! An old servant like Bell – my own old nurse. It is too
cruel!' cried Mrs Fausset, forgetting herself in her anger.

Fay stood tall and straight in the sunshine outside the tent, wondering at the storm. She had an instinctive apprehension that Mrs Fausset's anger was humiliating to her. She knew not why, but she felt a sense of despair darker than any other evil moment in her life; and yet her evil moments had been many.

'You need not be afraid that I shall ask Mildred to call me sister,' she said. 'I love her dearly, but I hate everybody else in this house.'

'You are a wicked, ungrateful girl,' exclaimed Mrs Fausset, 'and I am very sorry I ever saw your face.'

Fay drew herself up, looked at the speaker indignantly for a moment or so, and then walked quietly away towards the house.

She passed the footman with the tea-tray as she crossed the lawn, and a little further on she passed John Fausset, who looked at her wonderingly.

Mildred burst out crying.

'How unkind you are, mamma!' she sobbed. 'If I mayn't call her my sister I shall always love her like a sister – always, always, always.'

'What is the matter with my Mildred?' asked Mr Fausset, arriving at this moment.

'Nothing. She has only been silly,' his wife answered pettishly.

'And Fay – has she been silly, too?'

'Fay, your *protégée*, has been most impertinent to me. But I suppose that does not count.'

'It does count, for a good deal, if she has been intentionally impertinent,' answered Fausset gravely.

He looked back after Fay's vanishing figure with a troubled expression. He had so sighed for peace. He had hoped that the motherless girl might be taken into his home and cared for and made happy, without evil feeling upon any one's part; and now he could see by his wife's countenance that the hope of union and peace was at an end.

'I don't know what you mean about intention,' said his wife; 'I only know that the girl you are so fond of has just said she hates everybody in this house except Mildred. That sounds rather like intentional impertinence, I think.'

'Go and play, darling,' said Fausset to his child; 'or run after Fay, and bring her back to tea.'

'You show a vast amount of consideration for your wife,' said Mrs Fausset.

'My dear Maud, I want you to show a little more consideration for that girl, who has been so devoted to Mildred all through her illness, and who has one very strong claim upon a mother's heart – she is motherless.'

'I should think more of that claim, perhaps, if I knew who her mother was, and what she was to you,' said Maud Fausset.

'She was once near and dear to me. That is all I can tell you, Maud; and it ought to be enough.'

'It is more than enough,' his wife answered, trembling from head to foot, as she rose from her low chair, and walked away from the tent.

John Fausset looked after her irresolutely, went a few steps as if he meant to follow her, and then turned back to the tent, just as Mildred reappeared with Fay from another direction.

'We three will have tea together,' he exclaimed, with demonstrative cheerfulness. 'Mamma is not very well, Mildred; she has gone back to the house. You shall pour out my tea.'

He seated himself in his wife's chair, and Mildred sat on his knee, and put her arms round his neck, and adored him with all her power of adoration. Her household divinity had ever been the father. Perhaps her baby mind had found out the weakness of one parent and the strength of the other.

'Fay shall pour out the tea,' she said, with a sense of self-sacrifice. 'It will be a treat for Fay.'

So Fay poured out the tea, and they all three sat in the tent, and were happy and merry – or seemingly so, perhaps, as concerned John Fausset – for one whole sunshiny hour, and for the first time Fay felt that she was not an outsider. Yet there lurked in her mind the memory of Mrs Fausset's anger, and that memory was bitter.

'What am I, that almost everybody should be rude to me?' she asked herself, as she sat alone that night after Mildred had gone to bed.

From the open windows below came the languid sweetness of a nocturne by Chopin. Mrs Fausset was playing her husband to sleep after dinner. Sure token of reconciliation between husband and wife.

The doctor came next morning. He appeared upon alternate days now, and looked at Mildred in a casual manner, after exhausting the local gossip with Mrs Fausset. This morning he and Mrs Fausset were particularly confidential before the patient was sent for.

'Admirable!' he exclaimed, when he had looked at her tongue and felt her pulse; 'we are as nearly well as we can be. All we want now is a little sea-air to set us up for the winter. The great point, my dear madam' – to Mrs Fausset – 'is to avoid all risk of *sequelae*. A fortnight at Brighton or Eastbourne will restore our little friend to perfect health.'

There were no difficulties in the way of such people as the Faussets, no question of ways and means. Bell was sent for, and despatched to Eastbourne by an afternoon train. She was to take lodgings in a perfect position, and of impeccable repute as to sanitation. Mildred was to follow next day, under convoy of Meta and the under-butler, a responsible person of thirty-five.

'Fay must go, too,' exclaimed Mildred; whereupon followed a tragic scene.

Fay was not to go to Eastbourne. No reasons were assigned for the decision. Mildred was to ride a donkey; she was to have a pony-carriage at her disposition; but she was to be without Fay for a whole fortnight. In a fortnight she would be able to come home again.

'How many days are there in a fortnight?' she asked piteously.

'Fourteen.'

'O Fay, fourteen days away from you!' she exclaimed, clinging with fond arms round Fay's neck, and pulling down the dark head on a level with her own bright hair.

Fay was pale, but tearless, and said not a word. She let Mildred kiss her, and kissed back again, but in a dead silence. She went into the hall with the child, and to the carriage-door, and they kissed each other on the doorstep, and they kissed at the carriage-window; and then the horses trotted away along the gravel drive, and Fay had a last glimpse of the fair head thrust out of the window, and the lilies and roses of a child's face framed in pale gold hair.

It was a little more than a fortnight before Bell and her charge went back to The Hook. Mildred had sorely missed her playfellow, but had consoled herself with a spade and pail on the beach, and a donkey of venerable aspect, whose chief distinction was his white linen panoply, on the long dusty roads.

Mrs Fausset was not at home to receive her daughter. She had a superior duty at Chertsey, where people of some social importance were giving a lawn-party. The house seemed empty and silent, and all its brightness and graceful furniture, and flowers in the hall and on the staircase, could not atone for that want of human life.

'Where is Fay?' cried Mildred, taking alarm.

Nobody answered a question which was addressed to everybody.

'Fay, Fay, where are you?' cried the child, and then rushed up-stairs to the schoolroom, light as a lapwing, distracted with that sudden fear. 'Fay, Fay!' The treble cry rang through the house.

No one in the schoolroom, nor in Mildred's bedroom, nor in the little room where Fay had slept, nor in the drawing-rooms, whither Mildred came running, after that futile quest up-stairs.

Bell met her in the hall, with a letter in her hand.

'Your mamma wished to break it to you herself, miss,' said Bell. 'Miss Fay has gone.'

'Gone, where?'

'To Brussels.'

'Where is Brussels?'

'*I* believe, miss, that it is the capital of Belgium.'

Mildred tore open the letter, which Bell read aloud over the child's shoulder.

'I hope you won't be grieved at losing your playfellow, my dearest pet. Fay is dreadfully backward in her education, and has no manners. She has gone to a finishing-school at Brussels, and you may not see her again for some years.'

And so the years go by, and this story passes on to a time when the child Mildred is a child no more, but the happy mother of a fair young daughter, and the wife of an idolised husband.

CHAPTER V

WITHOUT THE WOLF

'Father,' said Lola, 'there are ever so many people in the village ill with fever. Isn't it sad?'

Mr and Mrs Greswold, of Enderby Manor, had been submitting to a fortnight's dissipation in London, and this was their first Sunday at home after that interval. They had returned late on the previous night, and house and gardens had all the sweetness and freshness of a scene to which one is restored after absence. They had spent the summer morning in the little village church with their daughter; and now they were enjoying the leisure interval between church and luncheon.

George Greswold sat in a lounging-chair under a cedar within twenty yards of the dining-room windows, and Lola was hanging about him as he read the *Athenaeum*, caressing him with little touches of light hands upon his hair or his coat-collar, adoring him with all her might after the agony of severance.

She was his only child, and the love between them was passing the love of the father and daughter of every-day life. It was an almost romantic attachment.

Like most only daughters, Lola was precocious, far in advance of her years in thoughtfulness and emotion, though perhaps a little behind the average girl of twelve in the severities of feminine education. She had been her mother's chief companion ever since she could speak, the confidante of all that mother's thoughts and fancies, which were as innocent as those of childhood itself. She had read much more than most girls of her age, and had been made familiar with poets whose names are only known to the schoolgirl in a history of literature. She knew a good deal about the best books in European literature; but, most of all, she knew the hearts and minds of her father and mother, their loves and likings, their joys and sorrows. She had never been shut out from their confidence; she had never been told to go and play when they wanted to talk to each other. She had sat with them, and walked and ridden and driven with them ever since she was old enough to dispense with her nurse's arms. She had lived her young life with them, and had been a part of their lives.

George Greswold looked up from his *Athenaeum* in quick alarm.

'Fever!' he exclaimed, 'fever at Enderby!'

'Strange, isn't it, father? Everybody is wondering about it. Enderby has always been such a healthy village, and you have taken such pains to make it so.'

'Yes, love, I have done my best. I am a landlord for pleasure, and not for gain, as you and mother know.'

'And what seems strangest and worst of all,' continued Lola, 'is that this dreadful fever has broken out among the people you and mother and I are fondest of – our old friends and pensioners – and the children we know most about. It seems so hard that those you and mother have helped the most should be the first to be ill.'

'Yes, love, that must seem very hard to my tender-hearted darling.'

Her father looked up at her fondly as she stood behind his chair, her white arm leaning upon his shoulder. The summer was in its zenith. It was strawberry-time, rose-time, haymaking-time – the season of nightingales and meadow-sweet and tall Mary lilies, and all those lovely things that cluster in the core of summer's great warm heart. Lola was all in white – a loose muslin frock, straight from shoulder to instep. Her thick gold hair fell straight as her frock below her ungirdled waist, and, in her white and gold, she had the look of an angel in an early Italian picture. Her eyes were as blue as that cloudless sky of midsummer which took a deeper azure behind the black-green branches of the cedar.

'My pet, I take it this fever is some slight summer malady. Cottagers are such ravens. They always make the worst of an illness.'

'O, but they really have been very bad. Mary Martin has had the fever, but she is getting better. And there's Johnny Giles; you know what a strong boy *he* is. He's very bad, poor little chap – so delirious; and I do feel so sorry for his poor mother. And young Mrs Peter has it, and two of her children.'

'It must be contagious,' cried Greswold, seizing his daughter's round white arm with an agitated movement. 'You have not been to see any of them, have you, Lola?' he asked, looking at her with unspeakable anxiety.

'No; Bell wouldn't let me go to see any of them; but of course I have taken them things every day – wine and beef-tea and jelly, and everything we could think of; and they have had as much milk as they liked.'

'You should not have gone yourself with the things, darling. You should have sent them.'

'That would seem so unkind, as if one hardly cared; and Puck with nothing to do all the time but to drag me about. It was no trouble to go myself. I did not even go inside the cottages. Bell said I mustn't.'

'Bell was right. Well, I suppose there is no harm done if you didn't go into any of the cottages; and it was very sweet of you to take the things yourself; like Red Riding Hood, only without the wolf. There goes the gong. I hope you are hungry.'

'Not very. The weather is too warm for eating anything but strawberries.'

He looked at her anxiously again, ready to take alarm at a word.

'Yes, it is too warm in this south-western country,' he said nervously. 'We'll go to Scotland next week.'

'So soon?'

'Why not a little sooner than usual, for once in a way?'

'I shall be sorry to go away while the people are ill,' she said gravely.

George Greswold forgot that the gong had sounded. He sat, leaning forward, in a despondent attitude. The very mention of sickness in the land had unhinged him. This child was so dear to him, his only one. He had done all that forethought, sense, and science could do to make the village which lay at his doors the perfection of health and purity. Famous sanitarians had been entertained at the Manor, and had held counsel with Mr Greswold upon the progress of sanitation, and its latest developments. They had wondered with him over the blind ignorance of our forefathers. They had instructed him how to drain his house, and how to ventilate and purify his cottages. They had assured him that, so far as lay within the limits of human intelligence, perfection had been achieved in Enderby village and Enderby Manor House.

And now his idolised daughter hung over his chair and told him that there was fever raging in the land, his land; the land which he loved as if it were a living thing, and on which he had lavished care and money ever since he had owned it. Other men might consider their ancestral estates as something to be lived upon; George Greswold thought of his forefathers' house and lands as something to be lived for. His cottages were model cottages, and he was known far and wide as a model landlord.

'George, are you quite forgetting luncheon?' asked a voice from one of the open windows, and he looked up to see a beautiful face looking out at him, framed in hair of Lola's colour.

'My dear Mildred, come here for a moment?' he said, and his wife went to him, smiling still, but with a shade of uneasiness in her face.

'Go in, pet. We'll follow you directly,' he said to his daughter; and then he rose slowly, with an air of being almost broken down by a great trouble, and put his hand through his wife's arm, and led her along the velvet turf beyond the cedar.

'Mildred, have you heard of this fever?'

'Yes; Louisa told me this morning when she was doing my hair. It seems to be rather bad; but there cannot be any danger, surely, after all you have done to make the cottages perfect in every way?'

'One cannot tell. There may be a germ of evil brought from somewhere else. I am sorry Lola has been among the people.'

'O, but she has not been inside any of the cottages. Bell took care to prevent that.'

'Bell was wise, but she might have done better still. She should have telegraphed to us. Lola must not go about any more. You will see to that, won't you, dearest? Before the end of the week I will take you both to Scotland.'

'Do you really suppose there can be danger?' she asked, growing very pale.

'No, no, I don't apprehend danger. Only it is better to be over-cautious than over-bold. We cannot be too careful of our treasure.'

'No, no, indeed,' answered the mother, with a piteous look.

'Mother,' called Lola from the window, 'are you ever coming? Pomfret will be late for church.'

Pomfret was the butler, whose convenience had to be studied upon Sundays. The servants dined while the family were at luncheon, and almost all the establishment went to afternoon service, leaving a footman and an under-housemaid in sole possession of the grave old manor-house, where the silence had a solemnity as in some monastic chapel. Lola was anxious that luncheon should begin, and Pomfret be dismissed to eat his dinner.

This child of twelve had more than a woman's forethought. She spent her life in thinking about other people; but of all those whom she loved, and for whom she cared, her father was first and chief. For him her love was akin to worship.

She watched his face anxiously now, as she took her seat at his right hand, and was silent until Pomfret had served the soup and retired, leaving all the rest of the luncheon on the table, and the wine on a dumb-waiter by his master's side.

There was always a cold lunch on Sundays, and the evening meal was also cold, a compromise between dinner and supper, served at nine o'clock, by which time the servants had gratified their various tastes for church or chapel, and had enjoyed an evening walk. There was no parsonage in England where the day of rest was held in more reverence than it was at Enderby Manor.

Mr Greswold was no bigot, his religion in no wise savoured of the over-good school; but he was a man of deep religious convictions; and he had been brought up to honour Sunday as a day set apart.

The Sunday parties and Sunday amusements of fashionable London were an abomination to him, though he was far too liberal-minded to wish to shut museums and picture-galleries against the people.

'Father,' said Lola, when they were alone, 'I'm afraid you had your bad dream last night.'

Greswold looked at her curiously.

'No, love, my dreams were colourless, and have left not even a remembrance.'

'And yet you look sorrowful, just as you always look after your bad dream.'

'Your father is anxious about the cottagers who are ill, dearest,' said Mrs Greswold. 'That is all.'

'But you must not be unhappy about them, father dear. You don't think that any of them will die, do you?' asked Lola, drawing very near him, and looking up at him with awe-stricken eyes.

'Indeed, my love, I hope not. They shall not die, if care can save them. I will walk round the village with Porter this afternoon, and find out all about the trouble. If there is anything that he cannot understand, we'll have Dr Hutchinson over from Southampton, or a physician from London if necessary. My people shall not be neglected.'

'May I go with you this afternoon, father?'

'No, dearest, neither you nor mother must leave the grounds till we go away. I will have no needless risks run by my dear ones.'

Neither mother nor daughter disputed his will upon this point. He was the sole arbiter of their lives. It seemed almost as if they lived only to please him. Both would have liked to go with him; both thought him over-cautious; yet neither attempted to argue the point. Happy household in which there are no arguments upon domestic trifles, no bickerings about the infinitesimals of life!

Enderby Manor was one of those ideal homes which adorn the face of England and sustain its reputation as the native soil of domestic virtues, the country in which good wives and good mothers are indigenous.

There are many such ideal homes in the land as to outward aspect, seen from the high-road, across park or pasture, shrubbery or flower-garden; but only a few of these sustain the idea upon intimate knowledge of the interior.

Here, within as well as without, the atmosphere was peace. Those velvet lawns and brilliant flower-beds were not more perfect than the love between husband and wife, child and parents. No cloud had ever shadowed that serene heaven of domestic peace. George Greswold had married at thirty a girl of eighteen who adored him; and those two had lived for each other and for their only child ever since. All outside the narrow circle of family love counted only as the margin or the framework of life. All the deepest and sweetest elements of life were within the veil. Mildred Greswold could not conceive a fashionable woman's existence – a life given up to frivolous occupations and futile excitements – a life of empty pleasure faintly flavoured with art, literature, science, philanthropy, and politics, and fancying itself eminently useful and eminently progressive. She had seen such an existence in her childhood, and had wondered that any reasoning creature could so live. She had turned her back upon the modish world when she married George Greswold, and had surrendered most of the delights of society to lead quiet days in her husband's ancestral home, loving that old house for his sake, as he loved it for the sake of the dead.

They were not in outer darkness, however, as to the movement of the world. They spent a fortnight at Limmers occasionally, when the fancy moved them. They saw all the pictures worth seeing, heard a good deal of the best music, mixed just enough in society to distinguish gold from tinsel, and to make a happy choice of friends.

They occasionally treated themselves to a week in Paris, and their autumn holidays were mostly spent in a shooting-box twenty miles beyond Inverness. They came back to the Manor in time for the pheasant-shooting, and the New Year generally began with a house-party which lasted with variations until the hunting was all over, and the young leaves were green in the neighbouring forest. No lives could have been happier, or fuller of interest; but the interest all centred in home. Farmers and cottagers on the estate were cared for as a part of home; and the estate itself was loved almost as a living thing by husband and wife, and the fair child who had been born to them in the old-fashioned house.

The grave red-brick manor-house had been built when William III was King; and there were some Dutch innovations in the Old English architecture, notably a turret or pavilion at the end of each wing, and a long bowling-green on the western side of the garden. The walls had that deep glowing red which is only seen in old brickwork, and the black glazed tiles upon the hopper roof glittered in the sunlight with the prismatic hues of antique Rhodian glass. The chief characteristic of the interior was the oak-panelling, which clothed the rooms and corridors as in a garment of sober brown, and would have been suggestive of gloom but for the pictures and porcelain which brightened every wall, and the rich colouring of brocaded curtains and tapestry *portières*. The chief charm of the house was the aspect of home life, the books and musical instruments, the art treasures, and flowers, and domestic trifles to be seen everywhere; the air which every room and every nook and corner had of being lived in by home-loving and home-keeping people.

The pavilion at the end of the south-west wing was Lola's special domain, that and the room communicating with it. That pretty sitting-room, with dwarf book-shelves, water-colour pictures, and Wedgwood china, was never called a schoolroom. It was Lola's study.

'There shall be no suggestion of school in our home,' said George Greswold.

It was he who chose his daughter's masters, and it was often he who attended during the lesson, listening intently to the progress of the work, and as keenly interested in the pupil's progress as the pupil herself. Latin he himself taught her, and she already knew by heart those noblest of Horace's odes which are fittest for young lips. Their philosophy saddened her a little.

'Is life always changing?' she asked her father; 'must one never venture to be quite happy?'

The Latin poet's pervading idea of mutability, inevitable death, and inevitable change impressed her with a flavour of sadness, child as she was.

'My dearest, had Horace been a Christian, as you are, and had he lived for others, as you do, he would not have been afraid to call himself happy,' answered George Greswold. 'He was a Pagan, and he put on the armour of philosophy for want of the armour of faith.'

These lessons in the classics, taking a dead language not as a dry study of grammar and dictionary, but as the gate to new worlds of poetry and philosophy, had been Lola's delight. She was in no wise unpleasantly precocious; but she was far in advance of the conventional schoolroom child, trained into characterless uniformity by a superior governess. Lola had never been under governess rule. Her life at the Manor had been as free as that of the butterflies. There was only Bell to lecture her – white-haired Mrs Bell, thin and spare, straight as an arrow, at seventy-four years of age, the embodiment of servants'-hall gentility, in her black silk afternoon gown and neat cambric cap – Bell, who looked after Lola's health, and Lola's rooms, and was for ever tidying the drawers and tables, and lecturing upon the degeneracy of girlhood. It was her boast to have nursed Lola's grandmother, as well as Lola's mother, which seemed going back to the remoteness of the dark ages.

Enderby Manor was three miles from Romsey, and within riding or driving distance of the New Forest and of Salisbury Cathedral. It lay in the heart of a pastoral district watered by the Test, and was altogether one of the most enjoyable estates in that part of the country.

Before luncheon was finished a messenger was on his way to the village to summon Mr Porter, more commonly Dr Porter, the parish and everybody's doctor, an elderly man of burly figure, close-cropped gray hair, and yeoman-like bearing – a man born on the soil, whose father and grandfather and great-grandfather had cured or killed the inhabitants of Enderby parish from time immemorial. Judging from the tombstones in the pretty old churchyard, they must have cured more than they killed; for those crumbling moss-grown stones bore the record of patriarchal lives, and the union near Enderby was a museum of incipient centenarians.

Mr Porter came into the grave old library at the Manor looking more serious than his wont, perhaps in sympathy with George Greswold's anxious face, turned towards the door as the footman opened it.

'Well, Porter, what does it all mean, this fever?' asked Greswold abruptly.

Mr Porter had a manner of discussing a case which was all his own. He always appealed to his patient with a professional air, as if consulting another medical authority, and a higher one than himself. It was flattering, perhaps, but not always satisfactory.

'Well, you see, there's the high temperature – 104 in some cases – and there's the inflamed throat, and there's headache. What do *you* say?'

'Don't talk nonsense, Porter; you must know whether it is an infectious fever or not. If you don't know, we'll send to Southampton for Hutchinson.'

'Of course, you can have him if you like. I judge more by temperature than anything – the thermometer is a safer guide than the pulse, as you know. I took their temperatures this morning before I went to church: only one case in which there was improvement – all the others decidedly worse; very strongly developed cases of malignant fever – typhus or typhoid – which, as you know, by Jenner's differentiation of the two forms——'

'For God's sake, man, don't talk to me as if I were a doctor, and had your ghoulish relish of disease! If you have the slightest doubt as to treatment, send for Hutchinson.'

He took a sheaf of telegraph-forms from the stand in front of him, and began to write his message while he was talking. He had made up his mind that Dr Hutchinson must come to see these humble sufferers, and to investigate the cause of evil. He had taken such pains to create a healthy settlement, had spared no expense; and for fifteen years, from the hour of his succession until now, all had gone well with him. And now there was fever in the land, fever in the air breathed by those two beloved ones, daughter and wife.

'I have been so happy; my life has been cloudless, save for one dark memory,' he said to himself, covering his face with his hands as he leaned with his elbows on the table, while Mr Porter expatiated upon the cases in the village, and on fever in general.

'I have tested the water in all the wells – perfectly pure. There can be nothing amiss with the milk, for all my patients are on Mrs Greswold's list, and are getting their milk from your own dairy. The drainage is perfection – yet here we have an outbreak of fever, which looks remarkably like typhoid?'

'Why not say at once that it is typhoid?'

'The symptoms all point that way.'

'You say there can be nothing amiss with the milk. You have not analysed it, I suppose?'

'Why should I? Out of your own dairy, where everything is managed in the very best way – the perfection of cleanliness in every detail.'

'You ought to have analysed the milk, all the same,' said Greswold thoughtfully. 'The strength of a chain is its weakest link. There may be some weak link here, though we cannot put our fingers upon it – yet. Are there many cases?'

'Let me see. There's Johnny Giles, and Mrs Peter and her children, and Janet Dawson, and there's Andrew Rogers, and there's Mary Rainbow,' began Mr Porter, counting on his fingers as he went on, until the list of sufferers came to eleven. 'Mostly youngsters,' he said in conclusion.

'They ought to have been isolated,' said Greswold. 'I will get out plans for an infirmary to-morrow. There is the willow-field, on the other side of the village, a ridge of high ground sloping down towards the parish drain, with a southern exposure, a capital site for a hospital. It is dreadful to think of fever-poison spreading from half-a-dozen different cottages. Which was the first case?'

'Little Rainbow.'

'That fair-haired child whom I used to see from my dressing-room window every morning as she went away from the dairy, tottering under a pitcher of milk? Poor little Polly! She was a favourite with us all. Is she very ill?'

'Yes, I think hers is about the best case,' answered the doctor unctuously; 'the others are a little vague; but there's no doubt about *her*, all the symptoms strongly marked – a very clear case.'

'Is there any danger of a fatal termination?'

'I'm afraid there is.'

'Poor little Polly – poor pretty little girl! I used to know it was seven o'clock when I saw that bright little flaxen head flit by the yew hedge yonder. Polly was as good a timekeeper as any clock in the village. And you think she may die? You have not told Lola, I hope?'

'No, I have not let out anything about danger. Lola is only too anxious already.'

'I will put the infirmary in hand to-morrow; and I will take my wife and daughter to Scotland on Tuesday.'

'Upon my word, it will be a very good thing to get them away. These fever cases are so mysterious. There's no knowing what shape infection may take. I have the strongest belief in your system of drainage——'

'Nothing is perfect,' said Greswold impatiently. 'The science of sanitation is still in its infancy. I sometimes think we have not advanced very far from the knowledge of our ancestors, whose homes were desolated by the Black Death. However, don't let us talk, Porter. Let us act, if we can. Come and look at the dairy.'

'You don't apprehend evil there?'

'There are three sources of typhoid poison – drainage, water, milk. You say the drains and the water are good, and that the milk comes from my own dairy. If you are right as to the first and second, the third must be wrong, no matter whose dairy it may come from.'

He took up his hat, and went out of the house with the doctor. Gardens and shrubberies stretched before them in all their luxuriance of summer verdure, gardens and shrubberies which had been the delight and pride of many generations of Greswolds, but loved more dearly by none than by George Greswold and his wife. In Mildred's mind the old family house was a part of her husband's individuality, an attribute rather than a mere possession. Every tree and every shrub was sacred. These, his mother's own hands had cropped and tended; those, grandfathers and great-grandfathers and *arrière* great-grandfathers had planted in epochs that distance has made romantic.

On the right of the hall-door a broad gravel path led in a serpentine sweep towards the stables, a long, low building spread over a considerable area, and hidden by shrubberies. The dairy was a little further off, approached by a winding walk through thickets of laurel and arbutus. It had been originally a barn, and was used as a receptacle for all manner of out-of-door lumber when Mildred came to the Manor. She had converted the old stone building into a model dairy, with outside gallery and staircase of solid woodwork, and with a Swiss roof. Other buildings had been added. There were low cowhouses, and tall pigeon-houses, and a picturesque variety of gables and elevations which was delightful to the eye, seen on a summer afternoon such as this June Sunday, amidst the perfume of clove carnations and old English roses, and the cooing of doves.

Mrs Greswold's Channel Island cows were her delight – creatures with cream-coloured coats, black noses, and wistful brown eyes. Scarcely a day passed on which she did not waste an hour or so in the cowhouses or in the meadows caressing these favourites. Each cow had her name painted in blue and white above her stall, and the chief, or duchess of the herd, was very severe in the maintenance of cowhouse precedence, and knew how to resent the insolence of a new-comer who should presume to cross the threshold in advance of her.

The well is poisned.

The dairy itself had a solemn and shadowy air, like a shrine, and was as pretty as the dairy at Frogmore. The walls were lined with Minton tiles, the shallow milk-pans were of Doulton pottery, and quaintly-shaped pitchers of bright colours were ranged on china brackets along the walls. The windows were latticed, and a pane of ruby, rose, or amethyst appeared here and there among the old bottle-green glass, and cast a patch of coloured light upon the cool marble slab below.

The chief dairy-woman lived at an old-fashioned cottage on the premises, with her husband, the cowkeeper; and their garden, which lay at the back of the cowhouses and dairy, was the ideal old English garden, in which flowers and fruit strive for the mastery. In a corner of this garden, close to the outer offices of the cottage, among rows of peas, and summer cabbages, and great overgrown lavender-bushes and moss-roses, stood the old well, with its crumbling brick border and ancient spindle, a well that had been dug when the old manor-house was new.

There were other water arrangements for Mrs Greswold's dairy, a new artesian well, on a hill a quarter of a mile from the kitchen-garden, a well that went deep down into the chalk, and was famous for the purity of its water. All the drinking-water of the house was supplied from this well, and the water was laid on in iron pipes to dairy and cowhouses. All the vessels used for milk or cream were washed in this water; at least, such were Mr Greswold's strict orders – orders supposed to be carried out under the supervision of his bailiff and housekeeper.

Mr Porter looked at a reeking heap of stable manure that sprawled within twenty feet of the old well with suspicion in his eye, and from the manure-heap he looked at the back premises of the old cob-walled cottage.

'I'm afraid there may have been soakage from that manure-heap into the well,' he said; 'and if your dairy vessels are washed in that water——'

'But they never are,' interrupted Mr Greswold; 'that water is used only for the garden – eh, Mrs Wadman?'

The dairy-woman was standing on the threshold of her neat little kitchen, curtseying to her master, resplendent in her Sunday gown of bright blue merino, and her Sunday brooch, containing her husband's photograph, coloured out of knowledge.

'No, of course not, sir; leastways, never except when there was something wrong with the pipes from the artesian.'

'Something wrong; when was that? I never heard of anything wrong.'

'Well, sir, my husband didn't want to be troublesome, and Mr Thomas he gave the order for the men from Romsey, that was on the Saturday after working-hours, and they was to come as it might be on the Monday morning, and they never come near; and Mr Thomas he wrote and wrote, and my husband he says it ain't no use writing, and he takes the pony and rides over to Romsey in his overtime, and he complains about the men not coming, and they tells him there's a big job on at Broadlands and not a plumber to be had for love or money; but the pipes is all right *now*, sir.'

'Now? Since when have they been in working order?'

'Since yesterday, sir. Mr Thomas was determined he'd have everything right before you came back.'

'And how long have you been using that water,' pointing to the well, with its moss-grown brickwork and flaunting margin of yellow stonecrop, 'for dairy purposes?'

'Well, you see, sir, we was obliged to use water of some kind; and there ain't purer or better water than that for twenty mile round. I always use it for my kettle every time I make tea for me or my master, and never found no harm from it in the last fifteen years.'

'How long have you used it for the dairy?' repeated George Greswold angrily; 'can't you give a straight answer, woman?'

Mrs Wadman could not: had never achieved a direct reply to a plain question within the memory of man.

'The men was to have come on the Monday morning, first thing,' she said, 'and they didn't come till the Tuesday week after that, and then they was that slow——'

George Greswold walked up and down the garden path, raging.

'She won't answer!' he cried. 'Was it a week – a fortnight – three weeks ago that you began to use that water for your dairy?' he asked sternly; and gradually he and the doctor induced her to acknowledge that the garden well had been in use for the dairy nearly three weeks before yesterday.

'Then that is enough to account for everything,' said Dr Porter. 'First there is filtration of manure through a gravelly soil – inevitable – and next there is something worse. She had her sister here from Salisbury – six weeks ago – down with typhoid fever three days after she came – brought it from Salisbury.'

'Yes, yes – I remember. You told me there was no danger of infection.'

'There need have been none. I made her use all precautions possible in an old-fashioned cottage; but however careful she might be, there would be always the risk of a well – close at hand like that one – getting tainted. I asked her if she ever used that water for anything but the garden, and she said no, the artesian well supplied every want. And now she talks about her kettle, and tells us coolly that she has been using that polluted water for the last three weeks – and poisoning a whole village.'

'Me poisoning the village! O Dr Porter, how can you say such a cruel thing? Me, that wouldn't hurt a fly if I knew it!'

'Perhaps not, Mrs Wadman; but I'm afraid you've hurt a good many of your neighbours without knowing it.'

George Greswold stood in the pathway silent and deadly pale. He had been so happy for the last thirteen years – a sky without a cloud – and now in a moment the clouds were closing round him, and again all might be darkness, as it had been once before in his life. Calamity for which he felt himself unaccountable had come upon him before – swift as an arrow from the bow – and now again he stood helpless, smitten by the hand of Fate.

He thought of the little village child, with her guileless face, looking up at his window as she tripped by with her pitcher. His dole of milk had been fatal to the simple souls who had looked up to him as a Providence. He had taken such pains that all should be sweet and wholesome in his people's cottages; he had spent money like water, and had lectured them and taught them; and lo! from his own luxurious home the evil had gone forth. Careless servants, hushing up a difficulty, loth to approach him with plain facts lest they should be considered troublesome, had wrought this evil, had spread disease and death in the land.

And his own and only child, the delight of his life, the apple of his eye – that tainted milk had been served at her table! Amidst all that grace of porcelain and flowers the poison had lurked, as at the cottagers' board. What if she, too, should suffer?

He meant to take her away in a day or two – now – now when the cause of evil was at work no longer. The thought that it might be too late, that the germ of poison might lurk in the heart of that fair flower, filled him with despair.

Mrs Wadman had run into her cottage, shedding indignant tears at Dr Porter's cruelty. She came out again, with a triumphant air, carrying a tumbler of water.

'Just look at it, sir,' she said; 'look how bright and clear it is. There never was better water.'

'My good woman, in this case brightness and clearness mean corruption,' said the doctor. 'If you'll give me a pint of that water in a bottle I'll take it home with me, and test it before I sleep to-night.'

CHAPTER VI

'AH! PITY! THE LILY IS WITHERED'

George Greswold left the dairy-garden like a man stricken to death. He felt as if the hand of Fate were on him. It was not his fault that this evil had come upon him, that these poor people whom he had tried to help suffered by his bounty, and were perhaps to die for it. He had done all that human foresight could do; but the blind folly of his servants had stultified his efforts. Nothing in a London slum could have been worse than this evil which had come about in a gentleman's ornamental dairy, upon premises where money had been lavished to secure the perfection of scientific sanitation.

Mr Porter murmured some hopeful remark as they went back to the house.

'Don't talk about it, Porter,' Greswold answered impatiently; 'nothing could be worse – nothing. Do all you can for these poor people – your uttermost, mind, your uttermost. Spare neither time nor money. Save them, if you can.'

'You may be assured I shall do my best. There are only three or four very bad cases.'

'Three or four! My God, how horrible! Three or four people murdered by the idiocy of my servants.'

'Joe Stanning – not much chance for him, I'm afraid – and Polly Rainbow.'

'Polly – poor pretty little Polly! O Porter, you *must* save her! You must perform a miracle, man. That is what genius means in a doctor. The man of genius does something that all other doctors have pronounced impossible. You will have Hutchinson over to-morrow. He may be able to help you.'

'If she live till to-morrow. I'm afraid it's a question of a few hours.'

George Greswold groaned aloud.

'And my daughter has been drinking the same tainted milk. Will she be stricken, do you think?' he asked, with an awful calmness.

'God forbid! Lola has such a fine constitution and the antecedent circumstances are different. I'll go and have a look at my patients, and come back to you late in the evening with the last news.'

They parted by a little gate at the corner of a thick yew hedge, which admitted Mr Greswold into his wife's flower-garden: a very old garden, which had been the care and delight of many generations; a large square garden, with broad flower-beds on each side, a stone sundial in the centre of a grass-plot, and a buttressed wall at the end, a massive old wall of vermilion brickwork, honeycombed by the decay of centuries, against which a double rank of hollyhocks made a particoloured screen, while flaunting dragon's-mouth and yellow stonecrop made a flame of colour on the top.

There was an old stone summer-house in each angle of that end wall, temples open to the sun and air, and raised upon three marble steps, stained with moss and lichen.

Charming as these antique retreats were to muse or read in, Mildred Greswold preferred taking tea on the lawn, in the shadow of the two old cedars. She was sitting in a low garden-chair, with a Japanese tea-table at her side, and a volume of Robertson's sermons on her lap.

It was a rule of life at Enderby Manor that only books of pious tendency should be read on Sundays. The Sunday library was varied and well chosen. Nobody ever found the books dull or the day too long. The dedication of that one day in seven to godliness and good works had never been an oppression to Mildred Greswold.

She remembered her mother's Sundays – days of hasty church, and slow elaborate dressing for afternoon or evening gaieties; days of church parade and much praise of other people's gowns and depreciation of other people's conduct; days of gadding about and running from place to place; Sunday luncheons, Sunday musical parties, Sunday expeditions up the river, Sunday in the studios, Sunday at Richmond or Greenwich. Mrs Greswold remembered the fussy emptiness of that fashionable Sunday, and preferred sermons and tranquil solitude in the manor gardens.

Solitude meant a trinity of domestic love. Husband, wife, and daughter spent their Sundays together. Those were blessed days for the wife and daughter, since there were no business engagements, no quarter-sessions, or interviews with the bailiff, or letter-writing, to rob them of the society they both loved best in the world. George Greswold devoted his Sundays entirely to his Creator and his home.

'Where is Lola?' he asked, surprised to find his wife alone at this hour.

'She has a slight headache, and I persuaded her to lie down for an hour or so.'

The father's face blanched. A word was enough in his overwrought condition.

'Porter must see her,' he said; 'and I have just let him leave me. I'll send some one after him.'

'My dear George, it is nothing; only one of her usual headaches.'

'You are sure she was not feverish?'

'I think not. It never occurred to me. She has often complained of headache since she began to grow so fast.'

'Yes, she has shot up like a tall white Lily – my lily!' muttered the father tenderly.

He sank into a chair, feeling helpless, hopeless almost, under that overpowering sense of fatality – of undeserved evil.

'Dear George, you look so ill this afternoon,' said his wife, with tender anxiety, laying her hand on his shoulder, and looking earnestly at him, as he sat there in a downcast attitude, his arms hanging loosely, his eyes bent upon the ground. 'I'm afraid the heat has overcome you.'

'Yes, it has been very hot. Do me a favour, Mildred. Go into the house, and send somebody to find Porter. He was going the round of the cottages where there are sick people. He can easily be found. I want him to see Lola, at once.'

George is a religious man --

'I'll send after him, George; but, indeed, I don't see any need for a doctor. Lola is so strong; her headaches pass like summer clouds. O George, you don't think that *she* is going to have fever, like the cottagers!' cried Mildred, full of a sudden terror.

'No, no; of course not. Why should she have the fever? But Porter might as well see her at once – at once. I hate delay in such cases.'

His wife hurried away without a word. He had imbued her with all his own fears.

He sat in the garden, just as she had left him, motionless, benumbed with sorrow. There might, indeed, be no ground for this chilling fear; others might die, and his beloved might still go unscathed. But she had been subjected to the same poison, and at any moment the same symptoms might show themselves. For the next week or ten days he must be haunted by a hideous spectre. He would make haste to get his dearest one away to the strong fresh mountain air, to the salt breath of the German Ocean; but if the poison had already tainted that young life, mountain and sea could not save her from the fever. She must pass through the furnace, as those others were passing.

'Poor little Polly Rainbow! The only child of a widow; the only one; like mine,' he said to himself.

He sat in the garden till dusk, brooding, praying dumbly, unutterably sad. The image of the widow of Nain was in his mind while he sat there. The humble funeral train, the mourning mother, and that divine face shining out of the little group of peasant faces, radiant with intellect and faith – among them, but not of them – and the uplifted hand beckoning the dead man from the bier.

'The age of miracles is past,' he thought: 'there is no Saviour in the land to help *me!* In my day of darkness Heaven made no sign. I was left to suffer as the worms suffer under the plough-share, and to wriggle back to life as best I could, like them.'

It was growing towards the summer darkness when he rose and went into the house, where he questioned the butler, whom he met in the hall. Mr Porter had been brought back, and had seen Miss Greswold. He had found her slightly feverish, and had ordered her to go to bed. Mrs Greswold was sitting with her. Did Dr Porter seem anxious? No, not at all anxious; but he was going to send Miss Laura some medicine before bedtime.

It was after nine now, but Greswold could not stay in the house. He wanted to know how it fared with his sick tenantry – most of all with the little flaxen-haired girl he had so often noticed of late.

He went out into the road that led to the village, a scattered colony, a cottage here and there, or a cluster of cottages and gardens on a bit of rising ground above the road. There was a common a little way from the Manor, a picturesque, irregular expanse of hollows and hillocks, skirted by a few cottages, and with a fir plantation shielding it from the north. Mrs Rainbow's cottage stood between the common and the fir-wood, an old half-timbered cottage, very low, with a bedroom in the roof, and a curious dormer-window, with a thatched arch projecting above the lattice, like an overhanging eyebrow. The little garden was aflame with scarlet bean-blossom, roses, and geraniums, and the perfume of sweet-peas filled the air.

Greswold heard the doctor talking in the upper chamber as he stood by the gate. The deep, grave tones were audible in the evening stillness, and there was another sound that chilled the Squire's heart: the sound of a woman's suppressed weeping.

He waited at the gate. He had not the nerve to go into the cottage and face that sorrowing widow. It seemed to him as if the child's peril were his fault. It was not enough that he had taken all reasonable precautions. He ought to have foreseen the idiocy of his servants. He ought to have been more on the alert to prevent evil.

The great round moon came slowly up out of a cluster of Scotch firs. How black the branches looked against that red light! Slowly, slowly gliding upward in a slanting line, the moon stole at the back of those black branches, and climbed into the open sky.

How often Lola had watched such a moonrise at his side, and with what keen eyes she had noted the beauty of the spectacle! It was not that he had trained her to observe and to feel the loveliness of nature. With her that feeling had been an instinct, born with her, going before the wisdom of maturity, the cultivated taste of travelled experience.

To-night she was lying in her darkened room, the poor head heavy and painful on the pillow. She would not see the moon rising slowly yonder in that cloudless sky.

'No matter; she will see it to-morrow, I hope,' he said to himself, trying to be cheerful. 'I am a morbid fool to torment myself; she has been subject to headaches of late. Mildred is right.'

And then he remembered that death and sorrow were near – close to him as he stood there watching the moon. He remembered poor little Polly Rainbow, and desponded again.

A woman's agonised cry broke the soft summer stillness, and pierced George Greswold's heart.

'The child is dead!' he thought.

Yes, poor little Polly was gone. The widow came out to the gate presently, sobbing piteously, and clasped Mr Greswold's hand and cried over it, broken down by her despair, leaning against the gate-post, as if her limbs had lost the power to bear her up.

'O, sir, she was my all!' she sobbed; 'she was my all!'

She could say no more than this, but kept repeating it again and again. 'She was all I had in the world; the only thing I cared for.'

George Greswold touched her shoulder with protecting gentleness. There was not a peasant in the village for whom he had not infinite tenderness – pitying their infirmities, forgiving their errors, inexhaustible in benevolence towards them all. He had set himself to make his dependents happy as the first duty of his position. And yet he had done them evil unwittingly. He had cost this poor widow her dearest treasure – her one ewe lamb.

'Bear up, if you can, my good soul,' he said; 'I know that it is hard.'

'Ah, sir, you'd know it better if it was your young lady that was stricken down!' exclaimed the widow bitterly; and the Squire walked away from the cottage-gate without another word.

Yes, he would know it better then. His heart was heavy enough now. What would it be like if *she* were smitten?

She was much the same next day: languid, with an aching head and some fever. She was not very feverish. On the whole, the doctor was hopeful, or he pretended to be so. He could give no positive opinion yet, nor could Dr Hutchinson. They were both agreed upon that point; and they were agreed that the polluted water in the garden well had been the cause of the village epidemic. Analysis had shown that it was charged with poisonous gas.

Mr Greswold hastened his preparations for the journey to Scotland with a feverish eagerness. He wrote to engage a sleeping-carriage on the Great Northern. They were to travel on Thursday, leaving home before noon, dining in town, and starting for the North in the evening. If Lola's illness were indeed the slight indisposition which everybody hoped it was, she might be quite able to travel on Thursday, and the change of air and the movement would do her good.

'She is always so well in Scotland,' said her father.

No, there did not seem much amiss with her. She was very sweet, and even cheerful, when her father went into her room to sit beside her bed for a quarter of an hour or so. The doctors had ordered that she should be kept very quiet, and a hospital nurse had been fetched from Salisbury to sit up at night with her. There was no necessity for such care, but it was well to do even a little too much where so cherished a life was at stake. People had but to look at the father's face to know how precious that frail existence was to him. Nor was it less dear to the mother; but she seemed less apprehensive, less bowed down by gloomy forebodings.

Yes, Lola was quite cheerful for those few minutes in which her father sat by her side. The strength of her love overcame her weakness. She lolais over

forgot the pain in her head, the weariness of her limbs, while he was there. She questioned him about the villagers.

'How is little Polly going on?' she asked.

He dared not tell the truth. It would have hurt him too much to speak to her of death.

'She is going on very well; all is well, love,' he said, deceiving her for the first time in his life.

This was on Tuesday, and the preparations for Scotland were still in progress. Mr Greswold's talk with his daughter was all of their romantic Highland home, of the picnics and rambles, the fishing excursions and sketching parties they would have there. The nurse sat in a corner and listened to them with a grave countenance, and would not allow Mr Greswold more than ten minutes with his daughter.

He counted the hours till they should be on the road for the North. There would be the rest of Tuesday and all Wednesday. She would be up and dressed on Wednesday, no doubt; and on Thursday morning the good old gray carriage-horses would take them all off to Romsey Station – such a pretty drive on a summer morning, by fields and copses, with changeful glimpses of the silvery Test.

Dr Hutchinson came on Tuesday evening, and found his patient not quite so well. There was a long conference between the two doctors, and then the nurse was called in to receive her instructions; and then Mr Greswold was told that the journey to Scotland must be put off for a fortnight at the very least.

He received the sentence as if it had been his death-warrant. He asked no questions. He dared not. A second nurse was to be sent over from Southampton next morning. The two doctors had the cool, determined air of men who are preparing for a battle.

Lola was light-headed next morning; but with intervals of calmness and consciousness. She heard the church bell tolling, and asked what it meant.

'It's for Polly Rainbow's funeral,' answered the maid who was tidying the room.

'O, no,' cried Lola, 'that can't be! Father said she was better.'

And then her mind began to wander, and she talked of Polly Rainbow as if the child had been in the room: talked of the little girl's lessons at the parish school, and of a prize that she was to get.

After that all was darkness, all was despair – a seemingly inevitable progress from bad to worse. Science, care, love, prayers – all were futile; and the bell that had tolled for the widow's only child tolled ten days afterwards for Lola.

It seemed to George Greswold as those slow strokes beat upon his brain, heavily, heavily, like minute guns, that all the hopes and cares and

Poor George [handwritten annotation]

joys and expectations life had held for him were over. His wife was on her knees in the darkened house from which the funeral train was slowly moving, and he had loved her passionately; and yet it seemed to him as if the open car yonder, with its coffin hidden under snow-white blossoms, was carrying away all that had ever been precious to him upon this earth.

'She was the morning, with its promise of day,' he said to himself. 'She was the spring-time, with its promise of summer. While I had her I lived in the future; henceforward I can only live in the present. I dare not look back upon the past!'

heart wrenching poignant words of woe.

CHAPTER VII

DRIFTING APART

George Greswold and his wife spent the rest of that fatal year in a villa on the Lake of Thun, an Italian villa, with a campanello tower, and a long white colonnade, and stone balconies overhanging lawn and gardens, where the flowers grew in a riotous profusion. The villa was midway between two of the boat-stations, and there was no other house near, and this loneliness was its chief charm for those two heart-broken mourners. They yearned for no sympathy, they cared for no companionship – hardly even for that of each other, close as the bond of love had been till now. Each seemed to desire above all things to be alone with that great grief – to hug that dear, sad memory in silence and solitude. Only to see them from a distance, from the boat yonder, as it glided swiftly past that flowery lawn, an observer would have guessed at sorrow and bereavement from the mere attitude of either mourner – the man sitting with his head bent forward, brooding on the ground, the unread newspaper lying across his knee; the woman on the other side of the lawn, beyond speaking distance, half reclining in a low basket-chair, with her hands clasped above her head, gazing at the distant line of snow mountains in listless vacancy. The huge tan-coloured St Bernard, snapping with his great cavern-like jaws at infinitesimal flies, was the only object that gave life to the picture.

The boats went by in sunshine and cloud, the boats went by under torrential rain, which seemed to fuse lake and mountains, villas and gardens, into one water chaos; the boats went by, and the days passed like the boats, and made no difference in the lives of those two mourners. Nothing could ever make any difference to either of them for evermore, it seemed to Mildred. It was as if some spring had broken in the machinery of life. Even love seemed dead.

'And yet he was once so fond of me, and I of him,' thought the wife, watching her husband's face, with its curious look of absence — the look of a window with the blind down.

There were times when that look of utter abstraction almost frightened Mildred Greswold. It was an expression she had seen occasionally during her daughter's lifetime, and which had always made her anxious. It was the look about which Lola used to say when they all met at the breakfast-table.

'Papa has had his bad dream again.'

That bad dream was no invention of Lola's, but a stern reality in George Greswold's life. He would start up from his pillow in an agony, muttering broken sentences in that voice of the sleeper which seems always different from his natural voice — as if he belonged to another world. Cold beads of sweat would start out upon his forehead, and the wife would put her arms round him and soothe him as a mother soothes her frightened child, until the muttering ceased and he sank upon his pillow exhausted, to lapse into quiet sleep, or else awoke and recovered calmness in awakening.

The dream — whatever it was — always left its mark upon him next day. It was a kind of nightmare, he told his wife, when she gently questioned him, not urging her questions lest there should be pain in the mere recollection of that horrid vision. He could give no graphic description of that dream. It was all confusion — a blurred and troubled picture; but that confusion was in itself agony.

Rarely were his mutterings intelligible; rarely did his wife catch half-a-dozen consecutive words from those broken sentences; but once she heard him say,

'The cage — the cage again — iron bars — like a wild beast!'

And now that absent and cloudy look which she had seen in her husband's face after the bad dream was there often. She spoke to him sometimes, and he did not hear. She repeated the same question twice or thrice, in her soft low voice, standing close beside him, and he did not answer. There were times when it was difficult to arouse him from that deep abstraction; and at such times the utter blankness and solitude of her own life weighed upon her like a dead weight, an almost unbearable burden.

'What is to become of us both in all the long years before us?' she thought despairingly. 'Are we to be always far apart — living in the same house, spending all our days together, and yet divided?'

She had married before she was eighteen, and at one-and-thirty was still in the bloom of womanhood, younger than most women of that age; for her life had been subject to none of those vicissitudes and fevers which age women of the world. She had never kept a secret from her husband, never trembled at opening a milliner's account, or blushed at the delivery of a surreptitious letter. The struggles for preëminence, the social race in which some women waste their energies and strain their nerves, were unknown to her. She had lived at Enderby Manor as the flowers lived, rejoicing in the air and the sunshine, drinking out of a cup of life in which there mingled no drop of poison. Thus it was that not one line upon the transparent skin marked the passage of a decade. The violet eyes had the limpid purity, and the emotional lips had the tender carnation, of girlhood. Mildred Greswold was as beautiful at thirty-one as Mildred Fausset had been at seventeen. And yet it seemed to her that life was over, and that her husband had ceased to care for her.

Many and many an hour in that lovely solitude beside the lake she sat with hands loosely clasped in her lap or above her head, with her books lying forgotten at her feet – all the newest books that librarians could send to tempt the jaded appetite of the reader – and her eyes gazing vacantly over the blue of the lake or towards the snow-peaks on the horizon. Often in these silent musings she recalled the past, and looked at the days that were gone as at a picture.

She remembered just such an autumn as this, a peerless autumn spent with her father at The Hook – spent for the most part on the river and in the garden, the sunny days and moonlit nights being far too lovely for any one to waste indoors. Her seventeenth birthday was not long past. It was just ten years since she had come home to that house to find Fay had vanished from it, and to shed bitter tears for the loss of her companion. Never since that time had she seen Fay's face. Her questions had been met coldly or angrily by her mother; and even her father had answered her with unsatisfactory brevity.

All she could learn was that Fay had been sent to complete her education at a finishing-school at Brussels.

'At school! O, poor Fay! I hope she is happy.'

'She ought to be,' Mrs Fausset answered peevishly. 'The school is horridly expensive. I saw one of the bills the other day. Simply *enormous*. The girls are taken to the opera, and have all sorts of absurd indulgences.'

'Still, it is only school, mother, not home,' said Mildred compassionately.

This was two years after Fay had vanished. No letter had ever come from her to Mildred, though Mildred was able to write now, in her own sprawling childish fashion, and would have been delighted to answer any such letter. She had herself indited various epistles to her friend, but had not succeeded in getting them posted. They had drifted to the waste-paper basket, mute evidences of wasted affection.

As each holiday time came round the child asked if Fay were coming home, always to receive the same saddening negative.

One day, when she had been more urgent than usual, Mrs Fausset lost temper and answered sharply,

'No, she is not coming. She is never coming. I don't like her, and I don't intend ever to have her in any house of mine, so you may as well leave off plaguing me about her.'

'But, mother, why don't you like her?'

'Never mind why. I don't like her. That is enough for you to know.'

'But, mother, if she is father's daughter and my sister, you ought to like her,' pleaded Mildred very much in earnest.

'How dare you say that! You must never say it again – you are a naughty, cruel child to say such things!' exclaimed Mrs Fausset, beginning to cry.

'Why naughty? why cruel? O, mother!' and Mildred cried too.

She clasped her arms round her mother's neck and sobbed aloud.

'Dear mother, indeed I'm not naughty,' she protested, 'but Bell said Fay was papa's daughter. "Of course she's his daughter," Bell said; and if she's father's daughter, she's my sister, and it's wicked not to love one's sister. The psalm I was learning yesterday says so, mother. "Behold how good and how pleasant it is for brethren to dwell together in unity!" And it means sisters just the same, Miss Colville said, when I asked her; and I do love Fay. I can't help loving her.'

'You must never speak her name again to me,' said Mrs Fausset resolutely. 'I shall leave off loving you if you pester me about that odious girl!'

'Then wasn't it true what Bell said?'

'Of course not.'

'Mother, would it be wrong for papa to have a daughter?' asked Mildred, perplexed by this mysterious resentment for which she could understand no cause.

'Wrong! It would be *infamous*.'

'Would God be angry?' asked the child, with an awe-stricken look. 'Would it be wicked?'

'It would be the worst possible insult to *me*,' said Lord Castle-Connell's daughter, ignoring the minor question.

After this Mildred refrained from all further speech about the absent girl to her mother; but as the years went by she questioned her father from time to time as to Fay's whereabouts.

'She is very well off, my dear. You need not make yourself unhappy about her. She is with a very nice family, and has pleasant surroundings.'

'Shall I never see her again, father?'

'Never's a long day, Mildred. I'll take you to see her by and by when there is an opportunity. You see, it happens unfortunately that your mother does not like her, so it is better she should not come here. It would not be pleasant for her – or for me.'

He said this gravely, with a somewhat dejected look, and Mildred felt somehow that even to him it woud be better to talk no more of her lost companion.

died

As the years went by Mrs Fausset changed from a woman of fashion to a nervous valetudinarian. It was not that she loved pleasure less, but her beauty and her health had both begun to dwindle and fade at an age when other women are in their prime. She fretted at the loss of her beauty – watched every wrinkle, counted every gray hair, lamented over every change in the delicate colouring which had been her chief charm.

'How pretty you are growing, Mildred!' she exclaimed once, with a discontented air, when Mildred was a tall slip of fourteen. 'You are just what I was at your age. And you will grow prettier every day until you are thirty, and then I daresay you will begin to fade as I have done, and feel an old woman as I do.'

It seemed to her that her own charms dwindled as her daughter grew. As the bud unfolded, the flower faded. She felt almost as if Mildred had robbed her of her beauty. She would not give up the pleasures and excitement of society. She consulted half-a-dozen fashionable physicians, and would not obey one of them. They all prescribed the same repulsive treatment – rest, early hours, country air, with gentle exercise; no parties, no excitement, no strong tea.

Mrs Fausset disobeyed them all, and from only fancying herself ill grew to be really ill; and from chronic lassitude developed organic disease of the heart.

She lingered nearly two years, a confirmed invalid, suffering a good deal, and giving other people a great deal of trouble. She died soon after Mildred's sixteenth birthday, and on her death-bed she confided freely in her daughter, who had attended upon her devotedly all through her illness, neglecting everything else in the world for her mother's sake.

'You are old enough to understand things that must once have seemed very mysterious to you, Mildred,' said Mrs Fausset, lying half-hidden in the shadow of guipure bed-curtains, with her daughter's hand clasped in hers, perhaps forgetting how young that daughter was in her own yearning for sympathy. 'You couldn't make out why I disliked that horrid girl so much, could you?'

'No, indeed, mother.'

'I hated her because she was your father's daughter, Mildred – his natural daughter; the child of some woman who was not his wife. You are old enough now to know what that means. You were reading *The Heart of Midlothian* to me last week. You know, Mildred?'

Yes, Mildred knew. She hung her head at the memory of that sad story, and at the thought that her father might have sinned like George Staunton.

'Yes, Mildred, she was the child of some woman he loved before he married me. He must have been desperately in love with the woman, or he would never have brought her daughter into my house. It was the greatest insult he could offer to me.'

Mrs F confides in Mildred about Fay

'Was it, mother?'

'Was it? Why, of course it was. How stupid you are, child!' exclaimed the invalid peevishly, and the feverish hand grew hotter as she talked.

Mildred blushed crimson at the thought of this story of shame. Poor Fay! poor, unhappy Fay! And yet her strong common sense told her that there were two sides to the question.

'It was not Fay's fault, mother,' she said gently. 'No one could blame Fay, or be angry with *her*. And if the – wicked woman was dead, and father had repented, and was sorry, was it very wrong for him to bring my sister home to us?'

'Don't call her your sister!' exclaimed Mrs Fausset, with a feeble scream of angry alarm; 'she is not your sister – she is no relation – she is nothing to you. It was an insult to bring her across my threshold. You must be very stupid, or you must care very little for *me*, if you can't understand that. His conduct proved that he had cared for that low, common woman – Fay's mother – more than ever he cared for me; perhaps he thought her prettier than me,' said the invalid in hysterical parenthesis, 'and I have never known a happy hour since.'

'O, mamma dear, not in all the years when you used to wear such lovely gowns, and go to so many parties?' protested the voice of common sense.

'I only craved for excitement because I was miserable at heart. I don't think you can half understand a wife's feelings, Mildred, or you wouldn't say such foolish things. I wanted you to know this before my death. I want you to remember it always, and if you meet that odious girl avoid her as you would a pestilence. If your father should attempt to bring her here, or to Parchment Street, after I am gone——'

'He will not, mother. He will respect your wishes too much – he will be too sorry,' exclaimed Mildred, bending down to kiss the hot, dry hand, and moistening it with her tears.

The year of mourning that began soon after this conversation was a very quiet interval for father and daughter. They travelled a little, spent six months in Leipsic, where Mildred studied the piano under the most approved masters, a couple of months in Paris, where her father showed her all the lions in a tranquil, leisurely way that was very pleasant; and then they went down to The Hook, and lived there in happy idleness on the river and in the gardens all through a long and lovely summer.

Both were saddened at the sight of an empty chair – one sacred corner in all the prettiest rooms – where Maud Fausset had been wont to sit, a graceful languid figure, robed in white, or some pale delicate hue even more beautiful than white in contrast with the background of palms and flowers, Japanese screen or Indian curtain. How pretty she had looked

sitting there, with books and scent-bottles, and dainty satin-lined basket
full of some light frivolous work, which progressed by stages of half-a-
dozen stitches a day! Her fans, her Tennyson, her palms, and perfumes –
all had savoured of her own fragile bright-coloured loveliness. She was
gone; and father and daughter were alone together – deeply attached to
each other, yet with a secret between them, a secret which made a
darkening shadow across the lives of both.

Whenever John Fausset wore a look of troubled thought Mildred
fancied he was brooding upon the past, thinking of that erring woman
who had borne him a child, the child he had tried to fuse into his own
family, and to whom her own childish heart had yearned as to a sister.

'It must have been instinct that made me love her,' she said to herself;
and then she would wonder idly what the fair sinner who had been Fay's
mother was like, and whether her father had really cared more for that
frail woman than for his lawful wife.

'Poor pretty mamma! he seemed to doat upon her,' thought Mildred. 'I
cannot imagine his ever having loved any one so well. I cannot imagine
his ever having cared for any other woman in this world.'

The formless image of that unknown woman haunted the girl's
imagination. She appeared sometimes with one aspect, sometimes
another – darkly beautiful, of Oriental type, like Scott's Rebecca, or fair
and lowly-born like Effie Deans – poor fragile Effie, fated to fall at the
first temptation. Poetry and fiction were full of suggestions about that
unknown influence in her father's life; but every thought of the past
ended in a sigh of pity for that fair wife whose domestic happiness had
been clouded over by that half-discovered mystery.

Never a word did she breathe to her father upon this forbidden subject;
never a word to Bell, who was still at the head of affairs in both Mr
Fausset's houses, and who looked like a grim and stony repository of
family secrets.

CHAPTER VIII

'SUCH THINGS WERE'

Mildred had been motherless for a year when that new love began to
grow which was to be stronger and closer than the love of mother or
father, and which was to take possession of her life hereafter and
transplant her to a new soil.

How well she remembered that summer afternoon on which she and
George Greswold met for the first time! – she a girl of seventeen,

fresh, simple-minded, untainted by that life of fashion and frivolity which she had seen only from the outside, looking on as a child at the follies of men and women – he her senior by thirteen years, and serious beyond his age. Her father and his father had been companions at the University, as undergraduates, with full purses and a mutual delight in fox-hunting and tandem-driving; and it was this old Oxford friendship which was the cause of George Greswold's appearance at The Hook on that particular summer afternoon. Mr Fausset had met him on a house-boat at Henley Regatta, had been moved by the memory of the past on discovering that Greswold was the son of George Ransome of Magdalen, and had brought his friend's son home to introduce to his daughter. It was not altogether without ulterior thought, perhaps, that he introduced George Greswold into his home. He had a theory that the young men of this latter day were for the most part a weak-kneed and degenerate race; and it had seemed to him that this tall, broad-shouldered young man with the marked features, dark eyes, and powerful brow was of a stronger type than the average bachelor.

'A pity that he is rather too old for Mildred,' he said to himself, supposing that his daughter would hardly feel interested in a man who was more than five-and-twenty.

Mildred could recall his face as she saw it for the first time, to-day in her desolation, sitting idly beside the lake, while the rhythmical beat of the paddle-wheels died away in the distance. That grave dark face impressed her at once with a sense of power. She did not think the stranger handsome, or fascinating, or aristocratic, or elegant; but she thought of him a great deal, and she was silent and shy in his presence, let him come as often as he might.

He was in mourning for his mother, to whom he had been deeply attached, and who had died within the last three months, leaving him Enderby Manor and a large fortune. His home life had not been happy. There had been an antagonism between him and his father from his boyhood upwards, and he had shaken the dust of the paternal house off his feet, and had left England to wander aimlessly, living on a small income allowed him by his mother, and making a little money by literature. He was a second son, a person of no importance, except to the mother, who doted upon him.

Happily for this younger son his mother was a woman of fortune, and on her death George Ransome inherited Enderby Manor, the old house in which generations of Greswolds had come and gone since Dutch William was King of England. There had been a much older house pulled down to make room for that red brick mansion, and the Greswolds had been lords of the soil since the Wars of the Roses – red-rose to the heart's core, and loyal to an unfortunate king, whether Plantagenet, Tudor, or Stuart.

By the conditions of his mother's will, George Ransome assumed her family name and arms, and became George Ransome Greswold in all legal documents henceforward; but he signed himself George Greswold, and was known to his friends by that name. He had not loved his father nor his father's race.

He came to The Hook often in that glorious summer weather. At the first he was grave and silent, and seemed oppressed by sad memories; but this seemed natural in one who had so lately lost a beloved parent. Gradually the ice melted, and his manner brightened. He came without being bidden. He contrived to make himself, as it were, a member of the family, whose appearance surprised nobody. He bought a steam-launch, which was always at Mr Fausset's disposal, and Miss Fausset went everywhere with her father. She recalled those sunlit days now, with every impression of the moment; the ever-growing sense of happiness; the silent delight in knowing herself beloved; the deepening reverence for the man who loved her; the limitless faith in his power of heart and brain; the confiding love which felt a protection in the very sound of his voice. Yes, those had been happy days – the rosy dawning of a great joy that was to last until the grave, Mildred Fausset had thought; and now, after thirteen years of wedded love, they had drifted apart. Sorrow, which should have drawn them nearer together, had served only to divide them.

'O, my lamb, if you could know in your heavenly home how much your loss has cost us!' thought the mother, with the image of that beloved child before her eyes.

There had been a gloomy reserve in George Greswold's grief which had held his wife at a distance, and had wounded her sorrowful heart. He was selfish in his sorrow, forgetting that her loss was as great as his. He had bowed his head before inexorable Fate, had sat down in dust and ashes, and brooded over his bereavement, solitary, despairing. If he did not curse God in his anguish, it was because early teaching still prevailed, and the habits of thought he had learned in childhood were not lightly to be flung off. Upon one side of his character he was a Pagan, seeing in this affliction the hand of Nemesis, the blind Avenger.

They left Switzerland in the late autumn, and wintered in Vienna, where Mr Greswold gave himself up to study, and where neither he nor his wife took any part in the gaieties of the capital. Here they lived until the spring, and then, even in the depths of his gloom, a yearning came upon George Greswold to see the home of his race, the manor which he had loved as if it were a living thing.

'Mildred, do you think you could bear to be in the old home again?' he asked his wife suddenly, one morning at breakfast.

'I could bear anything better than the life we lead here,' she answered, her eyes filling with tears.

'We will go back, then – yes, even if it is only to look upon our daughter's grave.'

They went back to England and to Enderby Manor within a week after that conversation. They arrived at Romsey Station one bright May afternoon, and found the gray horses waiting to carry them to the old house. How sad and strange it seemed to be coming home without Lola! She had always been their companion in such journeys, and her eager face and glad young voice, on the alert to recognise the first familiar points of the landscape, hill-top, or tree, or cottage that indicated home, had given an air of gaiety to every-day life.

The old horses took them back to the Manor, but not the old coachman. A great change in the household had come about after Lola's funeral. George Greswold had been merciless to those servants whose carelessness had brought about that great calamity, which made seven new graves in the churchyard before all was done. He dismissed his bailiff, Mrs Wadman and her husband, an under-dairymaid and a cowman, and his housekeeper, all of whom he considered accountable for the use of that foul water from the old well – accountable, inasmuch as they had given him no notice of the evil, and had exercised no care or common sense in their management of the dairy. These he dismissed sternly, and that party feeling which rules among servants took this severity amiss, and several other members of the household gave warning.

'Let it be a clean sweep, then,' said Mr Greswold to Bell, who announced the falling-away of his old servants. 'Let there be none of the old faces here when we come back next year – except yours. There will be plenty of time for you to get new people.'

'A clean sweep' suited Bell's temper admirably. To engage new servants who should owe their places to her, and bow themselves down before her, was a delight to the old Irishwoman.

Thus it was that all things had a strange aspect when Mildred Greswold reëntered her old home. Even the rooms had a different air. The new servants had arranged the furniture upon new lines, not knowing that old order which had been a part of daily life.

'Let us go and look at *her* rooms first,' said Mildred softly; and husband and wife went silently to the rooms in the south wing – the octagon-room with its dwarf bookcases and bright bindings, its proof-engravings after Landseer – pictures chosen by Lola herself. Here nothing was changed. Bell's own hands had kept all things in order. No unfamiliar touch had disturbed the relics of the dead.

Mrs Greswold stayed in that once happy scene for nearly an hour. It was hard to realise that she and her daughter were never to be together again, they who had been almost inseparable – who had sat side by side by yonder window or yonder hearth in all the changes of the seasons. There was the piano at which they had played and sung together. The music-stand still contained the prettily-bound volumes – sonatinas by Hummel and Clementi – easy duets by Mozart, national melodies, Volks-Lieder. In music the child had been in advance of her years. With the mother music was a passion, and she had imbued her daughter with her own tastes in all things. The child's nature had been a carrying on and completing of the mother's character, a development of all the mother's gifts.

She was gone, and the mother's life seemed desolate and empty – the future a blank. Never in her life had she so much needed her husband's love – active, considerate, sympathetic – and yet never had he seemed so far apart from her. It was not that he was unkind or neglectful, it was only that his heart made no movement towards hers; he was not in sympathy with her. He had wrapped himself in his grief as in a mantle; he stood aloof from her, and seemed never to have understood that her sorrow was as great as his own.

He left her on the threshold of Lola's room. It might be that he could not endure the sight of those things which she had looked at weeping, in an ecstasy of grief. To her that agony of touch and memory, the aspect of things that belonged to the past, seemed to bring her lost child nearer to her – it was as if she stretched her hands across the gulf and touched those vanished hands.

'Poor piano!' she sighed; 'poor piano, that she loved.'

She touched the keys softly, playing the opening bars of *La ci darem la mano*. It was the first melody they had played together, mother and child – arranged easily as a duet. Later they had sung it together, the girl's voice clear as a bird's, and seeming to need training no more than a bird's voice. These things had been, and were all over.

'What shall I do with my life?' cried the mother despairingly; 'what shall I do with all the days to come – now she is gone?'

She left those rooms at last, locking the doors behind her, and went out into the garden. The grand old cedars cast their broad shadows on the lawn. The rustic chairs and tables were there, as in the days gone by, when that velvet turf under the cedars had been Mrs Greswold's summer parlour. Would she sit there ever again? she wondered: could she endure to sit there without Lola?

There was a private way from the Manor gardens into the churchyard, a short cut to church by which mother and daughter had gone twice on every Sunday ever since Lola was old enough to know what Sunday meant. She went by this path in the evening stillness to visit Lola's grave.

She gathered a few rosebuds as she went.

'Flowers for my blighted flower,' she murmured softly.

All was still and solemn in the old churchyard shadowed by sombre yews – a churchyard of irregular levels and moss-grown monuments enclosed by rusty iron railings, and humbler headstones of crumbling stone covered over with an orange-coloured lichen which was like vegetable rust.

The names on these were for the most part illegible, the lettering of a fashion that has passed away; but here and there a brand-new stone perked itself up among these old memorials with an assertive statement about the dead.

Lola's grave was marked by a large white marble cross, carved in *alto relievo* on the level slab. The inscription was of the simplest:

'Laura, the only child of George and Mildred Greswold, aged twelve.'

There were no words of promise or of consolation upon the stone.

On one side of the grave there was a large mountain-ash, whose white blossoms and delicate leaves made a kind of temple above the marble slab; on the other, an ancient yew cast its denser shade. Mildred knelt down in the shadow, and let her head droop over the cold stone. There was a skylark singing in the blue vault high above the old Norman tower – a carol of joy and glad young life, as it seemed to Mildred, sitting in the dust. What a mockery that joyousness of spring-time and Nature seemed!

She knew not how long she had knelt there in silent grief when the branches rustled suddenly, as if a strong arm had parted them, and a man flung himself down heavily upon a turf-covered mound – a neglected, nameless grave – beside Lola's monument. She did not stir from her kneeling attitude, or lift her head to look at the new-comer, knowing that the mourner was her husband. She had heard his footsteps approaching, heavy and slow in the stillness of the place.

The trunk of the tree hid her from that other mourner as she knelt there. He thought himself alone; and, in the abandonment of that fancied solitude, he groaned aloud, as Job may have groaned, sitting among ashes.

'Judgment!' he cried, 'judgment!' and then, after an interval of silence, he cried again, 'judgment!'

That one word, so repeated, seemed to freeze all the blood in her veins. What did it mean, that exceeding bitter cry,

'Judgment!'

CHAPTER IX

THE FACE IN THE CHURCH

Two months had gone since that first visit to Lola's grave, when the husband and wife had knelt so near each other, and yet so far apart in the infinite mystery of human consciousness; he with his secret thoughts and secret woes, which she had never fathomed. He, unaware of her neighbourhood; she, chilled by a vague suspicion and sense of estrangement which had been growing upon her ever since her daughter's death.

It was summer again, the ripe full-blown summer of mid-July. The awful anniversary of their bereavement had passed in silence and prayer. All things at Enderby looked as they had looked in the years that were gone, except the faces of the servants, which were for the most part strange. That change of the household made a great change in life to people so conservative as George Greswold and his wife; and the old home seemed so much the less like home because of that change. The Squire of Enderby felt that his popularity was lessened in the village for which he had done so much. His severe dealing with the offenders had pleased nobody, not even the sufferers from the epidemic, whose losses he had avenged. He had shown himself implacable; and there were many who said he had been unjust.

'It was hard upon Wadman and his wife to be turned off after twenty years' faithful service,' said one of the villagers. 'The Squire may go a long way before he'll get as good a bailiff as Thomas,' said another.

For the first time since he had inherited the estate George Greswold felt himself surrounded by an atmosphere of discontent, and even dislike. His tenants seemed afraid of him, and were reticent and moody when he talked to them, which he did much seldomer than of old, making a great effort in order to appear interested in their affairs.

Mildred's life during those summer weeks, while the roses were opening and all the flowers succeeding each other in a procession of loveliness, had drifted along like a slow dull stream that crawls through a desolate swamp. There was neither beauty nor colour in her existence; there was a sense of vacuity, an aching void. Nothing to hope for, nothing to look back upon.

She did not abandon herself slavishly to her sorrow. She tried to resume the life of duty which had once been so full of sweetness, so rich in its rewards for every service. She went about among the cottagers as of old; she visited the shabby gentilities on the fringe of the market town, the annuitants and struggling families, the poor widows and elderly spinsters, who had quite as much need of help as the cottagers, and

whom it had always been her delight to encourage and sustain with
friendliness and sympathy, as well as with delicate benefactions, gifts that
never humiliated the recipient. She took up the thread of her work in the
parish schools; she resumed her old interest in the church services and
decorations, in the inevitable charity bazaar or organ-fund concert. She
played her part in the parish so well that people began to say,

'Mrs Greswold is getting over her loss.'

In him the shock had left a deeper mark. His whole aspect was
changed. He looked ten years older than before the coming of sorrow;
and though people loved her better, they pitied him more.

'She has more occupations and pursuits to interest her,' said Mr
Rollinson, the curate. 'She is devoted to music, and that employs her
mind.'

Yes, music was her passion; but in these days of mourning even music
was allied to pain. Every melody she played, every song she sang, recalled
the child whose appreciation of that divine art had been far beyond her
years. They had sung and played together. Often singing alone in the
summer dusk, in that corner of the long drawing-room, where Lola's
babyish chair still stood, she had started, fancying she heard that other
voice mingling with her own – the sweet clear tones which had sounded
seraphic even upon earth.

O, was she with the angels now; or was it all a fable, that fond vision of
a fairer world and an angelic choir, singing before the great white throne?
To have lost such a child was almost to believe in the world of seraphim
and cherubim, of angels and purified spirits. Where else could she be?

Husband and wife lived together, side by side, in a sad communion that
seemed to lack the spirit of unity. The outward semblance of confiding
affection was there, but there was something wanting. He was very good
to her – as kind, as attentive, and considerate as in their first year of
marriage; and yet there was something wanting.

She remembered what he had been when he came as a stranger to
The Hook; and it seemed to her as if the glass of Time had been turned
backwards for fourteen years, and that he was again just as he had been
in those early days, when she had watched him, curiously interested in
his character as in a mystery. He was too grave for a man of his years –
and with a shade of gloom upon him that hinted at a more than
common grief. He had been subject to lapses of abstraction, as if his
mind had slipped back to some unhappy past. It was only when he had
fallen in love and was wholly devoted to her that the shadow passed
away, and he began to feel the joyousness of life and the fervour of
ardent hopes. Then the old character dropped off him like the serpent's
slough, and he became as young as the youngest – boyish even in his
frank felicity.

This memory of her first impressions about him was so strong with her that she could not help speaking of it one evening after dinner when she had been playing one of Beethoven's grandest adagios to him, and they were sitting in silence, she by the piano, he far away by an open window on a level with the shadowy lawn, where the great cedars rose black against the pale gray sky.

'George, do you remember my playing that adagio to you for the first time?'

'I remember you better than Beethoven. I could scarcely think of the music in those days for thinking so much of you.'

'Ah, but the first time you heard me play that adagio was before you had begun to care for me – before you had cast your slough.'

'What do you mean?'

'Before you had come out of your cloud of sad memories. When first you came to us you lived only in the past. I doubt if you were more than half-conscious of our existence.'

She could only distinguish his profile faintly defined against the evening gray as he sat beside the window. Had she seen the expression of his face, its look of infinite pain, she would hardly have pursued the subject.

'I had but lately lost my mother,' he said gravely.

'Ah, but that was a grief which you did not hide from us. You did not shrink from our sympathy there. There was some other trouble, something that belonged to a remoter past, over which you brooded in secret. Yes, George, I know you had some secrets then – that divided us – and – and——' falteringly, with tears in her voice – 'I think those old secrets are keeping us asunder now, when our grief should draw us nearer together.'

She had left her place by the piano, and had gone to him as she spoke, and now she was on her knees beside him, clinging to him tearfully.

'George, trust me, love me,' she pleaded.

'My beloved, do I not love you?' he protested passionately, clasping her in his arms, kissing away her tears, soothing her as if she had been a child. 'My dearest and best, from the first hour I awakened to a new life in your love my truth has never wavered, my heart has never known change.'

'And yet you are changed – since our darling went – terribly changed.'

'Do you wonder that I grieve for her?'

'No, but you grieve apart – you hold yourself aloof from me.'

'If I do it is because I do not want you to share my burden, Mildred. Your sorrow may be cured, perhaps – mine never can be. Time may be merciful to you – for me time can do nothing.'

'Dearest, what hope can there be for me that you do not share? – the Christian's hope of meeting our loved one hereafter. I have no other hope.'

'I hardly know if I have that hope,' he answered slowly, with deepest despondency.

'And yet you are a Christian.'

'If to endeavour to follow Christ, the Teacher and Friend of humanity, is to be a Christian – yes.'

'And you believe in the world to come?'

'I try so to believe, Mildred. I try. Faith in the Kingdom of Heaven does not come easily to a man whose life has been ruled by the inexorable Fates. Not a word, darling; let us not talk of these things. We know no more than Socrates knew in his dungeon; no more than Roger Bacon knew in his old age – unheard, buried, forgotten. Never doubt my love, dearest. That is changeless. You and Lola were the sunshine of my life. You shall be my sunshine henceforward. I have been selfish in brooding over my sorrow; but it is the habit of my mind to grieve in silence. Forgive me, dear wife; forgive me.'

He clasped her in his arms, and again she felt assured of her husband's affection; but she knew all the same that there was some sorrow in his past life which he had kept hidden from her, which he meant her never to know.

Many a time in their happy married life she had tried to lead him to talk of his boyhood and youth. About his days at Eton and Oxford he was frank enough, but he was curiously reticent about his home life and about those years which he had spent travelling over the Continent after he had left his father's house for good.

'I was not happy at home, Mildred,' he told her one day. 'My father and I did not get on together, as the phrase goes. He was very fond of my elder brother. They had the same way of thinking about most things. Randolph's marriage pleased my father, and he looked to Randolph to strengthen the position of our family, which had been considerably reduced by his own extravagance. He would have liked my mother's estate to have gone to the elder son; but she had full disposing power, and she made me her heir. This set my father against me, and there came a time when, dearly as I loved my mother, I found that I could no longer live at home. I went out into the world, a lonely man; and I only came back to the old home after my father's death.'

This was the fullest account of his family history that George Greswold had given his wife. From his reserve in speaking of his father she divined that the balance of wrong had been upon the side of the parent rather than of the son. Had a man of her husband's temper been the sinner he would have frankly confessed his errors. Of his mother he spoke with undeviating love; and he seemed to have been on friendly terms with his brother.

On the morning after that tearful talk in the twilight Mr Greswold startled his wife from a pensive reverie as they sat at breakfast in the garden. They always breakfasted out of doors on fine summer mornings. They had made no change in old customs since their return, as some mourners might have done, hoping to blunt the keen edge of memory by an alteration in the details of life. Both knew too well how futile any such alteration of their surroundings would be. They remembered Lola no more vividly at Enderby than they had remembered her in Switzerland.

'My dearest, I have been thinking of you incessantly since last night, and of the loneliness of your life,' George Greswold began seriously, as he sat in a low basket-chair, sipping his coffee, with his favourite setter Kassandra at his feet; an Irish dog that had been famous for feather in days gone by, but who had insinuated herself into the family affections, and had got herself accepted as a household companion to the ruin of her sporting qualities. Kassandra went no more with the guns. Her place was the drawing-room or the lawn.

'I can never be lonely, George, while I have you. There is no other company I can ever care about henceforward.'

'Let me always be the first, dear; but you should have female companionship of some kind. Our house is empty and voiceless. There should be some young voice – some young footstep——'

'Do you mean that I ought to hire a girl to run up and down stairs, and laugh in the corridors, as Lola used? O, George, how can you!' exclaimed Mildred, beginning to cry.

'No, no, dear. I had no such thought in my mind. I was thinking of Randolph's daughter. You seemed to like her when she and her sister were here two years ago.'

'Yes, she was a nice, bright girl then, and my darling was pleased with her. How merry they were together, playing battledore and shuttlecock over there by the yew hedge! Don't ask me ever to see that girl again, George. It would make my heart ache.'

'I am sorry to hear you say that, Mildred. I was going to ask you to have her here on a good long visit. Now that Rosalind is married, Pamela has no home of her own. Rosalind and her husband like having her occasionally – for a month or six weeks at a time; but Sir Henry Mountford's house is not Pamela's home. She would soon begin to feel herself an incubus. The Mountfords are very fond of society, and just a little worldly. They would soon be tired of a girl whose presence was no direct advantage. I have been thinking that with us Pamela would never be in the way. You need not see too much of her in this big house. There would be plenty of room for her to carry on her own pursuits and amusements without boring you; and when you wanted her she would be at hand, a bright companionable girl, who would grow fonder of you every day.'

'I could not endure her fondness. I could not endure any girl's companionship. Her presence would only remind me of my loss.'

'Dearest, I thought we were both agreed that, as nothing can make us forget our darling, it cannot matter to us how often we are reminded of her.'

'Yes, by silent, unreasoning things like Kassandra,' touching the dog's tawny head with a caressing hand; 'or the garden – the trees and flowers she loved – her books – her piano. Those things may remind us of our darling without hurting us. But to hear a girl's voice calling me – as she used to call me from the garden on summer mornings – to hear a girl's laughter——'

'Yes, it would be painful, love, at first. I can understand that, Mildred. But if you can benefit an orphan girl by having her here, I know your kind heart will not refuse. Let her come for a few weeks, and if her presence pains you she shall stay no longer. She shall not be invited again. I would not ask you to receive a stranger, but my brother's daughter is near me in blood.'

'Let her come, George,' said Mildred impulsively; 'I am very selfish – thinking only of my own feelings. Let her come. How strangely this talk of ours reminds me of something that happened when I was a child!'

'What was that, Mildred?'

'You have heard me speak of Fay, my playfellow?'

'Yes.'

'I remember the evening my father asked mamma to let her come to us. It seemed just now as if you were using his very words; and yet all things were different.'

Mildred had told him very little about that childish sorrow of hers. She had shrunk from any allusion to the girl whose existence bore witness against her father. She, too, fond and frank as she was, had kept her own counsel, had borne the burden of a secret.

'Yes, I have heard you speak of the girl you called Fay, and of whom you must have been very fond, for the tears came into your eyes when you mentioned her. Did she live with you long?'

'Oh, no, a very short time! She was sent to school – to a finishing-school at Brussels.'

'Brussels!' he repeated, with a look of surprise.

'Yes. Do you know anything about Brussels schools?'

'Nothing personally. I have heard of girls educated there. And what became of your playfellow after the Brussels school?'

'I never heard.'

'And you never tried to find out?'

'Yes, I asked my mother; but there was a prejudice in her mind against poor Fay. I would rather not talk about her, George.'

Her vivid blush, her evident confusion, perplexed her husband. There was some kind of mystery, it seemed – some family trouble in the background, or Mildred, who was all candour, would have spoken more freely.

'Then may I really invite Pamela?' he asked after a brief silence, during which he had responded to the endearments of Kassandra, too well fed to have any design upon the dainties on the breakfast-table, and only asking to be loved.

'I will write to her myself, George. Where is she?'

'Not very far off. She is at Cowes with the Mountfords, on board Sir Henry's yacht the Gadfly. You had better send your letter to the post-office, marked Gadfly.'

The invitation was despatched by the first post; Miss Greswold was asked to come to the Manor as soon as she liked, and to stay till the autumn.

The next day was Sunday, and Mr and Mrs Greswold went to church together by the path that led them within a few paces of Lola's grave.

For the first time since her daughter's death Mildred had put on a light gown. Till to-day she had worn only black. This morning she came into the vivid sunlight in a pale gray gown of soft lustreless silk, and a neat little gray straw bonnet, which set off the fairness of her skin and the sheen of her golden hair. The simple fashion of her gown became her tall, slim figure, which had lost none of the grace of girlhood. She was the prettiest and most distinguished-looking woman in Enderby Church, although there were more county families represented there upon that particular Sunday than are often to be seen in a village church.

The Manor House pew was on one side of the chancel, and commanded a full view of the nave. The first lesson was long, and while it was being read Mildred's eyes wandered idly along the faces in the nave, recognising countenances that had been familiar to her ever since her marriage, until that wandering gaze stopped suddenly, arrested by a face that was strange.

She saw this strange face between other faces – as it were in a cleft in the block of people. She saw it at the end of a vista, with the sunlight from the chancel window full upon it – a face that impressed her as no face of a stranger had ever done before.

It looked like the face of Judas, she thought; and then in the next moment was ashamed of her fancy.

'It is only the colouring, and the effect of the light upon it,' she told herself. 'I am not so weak as to cherish the vulgar prejudice against that coloured hair.'

'That coloured hair' was of the colour which a man's enemies call red and his friends auburn or chestnut. It was of that ruddy brown which Titian has immortalised in more than one Venus, and without which Potiphar's wife would be a nonentity.

The stranger wore a small pointed beard of this famous colouring. His eyes were of a reddish brown, large, and luminous, his eyebrows strongly arched; his nose was a small aquiline; his brow was wide and lofty, slightly bald in front. His mouth was the only obviously objectionable feature. The lips were finely moulded, from a Greek sculptor's standpoint, and would have done for a Greek Bacchus, but the expression was at once crafty and sensual. The auburn moustache served to accentuate rather than to conceal that repellant expression. Mildred looked at him presently as he stood up for the *Te Deum*.

He was tall, for she saw his head well above intervening heads. He looked about five-and-thirty. He had the air of being a gentleman.

'Whoever he is, I hope I shall never see him again,' thought Mildred.

CHAPTER X

THERE IS ALWAYS THE SKELETON

When Mr and Mrs Greswold left the church, the stranger was taking his place in the Hillersdon wagonette, a capacious vehicle, drawn by a pair of upstanding black-brown horses, set off by servants in smart liveries of dark brown and gold.

Mildred gave a sigh of relief. If the stranger was a visitor at Riverdale it was not likely that he would stay long in the neighbourhood, or be seen again for years to come. The guests at Riverdale were generally birds of passage; and the same faces seldom appeared there twice. Mr and Mrs Hillersdon of Riverdale were famous for their extensive circle, and famous for bringing new people into the county. Some of their neighbours said it was Mr Hillersdon who brought the people there, and that Mrs Hillersdon had nothing to do with the visiting list; others declared that husband and wife were equally fickle and equally frivolous.

Riverdale was one of the finest houses within ten miles of Romsey, and it was variously described by the local gentry. It was called a delightful house, or it was called a curious house, according to the temper of the speaker. Its worst enemy could not deny that it was a splendid house – spacious, architectural, luxurious, with all the appendages of wealth and dignity – nor could its worst enemy deny its merit as one of the most hospitable houses in the county.

Mr
+ Mrs   Hillersdon ---

Notwithstanding this splendour and lavish hospitality, the local magnates did not go to Riverdale, and the Hillersdons were not received in some of the best houses. Tom Hillersdon was a large landowner, a millionaire, and a man of good family; but Tom Hillersdon was considered to have stranded himself in middle life by a marriage which in the outer world was spoken of vaguely as 'unfortunate,' but which the straitlaced among his neighbours considered fatal. No man who had so married could hold up his head among his friends any more; no man who had so married could hope to have his wife received in decent people's houses. In spite of which opinion prevailing among Tom Hillersdon's oldest friends Mrs Hillersdon contrived to gather a good many people round her, and some of them the most distinguished in the land. She had Cabinet Ministers, men of letters, and famous painters among her guests. She had plenty of women friends – of a sort: attractive women, intellectual and enlightened women; sober matrons, bread-and-butter girls; women who doated on Mrs Hillersdon, and, strange to say, had never heard her history.

And yet Hillersdon's wife had a history scarcely less famous than that of Cleopatra or Nell Gwynne. Louise Hillersdon was once Louise Lorraine, the young adventuress whose Irish gray eyes had set all London talking when the Great Exhibition of '62 was still a monstrous iron skeleton, and when South Kensington was in its infancy. Louise Lorraine's extravagance, and Louise Lorraine's devotees, from German princes and English dukes downwards, had been town-talk. Her box at the opera had been the cynosure of every eye; and Paris ran mad when she drove in the Bois, or exhibited her diamonds in the Rue Lepelletier; or supped in the small hours at the Café de Paris, with the topmost strawberries in the basket. Numerous and conflicting were the versions of her early history – the more sensational chronicles describing her as the Aphrodite of the gutter. Some people declared that she could neither read nor write, and could not stir without her amanuensis at her elbow; others affirmed that she spoke four languages, and read a Greek play or a chapter of Thucidydes every night, with her feet on the fender, while her maid brushed her hair. The sober truth lay midway between these extremes. She was the daughter of a doctor in a line regiment; she was eminently beautiful, very ignorant, and very clever. She wrote an uneducated hand, never read anything better than a sentimental novel, sang prettily, and could accompany her songs on the guitar with a good deal of dash and fire. To this may be added that she was an adept in the art of dress, had as much tact and finesse as a leader of the old French noblesse, and more audacity than a Parisian cocotte in the golden age of Cocotterie. Such she was when Tom Hillersdon, Wiltshire squire, and millionaire, swooped like an eagle upon this fair dove, and bore her off to his eerie. There was howling and gnashing of teeth among those many admirers who were all thinking seriously about making the lovely Louise a *bonâ fide* offer; and it was felt in a certain set that Tom Hillersdon had done a valiant and victorious deed; but his country friends were of one accord in the idea that Hillersdon had wrecked himself for ever.

The Squire's wife came to Riverdale, and established herself there with as easy an air as if she had been a duchess. She gave herself no trouble about the county families. London was near enough for the fair Louise, and she filled her house – or Tom Hillersdon filled it – with relays of visitors from the great city. Scarcely had she been settled there a week when the local gentry were startled at seeing her sail into church with one of the most famous English statesmen in her train. Upon the Sunday after she was attended by a great painter and a well-known savant; and besides these she had a pew full of smaller fry – a lady novelist, a fashionable actor, a celebrated Queen's Counsel, and a county member.

'Where does she get those men?' asked Lady Marjorie Danefled, the Conservative member's wife; 'surely they can't *all* be – reminiscences.'

It had been supposed while the newly-wedded couple were on their honeymoon that the lady's arrival at Riverdale would inaugurate a reign of profanity – that Sunday would be given over to Bohemian society, café-chantant songs, champagne, and cigarette-smoking. Great was the surprise of the locality, therefore, when Mrs Hillersdon appeared in the Squire's pew on Sunday morning, neatly dressed, demure, nay, with an aspect of more than usual sanctity; greater still the astonishment when she reappeared in the afternoon, and listened meekly to the catechising of the school-children and to the baptism of a refractory baby; greater even yet when it was found that these pious practices were continued, that she never missed a Saint's-Day service, that she had morning prayers for family and household, and that she held meetings of an evangelical character in her drawing-room – meetings at which curates from outlying parishes gathered like a flock of crows, and at which the excellence of the tea and coffee, pound-cake and muffins, speedily became known to the outside world.

Happily for Tom Hillersdon these pious tendencies did not interfere with his amusements or the pleasantness of his domestic life. Riverdale was enlivened by a perennial supply of lively or interesting people. Notoriety of some kind was a passport to the Hillersdons' favour. It was an indication that a man was beginning to make his mark when he was asked to Riverdale. When he had made his mark he might think twice about going. Riverdale was the paradise of budding celebrities.

So to-day, seeing the stranger get into the Hillersdon wagonette, Mrs Greswold opined that he was a man who had made some kind of reputation. He could not be an actor with that beard. He was a painter, perhaps. She thought he looked like a painter.

The wagonette was full of well-dressed women and well-bred men, all with an essentially metropolitan – or cosmopolitan – air. The eighteen-carat stamp of 'county' was obviously deficient. Mrs Hillersdon had her own carriage – a barouche – which she shared with an elderly lady, who looked as correct as if she had been a bishop's wife. She was on bowing terms with Mrs Greswold. They had met at hunt-balls and charity bazaars, and at various other functions from which the wife of a local landowner can hardly be excluded – even when she has a history.

Mildred thought no more of the auburn-haired stranger after the wagonette had disappeared in a cloud of summer-dust. She strolled slowly home with her husband by a walk which they had been in the habit of taking on fine Sundays after morning service, but which they had never trodden together since Lola's death. It was a round which skirted the common, and took them past a good many of the cottages, and their tenants had been wont to loiter at their gates on fine Sundays, in the hope of getting a passing word with the Squire and his wife. There had been something patriarchal, or clannish, in the feeling between landlord and tenant, labourer and master, which can only prevail in a parish where the chief landowner spends the greater part of his life at home.

To-day every one was just as respectful as of old; curtsies were as low and tones as reverential; but George Greswold and his wife felt there was a difference, all the same. A gulf had been cleft between them and their people by last summer's calamity. It was not the kindred of the dead in whom this coolness was distinguishable. The bereaved seemed drawn nearer to their Squire by an affliction which had touched him too. But in Enderby parish there was a bond of kindred which seemed to interlink the whole population. There were not above three family names in the village, and everybody was everybody else's cousin, when not a nearer relative. Thus, in dismissing his bailiff and dairy people, Mr Greswold had given umbrage to almost all his cottagers. He was no longer regarded as a kind master. A man who could dismiss a servant after twenty years' faithful service was, in the estimation of Enderby parish, a ruthless tyrant – a master whose yoke galled every shoulder.

'Him seemed to be so fond of we all,' said Luke Thomas, the village wheelwright, brother of that John Thomas who had been Mr Greswold's bailiff, and who was now dreeing his weird in Canada; 'and yet offend he, and him can turn and sack yer as if yer was a thief – sweep yer off his premises like a handful o'rubbish. Faithful service don't count with he.'

George Greswold felt the change from friendly gladness to cold civility. He could see the altered expression in all those familiar faces. The only sign of affection was from Mrs Rainbow, standing at her cottage gate in decent black, with sunken cheeks worn pale by many tears. She burst out crying at sight of Mildred Greswold, and clasped her hand in a fervour of sympathy.

'O, to think of your sweet young lady, ma'am! that you should lose her, as I lost my Polly!' she sobbed; and the two women wept together – sisters in affliction.

'You don't think we are to blame, do you, Mrs Rainbow?' Mildred said gently.

'No, no, indeed, ma'am. We all know it was God's will. We must kiss the rod.'

'What fatalists these people are!' said Greswold, as he and his wife walked homeward by the sweet-smelling common, where the heather showed purple here and there, and where the harebells were beginning to dance upon the wind. 'Yes, it is God's will; but the name of that God is Nemesis.'

Husband and wife were almost silent during luncheon. Both were depressed by that want of friendliness in those who had been to them as familiar friends. To have forfeited confidence and affection was hard when they had done so much to merit both. Mildred could but remember how she and her golden-haired daughter had gone about amongst those people, caring for all their needs, spiritual and temporal, never approaching them from the standpoint of superiority, but treating them verily as friends. She recalled long autumn afternoons in the village reading-room, when she and Lola had presided over a bevy of matrons and elderly spinsters, she reading aloud to them while they worked, Lola threading needles to save elderly eyes, sewing on buttons, indefatigable in giving help of all kinds to those village sempstresses. She had fancied that those mothers' meetings, the story-books, and the talk had brought them all into a bond of affectionate sympathy; and yet one act of stern justice seemed to have cancelled all obligations.

Mr Greswold lighted a cigar after lunch, and went for a ramble in those extensive copses which were one of the charms of Enderby Manor, miles and miles of woodland walks, dark and cool in the hottest day of summer – lonely footpaths where the master of Enderby could think his own thoughts without risk of coming face to face with any one in that leafy solitude. The Enderby copses were cherished rather for pleasure than for profit, and were allowed to grow a good deal higher and a good deal wilder and thicker than the young wood upon neighbouring estates.

Mildred went to the drawing-room and to her piano, after her husband, her chief companion and confidant now that Lola was gone. Music was her passion – the only art that moved her deeply, and to sit alone wandering from number to number of Beethoven and Mozart, Bach or Mendelssohn, was the very luxury of loneliness.

Adhering in all things to the rule that Sunday was not as other days, she had her library of sacred music apart from other volumes, and it was sacred music only which she played on Sundays. Her *répertoire* was large, and she roamed at will among the classic masters of the last two hundred years, but for sacred music Bach and Mozart were her favourites.

She was playing a Gloria by the latter composer when she heard a carriage drive past the windows, and looked up just in time to catch a glimpse of a profile that startled her with a sudden sense of strangeness and familiarity. The carriage was a light T-cart, driven by a groom in the Hillersdon livery.

A visitor from Riverdale was a novelty, for, although George Greswold and Tom Hillersdon were friendly in the hunting-field, Riverdale and the Manor were not on visiting terms. The visit was for her husband, Mildred concluded, and she went on playing.

The door was opened by the new footman, who announced 'Mr Castellani.'

Mrs Greswold rose from the piano to find herself face to face with the man whose countenance, seen in the distance, in the light of the east window, had reminded her of Judas. Seen as she saw him now, in the softer light of the afternoon, standing before her with a deprecating air in her own drawing-room, the stranger looked altogether different, and she thought he had a pleasing expression.

He was tall and slim, well dressed in a subdued metropolitan style; and he had an air of distinction and elegance which would have marked him anywhere as a creature apart from the common herd. It was not an English manner. There was a supple grace in his movements which suggested a Southern origin. There was a pleading look in the full brown eyes which suggested an emotional temperament.

'An Italian, no doubt,' thought Mildred, taking this Southern gracefulness in conjunction with the Southern name.

She wondered on what pretence this stranger had called, and what could be his motive for coming.

'Mrs Greswold, I have to apologise humbly for presenting myself without having first sent you my credentials and waited for your permission to call,' he said, in very perfect English, with only the slightest Milanese accent; and then he handed Mrs Greswold an unsealed letter, which he had taken from his breast-pocket.

She glanced at it hastily, not a little embarrassed by the situation. The letter was from an intimate friend, an amateur *littérateur*, who wrote graceful sonnets and gave pleasant parties:

'I need not excuse myself, my dear friend, for making Mr Castellani known to you in the flesh, as I have no doubt he is already familiar to you in the spirit. He is the anonymous author of *Nepenthe*, the book that *almost every one* has been reading and *quite every one* has been talking about

Castellani visits Mildred -

this season. Only the few can *understand* it; but you are of those few, and I feel assured your *deepest* feelings have been stirred by that *most exceptional* work. How delicious it must be with you among green lanes and English meadows! We are just rushing off to a land of extinct volcanoes for my poor husband's annual cure. *A vous de coeur,*

DIANA TOMKISON.'

'Pray sit down,' said Mildred, as she finished her gushing friend's note; 'my husband will be in presently – I hope in time to see you.'

'Pardon me if, in all humility, I say it is *you* I was especially anxious to see, to know, if it were possible – delightful as it will be also to know Mr Greswold. It is with your name that my past associations are interwoven.'

'Indeed! How is that?'

'It is a long story, Mrs Greswold. To explain the association I must refer to the remote past. My grandfather was in the silk trade, like your grandfather.'

Mildred blushed; the assertion came upon her like an unpleasant surprise. It was a shock. That great house of silk merchants from which her father's wealth had been derived had hardly ever been mentioned in her presence. Lord Castle-Connell's daughter had never grown out of the idea that all trade is odious, and *her* daughter had almost forgotten that her father had ever been in trade.

'Yes, when the house of Fausset was in its infancy the house of Felix & Sons, silk manufacturers and silk merchants, was one of the largest on the hillside of old Lyons. My great-grandfather was one of the richest men in Lyons, and he was able to help the clever young Englishman, your grandfather, who came into his house as corresponding clerk, to perfect himself in the French language, and to find out what the silk trade was like. He had a small capital, and when he had learnt something about the trade, he established himself near St Paul's Churchyard as a wholesale trader in a very small way. He had no looms of his own in those days; and it was the great house of Felix, and the credit given him by that house, which enabled him to hold his own, and to make a fortune. When your father began life the house of Felix was on the wane. Your grandfather had established a manufactory of his own at Lyons. Felix & Sons had grown old-fashioned. They had forgotten to march with the times. They had allowed themselves to go to sleep; and they were on the verge of bankruptcy when your father came to their rescue with a loan which enabled them to tide over their difficulties. They had had a lesson, and they profited by it. The house of Felix recovered its ascendency, and the loan was repaid before your father retired from business.'

'I am not surprised to hear that my father was generous. I should have been slow to believe that he could have been ungrateful,' said Mildred softly.

'Your name is among my earliest recollections,' pursued Castellani. 'My mother was educated at a convent at Roehampton, and she was very fond of England and English people. The first journey I can distinctly remember was a journey to London, which occurred when I was ten years old. I remember my father and mother talking about Mr Fausset. She had known him when she was a little girl. He used to stay in her father's house when he came to Lyons on business. She would like to have seen him and his wife and daughter, for old times' sake; but she had been told that his wife was a lady of rank, and that he had broken off all associations with his trading career. She was too diffident to intrude herself upon her father's old ally. One day our carriage passed yours in the Park. Yes, I saw you, a golden-haired child – yes, madam, saw you with these eyes – and the vision has stayed with me, a sunny remembrance of my own childhood. I can see that fair child's face in this room to-day.'

'You should have seen my daughter,' faltered Mildred sadly.

'You have a daughter?' said the stranger eagerly.

'I *had* a daughter. She is gone. I only put off my black gown yesterday; but my heart and mind will wear mourning for her till I go to my grave.'

'Ah, madam, how deeply I sympathise with such a grief!' murmured Castellani.

He had a voice of peculiar depth and beauty – one of those rare voices whose every tone is music. The pathos and compassion in those few commonplace words moved Mildred to sudden tears. She commanded herself with an effort.

'I am much interested in your reminiscences,' she said, after a brief pause. 'My father was very dear to me. My mother came of an old Irish family, and the Irish, as you know, are apt to be over-proud of high birth. I had never heard my father's commercial life spoken about until to-day. I only knew him as an idle man, without business cares of any kind, able to take life pleasantly. He used to spend two or three months of every year under this roof. It was a terrible blow to me when we lost him six years ago, and I think my husband mourned him almost as deeply as I did. But tell me about your book. Are you really the author of *Nepenthe*, that nameless author who has been so much discussed?'

'And who has been identified with so many distinguished people – Mr Gladstone – Cardinal Newman.'

'Mr Swinburne – Mr Browning. I have heard all kinds of speculations. And is it really you?'

'Yes, it is I. To you I may plead guilty, since, unfortunately, the authorship of *Nepenthe* is now *le secret de Polichinelle*.'

'It is a – strange book,' said Mildred. 'My husband and I were both interested in it, and impressed by it. But your book saddened us both. You seem to believe in nothing.'

Castellani nihilistic

A hint at something mysterious

Mrs Hillerdon's discussed

'"Seems," madam! nay, I know not "seems;" but perhaps I am not so bad as you think me. I am of Hamlet's temper – inquiring rather than disbelieving. To live is to doubt. And I own that I have seen enough of this life to discover that the richest gift Fate can give to man is the gift of forgetfulness.'

'I cannot think that. I would not forget, even if I could. It would be treason to forget the beloved ones we have lost.'

'Ah, Mrs Greswold, most men have worse memories than the memory of the dead. The wounds we want healed are deeper than those made by Death; his scars we can afford to look upon. There are wounds that have gone deeper, and that leave an uglier mark.'

There was a pause. Mr Castellani made no sign of departure. He evidently intended to wait for the Squire's return. Through the open windows of a second drawing-room, divided from the first by an archway, they could see the servants setting out the tea-table on the lawn. A Turkey carpet was spread under the cedar, and there were basket-chairs of various shapes, cushioned, luxurious, and two or three small wicker-tables of different colours, and a milking-stool or two, and all the indications of outdoor life. The one thing missing was that aerial figure, robed in white, which had been wont to flit about among the dancing shadows of branch and blossom – a creature as evanescent as they, it seemed to that mourning mother who remembered her to-day.

'Are you staying long at Riverdale?' asked Mildred presently, by way of conversation.

'If Mrs Hillersdon would be good enough to have me, I would stay another fortnight. The place is perfect, the surrounding scenery has your true English charm, and my hostess is simply delightful.'

'You like her?' asked Mildred, interested.

No woman can help being curious about a woman with such a history as Mrs Hillersdon's. All the elements of romance and mystery seem, from the feminine standpoint, to concentre in such a career. How many hearts has such a woman broken; how many lives has she ruined; how often has she been on the brink of madness or suicide? – she, the placid matron, with her fat carriage-horses, and powdered footmen, and big prayer-book, and demure behaviour, and altogether bourgeois surroundings.

'Like her? Yes; she is such a clever woman.'

'Indeed!'

'Yes, she is a marvel – the cleverest woman I know.'

He laid a stress on the superlative. His praise might mean anything – might be a hidden sneer. He might praise as the devil prays – backwards. Mildred had an uncomfortable feeling that he was not in earnest.

'Have you known her long?' she asked.

'Not very long; only this season. I am told that she is fickle, or that other people are fickle, and that she seldom knows any one more than a season. But I do not mean to be fickle; I mean to be a house-friend at Riverdale all my life if she will let me. She is a very clever woman, and thoroughly artistic.'

Mildred had not quite grasped the modern significance of this last word.

'Does Mrs Hillersdon paint?' she asked.

'No, she does not paint.'

'She plays – or sings, I suppose?'

'No. I am told she once sang Spanish ballads with a guitar accompaniment; but the people who remember her singing tell me that her arms were the chief feature in the performance. Her arms are lovely to this day. No; she neither paints, nor plays, nor sings; but she is supremely artistic. She dresses as few women of five-and-forty know how to dress – dresses so as to make one think five-and-forty the most perfect age for a woman; and she has a marvellous appreciation of art, of painting, of poetry, of acting, of music. She is almost the only woman to whom I have ever played Beethoven who has seemed to me thoroughly *simpatica*.'

'Ah!' exclaimed Mildred, surprised, 'you yourself play, then?'

'It is hardly a merit in me,' answered Castellani modestly; 'my father was one of the finest musicians of his time in Italy.'

'Indeed!'

'You are naturally surprised. His genius was poorly appreciated. His name was hardly known out of Milan and Brussels. Strange to say, those stolid Flemings appreciated him. His work was over the heads of the vulgar public. He saw such men as Verdi and Gounod triumphant, while he remained obscure.'

'But surely you admire Verdi and Gounod?'

'In their places, yes; both are admirable; but my father's place should have been in a higher rank of composers. But let me not plague you about him. He is dead, and forgotten. He died crownless. I heard you playing Mozart's "Gloria" as I came in. You like Mozart?'

'I adore him.'

'Yes, I know there are still people who like his music. Chopin did; asked for it on his death-bed,' said Castellani, with a wry face, as if he were talking of a vulgar propensity for sauerkraut or a morbid hankering for asafoetida.

'How I wish you would play something while we are waiting for my husband!' said Mildred, seeing her visitor's gaze wandering to the open piano.

'If you will go into the garden and take your tea, I will play with delight while you take it. I doubt if I could play to you in cold blood. I know you are critical.'

'And you think I am not *simpatica*,' retorted Mildred, laughing at him. She was quite at her ease with him already, all thought of that Judas face in the church being forgotten. His half-deferential, half-caressing manner; his easy confidences about himself and his own tastes, had made her more familiar with his individuality in the space of an hour than she would have been with the average Englishman in a month. She did not know whether she liked or disliked him; but he amused her, and it was a new sensation for her to feel amused.

She sauntered softly out to the lawn, and he began to play.

Heavens, what a touch! Was it really *her* piano which answered with tones so exquisite − which gave forth such thrilling melody? He played an improvised arrangement of Schubert's 'Ave Maria,' and she stood entranced till the last dying *arpeggio* melted into silence. No one could doubt that he came of a race gifted in music.

'Pray don't leave the piano,' she said softly, from her place by the open window.

'I will play till you call me away,' he answered, as he began Chopin's Etude in C sharp minor.

That weird and impassioned composition reached its close just as George Greswold approached from a little gate on the other side of the lawn. Mildred went to meet him, and Castellani left the piano and came out of the window to be presented to his host.

Nothing could be more strongly marked than the contrast between the two men, as they stood facing each other in the golden light of afternoon. Greswold, tall, broad-shouldered, rugged-looking, in his rough brown heather suit and deerstalker cap, carrying a thick stick, with an iron fork at the end of it, for the annihilation of chance weeds in his peregrinations. His fine and massive features had a worn look, his cheeks were hollow, his dark hair and beard were grizzled here and there, his dark complexion had lost the hue of youth. He looked ten years older than his actual age.

Before him stood the Italian, graceful, gracious in every line and every movement; his features delicately chiselled, his eyes dark, full, and bright; his complexion of that milky pallor which is so often seen with hair tending towards red; his brown beard of silkiest texture; his hands delicately modelled and of ivory whiteness; his dress imbued with all the grace which a fashionable tailor can given to the clothes of a man who cultivates the beautiful, even in the barren field of nineteenth-century costume. It was impossible that so marked a contrast could escape Mildred's observation altogether; yet she perceived it dimly. The picture came back to her memory afterwards in more vivid colours.

She made the necessary introduction, and then proceeded to pour out the tea, leaving the two men to talk to each other.

'Your name has an Italian sound,' Greswold said presently.

'It is a Milanese name. My father was a native of Milan; my mother was French, but she was educated in England, and all her proclivities were English. It was at her desire my father sent me to Rugby, and afterwards to Cambridge. Her fatal illness called me back to Italy immediately after I had got my degree, and it was some years before I again visited England.'

'Were you in Italy all that time?' asked Greswold, looking down absently, and with an unwonted trouble in his face.

Mildred sat at the tea-table, the visitor waiting upon her, insisting upon charging himself with her husband's cup as well as his own; an attention and reversal of etiquette of which Mr Greswold seemed unconscious. Kassandra had returned with her master from a long walk, and was lying at his feet in elderly exhaustion. She saluted the stranger with a suppressed growl when he approached with the teacups. Kassandra adored her own people, but was not remarkable for civility to strangers.

'Yes; I wasted four or five years in the South – in Florence, in Venice, or along the Riviera, wandering about like Satan, not having made up my mind what to do in the world.'

Greswold was silent, bending down to play with Kassandra, who wagged her tail with a gentle largo movement, in grateful contentment.

'You must have heard my father's name when you were at Milan,' said Castellani. 'His music was fashionable *there*.'

Mildred looked up with a surprised expression. She had never heard her husband talk of Milan, and yet this stranger mentioned his residence there as if it were an established fact.

'How did you know I was ever at Milan?' asked Greswold, looking up sharply.

'For the simplest of reasons. I had the honour of meeting you on more than one occasion at large assemblies, where my insignificant personality would hardly impress itself upon your memory. And I met you a year later at Lady Lochinvar's palace at Nice, soon after your first marriage.'

Mildred looked up at her husband. He was pale as ashes, his lips whitening as she gazed at him. She felt her own cheeks paling; felt a sudden coldness creeping over her, as if she were going to faint. She watched her husband dumbly, expecting him to tell this man that he was mistaken, that he was confounding him, George Greswold, with some one else; but Greswold sat silent, and presently, as if to hide his confusion, bent again over the dog, who got up suddenly and licked his face in a gush of affection – as if she knew – as if she knew.

He had been married before, and he had told his wife not one word of that first marriage. There had been no hint of the fact that he was a widower when he asked John Fausset for his daughter's hand.

CHAPTER XI

THE BEGINNING OF DOUBT

Enderby Church clock struck six. They heard every chime, slow and clear in the summer stillness, as they sat in the broad shadow of the cedar, silent all three.

It seemed as if the striking of the clock were the breaking of a spell.

'So late?' exclaimed Castellani, in a cheery voice; 'and I promised Mrs Hillersdon to be back in time to drive to Romsey for the evening service. The old Abbey Church of Romsey, she tells me, is a thing to dream about. There is no eight-o'clock dinner at Riverdale on Sundays. Every one goes to church somewhere, and we sup at half-past nine, and after supper there is sometimes extempore prayer – and sometimes there are charades or dumb crambo. *C'est selon.* When the Prince was there they had dumb crambo. Good-bye. I am almost ashamed to ask if I may ever come again, after having bored you for such an unconscionable time.'

He had the easiest air possible, and seemed totally unconscious of any embarrassment caused by his allusions to the past; and yet in both faces, as he looked from one to the other, he must have seen the strongest indications of trouble.

Mrs Greswold murmured something to the effect that she would be glad to see him at any time, a speech obviously conventional and unmeaning. Mr Greswold rose hastily and accompanied him to the hall-door, where the cart still waited for him, the groom fixed as a statue of despondency.

Mr Castellani was inclined to be loquacious to the last. Greswold was brief almost to incivility. He stood watching the light cart roll away, and then went slowly back to the garden and to his seat under the cedar.

He seated himself without a word, looking earnestly at his wife, whose drooping head and fixed attitude told of deepest thought. So they sat for some minutes in dead silence, Kassandra licking her master's pendant hand, as he leaned forward with his elbow on his knee, infinitely sorry for him.

Mildred was the first to break that silence.

'George, why did you not tell me,' she began in a low faltering voice, 'that I was not your first wife? What reason could there be for concealment between you and me? I so trusted you; I so loved you. Nothing you could have told would have changed me.'

'Dearest, there was one reason, and a powerful one,' answered George Greswold firmly, meeting the appealing look of her eyes with a clear and steady gaze. 'My first marriage is a sad remembrance for me – full of trouble. I did not care to tell you that miserable story, to call a dreaded ghost out of the grave of the past. My first marriage was the one great sorrow of my life, but it was only an episode in my life. It left me as lonely as it found me. There are very few who know anything about it. I am sorry that young man should have come here to trouble us with his uninvited reminiscences. For my own part, I cannot remember having ever seen his face before.'

'I am sorry you should have kept such a secret from me,' said Mildred. 'It would have been so much wiser to have been candid. Do you think I should not have respected your sad memories? You had only to say to me "Such things were; but let us not talk of them." It would have been more manly; it would have been kinder to me.'

'Say that I was a coward, if you like; that I am still a coward, where those memories are concerned,' said Greswold.

The look of agony in his face melted her in a moment. She threw herself on her knees beside his chair, she and the dog fawning upon him together.

'Forgive me, forgive me, dearest,' she pleaded, 'I will never speak to you of this again. Women are so jealous – of the past most of all.'

'Is that all?' he said: 'God knows you have little need. Let us say no more, Mildred. The past is past: neither you nor I can alter it. Memory is inexorable. God Himself cannot change it.'

'I will contrive that Mr Castellani shall not come here again, George, if you object to see him.'

'Pray don't trouble yourself. I would not have such a worm suppose that he could be obnoxious to me.'

'Tell me what you think of him,' she asked, in a lighter tone, anxious to bring back the easy mood of every-day life. 'He seems very clever, and he is rather handsome.'

'What do I think of the trumpet-ash on the verandah yonder? A beautiful parasite, which will hold on anywhere in the sunshine. Mr Castellani is of the same family, I take it – studies his own interests first, and chooses his friends afterwards. He will do admirably for Riverdale.'

'He plays divinely. His touch transformed my piano.'

'He looks the kind of man who would play the piano,' said Greswold, with ineffable contempt, looking down at his own sunburnt hands,

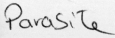

Parasite

hardened by exposure to all weathers, broadened by handling gun and punt-pole, and by half-a-dozen other forms of out-door exercise. 'However, I have no objection to him, if he serve to amuse you and Pamela.'

He spoke with a kind of weary indifference, as of a man who cared for very little in life; and then he rose slowly, took up his stick, and strolled off to the shrubbery.

Pamela appeared on the following afternoon with boxes, bags, music-books, racquets, and parasols, in a proportion which gave promise of a long visit. She had asked as a tremendous favour to be allowed to bring Box – otherwise Fitz-Box – her fox-terrier, son of Sir Henry Mountford's Box, great-grandson of Brockenhurst Joe, through that distinguished animal's daughter Lyndhurst Jessie, and on the paternal side a lineal descendant of Mr Murchison's Cracknel.

'I hope you won't mind very much,' she wrote; 'but it would be death to him if I were to leave him behind. To begin with, his brother Fitz-Cox, who has a villanous temper, would inevitably kill him; and besides that, he would pine to death at not sleeping in my room at night, which he has done ever since he was a puppy. If you will let me bring him, I will answer for his good manners, and that he shall not be a trouble to any one.'

The descendant of Brockenhurst Joe rushed out into the garden, and made a lightning circuit of lawn and shrubberies, while his young mistress was kissing her Aunt Mildred, as she called her uncle's wife in the fulness of her affection.

'It is so very good of you to have me, and I am so delighted to come!' she said.

Mildred would have much preferred that she were anywhere else, yet could not help feeling kindly to her. She was a frank, bright-looking girl, with brown eyes, and almost flaxen hair; a piquant contrast, for the hair was genuine, and carried out in the eyebrows, which were only just a shade darker. Her complexion was fair to transparency, and she had just enough soft rosy bloom to light up the delicate skin. Her nose was slightly *retroussé*, her mouth was a little wider than she herself approved, and her teeth were perfection. She had a charming figure of the plump order, but its plumpness was a distress to her.

'Don't you think I get horribly stout?' she asked Mildred, when she was sitting at tea in the garden presently.

'You may be a little stouter than you were at sixteen, perhaps, but not at all too stout.'

'O, but I am! I know it, I feel it. Don't endeavour to spare my feelings, aunt. It is useless. I know I am fat. Rosalind says I ought to marry; but I tell her it's absurd. How can anybody ever care for me now I am fat? They would only want my money if they asked me to marry them,' concluded Pamela, clinging to the plural.

'My dear Pamela, do you wish me to tell you that you are charming, and all that you ought to be?' asked Mildred, laughing.

'O, no, no! I don't want you to spare my feelings. Everybody spares one's feelings. One grows up in ignorance of the horrors in one's appearance, because people *will* spare one's feelings. And then one sees oneself in a strange glass; or a boy in the street says something, and one knows the worst. I think I know the worst about myself. That is one comfort. How lovely it is here!' said Pamela, with a sudden change of mood, glancing at Mildred with a little pathetic look as she remembered the childish figure that must be for ever missing from that home picture.

'I am so glad to be with you,' she murmured softly, nestling up to Mildred's side, as they sat together on a rustic bench; 'let me be useful to you, let me be a companion to you, if you can.'

'You shall be both, dear.'

'How good to say that! And you won't mind Box?'

'Not the least. If he will be amiable to Kassandra.'

'He will. He has been brought up among other dogs. We are a very doggy family at the Hall. Would you think he was worth a hundred and fifty guineas?' asked Pamela will ill-concealed pride, as the scion of illustrious progenitors came up and put his long lean head in her hand, and conversed with her in a series of expressive snorts, as it were a conversational code.

'I hardly know what constitutes perfection in a fox-terrier.'

'No more do I; but I know he is perfect. He is said to be the image of Cracknel, only better. I tremble when I think that my possession of him hangs by a thread. He might be stolen at any moment.'

'You must be careful.'

'Yes, I cannot be too careful. Here comes Uncle George,' said Pamela, rising and running to meet Mr Greswold. 'O, Uncle George, *how* altered you are!'

She was always saying the wrong thing, after the manner of impulsive girls; and she was quick-witted enough to discover her mistake the instant after.

Happily the dogs furnished a ready diversion. She introduced Box, and expatiated upon his grand qualities. She admired and made friends with Kassandra, and then settled down almost as lightly as a butterfly, in spite of her plumpness, on a Japanese stool, to take her teacup from Mildred's hands.

She was perfectly at her ease by this time, and told her uncle and aunt all about her sister Rosalind, and Rosalind's husband, Sir Henry

Mountford, whom she summed up lightly as a nice old thing, and no end of fun. It was easy to divine from her discourse that Rainham Hall was not an especially intellectual atmosphere, not a school of advanced thought, or of any other kind of thought. Pamela's talk was of tennis, yachting, fishing, and shooting, and of the people who shared in those sports. She seemed to belong to a world in which nobody ever sat down except to eat, or stayed indoors except under stress of weather.

'I hear you have all manner of clever people in your neighbourhood,' she said by and by, having told all she had to tell about Rainham.

'Have we?' asked Greswold, smiling at her intensity.

'Yes, at Riverdale. They do say the author of *Nepenthe* is staying there, and that he is not a Roman Cardinal or an English statesman, but almost a young man – an Italian by birth – and *very* handsome. I would give worlds to see him.'

'It is not unlikely you may be gratified without giving anything,' answered her uncle. 'Mr Castellani was here yesterday afternoon, and threatened to repeat his visit.'

'Castellani! Yes, that is the name I heard. What a pretty name! And what is he like? Do tell me all about him, Aunt Mildred.'

She turned to the woman as the more likely to give her a graphic description. The average man is an undescribing animal.

Mildred made an effort at self-command before she spoke. Castellani counted for but little in her recent trouble. His revelation had been an accident, and its effect entirely dissociated from him. Yet the very thought of the man troubled her, and the dread of seeing him again was like a physical pain.

'I do not know what to say about his appearance,' she answered presently, slowly fanning herself with a great scarlet Japanese fan, pale and cool looking in her plain white gown with its black ribbons. The very picture of domestic peace, one would suppose, judging by externals only. 'I suppose there are people who would think him handsome.'

'Don't you, aunt?'

'No. I don't like the colour of his eyes or of his hair. They are of that reddish-brown which the Venetian painters are so fond of, but which always gives me an idea of falsehood and treachery. Mr Castellani is a very clever man, but he is not a man whom I could ever trust.'

'How nice!' cried Pamela, her face radiant with enthusiasm; 'a creature with red-brown hair, and eyes with a depth of falsehood in them. That is just the kind of man who might be the author of *Nepenthe*. If you had told me he was stout and rosy-cheeked, with pepper-and-salt whiskers and a fine, benevolent head, I would never have opened his book again.'

'You seem to admire this *Nepenthe* prodigiously,' said her uncle, looking at her with a calmly critical air. 'Is it because the book is the fashion, or from your own unassisted appreciation of it? I did not think you were a bookish person.'

'I'm not,' cried Pamela. 'I am a mass of ignorance. I don't know anything about science. I don't know the name of a single butterfly. I don't know one toadstool from another. But when I love a book it is a passion with me. My Keats has tumbled to pieces; my Shelley is disgracefully dirty. I have read *Nepenthe* six times, and I am waiting for the cheap edition, to keep it under my pillow. It has made me an Agnostic.'

'Do you know the dictionary meaning of that word?'

'I don't think I do; but I know I am an Agnostic. *Nepenthe* has unsettled all my old beliefs. If I had read it four years ago I should have refused to be confirmed. I am dying to know the author.'

'You like unbelievers, then?' said Mr Greswold.

'I adore men who dare to doubt, who are not afraid to stand apart from their fellow-men.'

'On a bad eminence?'

'Yes, on a bad eminence. What a sweet expression! I can never understand Goethe's *Gretchen*.'

'Why not?'

'How could she have cared for *Faust*, when she had the privilege of knowing *Mephistopheles*?'

Pamela Ransome had established herself in her pretty bedroom and dressing-room, and had supervised her maid while she unpacked and arranged all her belongings, before dinner-time. She came down to the drawing-room, at a quarter to eight, as thoroughly at her ease as if she had lived half her life at Enderby Manor. She was a kind of visitor who gives no trouble, and who drops into the right place instinctively. Mildred Greswold felt cheered by her presence, in spite of that ever-recurrent pang of memory which associated all young bright things with the sweet girl-child who should have grown to womanhood under that roof, and who was lying a little way off, under the ripening berries of the mountain-ash, and in the deep shadow of a century-old yew.

They were very quiet in the drawing-room after dinner; Greswold reading in a nook apart, by the light of his own particular lamp; his wife bending over an embroidery-frame in her corner near the piano, where she had her own special dwarf bookcase and her work-basket, and the *bonheur du jour* at which she sometimes wrote letters, her own little table scattered with old family miniatures by Angelica Kaufmann, Cosway, and Ross, and antique watches in enamelled cases, and boxes of porcelain and gold and silver, every one of which had its history. Every woman who lives much at home has some such corner, where the very atmosphere is full of home thoughts. She asked her niece to play, and to go on playing as long as she liked; and Pamela, pleased with the touch of the Broadwood grand, rang the changes upon Chopin, Schumann, Raff, and Brahms, choosing those compositions which least jarred upon the atmosphere of studious repose.

Mildred's needle moved slowly, as she sat in her low chair, with her hands in the lamp-light and her face in shadow, moved very slowly, and then stopped altogether, and the white hands lay idle in her lap, and the embroidery-frame, with its half-finished group of azaleas, slid from her knee to the ground. She was thinking – thinking of that one subject which had possessed her thoughts since yesterday afternoon; which had kept her awake through the brief darkness of the summer night and in the slow hours betwixt dawn and seven o'clock, when the entrance of the maid with the early cup of tea marked the beginning of the daily routine. In all those hours her thoughts had revolved round that one theme with an intolerable recurrence.

It was of her husband's first marriage she thought, and of his motive for silence about that marriage: that he who, in the whole course of their wedded lives, had been the very spirit of single-minded candour, should yet have suppressed this all-important event in his past history, was a fact in itself so startling and mysterious that it might well be the focus of a wife's troubled thoughts. He could not so have acted without some all-sufficient reason; and what manner of reason could that have been which had influenced him to conduct so entirely at variance with his own character?

What was there in the history of that marriage which had sealed his lips, which made it horrible to him to speak about it, even when fair dealing with the girl who was to be his wife should have constrained frankness?

Had he been cursed with a wicked wife; some beautiful creature, who had caught his heart in her toils, as a cat catches a bird, and had won him only to betray and to dishonour him? Had she blighted his life, branded him with the shame of a forsaken husband?

And then a hideous dread floated across her mind. What if that first wife were still living – divorced from him? Had she, Mildred Fausset, severely trained in the strictest principles of the Anglican Church – taught her creed by an ascetic who deemed divorce unchristian and an abomination, and who had always refused to marry those who had been divorced – had she, in whose life and mind religion and duty were as one feeling and one principle – had she been trapped into a union with a man whose wife yet lived, and in the sight of God was yet one with him – a wife who might crawl penitent to his feet some day, and claim him as her own again by the right of tears and prayers and a soul

Mildred speculates on George's first marriage

Mildred speculates - she was his...

cleansed from sin? Such a sinner must have some hold, some claim even to the last, upon the man who once was her husband, who once swore to cherish her and cleave to her, of whom it had once been said, 'And they two shall be one flesh.'

No; again and again, no. She could not believe George Greswold capable of such deep dishonour as to have concealed the existence of a divorced wife. No; the reason for that mysterious silence must be another reason than this.

She had sinned against him, it might be, and had died in her sin, under circumstances too sad to be told without infinite pain; and he, who had never in her experience shown himself wanting in moral courage, had in this one crisis of his life acted as the coward acts. He had kept silence where conscience should have constrained him to speak.

And then the wife's vivid fancy conjured up the image of that other wife. Her jealous fears depicted that wife of past years as a being to be loved and remembered until death – beautiful, fascinating, gifted with all the qualities that charm mankind. 'He can never care for me as he once cared for her,' Mildred told herself. 'She was his first love.'

His first – the first revelation of what love means to the passionate heart of youth. What a world there is in that! Mildred remembered how a new life began for her with the awakening of her love for George Greswold. What a strange sweet enchantment, what an intoxicating gladness which glorified the whole face of nature! The river, and the reedy islets, and the pollard willows, and the autumn sunsets – things so simple and familiar – had all taken new colours in that magical dawn of her first love.

She – that unknown woman – had been George Greswold's first love. Mildred envied her that brief life, whose sole distinction was to have been loved by him.

'Why do I imagine a mystery about her?' she argued, after long brooding. 'The only secret was that he loved her as he could never love me, and he feared to tell me as much lest I should refuse the remnant of a heart. It was out of kindness to me that he kept silence. It would have pained me too much to know how *she* had been loved.'

She knew that her husband was a man of exceeding sensitiveness; she knew him capable of almost woman-like delicacy. Was it altogether unnatural that such a man should have held back the history of his first marriage – with its passionate love, its heartbroken ending – from the enthusiastic girl who had given him all her heart, and to whom he could give so little in return?

'He may have seen how I loved him, and may have married me half out of pity,' she said to herself finally, with unspeakable bitterness.

Yet if this were so, could they have been so happy together, so completely united – save in that one secret of the past, that one dark regret which had revealed itself from time to time in an agonising dream? He had walked that dark labyrinth of sleep alone with his sorrow: there she could not follow him.

She remembered the awful sound of those broken sentences – spoken to shadows in a land of shadow. She remembered how acutely she had felt his remoteness as he sat up in bed, pale as death, his eyes open and fixed, his lips muttering. He and the dead were face to face in the halls of the past. *She* had no part in his life, or in his memory.

CHAPTER XII

'SHE CANNOT BE UNWORTHY'

Mr Castellani did not wait long before he availed himself of Mrs Greswold's permission to repeat his visit. He appeared on Friday afternoon, at the orthodox hour of half-past three, when Mildred and her niece were sitting in the drawing-room, exhausted by a long morning at Salisbury, where they had explored the cathedral, and lunched in the Close with a clever friend of George Greswold's, who had made his mark on modern literature.

'I adore Salisbury Close,' said Pamela, as she looked through the old-fashioned window to the old-fashioned garden; 'it reminds me of Honoria.'

She did not deem it necessary to explain what Honoria she meant, presuming a universal acquaintance with Coventry Patmore's gentle heroine.

The morning had been sultry, the homeward drive long, and both ladies were resting in comfortable silence, each with a book, when Castellani was announced.

Mildred received him rather coldly, trying her uttermost to seem thoroughly at ease. She introduced him to her niece, Miss Ransome.

'The daughter of the late Mr Randolph Ransome and the sister of Lady Mountford?' Castellani inquired presently, when Pamela had run out on the lawn to speak to Box.

'Yes. You seem to know everybody's belongings.'

'Why not? It is the duty of every man of the world, more especially of a foreigner. I know Mr Ransome's place in the Sussex Weald – a very fine property – and I know that the two ladies are co-heiresses, but that the Sussex estate is to descend to the eldest son of the elder daughter, or failing male issue there, to the son of the younger. Lady Mountford has a baby-son, I believe.

'Your information is altogether correct.'

'Why should it be otherwise? Mr Hillersdon and his wife discussed the family history to-day at luncheon, *apropos* to Miss Ransome's appearance in Romsey Church at the Saint's Day service yesterday.'

His frankness apologised for his impertinence, and he was a foreigner, which seems always to excuse a great deal.

Pamela came back again, after rescuing Box from a rough-and-tumble game with Kassandra. She looked rosy and breathless, and very pretty, in her pale-blue gown and girlish sash flying in the wind, and flaxen hair fluffed into a feathery pile on the top of her head, and honest brown eyes. She resumed her seat in the deep old window behind the end of the piano, and made believe to go on with some work, which she took in a tangled heap from a very untidy basket. Already Pamela had set the sign of her presence upon the drawing-rooms at Enderby, a trail of heterogeneous litter which was a part of her individuality. Screened by the piano, she was able to observe Castellani, as he stood leaning over the large central ottoman, with his knee on the cushioned seat, talking to Mrs Greswold.

He was the author of *Nepenthe*. It was in that character he interested her. She looked at him with the thought of his book full in her mind. It was one of those half-mad, wholly artificial compositions which delight girls and young men, and which are just clever enough, and have just enough originality to get talked about and written about by the cultured few. It was a love-story, ending tragically; a story of ruined lives and broken hearts, told in the autobiographical form, with a studied avoidance of all conventional ornament, which gave an air of reality where all was inherently false. Pamela thought it must be Castellani's own story. She fancied she could see the traces of those heart-breaking experiences, those crushing disappointments in his countenance, in his bearing even, and in the tones of his voice, which gave an impression of mental fatigue, as of a man worn out by a fatal passion.

The story of *Nepenthe* was as old as the hills – or at least as old as the Boulevard des Capucines and the Palais Royal. It was the story of a virtuous young man's love for an unvirtuous woman – the story of Demetrius and Lamia – the story of a man's demoralisation under the influence of incarnate falsehood, of the gradual lapse from good to evil, the gradual extinction of every belief and every scruple, the final destruction of a soul.

The wicked siren was taken, her victim was left; but left to expiate that miserable infatuation by an after-life of misery; left without a joy in the present or a hope in the future.

'He looks like it,' thought Pamela, remembering that final chapter.

Mrs Greswold was putting a few slow stitches into the azalea-leaves on her embroidery-frame, and listening to Mr Castellani with an air of polite indifference.

'Do you know that Riverdale is quite the most delightful house I have every stayed in?' he said; 'and I have stayed in a great many. And do you know that Mrs Hillersdon is heart-broken at your never having called upon her?'

'I am sorry so small a matter should touch Mrs Hillersdon's heart.'

'She feels it intensely. She told me so yesterday. Perfect candour is one of the charms of her character. She is as emotional and as transparent as a child. Why have you not called on her?'

'You forget that Riverdale is seven miles from this house.'

'Does not your charity extend so far? Are people who live seven miles off beyond the pale? I think you must visit a little further afield than seven miles. There must be some other reason.'

'There is another reason, which I had rather not talk about.'

'I understand. You consider Mrs Hillersdon a person not to be visited. Long ago, when you were a child in the nursery, Mrs Hillersdon was an undisciplined, inexperienced girl, and the world used her hardly. Is that old history never to be forgotten? Men, who know it all, have agreed to forget it: why should women, who only know a fragment, so obstinately remember?'

'I know nothing, and remember nothing, about Mrs Hillersdon. My friends are, for the most part, those of my husband's choice, and I pay no visits without his approval. He does not wish me to visit at Riverdale. You have forced me to give you a plain answer, Mr Castellani.'

'Why not? Plain truth is always best. I am sorry Mr Greswold has interdicted my charming friend. You can have no idea how excellent a woman she is, or how admirable a wife. Tom Hillersdon might have searched the county from border to border and not have found as good a woman – looked at as the woman best calculated to make him happy. And what delightful people she has brought about him! One of the most interesting men I ever met arrived yesterday, and is to preach the hospital sermon at Romsey next Sunday. He is an old friend of yours.'

'A clergyman, and an old friend of mine, at Riverdale!'

'A man of ascetic life and exceptional culture. I never heard any man talk of Dante better than he talked to me last night in a moonlight stroll on the terrace, while the other men were in the smoking-room.'

'Surely you do not mean Mr Cancellor, the Vicar of St Elizabeth's, Parchment Street?'

'That is the man – Clement Cancellor, Vicar of St Elizabeth's. He looks like a mediaeval monk just stepped out of one of Bellini's altar-pieces.'

'He is the noblest, most unselfish of men,' said Mildred warmly; 'he has given his life to doing good among rich and poor. It is so long since I have seen him. We have asked him to Enderby very often, but he has always been too busy to come. And to think that he should be in this neighbourhood and I know nothing about it; and to think that he should go to Riverdale rather than come here!'

'He had hardly any option. It was Mrs Hillersdon who asked him to preach on Hospital Sunday. She extorted a promise from him three months ago in London. The Vicar of Romsey was enchanted. "You are the cleverest woman I know," he said. "No one else could have got me such a great gun."'

'A great gun — Mr Cancellor a great gun! I can only think of him as I knew him when I was twelve years old: a tall, thin young man, in a very shabby coat — he was curate at St Elizabeth's then — very gaunt and hollow-cheeked, but with such a sweet smile. He used to come twice a week to teach me the history of the Bible and the Church. He made me love both.'

'He is gaunt and hollow-cheeked still, tall and bony and sallow, and he still wears a shabby coat. You will not find much difference in him, I fancy — only so many more years of hard work and self-sacrifice, ascetic living and nightly study. A man to know Dante as he does must have given years of his life to that one poet — and I am told that in literature Cancellor is an all-round man. His monograph on Pascal is said to be the best of a brilliant series of such studies.'

'I hope he will come to see his old pupil before he leaves the neighbourhood.'

'He means to do so. He was talking of it yesterday evening — asking Mrs Hillersdon if she was intimate with you — so awkward for poor Mrs Hillersdon.'

'I shall be very glad to see him again.'

'May I drive him over to tea to-morrow afternoon?'

'He will be welcome here at any time.'

'Or with any one? If Mrs Hillersdon were to bring him, would you still refuse to receive her?'

'I have never refused to receive her. We have met and talked to each other on public occasions. If Mr Cancellor likes her she cannot be unworthy.'

'May she come with him to-morrow?' persisted Castellani.

'If she likes,' faltered Mildred, wondering that any woman could so force an entrance to another woman's house.

She did not know that it was by such forced entrances Mrs Hillersdon had made her way in society until some of the best houses in London had been opened to her.

'If you are not in a hurry to leave us, I know my niece would much like to hear you play,' she said, feeling that the talk about Riverdale had been dull work for Pamela.

Miss Ransome murmured assent.

'If you will play something of Beethoven's,' she entreated.

'Do you object to Mozart?' he asked, forgetting his depreciation of the valet-musician's son a few days before. 'I feel more in the humour for that prince of dramatists. I will give you the supper in *Don Giovanni*. You shall see Leporello trembling. You shall hear the tramp of ghostly feet.'

And then, improvising upon a familiar theme, he gave his own version of that wonderful scene, and that music so played conjured up a picture as vivid as ever opera-house furnished to an enthralled audience.

Pamela listened in silent rapture. What a God-gifted creature this was, who had so deeply moved her by his pen, who moved her even more intensely by that magical touch upon the piano!

When he had played those last crashing chords which consigned the profligate to his doom, he waited for a minute or so, and then, softly, as if almost unawares, in mere absent-minded idleness, his hands wandered into the staccato accompaniment of the serenade, and, with the finest tenor Mildred had heard since she heard Sim Reeves, he sang those delicate and dainty phrases with which the seducer woos his last divinity.

He rose from the piano at the close of that lovely air, smiling at his hearers.

'I had no idea that you were a singer as well as a pianist,' said Mildred.

'You forget that music is my native tongue. My father taught me to play before he taught me to read, and I knew harmony before I knew my alphabet. I was brought up in the house of a man who lived only for music – to whom all stringed instruments were as his mother tongue. It was by a caprice that he made me play the piano – which he rarely touched himself.'

'He must have been a great genius,' said Pamela, with girlish fervour.

'Alas! no, he just missed greatness, and he just missed genius. He was a highly-gifted man – various – capricious – volatile – and he married a woman with just enough money to ruin him. Had he been obliged to earn his bread, he might have been great. Who can say? Hunger is the slave-driver, with his whip of steel, who peoples the Valhalla of nations. If Homer had not been a beggar – as well as blind – we might have had no story of Troy. Good-bye, Mrs Greswold. Good-bye,' shaking hands with Pamela. 'I *may* bring my hostess to-morrow?'

'I – I – suppose so,' Mildred answered feebly, wondering what her husband would think of such an invasion.

Yet, if Clement Cancellor, who to Mildred's mind had always seemed the ideal Christian priest, if he could tolerate and consort with her, could she, Mildred Greswold, persist in the Pharisee's part, and hold herself aloof from this neighbour, to whose good works and kindly disposition many voices had testified in her hearing?

CHAPTER XIII

SHALL SHE BE LESS THAN ANOTHER?

It was in all good faith that Clement Cancellor had gone to Riverdale. He had not gone there for the fleshpots of Egypt. He was a man of severely ascetic habits, who ate and drank as temperately as a disciple of that old faith of the East which is gaining a curious influence upon our new life of the West. For him the gratification of the senses, soft raiment, artistic furniture, thoroughbred horses and luxurious carriages, palm-houses and orchid-houses, offered no temptation. He stayed in Mrs Hillersdon's house because he was her friend, her friend upon the broadest and soundest basis on which friendship could be built. He knew all that was to be known about her. He knew her frailties of the past, her virtues in the present, her exalted hope in the future. From her own lips he had heard the story of Louise Lorraine's life. She had extenuated nothing. She had not withheld from him either the foulness of her sins or their number – nay, it may be that she had in somewise exaggerated the blackness of those devils whom he, Clement Cancellor, had cast out from her, enhancing by just so much the magnitude of the miracle he had wrought. She had held back nothing; but over every revelation she had contrived to spread that gloss which a clever woman knows how to give to the tale of her own wrong-doing. In every incident of that evil career she had contrived to show herself more sinned against than sinning; the fragile victim of overmastering wickedness in others; the martyr of man's treachery and man's passion; the sport of fate and circumstance. Had Mr Cancellor known the world he lived in half as well as he knew the world beyond he would hardly have believed so readily in the lady who had been Louise Lorraine: but he was too single-minded to doubt a repentant sinner whose conversion from the ways of evil had been made manifest by so many good works, and such unflagging zeal in the exercises of the Anglican Church.

Parchment Street, Grosvenor Square, is one of the fashionable streets of London, and St Elizabeth's, Parchment Street, had gradually developed, in Clement Cancellor's incumbency, into one of the most popular tabernacles at the West End. He whose life-desire had been to carry the lamp of the faith into dark places, to be the friend and teacher of the friendless and the untaught, found himself almost in spite of himself a fashionable preacher, and the delight of the cultured, the wealthy, and the aristocratic. In his parish of St Elizabeth's there was plenty of work for him to do – plenty of that work which he had chosen as the mission that had been given to him to fulfil. Behind those patrician streets where only the best-appointed carriages drew up, where only the best-dressed footmen ever pulled the bells or rattled long peals on high-art knockers, there were some of the worst slums in London, and it was in those slums that half Mr Cancellor's life was spent. In narrow alleys between Oxford and Wigmore Streets, and in the intricate purlieus of Marylebone Lane, the Anglican priest had ample scope for his labour, a vineyard waiting for the husbandman. And in the labyrinth hidden in the heart of West End London Mr Cancellor's chief coadjutor for the last twenty years had been Louise Hillersdon. Thoroughness was the supreme quality of Mrs Hillersdon's mind. Nothing stopped her. It was this temper which had given her distinction in the days when princes were her cupbearers and diamonds her daily tribute. There had been other women as beautiful, other women as fascinating; but there was not one who with beauty and fascination combined the audacity and resolution of Louise Lorraine. When Louise Lorraine took possession of a man's wits and a man's fortune that man was doomed. He was as completely gone as the lemon in the iron squeezer. A twist of the machine, and there is nothing left but broken rind and crushed pulp. A season of infatuation, and there was nothing left of Mrs Lorraine's admirer but shattered health and an overdrawn banking account. Estates, houses, friends, position, good name, all dropped away from the man whom Louise Lorraine brayed in her mortar. She spoke of him next season with half contemptuous pity. 'Did I know Sir Theodore Barrymore! Yes; he used to come to my parties sometimes. A nice fellow enough, but such a terrible fool.'

When Louise Lorraine married Tom Hillersdon, and took it into her head to break away altogether from her past career, and to pose before the world as a beautiful Magdalen, she was clever enough to know that, to achieve any place in society, she must have a very powerful influence to help her. She was clever enough to discover that the one influence which a woman in her position could count upon was the influence of the Church. She was beautiful enough and refined enough to win friends among the clergy by the charm of her personality. She was rich enough to secure such friends, and bind them to herself by the splendour of her gifts, by her substantial aid in those good works which are to the priest as the very breath of his life. One man she could win by an organ; another lived only to complete a steeple; the third had been yearning for a decade for that golden hour when the cracked tintinnabulation which now summoned his flock should be exchanged for a fine peal of bells. Such men as these were only too easily won, and the drawing-rooms of Mr Hillersdon's house in Park Lane were rarely without the grace of some clerical figure in long frock-coat and Roman collar.

Clement Cancellor was of a sterner stuff, and not to be bought by bell or reredos, rood-screen or pulpit. Him Louise Hillersdon won by larger measures: to him she offered all that was spiritual in her nature: and this woman of strange memories was not without spiritual aspirations and real striving after godliness. Clement Cancellor was no pious simpleton, to be won by sentimental cant and crocodile tears. He knew truth from falsehood, had never in his life been duped by the jingle of false coin. He knew that Mrs Hillersdon's repentance had the true ring, albeit she was in some things still of the earth earthy. She had worked for him and with him in that wilderness of London as not one other woman in his congregation had ever worked. To the lost of her own sex she had been as a redeeming angel. Wretched women had blessed her with their expiring breath, had died full of hopes that might never have been awakened had not Louise Lorraine sat beside their beds. Few other women had ever so influenced the erring of her sex. She who had waded deep in the slough of sin knew how to talk to sinners.

Mr Cancellor never forgot her as he had seen her by the bed of death and in the haunts of iniquity. She could never be to him as the herd of women. To the mind of the preacher she had a higher value than one in twenty of those women of his flock whose unstained lives had never needed the cleansing of self-sacrifice and difficult works.

Thus it was that the Vicar of St Elizabeth's had never shrunk from acknowledging Mrs Hillersdon as his personal friend, had never feared to sit at her board, or to be seen with her in public; and in the work of Louise Lorraine's rehabilitation Clement Cancellor had been a tower of strength. And now this latest mark of friendship, this visit to her country home, and this appearance in the noble old Abbey Church at her solicitation, filled her cup of pride. These starched county people who had shunned her hospitalities were to see that one of the most distinguished preachers in the High Church party had given her his friendship and his esteem.

It had been something for her to have the Prince at Riverdale: it was still more to her to have Clement Cancellor.

Pamela was in a flutter of excitement all Saturday morning, in the expectation of Castellani's reappearance in the afternoon. She had heard Mr Cancellor preach, and was delighted at the idea of seeing him in the pleasant intimacy of afternoon tea. Had there been no such person as Castellani, her spirits would have been on tip-toe at the idea of conversing with the fashionable preacher – of telling him in a reverent under-tone of all those deep emotions his eloquence had inspired in her. But the author of *Nepenthe* possessed just that combination of qualities which commands the admiration of such a girl as Pamela. That exquisite touch on the piano, that perfect tenor voice, that exotic elegance of dress and figure, all had made their mark upon the sensitive plate of a girl's ardent fancy. 'If I had pictured to myself the man who wrote *Nepenthe*, I should have imagined just such a face, just such a style,' thought Pamela, quite forgetting that when first she had read the book she had made a very vivid picture of the author altogether the opposite of César Castellani – a dark man, lean as a whipping-post, grave as philosophy itself, with sombre black eyes, and ebon hair, and a complexion of antique marble. And now she was ready to accept the Italian, sleek, supple, essentially modern in every grace and attribute, in place of that sage of antique mould.

She went dancing about with the dogs all the morning, inciting the grave Kassandra to unwonted exertions, running in and out of the drawing-room, making an atmosphere of gaiety in the grave old house. Mildred's heart ached as she watched that flying figure in the white gown, youth, health, joyousness, personified.

'O, if my darling were but here, life might be full of happiness again,' she thought. 'I should cease to weary myself with wondering about that hidden past.'

Do what she would her thoughts still dwelt upon the image of that wife who had possessed George Greswold's heart before her. She knew that he must have loved that other woman whom he had sworn before God's altar to cherish. He was not the kind of man to marry for any motive but a disinterested love. That he had loved passionately, and that he had been wronged deeply, was Mildred's reading of the mystery. There had been a look of agony in his countenance when he spoke of the past that told of a sorrow too deep for words.

'He has never loved me as he once loved her,' thought Mildred, who out of the wealth of her own love had developed the capacity for that self-torture called jealousy.

It seemed to her that her husband had taken pains to avoid the old opportunities of confidential talk since that revelation of last Sunday. He had been more than usually engaged by the business details of his estate; and she fancied that he made the most of all those duties which he used once to perform with the utmost despatch, grudging every hour that was spent away from the home circle. He now complained of the new steward's ignorance, which threw so much extra work upon himself.

'After jogging on for years in the same groove with a man who knew every rood of my land, and the idiosyncrasies of every tenant, I find it hard work teaching a new man,' he told his wife.

This sounded reasonable enough, yet she could but think that since Sunday he had studiously avoided being alone with her. If he asked her to drive or walk with him, he secured Pamela's company before the excursion was planned.

'We must show you the country,' he said to his niece.

Mildred told him of the threatened incursion from Riverdale as they sat at luncheon with Pamela.

'I hope you don't mind my receiving Mrs Hillersdon,' she said.

'No, my dear Mildred, I think it would take a much worse woman than Mrs Hillersdon to do you any harm, or Pamela either. Whatever her early history may have been, she has made Tom Hillersdon an excellent wife, and she has been a very good friend to the poor. I should not have cared for you to cultivate Mrs Hillersdon, or the society she brings round her, at Riverdale——'

'Sir Henry says they have people from the music-halls,' interjected Pamela, in an awe-stricken voice.

'But if Mrs Hillersdon likes to come here with her clerical star——'

'Don't call him a star, George. He is highly gifted, and people have chosen to make him the fashion, but he is the most single-hearted and simple-minded man I ever met. No popularity could spoil him. I feel that if he holds out the hand of friendship to Mrs Hillersdon, she must be a good woman.'

'Let her come, Mildred, only don't let her coming open the door to intimacy. I would not have my wife the friend of any woman with a history.'

'And yet there are histories in most lives, George, and there is sometimes a mystery.'

She could not refrain from this little touch of bitterness, yet she was sorry the instant she had spoken, deeply penitent, when she saw the look of pain in the thoughtful face opposite her. Why should she wilfully wound him, purposely, needlessly, she who so fondly loved him, whose keenest pain was to think that he had loved any woman upon earth before he loved her?

'Will you be at home to help me to receive my old friend, George?' she said, as they rose from the table.

'Yes, I will be at home to welcome Cancellor, and to protect you from his _protégée's_ influence, if I can.'

They were all three in the drawing-room when the Riverdale party arrived. Mildred and Mrs Hillersdon met in somewise as old acquaintances, having been thrown together on numerous occasions, at hunt balls, charity bazaars, and other public assemblies. Pamela was the only stranger.

Although the scandalous romance of Louise Lorraine's career was called ancient history, she was still a beautiful woman. The delicate features, the pure tones of the alabaster skin, and the large Irish gray eyes, had been kindly dealt with by time. On the verge of fifty, Mrs Hillersdon might have owned only to forty, had she cared so far to palter with truth. Her charm was, however, now more in a fascinating personality than in the remains of a once dazzling loveliness. There was mind in the keen, bright face, with its sharply-cut lines, and those traces of intellectual wear which give a new grace, instead of the old one of youthful softness and faultless colouring. The bloom was gone from the peach, the brilliancy of youth had faded from those speaking eyes, but there was all the old sweetness of expression which had made Louise Lorraine's smile irresistible as the song of the lurlei in the days that were gone. Her dress was perfect, as it had always been from the day when she threw away her last cotton stocking, darned by her own fair hands, and took to dressing like a leader of the great world, and with perhaps even less concern for cost. She dressed in perfect harmony with her age and position. Her gown was of softest black silk, draped with some semi-diaphanous fabric and clouded with Chantilly lace. Her bonnet was of the same lace and gauze, and her tapering hand and slender wrist were fitted to perfection in a long black glove which met a cloud of lace just below the elbow.

At a period when almost every woman who wore black glittered with beads and bugles from head to foot, Mrs Hillersdon's costume was unembellished by a single ornament. The Parisian milliner had known how to obey her orders to the letter when she stipulated – *surtout point de jais* – and the effect was at once distinguished and refined.

Clement Cancellor greeted his old pupil with warm friendliness, and meekly accepted her reproaches for all those invitations which he had refused in the past ten years.

'You told me so often that it was impossible for you to come to Enderby, and yet you can go to my neighbour,' she said.

'My dear Mildred, I went to Riverdale because I was wanted at Romsey.'

'And do you think you were not wanted at Romsey before to-day? – do you think we should not have been proud to have you preach in our church here? People would have flocked from far and wide to hear you – yes, even to Enderby Church – and you might have aided some good work, as you are going to do to-morrow. How clever of Mrs Hillersdon to know how to tempt you down here!'

'You may be sure it is not the first time I have tried, Mrs Greswold,' said that lady, with her fascinating smile. 'Your influence would have gone further than mine, I daresay, had you taken half as much trouble as I have done.'

Mr Rollinson, the curate of Enderby, was announced at this moment. The Vicar was a rich man with another parish in his cure, and his own comfortable vicarage and his brother's family mansion being adjacent to the other church, Enderby saw him but seldom, whereby Mr Rollinson was a person of much more weight in the parish than the average clerical subaltern. Mildred liked him for his plain-sailing Christianity and unfailing kindness to the poor, and she had asked him to tea this afternoon, knowing that he would like to meet Clement Cancellor.

Castellani looked curiously unlike those three other men, with their grave countenances and unstudied dress; George Greswold roughly clad in shooting jacket and knickerbockers; the two priests in well-worn black. The Italian made a spot of brightness in that sombre assembly, the sunlight touching his hair and moustache with glints of gold, his brown velvet coat and light gray trousers suggestive of the studio rather than of rustic lanes, a gardenia in his button-hole, a valuable old intaglio fastening his white silk scarf, and withal a half-insolent look of amusement at those two priests and the sombre-visaged master of the house. He slipped with serpentine grace to the further side of the piano, where he contrived his first *tête-à-tête* with Pamela, comfortably sheltered by the great Henri Deux vase of gloxinias on the instrument.

Pamela was shy at first, and would hardly speak; then taking courage, told him how she had wondered and wept over *Nepenthe*, and thereupon they began to talk as if they were two kindred souls that had been kept too long apart by adverse fate, and thrilled with the new delight of union.

Round the tea-table the conversation was of a graver cast. After a general discussion of the threatening clouds upon the political and ecclesiastical horizon, the talk had drifted to a question which at this time was uppermost in the minds of men. The Deceased Wife's Sister's Bill had been thrown out by the Upper House during the last session, and everybody had been talking of that debate in which three princes of the blood royal had been attentive auditors. They had recorded their vote on the side of liberty of conscience, but in vain. Time-honoured prejudices had prevailed against modern enlightenment.

Clement Cancellor was a man who would have suffered martyrdom for his faith; he was generous, he was merciful, gentle, self-sacrificing, pure in spirit; but he was not liberal-minded. The old shackles hung heavily upon him. He could not love Wycliffe; and he could not forgive Cranmer. He was an ecclesiastic after the antique pattern. To him the marriage of a priest was a base paltering with the lusts of the flesh; and to him a layman's marriage with a dead wife's sister was unholy and abominable. He had been moved to indignation by the words that had been spoken and the pamphlets that had been written of late upon this question; and now, carried away by George Greswold's denunciation of that prejudiced majority by which the Bill had been rejected, Mr

Cancellor gave his indignation full vent, and forgot that he was speaking in a lady's drawing-room, and before feminine hearers.

He spoke of such marriages as unholy and immoral, he spoke of such households as accursed. Mildred listened to him, and watched him wonderingly, scared at this unfamiliar aspect of his character. To her he had ever been the gentlest of teachers; she saw him now pallid with wrath – she heard him breathing words of fire.

George Greswold took up the glove, not because he had ever felt any particular interest in this question, but because he hated narrow-minded opinions and clerical prejudices.

'Why should the sister of his wife be different to a man from all other women?' he asked. 'You may call her different – you may set her apart – you may say she must be to him as his own sister – her beauty must not touch him, the attractions that fascinate other men must have no influence over him. You may lay this down as a law – civil – canonical – what you will – but the common law of nature will override your clerical code, will burst your shackles of prejudice and tradition. Shall Rachel be withheld from him who was true and loyal to Leah? She has dwelt in his house as his friend, the favourite and playmate of his children. He has respected her as he would have respected any other of his wife's girl-friends; but he has seen that she was fair; and if God takes the wife, and he, remembering the sweetness of that old friendship, and his children's love, turns to her as the one woman who can give him back his lost happiness – is he to be told that this one woman can never be his, because she was the sister of his first chosen? She has come out of the same stock whose loyalty he has proved, she would bring to his hearth all the old sweet associations——'

'And she would *not* bring him a second mother-in-law. What a stupendous superiority she would have *there!*' interjected the jovial Rollinson, who had been wallowing in hot-buttered cakes and strong tea, until his usually roseate visage had become startlingly rubicund.

He was in all things the opposite of the Vicar of St Elizabeth's. He wrote poetry, made puns, played billiards, dined out at all the houses in the neighbourhood that were worth dining at, and was only waiting to marry until Tom Hillersdon should be able to give him a living.

Mr Cancellor reproved the ribald jester with a scathing look before he took up the argument against his host.

'If this Bill were to pass, no virtuous woman could live in the house of a married sister,' he said.

'That is as much as to say that no honest woman can live in the house of any married man,' retorted Greswold hotly. 'Do you think if a man is weak enough to fall in love with another woman under his wife's roof he is less likely to sin because your canonical law stares him in the face,

The bill

telling him, "Thou canst never wed her"? The married man who is inconstant to his wife is not influenced by the chances of the future. He is either a bold, bad man, whose only thought is to win the woman whom he loves at any cost of honour or conscience; or he is a weak fool, who drifts hopelessly to destruction, and in whom the resolution of to-day yields to the temptation of to-morrow. Neither the bold sinner nor the weak one is influenced by the consideration whether he can or cannot marry the woman he loves under the unlikely circumstance of his wife's untimely death. The man who does so calculate is the one man in so many thousands of men who will poison his wife to clear the way for his new fancy. I don't think we ought to legislate for poisoners. In plain words, if a married man is weak enough or wicked enough to be seduced by the charms of any woman who dwells beneath his roof, he will not be the less likely to fall because the law of the land has made that woman anathema maranatha, or because he has been warned from the pulpit that she is to be to him as his own flesh and blood, no dearer and no less dear than the sister beside whom he grew from infancy to manhood, and whom he has loved all his life, hardly knowing whether she is as beautiful as Hebe or as hideous as Tisyphone.'

'You are a disciple of the New Learning, Mr Greswold,' Cancellor said bitterly; 'the learning which breaks down all barriers and annihilates the Creator of all things – the learning which has degraded God from infinite power to infinitesimal insignificance, and which explains the genius of Plato and Shakespeare, Luther and Newton, as the ultimate outcome of an unconscious primeval mist.'

'I am no Darwinian,' replied Greswold coldly, 'but I would rather belong to his school of speculative inquiry than to the Calvinism which slew Servetus, or the Romanism which lit the death-pile of the Oxford martyrs.'

Mildred was not more anxious than Mrs Hillersdon to end a discussion which threatened angry feeling. They looked at each other in an agony, and then with a sudden inspiration Mildred exclaimed,

'If we could only persuade Mr Castellani to play to us! We are growing so terribly serious;' and then she went to Clement Cancellor, who was standing by the open window, and took her place beside him, while Mrs Hillersdon talked with Pamela and Castellani at the piano. 'You know what a privilege it is to *me* always to hear you talk,' she murmured in her sweet, subdued voice. 'You know how I have followed your teaching in all things. And be assured my husband is no materialist. We both cling to the old faith, the old hopes, the old promises. You must not misjudge him because of a single difference of opinion.'

'Forgive me, my dear Mildred,' replied Cancellor, touched by her submission. 'I did wrong to be angry. I know that to many good

Christians this question of marriage with a sister-in-law is a stumbling-block. I have taken the subject too deeply to heart perhaps – I, to whom marriage altogether seems outside the Christian priest's horizon. Perhaps I may exaggerate the peril of a wider liberty; but I, who look upon Henry VIII as the arch-enemy of the one vital Church – of which he might have been the wise and enlightened reformer – I, who trace to his unhallowed union with his brother's widow all the after evils of his career – must needs lift up my voice against a threatened danger.'

Castellani began Mendelssohn's 'Wedding March' with a triumphant burst that sounded like mockery. Do what the preacher might to assimilate earth to heaven, here there would still be marrying and giving in marriage.

After the march Mildred went over to the piano and asked Castellani to sing.

He smiled assent, and played the brief symphony to a ballad of Heine's, set by Jensen. The exquisite tenor voice, the perfect taste of the singer, held his audience spellbound. They listened in silence, and entreated him to sing again, and then again, till he had sung four of these jewel-like ballads, and they felt that it was impertinence to ask for more.

Mildred had stolen round to her own sheltered corner, half hidden by a group of tall palms. She sat with her hands clasped in her lap, her head bent. She could not see the singer. She only heard the low pathetic voice, slightly veiled. It touched her like no other voice that she had ever heard since, in her girlhood, she burst into a passion of sobs at first hearing Sim Reeves, when that divine voice touched some hyper-sensitive chord in her own organisation and moved her almost to hysteria. And now, in this voice of the man who of all other men she instinctively disliked, the same tones touched the same chord, and loosened the floodgates of her tears. She sat with streaming eyes, grateful for the sheltering foliage which screened her from observation.

She dried her eyes and recovered herself with difficulty when the singer rose from the piano and Mrs Hillersdon began to take leave. Mr Rollinson button-holed Castellani on the instant.

'You sing as if you had just come from the seraphic choir,' he said. 'You must sing for us on the seventh.'

'Who are "us"?' asked Castellani.

'Our concert in aid of the fund for putting a Burne-Jones window over the altar.'

'A concert in Enderby village? Is it to be given at the lock-up or in the pound?'

'It is to be given in this room. Mrs Greswold has been good enough to allow us the use of her drawing-room and her piano. Miss Ransome promises to preside at the buffet for tea and coffee.'

'It will be glorious fun,' exclaimed Pamela; 'I shall feel like a barmaid. I have always envied barmaids.'

'Daudet says there is one effulgent spot in every man's life – one supreme moment when he stands on the mountain-top of fortune and of bliss, and from which all the rest of his existence is a gradual descent. I wonder whether that afternoon will be your effulgent spot, Miss Ransome?' said Mrs Hillersdon laughingly.

'It will – it must. To superintend two great urns of tea and coffee – *almost* as nice as those delicious beer-engines one sees at Salisbury Station – to charge people a shilling for a small cup of tea, and sixpence for a penny sponge-cake. What splendid fun!'

'Will you help us, Mr Castleton?' asked the curate, who was not good at names.

'Mrs Greswold has only to command me. I am in all things her slave.'

'Then she will command you – she does command you,' cried the curate.

'If you will be so very kind——' began Mildred.

'I am only too proud to obey you,' answered Castellani, with more earnestness than the occasion required, drawing a little nearer to Mildred as he spoke; 'only too glad of an excuse to return to this house.'

Mildred looked at him with a half-frightened expression, and then glanced at Pamela. Did he mean mischief of some kind? Was this the beginning of an insidious pursuit of that frank girl, whose fortune was quite enough to tempt the casual adventurer?

'Of all men I have ever seen he is the last to whom I would entrust a girl's fate,' thought Mildred, determined to be very much on her guard against the blandishments of César Castellani.

She took the very worst means to ward off danger. She made the direful mistake of warning the girl against the possible pursuer that very evening when they were sitting alone after dinner.

'He is a man I could never trust,' she said.

'No more could I,' replied Pamela; 'but O, how exquisitely he sings!' and excited at the mere memory of that singing, she ran to the piano and began to pick out the melody of Heine's 'Ich weiss nicht was soll es bedeuten,' and sang the words softly in her girlish voice; and then slipped away from the piano with a nervous little laugh.

'Upon my word, Aunt Mildred, I am *traurig* myself at the very thought of that exquisite song,' she said. 'What a gift it is to sing like that! How I wish *I* were César Castellani!'

'What, when we have both agreed that he is not a good man?'

'Who cares about being *good?*' exclaimed Pamela, beside herself; 'three-fourths of the people of this world are good. But to be able to write a book that can unsettle every one's religion; to be able to make everybody miserable when one sings! Those are gifts that place a man on a level with the Greek gods. If I were Mr Castellani I should feel like Mercury or Apollo.'

'Pamela, you frighten me when you rave like that. Remember that, for all we know to the contrary, this man may be a mere adventurer, and in every way dangerous.'

'Why should we think him an adventurer? He told me all about himself. He told me that his grandfather was under obligations to your grandfather. He told me about his father, the composer, who wrote operas which are known all over Italy, and who died young, like Mozart and Mendelssohn. Genius is hereditary with him; he was suckled upon art. I have no doubt he is bad, irretrievably bad,' said Pamela, with unction; 'but don't try to persuade me that he is a vulgar adventurer who would try to borrow five-pound notes, or a fortune-hunter who would try to marry one for one's money,' concluded the girl, falling back upon her favourite form of speech.

CHAPTER XIV

LIFTING THE CURTAIN

The charity concert afforded César Castellani just the necessary excuse for going to Enderby Manor House as often as he liked, and for staying there as long as he liked. He was now on a familiar footing. He drove or rode over from Riverdale nearly every day during the three weeks that intervened between Mr Cancellor's sermon and the afternoon concert. He made himself the curate's right hand in all the details of the entertainment. He chose the music, he wrote the programme, he sent it to his favourite printer to be printed in antique type upon ribbed paper with ragged edges: a perfect gem in the way of a programme. He scoured the country round in quest of amateur talent, and was much more successful than the curate had been in the same quest.

'I'm astounded at your persuading Lady Millborough to show in the daylight,' said Rollinson, laughing. 'You have the tongue of the serpent to overcome her objection to the glare of the afternoon sun.'

'*Estote prudentes sicuti serpentes,*' said Castellani. 'There's a fine old ecclesiastic's motto for you. I know Lady Millborough rather dreads the effect of sunlight upon her *nacre Bernhardt*. She told me that she was never equal to singing in the afternoon: the glare of the sun always gave her a headache. But I assured her in the first place that there should be no glare –

that as an artist I abhorred a crude, white light – and that it should be my business to see that our concert-room was lighted upon purely aesthetic principles. We would have the dim religious light which painters and poets love. In the second place I assured her that she had as fine a contralto as Madame Alboni, on whose knees I had often sat as a child, and who gave me the emerald pin I was wearing.'

'My hat, what a man you are!' exclaimed Rollinson. 'But do you mean to say we are to give our concert in the dark?'

'We will not have the afternoon sun blinding half our audience. We will have the auditorium in a cool twilight, and we will have lamplight on our platform – just that mellow and flattering light in which elderly women look young and young women angelic.'

'We'll leave everything to you,' cried the curate. 'I think we ought to leave him free scope; ought we not, Mrs Greswold?'

Mildred assented. Pamela was enthusiastic. This concert was to be one of the events of her life. Castellani had discovered that she possessed a charming mezzo-soprano. She was to sing a duet with him. O, what rapture! A duet of his own composition, all about roses and love and death.

> "'Twere sweet to die as the roses die,
> If I had but lived for thee;
> A life as long as the nightingale's song
> Were enough for my heart and me.'

The words and the voices were interwoven in a melodious web; tenor and soprano entwined together – following and ever following like the phrases in an anthem.

The preparation of this one duet alone obliged Mr Castellani to be nearly every day at Enderby. A musician has inexhaustible patience in teaching his own music. Castellani hammered at every bar and every note with Pamela. He did not hesitate at unpleasant truth. She had received the most expensive instruction from a well-known singing-master, and, according to Castellani, everything she had been taught was wrong. 'If you had been left alone to sing as the birds sing you would be ever so much better off,' he said; 'the man has murdered a very fine organ. If I had had the teaching of you, you would have sung as well as Trebelli by this time.'

Pamela thrilled at the thought. O, to sing like some great singer – to be able to soar skyward on the wings of music – to sing as *he* sang! She had known him a fortnight by this time, and was deeply in love with him. In moments of confidence by the piano he called her Pamela, treating her almost as if she were a child, yet with a touch of gallantry always – an air

Pamela loves Castellani.

that said, 'You are beautiful, dear child, and you know it; but I have lived my life.' Before Mrs Greswold he was more formal, and called her Miss Ransome.

All barriers were down now between Riverdale and the Manor. Mrs Hillersdon was going to make an extra large house-party on purpose to patronise the concert. It was to be on the 7th of September: the partridge-shooting would be in full swing, and the shooters assembled. Mrs Greswold had been to tea at Riverdale. There seemed to be no help for it, and George Greswold was apparently indifferent.

'My dearest, your purity of mind will be in no danger from Mrs Hillersdon. Even were she still Louise Lorraine, she could not harm you – and you know I am not given to consider the *qu'on dira t'on* in such a case. Let her come here by all means, so long as she is not obnoxious to you.'

'She is far from that. I think she has the most delightful manners of any woman I ever met.'

'So, no doubt, had Circe, yet she changed men into swine.'

'Mr Cancellor would not believe in her if she were not a good woman.'

'I should set a higher value on Cancellor's opinion if he were more of a man of the world, and less of a bigot. See what nonsense he talked about the Deceased Wife's Sister's Bill.'

'Nonsense! O, George, if you knew how it distressed me to hear you take the other side – the unchristian side!'

'I can find no word of Christ's against such marriages, and the Church of old was always ready with a dispensation for any such union, if it was made worth the Church's while to be indulgent. It was the earnest desire of the Roman Catholic world that Philip should marry Elizabeth. You are Cancellor's pupil, Mildred, and I cannot wonder if he has made you something of a bigot.'

'He is the noblest and most unselfish of men.'

'I admit his unselfishness – the purity of his intentions – the tenderness of his heart; but I deny his nobility. Ecclesiastic narrow-mindedness spoils a character that might have been perfect had it been less hampered by tradition. Cancellor is a couple of centuries behind the time. His Church is the Church of Laud.'

'I thought you admired and loved him, George,' said Mildred regretfully.

'I admire his good qualities, I love him for his thoroughness; but our creeds are wide apart. I cannot even pretend to think as he thinks.'

This confession increased Mildred's sadness. She would have had her husband think as she thought, believe as she believed, in all spiritual things. The beloved child they had lost was waiting for them in heaven; and she would fain that they should both tread the same path to that better world where there would be no more tears, no more death – where day and night would be alike in the light of the great Throne. She shuddered at the thought of any difference of creed on her husband's part, shuddered at that beginning of divergence which might end in infidelity. She had been educated by Clement Cancellor, and she thought as he thought. It seemed to her that she was surrounded by an atmosphere of doubt. In the books she read, among the more cultivated people whom she met, she found the same tendency to speculative infidelity, pessimism, Darwinism, sociology, Pantheism, anything but Christian belief. The nearest approach to religious feeling seemed to be found in the theosophists, with their last fashionable Oriental improvements upon the teaching of Christ.

Clement Cancellor had trained her in the belief that there was one Church, one creed, one sovereign rule of life, outside which rigid boundary-line lay the dominion of Satan. And now, seeing her husband's antagonism to her pastor upon this minor point of the marriage law, she began to ask herself whether those two might not stand as widely apart upon graver questions – whether George Greswold might not be one of those half-hearted Christians who attend their parish church and keep Sunday sacred because it is well to set a good example to their neighbours and dependants, while their own faith is little more than a memory of youthful beliefs, the fading reflection of a sun that has sunk below the horizon.

She had discovered her husband capable of a suppression of truth that was almost as bad as falsehood; and now having begun to doubt his conscientiousness, it was not unnatural that she should begin to doubt his religious feeling.

'Had he been as deeply religious as I thought him, he would not have so deceived me,' she told herself, still brooding upon that mystery of his first marriage.

Castellani's presence in the house was a continual irritation to her. It tortured her to think that he knew more of her husband's past life than was known to her. She longed to question him, yet refrained, feeling that there would be unspeakable meanness, treachery even, in obtaining any information about her husband's past life except from his own lips. He had chosen to keep silence, he who could so easily have explained all things; and it was her duty to submit.

She tried to be interested in the concert, which involved a good deal of work for herself, as she was to play all the accompaniments, the piano part in a concertante duet by De Bériot with an amateur violin player, and a Hungarian march by a modern classic by way of overture. There were rehearsals nearly every day, with much talk and tea-drinking.

Enderby Manor seemed given over to bustle and gaiety – that grave old house, which to her mind ought to have been silent as a sepulchre, now that Lola's voice could sound there never more, except in dreams.

'People must think I am forgetting her,' she said to herself with a sigh, when half-a-dozen carriages had driven away from the door, after two hours of bustle and confusion, much discussion as to the choice of songs and the arrangement of the programme, which everybody wanted different.

'I cannot possibly sing "The Three Fishers" after Captain Scobell's "Wanderer,"' protested Lady Millborough. 'It would never do to have two dismal songs in succession.'

Yet when it was proposed that her ladyship's song should succeed Mr Rollinson's admirable rendering of George Grossmith's 'He was such a Careless Man,' she distinctly refused to sing immediately after a comic song.

'I am not going to take the taste of Mr Rollinson's vulgarity out of people's mouths,' she told Mildred, in an audible aside.

To these God-gifted vocalists the accompanist was as an inferior being, a person with a mere mechanical gift of playing anything set before her with taste and style. They treated her as if she had been a machine.

'If you wouldn't mind going over our duet just once more, I think we should feel more comfortable in it,' said one of the two Miss Tadcasters, who were to take the roof off, metaphorically, in the Norma duet.

Mildred toiled with unwavering good-nature, and suppressed her shudders at many a false note, and cast oil on the waters when the singers were inclined to quarrel. She was glad of the drudgery that kept her fingers and her mind occupied; she was glad of any distraction that changed the current of her thoughts.

It was the day before the concert. César Castellani had established himself as *l'ami de la maison*, a person who had the right to come in and out as he liked, whose coming and going made no difference to the master of the house. Had George Greswold's mind been less abstracted from the business of everyday life he might have seen danger to Pamela Ransome's peace of mind in the frequent presence of the Italian, and he might have considered it his duty, as the young lady's kinsman, to have restricted Mr Castellani's privileges. But the blow which had crushed George Greswold's heart a little more than a year ago had left him in somewise a broken man. He had lost all interest in the common joys and occupations of everyday life. His days were spent for the most part in long walks or rides in the loneliest places he could find, his only evening amusement was found in books, and those books of a kind which engrossed his attention and took him out of himself. His wife's companionship was always precious to him; but their intercourse had lost all its old gaiety and much of the old familiarity. There was an indefinable something which held them asunder even when they were sitting in the same room, or pacing side by side, just as of old, upon the lawn in front of the drawing-room, or idling in their summer parlour in the shade of the cedars.

Again and again in the last three weeks some question about the past had trembled upon Mildred's lips as she sat at work by the piano where Castellani played in dreamy idleness, wandering from one master to another, or extemporising after his own capricious fancies. Again and again she had struggled against the temptation and had conquered. No, she would not stoop to a meanness. She would not be disloyal to her husband by so much as one idle question.

To-day Castellani was in high spirits, proud of to-morrow's anticipated success, in which his own exertions would count for much. He sat at the piano in a leisure hour after tea. All the performers had gone, after the final adjustment of every detail. Mildred sat idle with her head resting against the cushion of a high-backed armchair, exhausted by the afternoon's labours. Pamela stood by the piano watching and listening delightedly as Castellani improvised.

'I will give you my musical transcript of St Partridge Day,' he said, smiling down at the notes as he played a lively melody with little rippling runs in the treble and crisp staccato chords in the bass. 'This is morning, and all the shooters are on tip-toe with delight – a misty morning,' gliding into a dreamy legato movement as he spoke. 'You can scarcely see the hills yonder, and the sun is not yet up. See there he leaps above that bank of purple cloud, and all is brightness,' changing to crashing chords in the bass and brilliant arpeggios in the treble. 'Hark! there is chanticleer. How shrill he peels in the morning air! The dogs are leaving the kennel – and now the gates are open, dogs and men are in the road. You can hear the steady tramp of the clumsy shooting-boots – your dreadful English boots – and the merry music of the dogs. Pointers, setters, spaniels, smooth beasts and curly beasts, shaking the dew from the hedgerows as they scramble along the banks, flying over the ditches – creatures of lightning swiftness; yes, even those fat heavy spaniels which seem made to sprawl and snap at flies in the sunshine or snore beside the fire.'

He talked in brief snatches, playing all the time – playing with the easy brilliancy, the unerring grace of one to whom music is a native tongue – as natural a mode of thought-expression as speech itself. His father had trained him to improvise, weaving reminiscences of all his favourite composers into those dreamy reveries. They had sat side by side, father and son, each following the bent of his own fancy, yet quick to adapt it

Castellani loves   Mildred

to the other, now leading, now following. They had played together as
Moscheles and Mendelssohn used to play, delighting in each other's
caprices.

'I hope I don't bore you very much,' said Castellani, looking up at
Mildred as she sat silent, the fair face and pale gold hair defined against
the olive brocade of the chair cushion.

He looked up at her in wondering admiration, as at a beautiful picture.
How lovely she was, with a loveliness that grew upon him, and took
possession of his fancy and his senses with a strengthening hold day by
day. It was a melancholy loveliness, the beauty of a woman whose life had
come to a dead stop, in whose breast hope and love were dead – or
dormant.

'Not dead,' he told himself, 'only sleeping. Whose shall be the spell to
awaken the sleepers? Who shall be the Orpheus to bring this sweet
Eurydice from the realms of Death?'

Such thoughts were in his mind as he sat looking at her, waiting for
her answer, playing all the while, telling her how fair she was in the
tenderest variations of an old German air whose every note breathed
passionate love.

'How sweet!' murmured Pamela; 'what an exquisite melody!' taking
some of the sweetness to herself. 'How could such sweetness weary any
one with the ghost of an ear? You are not bored by it, are you, aunt?'

'Bored? no, it is delightful,' answered Mildred, rousing herself from a
reverie. 'My thoughts went back to my childhood while you were
playing. I never knew but one other person who had that gift of
improvisation, and she used to play to me when I was a child. She was
almost a child herself, and of course she was very inferior to you as a
pianist; but she would sit and play to me for an hour in the twilight,
inventing new melodies, or playing recollections of old melodies,
describing in music. The old fairy tales are for ever associated with music
in my mind, because of those memories. I believe she was highly gifted
in music.'

'Music of a high order is not an uncommon gift among women of
sensitive temperament,' said Castellani musingly. 'I take it to be only
another name for sympathy. Want of musical feeling is want of sympathy.
Shakespeare knew that when he declared the non-musical man to be by
nature a villain. I could no more imagine *you* without the gift of music
than I could imagine the stars without the quality of light. Mr Greswold's
first wife was a good musician, as no doubt you know.'

'You heard her play – and sing?' faltered Mildred, avoiding a direct
reply.

The sudden mention of her dead rival's name had quickened the
beating of her heart. She had longed to question him and had refrained;

and now, without any act of hers, he had spoken, and she was going to hear something about that woman whose existence was a mystery to her, whose Christian name she had never heard.

'Yes, I heard her several times at parties at Nice. She was much admired for her musical talents. She was not a grand singer, but she had been well taught, and she had exquisite taste, and knew exactly the kind of music that suited her best. She was one of the attractions at the Palais Montano, where one heard only the best music.'

'I think you said the other day that you did not meet her often,' said Mildred. 'My husband could hardly have forgotten you had you met frequently.'

'I can scarcely say that we met frequently, and our meetings were such as Mr Greswold would not be very likely to remember. I am not a remarkable man now, and I was a very insignificant person fifteen years ago. I was only asked to people's houses because I could sing a little, and because my father had a reputation in the South as a composer. I was never introduced to your husband, but I was presented to his wife – as a precocious youth with some pretensions to a tenor voice – and I found her very charming – after her own particular style.'

'Was she a beautiful woman?' asked Mildred. 'I – I – have never talked about her to my husband, she died so young, and——'

'Yes, yes, I understand,' interrupted Castellani, as she hesitated. 'Of course you would not speak of her. There are things that cannot be spoken about. There is always a skeleton in every life – not more in Mr Greswold's past than in that of other people, perhaps, could we know all histories. I was wrong to speak of her. Her name escaped me unawares.'

'Pray don't apologise,' said Mildred, indignant at something in his tone, which hinted at wrongdoing on her husband's part. 'There can be no reason why you should keep silence – to me; though any mention of an old sorrow might wound him. I know my husband too well not to know that he must have behaved honourably in every relation of life – before I married him as well as afterwards. I only asked a very simple question: was my predecessor as beautiful as she was gifted?'

'No. She was charming, piquant, elegant, spirituelle, but she was not handsome. I think she was conscious of that want of beauty, and that it made her sensitive, and even bitter. I have heard her say hard things of women who were handsomer than herself. She had a scathing tongue and a capricious temper, and she was not a favourite with her own sex, though she was very much admired by clever men. I know that as a lad I thought her one of the brightest women I had ever met.'

'It was sad that she should die so young,' said Mildred.

Mmm - sad

She would not for worlds that this man should know the extent of her ignorance about the woman who had borne her husband's name. She spoke vaguely, hoping that he would take it for granted she knew all.

'Yes,' assented Castellani with a sigh, 'her death was infinitely sad.'

He spoke as of an event of more than common sadness — a calamity that had been in somewise more tragical than untimely death must needs be.

Mildred kept silence, though her heart ached with shapeless forebodings, and though it would have been an unspeakable relief to know the worst rather than to feel the oppression of this mystery.

Castellani rose to take leave. He was paler than he had been before the conversation began, and he had a troubled air. Pamela looked at him with sympathetic distress. 'I am afraid you are dreadfully tired,' she said, as they shook hands.

'I am never tired in this house,' he answered; and Pamela appropriated the compliment by her vivid blush.

Mildred shook hands with him mechanically and in silence. She was hardly conscious of his leaving the room. She rose and went out into the garden, while Pamela sat down to the piano and began singing her part in the everlasting duet. She never sang anything else nowadays. It was a perpetual carol of admiration for the author of *Nepenthe*.

> "'Twere sweet to die as the roses die,
> If I had but lived for thee;
> 'Twere sweet to fade as the twilight fades
> Over the western sea,'

she warbled, while Mildred paced slowly to and fro in front of the cedars, brooding over every word Castellani had spoken about her husband's first wife.

'Her death was infinitely sad.'

Why infinitely? The significance of the word troubled her. It conjured up all manner of possibilities. Why infinitely sad? All death is sad. The death of the young especially so. But to say even of a young wife's death that it was infinitely sad would seem to lift it out of the region of humanity's common doom. That qualifying word hinted at a tragical fate rather than a young life cut short by any ordinary malady. There had been something in Castellani's manner which accentuated the meaning of his words. That troubled look, that deep sigh, that hurried departure, all hinted at a painful story which he knew and did not wish to reveal.

He had in a manner apologised for speaking of George Greswold's first wife. There must have been a reason for that. He was not a man to say meaningless things out of *gaucherie*; not a man to blunder and equivocate from either shyness or stupidity. He had implied that Mr Greswold was not likely to talk about his first marriage – that he would naturally avoid any allusion to his first wife.

Why naturally? Why should he not speak of that past life? Men are not ordinarily reticent upon such subjects. And that a man should suppress the fact of a first marriage altogether would suggest memories so dark as to impel an honourable man to stoop to a tacit lie rather than face the horror of revelation.

She walked up and down that fair stretch of velvet turf upon which her feet had trodden so lightly in the happy years that were gone – gone never to be recalled, as it seemed to her, carrying with them all that she had ever known of domestic peace, of wedded bliss. Never again could they two be as they had been. The mystery of the past had risen up between them – like some hooded phantom, a vaguely threatening figure, a hidden face – to hold them apart for evermore.

'If he had only trusted me,' she thought despairingly, 'there is hardly any sin that I would not have forgiven for love of him. Why could he not believe in my love well enough to know that I should judge him leniently – if there had been wrong-doing on his side – if——'

She had puzzled over that hidden past, trying to penetrate the darkness, imagining the things that might have happened – infidelity on the wife's part – infidelity on the husband's side – another and fatal attachment taking the place of loyal love. Sin of some kind there must have been, she thought; for such dark memories could scarcely be sinless. But was husband or wife the sinner?

'Her death was infinitely sad.'

That sentence stood out against the dark background of mystery as if written in fire. That one fact was absolute. George Greswold's first wife had died under circumstances of peculiar sadness; so painful that Castellani's countenance grew pale and troubled at the very thought of her death.

'I cannot endure it,' Mildred thought at last, in an agony of doubt. 'I will not suffer this torture for another day. I will appeal to him. I will question him. If he values my love and my esteem he will answer faithfully. It must be painful for him, painful for me; but it will be far better for us both in the long-run. Anything will be better than these torturing fears. I am his wife, and I have a right to know the truth.'

The dressing-gong summoned her back to the house. Her husband was in the drawing-room half-an-hour afterwards, when she went down to dinner. He was still in his jacket and knickerbockers, just as he had come in from a long ramble.

'Will you forgive me if I dine with you in these clothes, Mildred, and you, Pamela?' to the damsel in white muslin, whom he had just surprised at the piano still warbling her honeyed strain about death and the roses; 'I came in five minutes ago – dead beat. I have been in the forest, and had a tramp with the deerhounds over Bramble Hill.'

'You walk too far, George. You are looking dreadfully tired.'

'I'm sure you needn't apologise for your dress on my account,' said Pamela. 'Henry is a perfect disgrace half his time. He hates evening-clothes, and I sometimes fear he hates soap-and-water. He can reconcile his conscience to any amount of dirt so long as he has his cold tub in the morning. He thinks that one sacrifice to decency justifies anything. I have had to sit next him at dinner when he came straight from rats,' concluded Pamela, with a shudder. 'But Rosalind is so foolishly indulgent. She would spoil twenty husbands.'

'And you, I suppose, would be a martinet to one?' said Greswold, smiling at the girl's animated face.

'It would depend. If I were married to an artist I could forgive any neglect of the proprieties. One does not expect a man of that kind to be the slave of conventionalities; but a commonplace person like Sir Henry Mountford has nothing to recommend him but his tailor.'

They went to dinner, and Pamela's prattle relieved the gloom which had fallen upon husband and wife. George Greswold saw that there were signs of a new trouble in his wife's face. He sat for nearly an hour alone with the untouched decanters before him, and with Kassandra's head upon his knee. The dog always knew when his thoughts were darkest, and would not be repulsed at such times. She was not obtrusive: she only wanted to bear him company.

It was nearly ten o'clock when he left the dining-room. He looked in at the drawing-room door, and saw his wife and his niece sitting at work, silent both.

'I am going to the library to write some letters, Mildred,' he said: 'don't sit up for me.'

She rose quickly and went over to him.

'Let me have half-an-hour's talk with you first, George,' she said, in an earnest voice: 'I want so much to speak to you.'

'My dearest, I am always at your service,' he answered quietly; and they went across the hall together, to that fine old room which was essentially the domain of the master of the house.

It was a large room with three long narrow windows – unaltered from the days of Queen Anne – looking out to the carriage-drive in the front of the house, and the walls were lined with books, in severely architectural bookcases. There was a lofty marble chimneypiece, richly decorated, and in front of the fireplace there was an old-fashioned knee-hole desk, at which Mr Greswold was wont to sit. There was a double reading-lamp ready-lighted for him upon this desk, and there was no other light in the room. By this dim light the sombre colouring of oak bookcases and maroon velvet window-curtains deepened to black. The spacious room had almost a funereal aspect, like that awful banqueting-hall to which Domitian invited his parasites and straightway frightened them to death.

'Well, Mildred, what is the matter?' asked Greswold, when his wife had seated herself beside him in front of the massive oak desk at which all the business of his estate had been transacted since he came to Enderby. 'There is nothing amiss, love, I hope, to make you so earnest?'

'There is something very much amiss, George,' she answered. 'Forgive me if I pain you by what I have to say – by the questions I am going to ask. I cannot help giving you pain, truly and dearly as I love you. I cannot go on suffering as I have suffered since that wretched Sunday afternoon when I discovered how you had deceived me – you whom I so trusted, so honoured as the most upright among men.'

'It is a little hard that you should say I deceived you, Mildred. I suppressed one fact which had no bearing upon my relations with you.'

'You must have signed your name to a falsehood in the register, if you described yourself as a bachelor.'

'I did not so describe myself. I confided the fact of my first marriage to your father on the eve of our wedding. I told him why I had been silent – told him that my past life had been steeped in bitterness. He was generous enough to accept my confidence and to ask no questions. My bride was too shy and too agitated to observe what I wrote in the register, or else she might have noted the word "widower" after my name.'

'Thank God you did not sign your name to a lie,' said Mildred, with a sigh of relief.

'I am sorry my wife of fourteen years should think me capable of falsehood on the document that sealed my fate with hers.'

'O, George, I know how true you are – how true and upright you have been in every word and act of your life since we two have been one. It is not in my nature to misjudge you. I *cannot* think you capable of wrong-doing to any one under strongest temptation. I cannot believe that Fate could set such a snare for you as could entrap you into one dishonourable act; but I am tortured by the thought of a past life of which I know nothing. Why did you hide your marriage from me when we were lovers? Why are you silent and secret now, when I am your wife, the other half of yourself, ready to sympathise with you, to share the burden of dark memories? Trust me, George. Trust me, dear love, and let us be again as we have been, united in every thought.'

'You do not know what you are asking me, Mildred,' said George Greswold, in his deep, grave voice, looking at her with haggard reproachful eyes. 'You cannot measure the torture you are inflicting by this aimless curiosity.'

'You cannot measure the agony of doubt which I have suffered since I knew that you loved another woman before you loved me – loved her so well that you cannot bear even to speak of that past life which you lived with her – regret her so intensely that now, after fourteen years of wedded life with me, the mere memory of that lost love can plunge you into gloom and despair,' said Mildred passionately.

That smothered fire of jealousy which had been smouldering in her breast for weeks broke out all at once in impetuous speech. She no longer cared what she said. Her only thought was that the dead love had been dearer than the living, that she had been cozened by a lover whose heart had never been wholly hers.

'You are very cruel, Mildred,' her husband answered quietly. 'You are probing an old wound, and a deep one, to the quick. You wrong yourself more than you wrong me by causeless jealousy and unworthy doubts. Yes, I did conceal the fact of my first marriage – not because I had loved my wife too well, but because I had not loved her well enough. I was silent about a period of my life which was one of intense misery – which it was my duty to myself to forget, if it were possible to forget – which it was perilous to remember. My only chance of happiness – or peace of mind – lay in oblivion of that bitter time. It was only when I loved you that I began to believe forgetfulness was possible. I courted oblivion by every means in my power. I told myself that the man who had so suffered was a man who had ceased to exist. George Ransome was dead. George Greswold stood on the threshold of a new life, with infinite capacities for happiness. I told myself that I might be a beloved and honoured husband – which I had never been – a useful member of society – which I had not been hitherto. Until that hour all things had been against me. With you for my wife all things would be in my favour. For thirteen happy years this promise of our marriage morning was fully realised; then came our child's death; and now comes your estrangement.'

'I am not estranged, George. It is only my dread of the beginning of estrangement which tortures me. Since that man spoke of your first wife, I have brooded perpetually upon that hidden past. It is weak, I know, to have done so. I ought to trust unquestioningly: but I cannot, I cannot. I love you too well to love without jealousy.'

'Well, let the veil be lifted then, since it must be so. Ask what questions you please, and I will answer them – as best I can.'

'You are very good,' she faltered, drawing a little nearer to him, leaning her head against his shoulder as she talked to him, and laying her hand on his as it lay before him on the desk, tightly clenched. 'Tell me, dear, were you happy with your first wife?'

'I was not.'

'Not even in the beginning?'

'Hardly in the beginning. It was an ill-advised union, the result of impulse.'

'But she loved you very dearly, perhaps.'

'She loved me – dearly – after her manner of loving.'

'And you did not love her?'

'It is a cruel thing you force me to say, Mildred. No, I did not love her.'

'Had you been married long when she died?'

She felt a quivering movement in the clenched hand on which her own lay caressingly, and she heard him draw a long and deep breath.

'About a year.'

'Her death was a sad one, I know. Did she go out of her mind before she died?'

'No.'

'Did she leave you – or do you any great wrong?'

'No.'

'Were you false to her, George – O, forgive me, forgive me – but there must have been something more sad than common sadness, and it might be that some new and fatal love——'

'There was no such thing,' he answered sternly. I was true to my duties as a husband. It was not a long trial – only a year. Even a profligate might keep faith for so short a span.'

'I see you will not confide in me. I will ask no more questions, George. That kind of catechism will not make us more in sympathy with each other. I will ask you nothing more – except – just one question – a woman's question. Was your first wife beautiful in your eyes?'

'She was not beautiful; but she was intellectual, and she had an interesting countenance – a face that attracted me at first sight. It was even more attractive to me than the faces of handsomer women. But if you want to know what your fancied rival was like you need not languish in ignorance,' with some touch of scorn. 'I have her photograph in this desk. I have kept it for my days of humiliation, to remind me of what I have been and what I may be again. Would you like to see it?'

'Yes, George, if it will not pain you too much to show it to me.'

'Do not talk of pain. You have stirred the waters of Marah so deeply that one more bitter drop cannot signify.' He unlocked his desk as he spoke, lifted the lid, which was sustained by a movable upright, and groped among the accumulation of papers and parchments inside.

The object for which he was seeking was at the back of the desk, under all the papers. He found it by touch: a morocco case containing a cabinet photograph. Mildred stood up beside him, with one hand on his shoulder as he searched.

He handed her the case without a word. She opened it in silence and looked at the portrait within. A small, delicately-featured face, with large dark eyes — eyes almost too large for the face — a slender throat, thin sloping shoulders — eyes that looked out of the picture with a strange intensity — a curious alertness in the countenance, as of a woman made up of nerves and emotions, a nature wanting the element of repose.

Mildred stared at the picture three or four seconds, and then with a choking sound like a strangled sob fell unconscious at her husband's feet.

BOOK THE SECOND
LACHESIS; OR THE METER OF DESTINY

CHAPTER I

A WIFE AND NO WIFE

Mr Castellani's existence was one of those social problems about which the idle world loves to speculate. There are a good many people in London to whom the idea of a fourth dimension is not half so interesting as the notion of a man who lives by his wits, and yet contrives to get himself dressed by a good tailor, and to obtain a footing in some of the best houses at the smart end of the town. This problem César Castellani had offered to the polite world of London for the last three seasons.

Who *is* Mr Castellani? was a question still asked by a good many people who invited the gentleman to their houses, and made much of him. He had not forced his way into society; nobody had the right to describe him as a pushing person. He had slipped so insidiously into his place in the social orbit that people had not yet left off wondering how he came there, or who had been his sponsors. This kind of speculation always stimulates the invention of the clever people; and these affected to know a good deal more about Mr Castellani than he knew about himself.

'He came with magnificent credentials, and an account was opened for him at Coutts's before he arrived,' said Magnus Dudley, the society poet, flinging back his long hair with a lazy movement of the large languid head. 'Of course, you know that he is a natural son of Cavour's?'

'Indeed! No, I never heard *that*. He is not like Cavour.'

'Of course not, but he is the image of his mother − one of the handsomest women in Italy − a Duchess, and daughter of a Roman Prince, who could trace his descent in an unbroken line from Germanicus. Castellani has the blood of Caligula in his veins.'

'He looks like it; but I have heard on pretty good authority that he is the son of a Milanese music-master.'

'There are people who will tell you his father wheeled a barrow and sold penny ices in Whitechapel,' retorted Magnus. 'People will say anything.'

Thus and in much otherwise did society speculate; and in the meantime Mr Castellani's circle was always widening. His book had been just audacious enough and just clever enough to hit the gold in the literary target. *Nepenthe* had been one of the successes of the season

before last: and Mr Castellani was henceforth to be known as the author
of *Nepenthe*. He had touched upon many things below the stars, and
some things beyond them. He had written of other worlds with the
confidence of a man who had been there. He had written of women
with the air of a Café de Paris Solomon; and he had written of men as if
he had never met one.

A man who could write a successful book, and could sing and play
divinely, was a person to be cultivated in feminine society. Few men
cared to be intimate with Mr Castellani, but among women his influence
was indisputable. He treated them with a servile deference which
charmed them, and he made them his slaves. No Oriental despot ever
ruled more completely than César Castellani did in half-a-dozen of those
drawing-rooms which give the tone to scores of other drawing-rooms
between Mayfair and Paris Tyne. He considered to be in request from
the dawn to the close of the London season. He had made a favour of
going to Riverdale; and now although it suited his purpose to be here,
he made a favour of staying.

'If it were not for the delight of being here, I should be in one of the
remotest valleys in the Tyrol, or wild bla Highlands. I have never stayed
in England so long after the end of the season. I feel longing to break
loose from the bonds of civilised propriety want to do this time of
the year. I want to go coastward, and away and then away again afterward.
I should like to go and live in a shanty, like the girl in Ouida's *In
Maremma*. My third—a ten cent of a day.'

This from a man who spent the greater part of his existence dawdling
in drawing-rooms and boudoirs sounded paradoxical; but paradoxes are
accepted graciously from a man who was written the book of the season.
Louise Hillersdon treated Castellani like a favourite son. At his bidding
she brought out the old guitar which had slumbered in its case for nearly
a decade, and sang the old Spanish songs, and struck the strings with the
old dashing sweep of a delicate hand, and graceful curve of a rounded
arm.

'When you sing I could believe you as young as Helen when Paris stole
her,' said Castellani, lolling along the sofa beside the low chair in which
she was sitting; 'I cease to envy the men who knew you when you were a
girl.'

'My dear Castellani, I feel old enough to be your grandmother; unless
you are really the person I sometimes take you for——'

'Who may that be?'

'The Wandering Jew.'

'No matter what my creed or where I have wandered, since I am so
happy as to find a haven here. Granted that I can remember Nero's
beautiful Empress, and Faustina, and all that procession of fair women

who illumine the Dark Ages – and Mary of Scotland, and Emma
Hamilton, blonde and brunette, pathetic and *espiègle*, every type, and
every variety. It is enough for me to find perfection here.'

'If you only knew how sick I am of that kind of nonsense!' said Mrs
Hillersdon, smiling at him, half in amusement, half in scorn.

'O, I know that you have drunk the wine of men's worship to satiety!
Yet if you and I had lived upon the same plane, I would have taught you
that among a hundred adorers one could love you better than all the rest.
But it is too late. Our souls may meet and touch perhaps thousands of
years hence in a new incarnation.'

'Do you talk this kind of nonsense to Mrs Greswold or her niece?'

'No; with them I am all dulness and propriety. Neither lady is *simpatica*.
Miss Ransome is a frank, good-natured girl – much too frank – with all
the faults of her species. I find the genus girl universally detestable.'

'Miss Ransome has about fifteen hundred a year. I suppose you know
that?'

'Has she really? If ever I marry I hope to do better than that,' answered
César with easy insolence. 'She would be a very nice match for a country
parson; that Mr Rollinson, for instance, who is getting up the concert.'

'Then Miss Ransome is not your attraction at Enderby? It is Mrs
Greswold who draws you.'

'Why should I be drawn?' he asked, with his languid air. 'I go there in
sheer idleness. They like me to make music for them; they fool me and
praise me; and it is pleasant to be fooled by two pretty women.'

'Does Mrs Greswold take any part in the fooling? She looks like
marble.'

'There is fire under that marble. Mrs Greswold is romantically in love
with her husband: but that is a complaint which is not incurable.'

'He is not an agreeable man,' said Louise, remembering how long
George Greswold and his wife had kept aloof from her. 'And he does not
look a happy man.'

'He is not happy.'

'You know something about him – more than we all know?' asked
Louise, with keen curiosity.

'Not much. I met him at Nice before he came into his property. He
was not a very fortunate person at that time, and he doesn't care to be
reminded of it now.'

'Was he out-at-elbows, or in debt?'

'Neither. His troubles did not take that form. But I am not a gossip.
Let the past be past, as Goethe says. We can't change it, and it is charity
to forget it. If we are not sure about what we touch and hear and see – or
fancy we hear and touch and see – in the present, how much less can we
be sure of any reality or external existence in the past! It is all done away

with – vanished. How can we know that it ever was? A grave here and there is the only witness; and even the grave and the name on the headstone may be only a projection of our own consciousness. We are such stuff as dreams are made of.'

'That is a politely circuitous manner of refusing to tell me anything about Mr Greswold when his name was Ransome. No matter. I shall find other people who know the scandal, I have no doubt. Your prevarication assures me that there was a scandal.'

This was on the eve of the concert at Enderby, at about the same hour when George Greswold showed Mildred his first wife's portrait. Castellani and his hostess were alone together in the lady's morning-room, while Hillersdon and his other guests were in the billiard-room on the opposite side of a broad corridor. Mrs Hillersdon had a way of turning over her visitors to her husband when they bored her. Gusts of loud talk and louder laughter came across the corridor now and again as they played pool. There were times when Louise was too tired of life to endure the burden of commonplace society. She liked to dream over a novel. She liked to talk with a clever young man like Castellani. His flatteries amused her, and brought back a faint flavour of youth and a dim remembrance of the day when all men praised her, when she had known herself without a rival. Now other women were beautiful, and she was only a tradition. She had toiled hard to live down her past, to make the world forget that she had ever been Louise Lorraine: yet there were moments in which she felt angry to find that old personality of hers so utterly forgotten, when she was tempted to cry out, 'What rubbish you talk about your Mrs Egremont, your Mrs Linley Varden, your professional beauties and fine lady actresses. Have you never heard of ME – Louise Lorraine?'

The drawing-rooms at Enderby Manor had been so transformed under Mr Castellani's superintendence, and with the help of his own dexterous hands, that there was a unanimous expression of surprise from the county families as they entered that region of subdued light and aesthetic draperies between three and half-past three o'clock on the afternoon of the concert.

The Broadwood grand stood on a platform in front of a large bay-window, draped as no other hand could drape a piano, with embroidered Persian curtains and many-hued Algerian stuffs, stripped with gold; and against the sweeping folds of drapery rose a group of tall golden lilies out of a shallow yellow vase. A cluster of gloxinias were massed near the end of the piano, and a few of the most artistic chairs in the house were placed about for the performers. The platform, instead of being as other platforms, in a straight line across one side of the room, was placed diagonally, so as to present the picturesque effect of an angle in the background, an angle lighted with clusters of wax-candles, against a forest of palms.

All the windows had been darkened save those in the further drawing-room, which opened into the garden, and even these were shaded by Spanish hoods, letting in coolness and the scent of flowers, with but little daylight. Thus the only bright light was on the platform.

The auditorium was arranged with a certain artistic carelessness: the chairs in curved lines to accommodate the diagonal line of the platform; and this fact, in conjunction with the prettiness of the stage, put every one in good temper before the concert began.

The concert was as other concerts: clever amateur singing, excellent amateur playing, fine voices cultivated to a certain point, and stopping just short of perfect training.

César Castellani's three little songs – words by Heine – music, Schubert and Jensen – were the hit of the afternoon. There were few eyes that were unclouded by tears, even among those listeners to whom the words were in an unknown language. The pathos was in the voice of the singer.

The duet was performed with *aplomb*, and elicited an encore, on which Pamela and Castellani sang the old-fashioned 'Flow on, thou shining river,' which pleased elderly people, moving them like a reminiscence of long-vanished youth.

Pamela's heart beat furiously as she heard the applause, and she curtsied herself off the platform in a whirl of delight. She felt that it was in her to be a great public singer – a second Patti – if – if she could be taught and trained by Castellani. Her head was full of vague ideas – a life devoted to music – three years' hard study in Italy – a *début* at La Scala – a world-wide renown achieved in a single night. She even wondered how to Italianise her name. Ransomini? No, that would hardly do. Pamelani – Pameletta? What awkward names they were – christian and surname both!

And then, crimsoning at the mere thought, she saw in large letters, 'MADAME CASTELLANI.'

How much easier to make a great name in the operatic world with a husband to fight one's battles and get the better of managers!

'With an income of one's own it ought to be easy to make one's way,' thought Pamela, as she stood behind the long table in the dining-room, dispensing tea and coffee, with the assistance of maids and footmen.

Her head was so full of these bewildering visions that she was a little less on the alert than she ought to have been for shillings and half-crowns, whereby a few elderly ladies got their tea and coffee for nothing, not being asked for payment, and preferring to consider the entertainment gratis.

Mildred's part of the concert was performed to perfection – not a false note in an accompaniment, or a fault in the *tempo*. Lady Millborough, a very exacting personage, declared she had never been so well supported in her *cheval de bataille*, the finale to *La Cenerentola*. But many among the audience remarked that they had never seen Mrs Greswold look so ill; and both Rollinson and Castellani were seriously concerned about her.

'You are as white as marble,' said the Italian. 'I know you are suffering.'

'I assure you it is nothing. I have not been feeling very well lately, and I had a sleepless night. There is nothing that need give any one the slightest concern. You may be sure I shall not break down. I am very much interested in the painted window,' she added, with a faint smile.

'It is not that I fear,' said Castellani, in a lower voice. 'It is of you and your suffering I am thinking.'

George Greswold did not appear at the concert: he was engaged elsewhere.

'I cannot think how Uncle George allowed himself to have an appointment at Salisbury this afternoon,' said Pamela. 'I know he doats on music.'

'Perhaps he doesn't doat upon it quite so well as to like to see his house turned topsy-turvy,' said Lady Millborough, who would have allowed every philanthropic scheme in the country to collapse for want of cash rather than suffer her drawing-room to be pulled about by amateur scene-shifters.

Mrs Hillersdon and her party occupied a prominent position near the platform; but that lady was too clever to make herself conspicuous. She talked to the people who were disposed to friendliness – their numbers had increased with the advancing years – and she placidly ignored those who still held themselves aloof from 'that horrid woman.' Nor did she in any way appropriate Castellani as her special *protégé* when the people round her were praising him. She took everything that happened with the repose which stamps the caste of Vere de Vere, and may often be found among women whom the Vere de Veres despise.

All was over: the last of the carriages had rolled away. Castellani had been carried off in Mrs Hillersdon's barouche, no one inviting him to stay at the Manor House. Rollinson lingered to repeat his effusive thanks for Mrs Greswold's help.

'It has been a glorious success,' he exclaimed; 'glorious! Who would have thought there was so much amateur talent available within thirty miles? And Castellani was a grand acquisition. We shall clear at least seventy pounds for the window. I don't know how I can ever thank you enough for giving us the use of your lovely rooms, Mrs Greswold, and for letting us pull them about as we liked.'

'That did not matter – much,' Mildred said faintly, as she stood by the drawing-room door in the evening light, the curate lingering to reiterate the assurance of his gratitude. 'Everything can be arranged again – easily.'

She was thinking, with a dull aching at her heart, that to her the pulling about and disarrangement of those familiar rooms hardly mattered at all. They were her rooms no longer. Enderby was never more to be her home. It had been her happy home for thirteen gracious years – years clouded with but one natural sorrow, in the loss of her beloved father. And now that father's ghost rose up before her, and said, 'The sins of the fathers shall be visited upon the children, and because of my sin you must go forth from your happy home and forsake the husband of your heart.'

She gave the curate an icy hand, and turned from him without another word.

'Poor soul, she is dead-beat!' thought Rollinson, as he trudged home to his lodgings over a joiner and builder's shop: airy and comfortable rooms enough, but odorous of sawdust, and a little too near the noises of the workshop.

He could but think it odd that he had not been asked to dine at the Manor, as he would have been in the ordinary course of events. He had told the builder's wife that he should most likely dine out, whereupon that friendly soul had answered, 'Why, of course they'll ask you, Mr Rollinson. You know they're always glad to see you.'

And now he had to return to solitude and a fresh-killed chop.

It was seven o'clock, and George Greswold had not yet come home from Salisbury. Very few words had passed between him and his wife since she fell fainting at his feet last night. He had summoned her maid, and between them they had brought her back to consciousness, and half carried her to her room. She would give no explanation of her fainting-fit when the maid had left the room, and she was lying on her bed, white and calm, with her husband sitting by her side. She told him that she was tired, and that a sudden giddiness had come upon her. That was all he could get from her.

'If you will ask me no questions, and leave me quite alone, I will try to sleep, so that I may be fit for my work in the concert to-morrow,' she pleaded. 'I would not disappoint them for worlds.'

'I don't think you need be over-anxious about them,' said her husband bitterly. 'There is more at stake than a painted window: there is your peace and mine. Answer me only one question,' he said, with intensity of purpose: 'had your fainting-fit anything to do with the portrait of my first wife?'

'I will tell you everything – after the concert to-morrow,' she answered; 'for God's sake leave me to myself till then.'

'Let it be as you will,' he answered, rising suddenly, wounded by her reticence.

He left the room without another word. She sprang up from her bed directly he was gone, ran to the door and locked it, and then flung herself on her knees upon the prie-dieu chair at the foot of a large ivory crucifix which hung in a deep recess beside the old-fashioned fireplace.

Here she knelt, in tears and prayer, deep into the night. Then for an hour or more she walked up and down the room, absorbed in thought, by the dim light of the night-lamp.

When the morning light came she went to a bookcase in a little closet of a room opening out of the spacious old bedroom – a case containing only devotional books, and of these she took out volume after volume – Taylor's *Rule of Conscience*, Hooker's *Religious Polity*, Butler, Paley – one after another, turning over the leaves, looking through the indexes – searching for something which she seemed unable to find anywhere.

'What need have I to see what others have thought?' she said to herself at last, after repeated failure; 'Clement Cancellor knows the right. I could have no better guide than his opinion, and he has spoken. What other law do I need? His law is the law of God.'

Not once did her eyes close in sleep all through that night, or in the morning hours before breakfast. She made an excuse for breakfasting in her dressing-room, a large, airy apartment, half boudoir. She was told that Mr Greswold had gone out early to see some horses at Salisbury, and would not be back till dinner-time. He was to be met at the station at half-past seven.

She had her morning to herself. Pamela was rehearsing her part in the duet, and in 'Flow on, thou shining river,' which was to be sung in the event of an encore. That occupation, and the arrangement of her toilet, occupied the young lady till luncheon – allowing for half-hourly rushes about the lawn and shrubberies with Box, whose health required activity, and whose social instincts yearned for companionship.

'He can't get on with only Kassandra; she hasn't intellect enough for him,' said Pamela.

It was only ten minutes before the arrival of the performers that Mrs Greswold went down-stairs, pale as ashes, but ready for the ordeal. She had put on a white gown with a little scarlet ribbon about it, lest black should make her pallor too conspicuous.

And now it was seven o'clock, and she was alone. The curate had been right in pronouncing her dead-beat; but she had some work before her yet. She had been writing letters in the morning. Two of these she now placed on the mantelpiece in her bedroom: one addressed to her husband, the other to Pamela.

She had a bag packed – not one of those formidable dressing-bags which weigh fifteen to twenty pounds – but a light Russia-leather bag, just large enough to contain the essentials of the toilet. She put on a neat little black bonnet and a travelling-cloak, and took her bag and umbrella, and went down to the hall. She had given orders that the carriage should call for her before going to the station, and she was at the door ready to step into it when it came round.

She told the groom that she was to be put down at Ivy Cottage, and was driven off unseen by the household, who were all indulging in a prolonged tea-drinking after the excitement of the concert.

Ivy Cottage was within five minutes' walk of Romsey Station: a little red cottage, newly built, with three or four ivy plants languishing upon a slack-baked brick wall, and just enough garden for the proverbial cat to disport himself in at his ease – the swinging of cats being no longer a popular English sport. There was nothing strange in Mrs Greswold alighting at Ivy Cottage – unless it were the hour of her visit – for the small brick box was occupied by two maiden ladies of small means: one a confirmed invalid; the other her patient nurse; whom the lady of Enderby Manor often visited, and in whom she was known to be warmly interested.

The coachman concluded that his mistress was going to spend a quarter of an hour with the two old ladies, while he went on and waited for his master at the station, and that he was to call for her on his return. He did not even ask for her orders upon this point, taking them for granted.

He was ten minutes too soon at the station, as every well-conducted coachman ought to be.

'I'm to call for my mistress, sir,' he said, as Mr Greswold stepped into the brougham.

'Where?'

'At Ivy Cottage, sir: Miss Fisher's.'

'Very good.'

The brougham pulled up at Ivy Cottage; and the groom got down and knocked a resounding peal upon the Queen Anne knocker, it being hardly possible nowadays to find a knocker that is not after the style of Queen Anne, or a newly-built twenty-five pound a year cottage in any part of rural England that does not offer a faint reminiscence of Bedford Park.

The groom made his inquiry of the startled little maid-of-all-work, fourteen years old last birthday, and already aspiring to better herself as a vegetable-maid in a nobleman's family.

Mrs Greswold had not been at Ivy Cottage that evening.

George Greswold was out of the brougham by this time, hearing the girl's answer.

'Stop where you are,' he said to the coachman, and ran back to the station, an evil augury in his mind.

He went to the up-platform, the platform at which he had alighted ten minutes before.

'Did you see Mrs Greswold here just now?' he asked the station-master, with as natural an air as he could command.

'Yes, sir. She got into the up-train, sir; the train by which you came. She came out of the waiting-room, sir, the minute after you left the platform. You must just have missed her.'

'Yes, I have just missed her.'

He walked up and down the length of the platform two or three times in the thickening dusk. Yes, he had missed her. She had left him. Such a departure could mean only severance – some deep wound – which it might take long to heal. It would all come right by and by. There could be no such thing as parting between man and wife who loved each other as they loved – who were incapable of falsehood or wrong.

What was this jealous fancy that had taken possession of her? This unappeasable jealousy of the dead past – a passion so strong that it had prompted her to rush away from him in this clandestine fashion, to torture him by all the evidences of an inconsolable grief. His heart was sick to death as he went back to the carriage, helpless to do anything except go to his deserted home, and see what explanation awaited him there.

It was half-past eight when the carriage drove up to the Manor House. Pamela ran out into the hall to receive him.

'How late you are, uncle!' she cried, 'and I can't find aunt. Everything is at sixes and sevens. The concert was a stupendous success – and – only think! – *I* was encored.'

'Indeed, dear!'

'Yes, my duet with him: and then we sang the other. They would have liked a third, only we pretended not to understand. It would have made all the others so fearfully savage if we had taken it.'

This speech was not a model of lucidity, but it might have been much clearer and yet unintelligible to George Greswold.

'Do you mind dining alone to-night, my dear Pamela?' he said, trying to speak cheerily. 'Your aunt is out – and I – I have some letters to write – and I lunched heavily at Salisbury.'

His heavy luncheon had consisted of a biscuit and a glass of beer at the station. His important business had been a long ramble on Salisbury Plain, alone with his troubled thoughts.

'Did your mistress leave any message for me?' he asked the butler.

'No, sir. Nobody saw my mistress go out. When Louisa went up to dress her for dinner she was gone, sir – but Louisa said there was a letter for you on the bedroom mantelpiece. Shall I send for it, sir?'

'No, no – I will go myself. Serve dinner at once. Miss Ransome will dine alone.'

George Greswold went to the bedroom – that fine old room, the real Queen Anne room, with thick walls and deep-set windows, and old window-seats, and capacious recesses on each side of the high oak chimneypiece, and richly-moulded wainscot, and massive panelled doors, a sober eighteenth-century atmosphere in which it is a privilege to exist – a spacious old room, with old Dutch furniture, of the pre-Chippendale era, and early English china, Worcester simulating Oriental, Chelsea striving after Dresden: a glorious old room, solemn and mysterious as a church in the dim light of a pair of wax-candles which Louisa the maid had lighted on the mantelpiece.

There, between the candles, appeared two letters: 'George Greswold, Esq.,' 'Miss Ransome.'

The husband's letter was a thick one, and the style of the penmanship showed how the pen had hurried along, driven by the electric forces of excitement and despair:

'MY BELOVED, – You asked me last night if the photograph which you showed me had anything to do with my fainting-fit. It had everything to do with it. That photograph is a portrait of my unhappy sister, my cruelly-used, unacknowledged sister; and I, who have been your wife fourteen years, know now that our marriage was against the law of God and man – that I have never been legally your wife – that our union from the first has been an unholy union, and for that unlawful marriage the hand of God has been laid upon us – heavily – heavily – in chastisement, and the darling of our hearts has been taken from us.

'"Whom He loveth He chasteneth." He has chastened us, George – perhaps to draw us nearer to Him. We were too happy, it may be, in this temporal life – too much absorbed by our own happiness, living in a charmed circle of love and gladness, till that awful chastisement came.

'There is but one course possible to me, my dear and honoured husband, and that course lies in life-long separation. I am running away from my dear home like a criminal, because I am not strong enough to stand face to face with you and tell you what must be. We must do our best to live out our lives asunder, George; we must never meet again as wedded lovers, such as we have been for fourteen years. God knows, my affection for you has grown and strengthened with every year of union, and yet it seems to me on looking back that my heart went out to you in all the fullness of an infinite love when first we stood, hand clasped in hand, beside the river. If you are angry with me, George – if you harden your heart against me because I do that which I know to be my duty, at least believe that I never loved you better than in this bitter hour of parting. I spent last night in prayer and thought. If there were any way of escape – any possibility of living my own old happy life with a clear conscience – I think God would have shown it to me in answer to my prayers; but there was no ray of light, no gleam of hope. Conscience answers sternly and plainly. By the law of God I have never been your wife, and His law commands me to break an unhallowed tie, although my heart may break with it.

'Do you remember your argument with Mr Cancellor? I never saw you so vehement in any such dispute, and you took the side which I can but think the side of the Evil One. That conversation now seems to me like a strange foreshadowing of sorrow – a lesson meant for my guidance. Little did I then think that this question could ever have any bearing on my own life; but I recall every word now, and I remember how earnestly my old master spoke – how ruthlessly he maintained the right. Can I doubt his wisdom, from whose lips I first learnt the Christian law, and in whom I first saw the true Christian life?

'I have written to Pamela, begging her to stay with you, to take my place in the household, and to be to you as an adopted daughter. May God be merciful to us both in this heavy trial, George! Be sure He will deal with us mercifully if we do our duty according to the light that is given to us.

'I shall stay to-night in Queen Anne's Gate with Mrs Tomkison. Please send Louisa to me to-morrow with luggage for a considerable absence from home. She will know what to bring. You can tell her that I am going abroad for my health. My intention is to go to some small watering-place in Germany, where I can vegetate, away from all beaten tracks, and from the people who know us. You may rely upon me to bear my own burden, and to seek sympathy and consolation from no earthly comforter.

'Do not follow me, George – should your heart urge you to do so. Respect my solemn resolution, the result of many prayers. – Your ever loving

'MILDRED.'

CHAPTER II

THE SINS OF THE FATHERS

George Greswold read his wife's letter a second time with increasing perplexity and trouble of mind. Her sister! What could this mean? She had never told him of the existence of a sister. She had been described by her father, by every one, as an only child. She had inherited the whole of her father's fortune.

'Her cruelly-used, unacknowledged sister.'

Those words indicated a social mystery, and as he read and re-read those opening lines of his wife's letter he remembered her reticence about that girl-companion from whom she had been parted so early. He remembered her blushing embarrassment when he questioned her about the girl she called Fay.

The girl had been sent to a finishing-school at Brussels, and Mildred had seen her no more.

His first wife had finished her education at Brussels. She had talked to him often of the fashionable boarding-school in the quaint old street near the Cathedral; and the slights she had endured there from other girls because of her isolation. There was no stint in the expense of her education. She had as many masters as she cared to have. She was as well dressed as the richest of her companions. But she was nobody, and belonged to nobody, could give no account of herself that would satisfy those merciless inquisitors.

His wife, Vivien Faux, the young English lady whom he had met at Florence. She was travelling in the care of an English artist and his wife, who spent their lives on the Continent. She submitted to no authority, had ample means, and was thoroughly independent. She did not get on very well with either the artist or his wife. She had a knack of saying disagreeable things, and a tongue of exceeding bitterness. A difficult subject the painter called her, and imparted to his particular friends in confidence that his wife and Miss Faux were always quarrelling. Vivien Faux, that was the name borne by the girl whom he met nineteen years ago at an evening-party in Florence; that was the name of the girl he had married, after briefest acquaintance, knowing no more about her than that she had a fortune of thirty thousand pounds when she came of age, and that the trustee and custodian of that fortune was a lawyer in Lincoln's Inn, who affected no authority over her, and put no difficulties in the way of her marrying.

He remembered now when he first saw Mildred Fausset something in her fresh young beauty, some indefinable peculiarity of expression or contour, had evolved the image of his dead wife, that image which never recurred to him without keenest pain. He remembered how strange that vague, indescribable resemblance had seemed to him, and how he had asked himself if it had any real existence, or were only the outcome of his own troubled mind, reverting involuntarily to an agonising memory.

'Her face may come back to me in the faces of other women, as it comes back to me in my miserable dreams,' he told himself.

But as the years went by he became convinced that the likeness was not imaginary. There were points of resemblance – the delicate tracing of the eyebrows, the form of the brow, the way the hair grew above the temples,

were curiously alike. He came to accept the likeness as one of those
chance resemblances which are common enough in life. It suggested to
him nothing more than that.

He went to the library with the letter still in his hand. His lamp was
ready lighted, and, the September evening being chilly, there was a wood
fire on the low hearth, which gave an air of cheerfulness to the sombre
room.

He rang and told the footman to send Mrs Bell to him.

Bell appeared, erect and severe of aspect as she had been four-and-
twenty years before; neatly dressed in black silk, with braided gray hair,
and a white lace cap.

'Sit down, Mrs Bell, I have a good many questions to ask you,' said
Greswold, motioning her to a chair on the further side of his desk.

He was sitting with his eyes fixed, looking at the spot where Mildred
had fallen senseless at his feet. He sat for some moments in a reverie, and
then turned suddenly, unlocked his desk, and took out the photograph
which he had shown Mildred last night.

'Did you ever see that face before, Bell?' he asked, handing her the
open case.

'Good gracious, sir, yes, indeed, I should think I did! but Miss Fay was
younger than that when she came to Parchment Street.'

'Did you see much of her in Parchment Street?'

'Yes, sir, a good deal, and at The Hook, too; a good deal more than I
watched to. *I* didn't hold with her being brought into our house, sir.'

'Why not?'

'I didn't think it was fair to my mistress.'

'But how was it unfair?'

'Well, sir, *I* don't wish to say anything against the dead, and Mr
Fausset was a liberal master to me, and I make no doubt that he died a
penitent man. He was a regular church-goer, and an upright man in all
his ways while *I* lived with him; but right is right; and *I* shall always
maintain that it was a cruel thing to a young wife like Mrs Fausset, who
doted on the ground he walked upon, to bring his natural daughter into
the house.'

'Mrs Bell, do you know that this is a serious accusation you are
bringing against a dead man?' said George Greswold solemnly. 'Now,
what grounds have you for saying that this girl' – with his hand upon the
photograph – 'was Mr Fausset's daughter?'

'What grounds, sir? *I* don't want any grounds. I'm not a lawyer to put
things in that way; but I know what I know. First and foremost, she was
the image of him; and next, why did he bring her home and want her to
be made one of the family, and treated as a sister by Miss Mildred?'

'She may have been the daughter of a friend.'

'People don't do that kind of thing – don't run the risk of making a wife miserable to oblige a friend,' retorted Bell scornfully. 'Besides, I say again, if she wasn't his own flesh and blood, why was she so like him?'

'She may have been the daughter of a near relation.'

'He had but one near relation in the world: his only sister, a young lady who was so difficult to please that she refused no end of good offers, and of such a pious turn that she has devoted her life to doing good for the last five-and-twenty years, to my certain knowledge. I hope, sir, you would not insinuate that *she* had a natural daughter?'

'She may have made a secret marriage, perhaps, known only to her brother.'

'She couldn't have done any such thing without my knowledge, sir. She was a girl at school at the time of Miss Fay's birth. Don't mix Miss Fausset up in it, pray, sir.'

'Was it you only who suspected Mr Fausset to be Miss Fay's father?'

'Only me, sir? Why, it was everybody: and, what was worst of all, my poor mistress knew it, and fretted over it to her dying day.'

'But you never heard Mr Fausset acknowledge the parentage?'

'No, sir, not to me; but I have no doubt he acknowledged it to his poor dear lady. He was an affectionate husband, and he must have been very much wrapped up in that girl, or he wouldn't have made his wife unhappy about her.'

With but the slightest encouragement from Mr Greswold, Bell expatiated on the subject of Fay's residence in the two houses, and the misery she had wrought there. She unconsciously exaggerated the general conviction about the master's relationship to his *protégée*, nor did she hint that it was she who first mooted the notion in the Parchment Street household. She left George Greswold with the belief that this relationship had been known for a fact to a great many people – that the tie between protector and protected was an open secret.

She dwelt much upon the child Mildred's love for the elder girl, which she seemed to think in itself an evidence of their sisterhood. She gave a graphic account of Mildred's illness, and described how Fay had watched beside her bed night after night.

'I saw her sitting there in her nightgown many a time when I went in the middle of the night to see if Mildred was asleep. I never liked Miss Fay, but justice is justice, and I must say, looking back upon all things,' said Mrs Bell, with a virtuous air, 'that there was no deception about her love for Miss Mildred. I may have thought it put on then; but looking back upon it now, I know that it was real.'

'I can quite understand that my wife must have been very fond of such a companion – sister or no sister – but she was so young that no doubt she soon forgot her friend. Memory is not tenacious at seven years old,' said Greswold, with an air of quiet thoughtfulness, cutting the leaves of a new book which had lain on his desk, the paper-knife marking the page where he had thrown it down yesterday afternoon.

'Indeed, she didn't forget, sir. You must not judge Miss Mildred by other girls of seven. She was – she was like Miss Lola, sir' – Bell's elderly voice faltered here. 'She was all love and thoughtfulness. She doted on Miss Fay, and I never saw such grief as she felt when she came back from the sea-side and found her gone. It was done for the best, and it was the only thing my mistress could do with any regard for her own self-respect; but even I felt very sorry Miss Fay had been sent away, when I saw what a blow it was to Miss Mildred. She didn't get over it for years; and though she was a good and dutiful daughter, I know that she and her mother had words about Miss Fay more than once.'

'She was very fond of her, was she?' murmured George Greswold, in an absent way, steadily cutting the leaves of his book. 'Very fond of her. And you have no doubt in your own mind, Mrs Bell, that the two were sisters?'

'Not the least doubt, sir. I never had,' answered Bell resolutely.

She waited for him to speak again, but he sat silent, cutting his way slowly through the big volume, without making one jagged edge, so steady was the movement of the hand that grasped the paper-knife. His eyes were bent upon the book; his face was in shadow.

'Is that all, sir?' Bell asked at last, when she had grown tired of his silence.

'Yes, Mrs Bell, that will do. Good-night.'

When the door closed upon her, he flung the book away from him, sprang to his feet, and began to pace the room, up and down its length of forty feet, from hearth to door.

'Sisters! – and so fond of each other!' he muttered. 'My God, this is fatality! In this, as in the death of my child, I am helpless. The wanton neglect of my servants cost me the idol of my heart. It was not my fault – not mine – but I lost her. And now I am again the victim of fatality – blind, impotent – groping in the dark web – caught in the inexorable net.'

He went back to his desk, and re-read Mildred's letter in the light of the lamp.

'She leaves me because our marriage is unholy in her eyes,' he said to himself. 'What will she think when she knows all – as she must know, I suppose, sooner or later? Sooner or later all things are known, says one of the wise ones of the earth. Sooner or later! She is on the track now. Sooner or later she must know – everything.'

He flung himself into a low chair in front of the hearth, and sat with his elbows on his knees staring at the fire.

'If it were that question of legality only,' he said to himself, 'if it were a question of Church, law, bigotry, prejudice, I should not fear the issue. My love for her, and hers for me, ought to be stronger than any such prejudice. It would need but the first sharp pain of severance to bring her back to me, my fond and faithful wife, willing to submit her judgment to mine, willing to believe, as I believe, that such marriages are just and holy, such bonds pure and true, all over the world, even though one country may allow and another disallow, one colony tie the knot and another loosen it. If it were *that* alone which parts us, I should not fear. But it is the past, the spectral past, which rises up to thrust us asunder. Her sister! And they loved each other as David and Jonathan loved, with the love whose inheritance is a life-long regret.'

CHAPTER III

THE VERDICT OF HER CHURCH

It was nearly eleven o'clock when Mrs Greswold arrived at Waterloo. There had been half-an-hour's delay at Bishopstoke, where she changed trains, and the journey had seemed interminable to the over-strained brain of that solitary traveller. Never before had she so journeyed, never during the fourteen years of her married life had she sat behind an engine that was carrying her away from her husband. No words could speak that agony of severance, or express the gloom of the future – stretching before her in one dead-level of desolation – which was to be spent away from him.

'If I were a Roman Catholic I would go into a convent to-morrow; I would lock myself for ever from the outer world,' she thought, feeling that the world could be nothing to her without her husband.

And then she began to ponder seriously upon those sisterhoods in which the Anglican Church is now almost as rich as the Roman. She thought of those women with whom she had been occasionally brought in contact, whom she had been able to help sometimes with her purse and with her sympathy, and she knew that when the hour came for her to renounce the world there would be many homes open to receive her, many a good work worthy of her labour.

'I am not like those good women,' she thought; 'the prospect seems to me so dreary. I have loved the world too well. I love it still, even after all that I have lost.'

She had telegraphed to her friend Mrs Tomkison, and that lady was at the terminus, with her neat little brougham, and with an enthusiastic welcome.

'It is so sweet of you to come to me!' she exclaimed; 'but I hope it is
not any worrying business that has brought you up to town so suddenly –
papers to sign, or anything of that kind.'

Mrs Tomkison was literary and aesthetic, and had the vaguest notions
upon all business details. She was an ardent champion of woman's rights,
sent Mr Tomkison off to the City every morning to earn money for her
milliners, decorators, fads, and *protégés* of every kind, and reminded him
every evening of his intellectual inferiority. She had an idea that women
of property were inevitably plundered by their husbands, and that it was
one of the conditions of their existence to be wheedled into signing away
their fortunes for the benefit of spendthrift partners, she herself being in
the impregnable position of never having brought her husband a
sixpence.

'No, it is hardly a business matter, Cecilia. I am only in town *en passant*. I
am going to my aunt at Brighton to-morrow. I knew you would give me a
night's shelter; and it is much nicer to be with you than to go to an hotel.'

The fact was, that of two evils Mildred had chosen the lesser. She had
shrunk from the idea of meeting her lively friend, and being subjected to
the ordeal of that lady's curiosity; but it had seemed still more terrible to
her to enter a strange hotel at night, and alone. She who had never
travelled alone, who had been so closely guarded by a husband's thoughtful
love, felt herself helpless as a child in that beginning of widowhood.

'I should have thought it simply detestable of you if you had gone to an
hotel,' protested Cecilia, who affected strong language. 'We can have a
delicious hour of confidential talk. I sent Adam to bed before I came out.
He is an excellent devoted creature – has just made what *he* calls a pot of
money on Mexican Street Railways; but he is a dreadful bore when one
wants to be alone with one's dearest friend. I have ordered a cosy little
supper – a few natives, only just in, a brace of grouse, and a bottle of the
only champagne which smart people will hear of nowadays.'

'I am so sorry you troubled about supper,' said Mildred, not at all
curious about the latest fashion in champagne. 'I could not take anything,
unless it were a cup of tea.'

'But you must have dined early, or hurriedly, at any rate. I hate that
kind of dinner – everything huddled over – and the carriage announced
before the *pièce de résistance*. And so you're going to your aunt. Is she ill?
Has she sent for you at a moment's notice? You will come into all her
money, no doubt; and I am told she is immensely rich.'

'I have never thought about her money.'

'I suppose not, you lucky creature. It will be sending coals to
Newcastle in your case. Your father left you so rich. I am told Miss
Fausset gives no end of money to her church people. She has put in two
painted windows at St Edmund's: a magnificent rose window over the

porch, and a window in the south transept by Burne Jones – a delicious design – St Cecilia sitting at an organ, with a cloud of cherubs. By the bye, talking of St Cecilia, how did you like my friend Castellani? He wrote me a dear little note of gratitude for my introduction, so I am sure you were very good to him.'

'I could not dishonour any introduction of yours; besides, Mr Castellani's grandfather and my father had been friends. That was a link. He was very obliging in helping us with an amateur concert.'

'How do you like him? But here we are at home. You shall tell me more while we are at supper.'

Mildred had to sit down to the oysters and grouse, whether she would or not. The dining-room was charming in the day-time, with its view of the Park. At night it might have been a room excavated from Vesuvian lava, so strictly classic were its terra-cotta draperies, its butter-boat lamps, and curule chairs.

'How sad to see you unable to eat anything!' protested Mrs Tomkison, snapping up the natives with gusto; for it may be observed that the people who wait up for travellers, or for friends coming home from the play, are always hungrier than those who so return. 'You shall have your tea directly.'

Mildred had eaten nothing since her apology for a breakfast. She was faint with fasting, but had no appetite, and the odour of grouse, fried bread-crumbs, and gravy sickened her. She withdrew to a chair by the fire, and had a dainty little tea-table placed at her side, while Mrs Tomkison demolished one of the birds, talking all the time.

'Isn't he a gifted creature?' she asked, helping herself to the second half of the bird.

Mildred almost thought she was speaking of the grouse.

'I mean Castellani,' said Cecilia, in answer to her interrogative look. 'Isn't he a heap of talent? You heard him play, of course, and you heard his divine voice? When I think of his genius for music, and remember that he wrote *that* book, I am actually wonderstruck.'

'The book is clever, no doubt,' answered Mildred thoughtfully, 'almost too clever to be quite sincere. And as for genius – well, I suppose his musical talent does almost reach genius; and yet what more can one say of Mozart, Beethoven, or Chopin? I think genius is too large a word for any one less than they.'

'But I say he is a genius,' cried Mrs Tomkison, elated by grouse and dry sherry (the champagne had been put aside when Mildred refused it). 'Does he not carry one out of oneself by his playing? Does not his singing open the floodgates of our hard, battered old hearts? No one ever interested me so much.'

'Have you known him long?'

'For the last three seasons. He is with me three or four times a week when he is in town. He is like a son of the house.'

'And does Mr Tomkison like him?'

'O, you know Adam,' said Cecilia, with an expressive shrug. 'You know Adam's way. *He* doesn't mind. "You always must have somebody hanging about you," he said, "so you may as well have that French fool as any one else." Adam calls all foreigners Frenchmen, if they are not obtrusively German. Castellani has been devoted to me; and I daresay I may have got myself talked about on his account,' pursued Cecilia, with the pious resignation of a blameless matron of five-and-forty, who rather likes to be suspected of an intrigue; 'but I can't help *that*. He is one of the few young men I have ever met who understands me. And then we are such near neighbours, and it is easy for him to run in at any hour. "You ought to give him a latchkey," says Adam; "it would save the servants a lot of trouble."'

'Yes, I remember; he lives in Queen Anne's Mansions,' Mildred answered listlessly.

'He has a suite of rooms near the top, looking over half London, and exquisitely furnished. He gives afternoon tea to a few chosen friends who don't mind the lift; and we have had a Materialisation in his rooms, but it wasn't a particularly good one,' added Mrs Tomkison, as if she were talking of something to eat.

The maid Louisa arrived at Queen Anne's Gate a little before luncheon on the following day. She brought a considerable portion of Mrs Greswold's belongings in two large basket-trunks, a portmanteau, and a dressing-bag. These were at once sent on to Victoria in the cab that had brought the young person and the luggage from Waterloo, while the young person herself was accommodated with dinner, table-beer, and gossip in the housekeeper's room. She also brought a letter for her mistress, a letter written by George Greswold late on the night before.

Mildred could hardly tear open the envelope for the trembling of her hands. How would he write to her? Would he plead against her decision? would he try to make her waver? would he set love against law, in such irresistible words as love alone can use? She knew her own weakness and his strength, and she opened his letter full of fear for her own resolution: but there was no passionate pleading.

The letter was measured almost to coldness:

'I need not say that your departure, together with your explanation of that departure, has come upon me as a crushing blow. Your reasons in your own mind are doubtless unanswerable. I cannot even endeavour to gainsay them. I could only seem to you as a special pleader, making the worse appear the better reason, for my own selfish ends. You know my opinion upon this hard-fought question of marriage with a deceased wife's sister; and you know how widely it differs from Mr Cancellor's view and yours – which, to my mind, is the view of the bigot, and not the Christian. There is no word in Christ's teaching to forbid such marriages. Your friend and master, Clement Cancellor, is of the school which sets the law-making of a mediaeval Church above the wisdom of Christ. Am I to lose my wife because Mr Cancellor is a better Christian than his Master?

'But granted that you are fixed in this way of thinking, that you deem it your duty to break your husband's heart, and make his home desolate, rather than tolerate the idea of union with one who was once married to your half-sister, let me ask you at least to consider whether you have sufficient ground for believing that my first wife was verily your father's daughter. In the first place, your only evidence of the identity between my wife and the girl you call Fay consists of a photograph which bears a striking likeness to the girl you knew, a likeness which I am bound to say Bell saw as instantly as you yourself had seen it. Remember, that the strongest resemblances have been found between those who were of no kin to each other; and that more than one judicial murder has been committed on the strength of just such a likeness.

'The main point at issue, however, is not so much the question of identity as the question whether the girl Fay was actually your father's daughter; and from my interrogation of Bell, it appears to me that the evidence against your father in this matter is one of impressions only, and, even as circumstantial evidence, too feeble to establish any case against the accused. Is it impossible for a man to be interested in an orphan girl, and to be anxious to establish her in his own home, as a companion for his only child, unless that so-called orphan were his own daughter, the offspring of a hidden intrigue? There may be stronger evidence as to Fay's parentage than the suspicions of servants or your mother's jealousy; but as yet I have arrived at none. You possibly may know much more than Bell knows, more than your letter implies. If it is not so, if you are acting on casual suspicions only, I can but say that you are prompt to strike a man whose heart has been sorely tried of late, and who had a special claim upon your tenderness by reason of that recent loss.

'I can write no more, Mildred. My heart is too heavy for many words. I do not reproach you. I only ask you to consider what you are doing before you make our parting irrevocable. You have entreated me not to follow you, and I will obey you, so far as to give you time for reflection before I force myself upon your presence; but I must see you before you leave England. I ask no answer to this letter until we meet. – Your unhappy husband

'GEORGE GRESWOLD.'

The letter chilled her by its calm logic – its absence of passion. There seemed very little of the lover left in a husband who could so write. His contempt for a law which to her was sacred shocked her almost as if it had been an open declaration of infidelity. His sneer at Clement Cancellor wounded her to the quick.

She answered her husband's letter immediately:

'Alas! my beloved,' she wrote, 'my reason for believing Fay to have been my sister is unanswerable. My mother on her death-bed told me of the relationship; told me the sad secret with bitter tears. Her knowledge of that story had cast a shadow on the latter years of her married life. I had seen her unhappy, without knowing the cause. On her death-bed she confided in me. I was almost a woman then, and old enough to understand what she told me. Women are so jealous where they love, George. I suffered many a sharp pang after my discovery of your previous marriage; jealous of that unknown rival who had gone before me, little dreaming that fatal marriage was to cancel my own.

'My mother's evidence is indisputable. She must have known. As I grew older I saw that there was that in my father's manner when Fay was mentioned which indicated some painful secret. The time came when I was careful to avoid the slightest allusion to my lost sister; but in my own mind and in my own heart I cherished her image as the image of a sister.

'I am grieved that you should despise Mr Cancellor and his opinions. My religious education was derived entirely from him. My father and mother were both careless, though neither was unbelieving. He taught me to care for spiritual things. He taught me to look to a better life than the best we can lead here; and in this dark hour I thank and bless him for having so taught me. What should I be now, adrift on a sea of trouble, without the compass of faith? I will steer by that, George, even though it carry me away from him I shall always devotedly love. – Ever, in severance as in union, your own

'MILDRED.'

She had written to Mr Cancellor early that morning, asking him to call upon her before three o'clock. He was announced a few minutes after she finished her letter, and she went to the drawing-room to receive him.

His rusty black coat and slouched hat, crumpled carelessly in his ungloved hand, looked curiously out of harmony with Mrs Tomkison's drawing-room, which was the passion of her life, the shrine to which she carried gold and frankincense and myrrh, in the shape of *rose du Barri* and *bleue du Roi* Sèvres, veritable old Sherraton tables and chairs, and commodes and cabinets from the boudoir of Marie Antoinette, a lady who must assuredly have sat at more tables and written at more escritoires than any other woman in the world. Give her Majesty only five minutes for every table and ten for every *bonheur du jour* attributed to her possession, and her married life must have been a good deal longer than the span which she was granted of joy and grief between the passing of the ring and the fall of the axe.

Unsightly as that dark figure showed amidst the delicate tertiaries of Lyons brocade and the bright colouring of satin-wood tables and Sèvres porcelain, Mr Cancellor was perfectly at his ease in Mrs Tomkison's drawing-room. He wasted very few of his hours in such rooms, albeit there were many such in which his presence was courted; but seldom as he appeared amidst such surroundings he was never disconcerted by them. He was not easily impressed by externals. The filth and squalor of a London slum troubled him no more than the artistic intricacies of a West End drawing-room, in which the *culte* of beauty left him no room to put down his hat. It was humanity for which he cared – persons, not things. His soul went straight to the souls he was anxious to save. He was narrow, perhaps; but in that narrowness there was a concentrative power that could work wonders.

One glance at Mildred's face showed him that she was distressed, and that her trouble was no small thing. He held her hand in his long lean fingers, and looked at her earnestly as he said:

'You have something to tell me – some sorrow?'

'Yes,' she answered, 'an incurable sorrow.'

She burst into tears, the first she had shed since she left her home, and sobbed passionately for some moments, leaning against the Trianon spinet, raining her tears upon the *Vernis Martin* in a way that would have made Mrs Tomkison's blood run cold.

'How weak I am!' she said impatiently, as she dried her eyes and choked back her sobs. 'I thought I was accustomed to my sorrow by this time. God knows it is no new thing! It seems a century old already.'

'Sit down, and tell me all about it,' said Clement Cancellor quietly, drawing forward a chair for her, and then seating himself by her side. 'I cannot help you till you have told me all your trouble; and you know I shall help you if I can. I can sympathise with you, in any case.'

'Yes, I am sure of that,' she answered sadly; and then, falteringly but clearly, she told him the whole story, from its beginning in the days of her childhood till the end yesterday. She held back nothing, she spared no one. Freely, as to her father confessor, she told all. 'I have left him for ever,' she concluded. 'Have I done right?'

'Yes, you have done right. Anything less than that would have been less than right. If you are sure of your facts as to the relationship – if Mr Greswold's first wife was your father's daughter – there was no other course open to you. There was no alternative.'

'And my marriage is invalid in law?' questioned Mildred.

'I do not think so. Law does not always mean justice. If this young lady was your father's natural daughter she had no status in the eye of the law. She was not your sister – she belonged to no one, in the eye of the law. She had no right to bear your father's name. So, if you accept the civil law for your guide, you may still be George Greswold's wife – you may ignore the tie between you and his first wife. Legally it has no existence.'

Mildred crimsoned, and then grew deadly pale. In the eye of the law her marriage was valid. She was not a dishonoured woman – a wife and no wife. She might still stand by her husband's side – go down to the grave as his companion and sweetheart. They who so short a time ago were wedded lovers might be lovers again, all clouds dispersed, the sunshine of domestic peace upon their pathway – if she were content to be guided by the law.

'Should you think me justified if I were to accept my legal position, and shut my eyes to all the rest?' she asked, knowing but too well what the answer would be.

'Should *I* so think! O Mildred, do you know me so little that you need ask such a question? When have I ever taken the law for my guide? Have I not defied that law when it stood between me and my faith? Am I not ready to defy it again were the choice between conscience and law forced upon me? To my mind your half-sister's position makes not one jot of difference. She was not the less your sister because of her parent's sin, and your marriage with the man who was her husband is not the less an incestuous marriage.'

The word struck Mildred like a whip – stung the wounded heart like the sharp cut of a lash.

'Not one word more,' she cried, holding up her hands as if to ward off a blow. 'If my union with my – very dear – husband was a sinful union, I was an unconscious sinner. The bond is broken for ever. I shall sin no more.'

Her tears came again; but this time they gathered slowly on the heavy lids, and rolled slowly down the pale cheeks, while she sat with her eyes fixed, looking straight before her, in dumb despair.

'Be sure all will be well with you if you cleave to the right,' said the priest, with grave tenderness, feeling for her as acutely as an ascetic can feel for the grief that springs from earthly passions and temporal loves, sympathising as a mother sympathises with a child that sobs over a broken toy. The toy is a futile thing, but to the child priceless.

'What are you going to do with your life?' he asked gently, after a long pause, in which he had given her time to recover her self-possession.

'I hardly know. I shall go to the Tyrol next month, I think, and choose some out-of-the-way nook, where I can live quietly; and then for the winter I may go to Italy or the south of France. A year hence perhaps I may enter a sisterhood; but I do not want to take such a step hurriedly.'

'No, not hurriedly,' said Mr Cancellor, his face lighting up suddenly as that pale, thin, irregular-featured face could lighten with the divine radiance from within; 'not hurriedly, not too soon; but I feel assured that it would be a good thing for you to do – the sovereign cure for a broken life. You think now that happiness would be impossible for you, anywhere, anyhow. Believe me, my dear Mildred, you would find it in doing good to others. A vulgar remedy, an old woman's recipe, perhaps, but infallible. A life lived for the good of others is always a happy life. You know the glory of the sky at sunset - there is nothing like it, no such splendour, no such beauty – and yet it is only a reflected light. So it is with the human heart, Mildred. The sun of individual love has sunk below life's horizon, but the reflected glory of the Christian's love for sinners brightens that horizon with a far lovelier light.'

'If I could feel like you; if I were as unselfish as you——' faltered Mildred.

'You have seen Louise Hillersdon – a frivolous, pleasure-loving woman, you think, perhaps; one who was once an abject sinner, whom you are tempted to despise. I have seen that woman kneeling by the bed of death; I have seen her ministering with unflinching courage to the sufferers from the most loathsome diseases humanity knows; and I firmly believe that those hours of unselfish love have been the brightest spots in her chequered life. Believe me, Mildred, self-sacrifice is the shortest road to happiness. No, I would not urge you to make your election hurriedly. Give yourself leisure for thought and prayer, and then, if you decide on devoting your life to good works, command my help, my counsel – all that is mine to give.'

'I know, I know that I have a sure friend in you, and that under heaven I have no better friend,' she answered quietly, glancing at the clock as she spoke. 'I am going to Brighton this afternoon, to spend a few days with my aunt, and to – tell her what has happened. She must know all about Fay. If there is any room for doubt she will tell me. My last hope is there.'

CHAPTER IV

NO LIGHT

Miss Fausset – Gertrude Fausset – occupied a large house in Lewes Crescent – with windows commanding all that there is of bold coast-line and open sea within sight of Brighton. Her windows looked eastward, and her large substantial mansion turned its back upon all the frivolities of the popular watering-place – upon its Cockney visitors of summer and its

November smartness, its aquarium and theatre, its London stars and Pavilion concerts, its carriages and horsemen – few of whom ever went so far east as Lewes Crescent; its brazen bands and brazen faces – upon everything except its church bells, which were borne up to Miss Fausset's windows by every west wind, and which sounded with but little intermission from no less than three tabernacles within half a mile of the crescent.

Happily Miss Fausset loved the sound of church bells, loved all things connected with her own particular church with the ardour which a woman who has few ties of kindred or friendship can afford to give to clerical matters. Nothing except serious indisposition would have prevented her attending matins at St Edmund's, the picturesque and semi-fashionable Gothic temple in a narrow side street within ten minutes' walk of her house; nor was she often absent from afternoon prayers, which were read daily at five o'clock to a small and select congregation. The somewhat stately figure of the elderly spinster was familiar to most of the worshippers at St Edmund's. All old Brightonians knew the history of that tall, slim maiden lady, richly clad after a style of her own, which succeeded in reconciling Puritanism with the fashion of the day; very dignified in her carriage and manners, with a touch of hauteur, as of a miserable sinner who knew that she belonged to the salt of the earth. Brightonians knew that she was Miss Fausset, sole survivor of the great house of Fausset & Company, silk merchants and manufacturers, St Paul's Churchyard and Lyons; that she had inherited a handsome fortune from her father before she was twenty, that she had refused a good many advantageous offers, had ranked as a beauty, and had been much admired in her time, that she had occupied the house in Lewes Crescent for more than a quarter of a century, and that she had taken a prominent part in philanthropic associations and clerical matters during the greater number of those years. No charity bazaar was considered in the way of success until Miss Fausset had promised to hold a stall; no new light in the ecclesiastical firmament of Brighton ranked as a veritable star until Miss Fausset had taken notice of him. She received everybody connected with Church and charitable matters. Afternoon tea in her drawing-room was a social distinction, and strangers were taken to her as to a Royal personage. Her occasional dinners – very rare, and never large – were talked of as perfection in the way of dining.

'It is easy for her to do things well,' sighed an overweighted matron, 'with her means, and no family. She must be inordinately rich.'

'Did she come into a very large fortune at her father's death?'

'O, I believe old Fausset was almost a millionaire, and he had only a son and a daughter. But it is not so much the amount she inherited as the amount she must have saved. Think how she must have nursed her income, with her quiet way of living! Only four indoor servants and a coachman; no garden, and one fat brougham horse. She must be rolling in money.'

'She gives away a great deal.'

'Nothing compared with what other people spend. Money goes a long way in charity. Ten pounds makes a good show on a subscription list; but what is it in a butcher's book? I daresay my three boys have spent as much at Oxford in the last six years as Miss Fausset has given in charity within the same time; and *we* are poor people.'

It pleased Miss Fausset to live quietly, and to spend very little money upon splendours of any kind. There was distinction enough for her in the intellectual ascendency she had acquired among those church-going Brightonians who thought exactly as she thought. Her spacious, well-appointed house; her experienced servants – cook, housemaid, lady's-maid, and butler; her neat little brougham and perfect brougham horse realised all her desires in the way of luxury. Her own diet was of an almost ascetic simplicity, and her servants were on board-wages; but she gave her visitors the best that the season or the fashion could suggest to an experienced cook. Even her afternoon tea was considered superior to everybody else's tea, and her table was provided with daintier cakes and biscuits than were to be seen elsewhere.

Her house had been decorated and furnished under her own direction, and was marked in all particulars by that grain of Puritanism which was noticeable in the lady's attire. The carpets and curtains in the two drawing-rooms were silver-gray; the furniture was French, and belonged to the period of the Directory, when the graceful lightness of the Louis Seize style was merging into the classicism of the Empire. In Miss Fausset's drawing-room there were none of those charming futilities which cumber the tables of more frivolous women. Here Mr Cancellor would have found room, and to spare, for his hat – room for a committee meeting, or a mission service, indeed – on that ample expanse of silvery velvet pile, a small arabesque pattern in different shades of gray.

The grand piano was the principal feature of the larger room, but it was not draped or disguised, sophisticated by flower-vases, or made glorious with plush, after the manner of fashionable pianos. It stood forth – a concert grand, in unsophisticated bulk of richly carved rosewood, a Broadwood piano, and nothing more. The inner room was lined with bookshelves, and had the air of a room that was meant for usefulness rather than hospitality. A large, old-fashioned rosewood secrétaire, of the Directory period, occupied the space at the side of the wide single window, which commanded a view of dead walls covered with Virginia creeper, and in the distance a glimpse of the crocketed spire of St Edmund's, a reproduction in little of one of the turrets of the Sainte Chapelle.

Two-thirds of the volumes in those tall bookcases were of a theological character; the remaining third consisted of those standard works which everybody likes to possess, but which only the superior few care to read.

Mildred had telegraphed in the morning to announce her visit, and she found her aunt's confidential man-servant, a German Swiss, and her aunt's neat little brougham waiting for her at the station. Miss Fausset herself was in the inner drawing-room ready to receive her.

There was something in the chastened colouring and perfect order of that house in Lewes Crescent which always chilled Mildred upon entering it after a long interval. It was more than three years since she had visited her aunt, and this afternoon in the fading light the silver-gray drawing-rooms looked colder and emptier than usual.

Miss Fausset rose to welcome her niece, and imprinted a stately kiss on each cheek.

'My dear Mildred, you have given me a very agreeable surprise,' she said; 'but I hope it is no family trouble that has brought you to me – so suddenly.'

She looked at her niece searchingly with her cold gray eyes. She was a handsome woman still, at fifty-seven years of age. Her features were faultless, and the oval of her face was nearly as perfect as it had been at seven-and-twenty. Her abundant hair was silvery gray, and worn *à la* Marie Antoinette, a style which lent dignity to her appearance. Her dinner-gown of dark gray silk fitted her tall, upright figure to perfection, and her one ornament, an antique diamond cross, half hidden by the folds of her lace fichu, was worthy of the rich Miss Fausset.

'Yes, aunt, it is trouble that has brought me to you – very bitter trouble; but it is just possible that you can help me to conquer it. I have come to you for help, if you can give it.'

'My dear child, you must know I would do anything in my power——' Miss Fausset began, with gentle deliberation.

'Yes, yes, I know,' Mildred answered, almost impatiently. 'I know that you will be sorry for me, but you may not be able to do anything. It is a forlorn hope. In such a strait as mine one catches at any hope.'

Her aunt's measured accents jarred upon her overstrung nerves. Her grief raged within her like a fever, and the grave placidity of the elder woman tortured her. There seemed no capacity for sympathy in this stately spinster who stood and scanned her with coldly inquisitive eyes.

'Can we be quite alone for a little while, aunt? Are you sure of no one interrupting us while I am telling you my troubles?'

'I will give an order. It is only half-past six, and we do not dine till eight. There is no reason we should be disturbed. Come and sit over here, Mildred, on this sofa. Your maid can take your hat and jacket to your room.'

Stray garments lying about in those orderly drawing-rooms would have been agony to Miss Fausset. She rang the bell, and told the servant to send Mrs Greswold's maid, and to take particular care that no visitor was admitted.

'I can see nobody this evening,' she said. 'If any one calls you will say I have my niece with me, and cannot be disturbed.'

Franz, the Swiss butler, bowed with an air of understanding the finest shades of feeling in that honoured mistress. He brought out a tea-table, and placed it conveniently near the sofa on which Mildred was sitting, and he placed upon it the neatest of salvers, with tiny silver teapot and Worcester cup and saucer, and bread and butter such as Titania herself might have eaten with an 'apricock' or a bunch of dewberries. Then he discreetly retired, and sent Louisa, who smelt of tea and toast already, though she could not have been more than ten minutes in the great stony basement, which would have accommodated a company of infantry just as easily as the spinster's small establishment.

Louisa took the jacket and hat and her mistress's keys, and withdrew to finish her tea and to discuss the motive and meaning of this extraordinary journey from Enderby to Brighton. The gossips over the housekeeper's tea-table inclined to the idea that Mrs Greswold had found a letter – a compromising letter – addressed to her husband by some lady with whom he had been carrying on an intrigue, in all probability Mrs Hillersdon of Riverdale.

'We all know who *she* was before Mr Hillersdon married her,' said Louisa; 'and don't tell me that a woman who has behaved liked that while she was young would ever be really prudent. Mrs Hillersdon must be fifty if she's a day; but she is a handsome woman still, and who knows? – she may have been an old flame of my master's.'

'That's it,' sighed Franz assentingly. 'It's generally an old flame that does the mischief. *Wir sind armer Thieren.*'

'And now, my dear, tell me what has gone wrong with you,' said Miss Fausset, seating herself on the capacious sofa – low, broad, luxurious, one of Crunden's masterpieces – beside her niece.

The rooms were growing shadowy. A small fire burned in the bright steel grate, and made the one cheerful spot in the room, touching the rich bindings of the books with gleams of light.

'O, it is a long story, aunt! I must begin at the beginning. I have a question to ask you, and your answer means life or death to me.'

'A question – to – ask – me?'

Miss Fausset uttered the words slowly, spacing them out, one by one, in her clear, calm voice – the voice that had spoken at committee meetings, and had laid down the law in matters charitable and ecclesiastical many times in that good town of Brighton.

'I must go back to my childhood, aunt, in the first place,' began
Mildred, in her low, earnest voice, her hands clasped, her eyes fixed upon
her aunt's coldly correct profile, between her and the light of the fire, the
wide window behind her, with the day gradually darkening after the
autumnal sunset. The three eastward-looking windows in the large room
beyond had a ghostly look, with their long guipure curtains closely
drawn against the dying light.

'I must go back to the time when I was seven years old, and my dear
father,' falteringly, and with tears in her voice, 'brought home his adopted
daughter, Fay – Fay Fausset, he called her. She was fourteen and I was
only seven, but I was very fond of her all the same. We took to each
other from the beginning. When we left London and went to The
Hook, Fay went with us. I was ill there, and she helped to nurse me. She
was very good to me – kinder than I can say, and I loved her as if she had
been my sister. But when I got well she was sent away – sent to a
finishing-school at Brussels, and I never saw her again. She had only lived
with us one short summer. Yet it seemed as if she and I had been
together all my life. I missed her sorely. I missed her for years afterwards.'

'My tender-hearted Mildred!' said Miss Fausset gently. 'It was like you
to give your love to a stranger, and to be so faithful to her memory!'

'O, but she was not a stranger! she was something nearer and dearer. I could
hardly have been so fond of her if there had not been some link between us.'

'Nonsense, Mildred! A warm-hearted child will take to any one near
her own age who is kind to her. Why should this girl have been anything
more than an orphan, whom your father adopted out of the generosity of
his heart?'

'O, she was something more! There was a mystery. Did you ever see
her, aunt? I don't remember your coming to Parchment Street or to The
Hook while she was with us.'

'No. I was away from England part of that year. I spent the autumn at
Baden with my friends the Templemores.'

'Ah, then you knew nothing of the trouble Fay made in our home –
most innocently? It is such a sad story, aunt. I can hardly bear to touch
upon it, even to you, for it cast a shadow upon my father's character. You
know how I loved and honoured him, and how it must pain me to say
one word that reflects upon him.'

'Yes, I know you loved him. You could not love him too well,
Mildred. He was a good man – a large-hearted, large-minded man.'

'And yet that one act of his, bringing poor Fay into his home, brought
unhappiness upon us all. My mother seemed set against her from the very
first; and on her death-bed she told me that Fay was my father's daughter.
She gave me no proof – she told me nothing beyond that one cruel fact.
Fay was the offspring of hidden sin. She told me this, and told me to

remember it all my life. Do you think, aunt, she was justified in this accusation against my father?'

'How can I tell, Mildred?' Miss Fausset answered coldly. 'My brother may have had secrets from me.'

'But did you never hear anything – any hint of this mystery? Did you never know anything about your brother's life in the years before his marriage which would serve as a clue? He could hardly have cared for any one – been associated with any one – and you not hear something——'

'If you mean did I ever hear that my brother had a mistress, I can answer no,' replied Miss Fausset, in a very unsympathetic voice. 'But men do not usually allow such things to be known to their sisters, especially to a younger sister, as I was by a good many years. He may have been – like other men. Few of them seem free from the stain of sin. But however that may have been, I know nothing about the matter.'

'And you do not know the secret of Fay's parentage – you, my father's only sister – his only surviving relation. Can you help me to find any one who knew more about his youth – any confidential friend – any one who can tell me whether that girl was really my sister?'

'No, Mildred. I have no knowledge of your father's friends. They are all dead and gone, perhaps. But what can it matter to you who this girl was? She is dead. Let the secret of her existence die with her. It is wisest, most charitable to do so.'

'Ah, you know she is dead!' cried Mildred quickly. 'Where and when did she die? How did you hear of her?'

'From your father. She died abroad. I do not remember the year.'

'Was it before my marriage?'

'Yes, I believe so.'

'Long before?'

'Two or three years, perhaps. I cannot tell you anything precisely. The matter was of no moment to me.'

'O aunt, it is life and death to *me*. She was my husband's first wife. She and I – daughters of one father – as I, alas! can but believe we were – married the same man.'

'I never heard your husband was a widower.'

'No, nor did I know it until a few weeks ago;' and then, as clearly as her distress of mind would allow, Mildred told how the discovery had been made.

'The evidence of a photograph – which may be a good or a bad likeness – is a small thing to go upon, Mildred,' said her aunt. 'I think you have been very foolish to make up your mind upon such evidence.'

'O, but there are other facts – coincidences! And nothing would make me doubt the identity of the original of that photograph with Fay Fausset. I recognised it at the first glance; and Bell, who saw it afterwards, knew the face immediately. There could be no error in that. The only question is about her parentage. I thought, if there were room for doubt in the face of my mother's death-bed statement, you could help me. But it is all over. You were my last hope,' said Mildred despairingly.

She let her face sink forward upon her clasped hands. Only in this moment did she know how she had clung to the hope that her aunt would be able to assure her she was mistaken in her theory of Fay's parentage.

'My dear Mildred,' began Miss Fausset, after a pause, 'the words you have just used – "death-bed statement" – seem to mean something very solemn, indisputable, irrevocable; but I must beg you to remember that your poor mother was a very weak woman and a very exacting wife. She was offended with my brother for his adoption of an orphan girl. I have heard her hold forth about her wrongs many a time, vaguely, not daring to accuse him before me; but still I could understand the drift of her thoughts. She may have nursed these vague suspicions of hers until they seemed to her like positive facts; and on her death-bed, her brain enfeebled by illness, she may have made direct assertions upon no other ground than those long-cherished suspicions and the silent jealousies of years. I do not think, Mildred, you ought to take any decisive step upon the evidence of your mother's jealousy.'

'My mother spoke with conviction. She must have known something – she must have had some proof. But even if it were possible she could have spoken so positively without any other ground than jealous feeling, there are other facts that cry aloud to me, evidences to which I dare not shut my eyes. Fay must have belonged to some one, aunt,' pursued Mildred, with growing earnestness, clasping her hands upon Miss Fausset's arm as they sat side by side in the gathering darkness. 'There must have been some reason – and a strong one – for her presence in our house. My father was not a man to act upon caprice. I never remember any foolish or frivolous act of his in all the years of my girlhood. He was a man of thought and purpose; he did nothing without a motive. He would not have charged himself with the care of that poor girl unless he had considered it his duty to protect her.'

'Perhaps not.'

'I am sure not. Then comes the question, who was she if she was not my father's daughter? He had no near relations, he had no bosom friend that I ever heard of – no friend so dear that he would deem it his duty to adopt that friend's orphan child. There is no other clue to the mystery that I can imagine. Can you, aunt, suggest any other solution?'

'No, Mildred, I cannot.'

'If there were no other evidence within my knowledge, my father's manner alone would have given me a clue to his secret. He so studiously evaded my inquiries about Fay – there was such a settled melancholy in his manner when he spoke of her.'

'Poor John! he had a heart of gold, Mildred. There never was a truer man than your father. Be sure of that, come what may.'

'I have never doubted that.'

There was a pause of some minutes after this. The two women sat in silence looking at the fire, which had burned red and hollow since Franz had last attended to it. Mildred sat with her head leaning against her aunt's shoulder, her hand clasping her aunt's hand. Miss Fausset sat erect as a dart, looking steadily at the fire, her lips compressed and resolute, the image of unfaltering purpose.

'And now, Mildred,' she began at last, in those measured accents which Mildred remembered in her childhood as an association of awe, 'take an old woman's advice, and profit by an old woman's experience of life if you can. Put this suspicion of yours on one side – forget it as if it had never been, and go back to your good and faithful husband. This suspicion of yours is but a suspicion at most, founded on the jealous fancy of one of the most fanciful women I ever knew. Why should George Greswold's life be made desolate because your mother was a bundle of nerves? Forget all you have ever thought about that orphan girl, and go back to your duty as a wife.'

Mildred started away from her aunt, and left the sofa as if she had suddenly discovered herself in contact with the Evil One.

'Aunt, you astound, you horrify me!' she exclaimed. 'Can *you* be so false to the conduct and principles of your whole life – can *you* put duty to a husband before duty to God? Have I not sworn to honour Him with all my heart, with all my strength; and am I to yield to the weak counsel of my heart, which would put my love of the creature above my honour of the Creator? Would you counsel me to persist in an unholy union – you whose life has been given up to the service of God – you who have put His service far above all earthly affections; you who have shown yourself so strong: can you counsel me to be so weak: and to let my love – my fond true love for my dear one – conquer my knowledge of the right? Who knows if my darling's death may not have been God's judgment upon iniquity – God's judgment——'

She had burst into sudden tears at the mention of her husband's name, with all that tenderness his image evolved; but at that word judgment she stopped abruptly with a half-hysterical cry, as a vision of the past flashed into her mind.

She remembered the afternoon of the return to Enderby, and how her husband had knelt by his daughter's grave, believing himself alone, and how there had come up from that prostrate figure a bitter cry:

'Judgment! judgment!'

Did he know? Was that the remorseful ejaculation of one who knew himself a deliberate sinner?

Miss Fausset endured this storm of reproof without a word. She never altered her attitude, or wavered in her quiet contemplation of the fading fire. She waited while Mildred paced up and down the room in a tempest of passionate feeling, and then she said, even more quietly than she had spoken before,

'My dear Mildred, I have given you my advice, conscientiously. If you refuse to be guided by the wisdom of one who is your senior by a quarter of a century, the consequences of your obstinacy must be upon your own head. I only know that if *I* had as good a man as George Greswold for my husband' – with a little catch in her voice that sounded almost like a sob – 'it would take a great deal more than a suspicion to part me from him. And now, Mildred, if you mean to dress for dinner, it is time you went to your room.'

In any other house, and with any other hostess, Mildred would have asked to be excused from sitting down to a formal dinner, and to spend the rest of the evening in her own room; but she knew her aunt's dislike of any domestic irregularity, so she went away meekly, and put on the black lace gown which Louisa had laid out for her, and returned to the drawing-room at five minutes before eight.

She had been absent half an hour, but it seemed to her as if Miss Fausset had not stirred since she left her. The lamps were lighted, the fire had been made up, and the silver-gray brocade curtains were drawn; but the mistress of the house was sitting in exactly the same attitude on the sofa near the fire, erect, motionless, with her thoughtful gaze fixed upon the burning coals in the bright steel grate.

Aunt and niece dined *tête-à-tête*, ministered to by the experienced Franz, who was thorough master of his calling. All the details of that quiet dinner were of an elegant simplicity, but everything was perfect after its fashion, from the soup to the dessert, from the Irish damask to the old English silver – everything such as befitted the station of a lady who was often spoken of as the rich Miss Fausset.

The evening passed in mournful quiet. Mildred played two of Mozart's sonatas at her aunt's request – sonatas which she had played in her girlhood before the advent of her first and only lover, the lover who was now left widowed and desolate in that time which should have been the golden afternoon of life. As her fingers played those familiar movements, her mind was at Enderby with the husband she had deserted. How was he bearing his solitude? Would he shut his heart against her in anger, teach himself to live without her? She pictured him in his accustomed corner of the drawing-room, with his lamp-lit table, and pile of books and papers, and Pamela seated on the other side of the room, and the dogs lying on the hearth, and the room all aglow with flowers in the subdued light of the shaded lamps; so different from these colourless rooms of Miss Fausset's, with their look as of vaulted halls, in which voices echo with hollow reverberations amidst empty space.

And then she thought of her own desolate life, and wondered what it was to be. She felt as if she had no strength of mind to chalk out a path for herself – to create for herself a mission. That sublime idea of living for others, of a life devoted to finding the lost ones of Israel – or nursing the sick – or teaching children the way of righteousness – left her cold. Her thoughts dwelt persistently upon her own loves, her own losses, her own ideal of happiness.

'I am of the earth earthy,' she thought despairingly, as her fingers lingered over a slow movement. 'If I were like Clement Cancellor, my own individual sorrow would seem as nothing compared with that vast sum of human suffering which he is always trying to lessen.'

'May I ask what your plans are for the future, Mildred?' said Miss Fausset, laying aside a memoir of Bishop Selwyn, which she had been reading while her niece played. 'I need hardly tell you that I shall be pleased to have you here as long as you care to stay; but I should like to know your scheme of life – in the event of your persistence in a separation from your husband.'

'I have made no definite plan, aunt; I shall spend the autumn in some quiet watering-place in Germany, and perhaps go to Italy for the winter.'

'Why to Italy?'

'It is the dream of my life to see that country, and my husband always refused to take me there.'

'For some good reason, no doubt.'

'I believe he had a dread of fever. I know of no other reason.'

'You are prompt to take advantage of your independence.'

'Indeed, aunt, I have no idea of that kind. God help me! my independence is a sorry privilege. But if any country could help me to forget my sorrows, that country would be Italy.'

'And after the winter? Do you mean to live abroad altogether?'

'I don't know what I may do. I have thoughts of entering a sisterhood by and by.'

'Well, you must follow your own course, Mildred. I can say no more than I have said already. If you make up your mind to renounce the world there are sisterhoods all over England, and there is plenty of good work to be done. Perhaps after all it is the best life, and that those are happiest who shut their minds against earthly affections.'

'As you have done, aunt,' said Mildred, with respect. 'I know how full of good works your life has been.'

'I have tried to do my duty according to my lights,' answered the spinster gravely.

The next day was cold and stormy, autumn with a foretaste of winter. Mildred went to the morning service with her aunt, in the bright new Gothic church which Miss Fausset's liberality had helped to create: a picturesque temple with clustered columns and richly floriated capitals, diapered roof, and encaustic pavement, and over all things the glow of many-coloured lights from painted windows. Miss Fausset spent the morning in visiting among the poor. She had a large district out in the London Road, in a part of Brighton of which the fashionable Brightonian hardly knoweth the existence.

Mildred sat in the back drawing-room all the morning, pretending to read. She took volume after volume out of the bookcase, turned over the leaves, or sat staring at a page for a quarter of an hour at a time, in hopeless vacuity of mind. She had brooded upon her trouble until her brain seemed benumbed, and nothing was left of that sharp sorrow but a dull aching pain.

After luncheon she went out for a solitary walk on the cliff-road that leads eastward. It was a relief to find herself alone upon that barren down, with the great stormy sea in front of her, and the busy world left behind. She walked all the way to Rottingdean, rejoicing in her solitude, dreading the return to the stately silver-gray drawing-room and her aunt's society. Looking down at the village nestling in the hollow of the hills, it seemed to her that she might hide her sorrows almost as well in that quiet nook as in the remotest valley in Europe; and it seemed to her also that this place of all others was best fitted for the establishment of any charitable foundation in a small way – for a home for the aged poor, for instance, or for orphan children. Her own fortune would amply suffice for any such modest foundation. The means were at her disposal. Only the will was wanting.

It was growing dusk when she went back to Lewes Crescent, so she went straight to her room and dressed for dinner before going to the drawing-room. The wind, with its odour of the sea, had refreshed her. She felt less depressed, better able to face a life-long sorrow, than before she went out, but physically she was exhausted by the six-mile walk, and she looked pale as ashes in her black gown, with its evening bodice, showing the alabaster throat and a large black enamel locket set with a monogram in diamonds – L G, Laura Greswold.

She entered the inner room. Her aunt was not there, and there was only one large reading-lamp burning on a table near the fire. The front drawing-room was in shadow. She went towards the piano, intending to play to herself in the twilight, but as she moved slowly in the direction of the instrument a strong hand played the closing bars of a fugue by Sebastian Bach, a chain of solemn chords that faded slowly into silence.

The hands that played those chords were the hands of a master. It was hardly a surprise to Mildred when a tall figure rose from the piano, and César Castellani stood before her in the dim light.

His hat and gloves were upon the piano, as if he had just entered the room.

'My dear Mrs Greswold, how delightful to find you here! I came to make a late call upon your aunt – she is always indulgent to my Bohemian indifference to etiquette – and had not the least idea that I should see you.'

'I did not know that you and my aunt were friends.'

'No?' interrogatively. 'That is very odd, for we are quite old friends. Miss Fausset was all goodness to me when I was an idle undergraduate.'

'Yet when you came to Enderby you brought an introduction from Mrs Tomkison. Surely my aunt would have been a better person——'

'No doubt; but it is just like me to take the first sponsor who came to hand. When I am in London I half live at Mrs Tomkison's, and I had heard her rave about you until I became feverishly anxious to make your acquaintance. I ought perhaps to have referred to Miss Fausset for my credentials – but I am *volage* by nature: and then I knew Mrs Tomkison would exaggerate my virtues and ignore my errors.'

Mildred went back to the inner room, and seated herself by the reading-lamp. Castellani followed her, and placed himself on the other side of the small octagon table, leaving only a narrow space between them.

'How pale you are!' he said, with a look of concern. 'I hope you are not ill?'

'No, I am only tired after a long walk.'

'I had no idea you had left Enderby.'

'Indeed!'

'You said nothing of your intention of leaving the neighbourhood the day before yesterday.'

'There was no occasion to talk of my plans,' Mildred answered coldly. 'We were all too anxious about the concert to think of any other matter.'

'Did you leave soon after the concert?'

'The same evening. I did not know you were leaving Riverdale.'

'O, I only stayed for the concert. I had protracted my visit unconscionably, but Mrs Hillersdon was good enough not to seem tired of me. I am in nobody's way, and I contrived to please her with my music. Did you not find her delightfully artistic?'

'I thought her manners charming; and she seems fond of music, if that is what you mean by being artistic.'

'O, I mean worlds more than that. Mrs Hillersdon is artistic to her fingers' ends. In everything she does one feels the artist. Her dress, her air, her way of ordering a dinner or arranging a room – her feeling for literature – she seldom reads – her feeling for form and colour – she cannot draw a line – her personality is the very essence of modern art. She is as a woman what Ruskin is as a man. Is Miss Ransome with you?'

'No, I have left her to keep house for me.'

It seemed a futile thing to make believe that all was well at Enderby, to ward off explanations, when before long the world must know that George Greswold and his wife were parted for ever. Some reason would have to be given. That thirst for information about the inner life of one's neighbours which is the ruling passion of this waning century must be slaked somehow. It was partly on this account, perhaps, that Mildred fancied it would be a good thing for her to enter a Sisterhood. The curious could be satisfied then. It would be said that Mrs Greswold had given up the world.

'She is a very sweet girl,' said Castellani thoughtfully; 'pretty too, a delicious complexion, hair that suggests Sabrina after a visit from the hairdresser, a delightful figure, and very nice manners – but she leaves me as cold as ice. Why is it that only a few women in the world have magnetic power? They are so few, and their influence is so stupendous. Think of the multitude of women of all nations, colours, and languages that go to make up one Cleopatra or one Mary Stuart.'

Miss Fausset came into the room while he was talking, and was surprised at seeing him in such earnest conversation with her niece.

'One would suppose you had known each other for years,' she said, as she shook hands with Castellani, looking from one to the other.

'And so we have,' he answered gaily. 'In some lives weeks mean years. I sometimes catch myself wondering what the world was like before I knew Mrs Greswold.'

'How long have you known her – without rodomontade?'

'For about a month, aunt,' replied Mildred. 'I have been asking Mr Castellani why he came to me with an introduction from my friend Mrs Tomkison, when it would have been more natural to present himself as a friend of yours.'

'O, he has always a motive for what he does,' Miss Fausset said coldly. 'You still stay to dinner, of course?' she added to Castellani.

'I am free for this evening, and I should like to stay, if you can forgive my morning coat.'

'I am used to irregularities from you. Give Mrs Greswold your arm.'

Franz was at the door, announcing the evening meal, and presently Mildred found herself seated at the small round table in the sombre spacious dining-room – a room with a bayed front, commanding an illimitable extent of sea – with César Castellani sitting opposite her. The meal was livelier than the dinner of last night. Castellani appeared unconscious that Mildred was out of spirits. He was full of life and gaiety, and had an air of happiness which was almost contagious. His conversation was purely intellectual, ranging through the world of mind and of fancy, scarcely touching things earthly and human; and thus he struck no jarring chord in Mildred's weary heart. So far as she could be distracted from the ever-present thought of loss and sorrow, his conversation served to distract her.

He went up to the drawing-room with the two ladies, and at Miss Fausset's request sat down to the piano. The larger room was still in shadow, the smaller bright with fire and lamplight.

He played as only the gifted few can play – played as one in whom music is a sixth sense, but to-night his music was new to Mildred. He played none of those classic numbers which had been familiar to her ever since she had known what music meant. His muse to-night was full of airy caprices, quips and cranks and wreathed smiles. It was operatic music, of the stage stagey; a music which seemed on a level with Watteau or Tissot in the sister art – gay to audacity, and sentimental to affectation. It was charming music all the same – charged with melody, gracious, complacent, uncertain, like an April day.

Whatever it was, every movement was familiar to Gertrude Fausset. She sat with her long ivory knitting-needles at rest on her lap – sat in a dreamy attitude, gazing at the fire and listening intently. Some melodies seemed to touch her almost to tears. The love of music ran in the Fausset family, and it was no surprise to Mildred to see her aunt so absorbed. What had an elderly spinster to live for if it were not philanthropy and art? And for the plastic arts – for pictures and porcelain, statuary or high-art furniture – Miss Fausset cared not a jot, as those barren drawing-rooms, with their empty walls and pallid colour, bore witness. Music she loved with unaffected devotion, and it was in nowise strange to find her the friend and patroness of César Castellani, opposite as were the opinions of the man who wrote *Nepenthe* and the woman who had helped to found the church of St Edmund the Confessor.

'Play the duet at the end of the second act,' she said, when he paused after a brilliant six-eight movement which suggested a joyous chorus.

He played a cantabile accompaniment, like the flow of summer seas, and then a plaintive melody for two voices – following, answering, echoing each other with tearful emphasis – a broken phrase here and there, as if the singer were choked by a despairing sob.

'What is the name of the opera, aunt?' asked Mildred; 'I never heard any of that music before.'

'He has been playing selections from different operas. That last melody is a duet in an opera called *La Donna del Pittore*.'

'By what composer? It sounded like Flotow.'

'It is not Flotow's. That opera was written by Mr Castellani's father.'

'I remember he told me his father had written operas. It is a pity his music was never known in England.'

'You had better say it was a pity his music was never fashionable in Paris. Had it been recognised there, English connoisseurs would have speedily discovered its merits. We are not a musical nation, Mildred. We find new planets, but we never discover new musicians. We took up Weber only to neglect him and break his heart. We had not taste enough to understand Mendelssohn's *Melusine*.'

'Mr Castellani's operas were popular in Italy, were they not?'

'For a time, yes; but the Italians are as capricious as we are dull. César tells me that his father's operas have not held the stage.'

'Were they fashionable in your time, aunt, when you were studying music at Milan?'

'Yes, they were often performed at that time. I used to hear them occasionally.'

'And you like them now. They are associated with your girlhood. I can understand that they must have a peculiar charm for you.'

'Yes, they are full of old memories.'

'Do you never play or sing yourself, aunt?'

'I play a little sometimes, when I am quite alone.'

'But never to give pleasure to other people? That seems unkind. I remember how proud my father was of your musical talent; but you would never let us hear you either at The Hook or in Parchment Street.'

'I have never cared to play or sing before an audience – since I was a girl. You need not wonder at me, Mildred. Different people have different ways of thinking. My pleasure in music of late years has been the pleasure of a listener. Mr Castellani is good enough to gratify me sometimes, as he has done to-night, when he has nothing better to do.'

'Do not say that,' exclaimed Castellani, coming into the glow of the hearth, and seating himself beside Miss Fausset's armchair. 'What can I have better to do than to commune with a sympathetic mind like yours – in the language of the dead? It is almost as if my father's vanished voice were speaking to you,' he said, in caressing tones, bending down to kiss the thin pale hand which lay idle on the arm of the chair.

CHAPTER V

THE FUTURE MIGHT BE DARKER

George Greswold was not the kind of man to sit down in idle submission to Fate under a great wrong or under a great loss. A feeling of blank despair had come upon him after his interview with Mrs Bell, in the solitude of those deserted rooms where every object spoke to him of his wife's absence – where the influence of her mind and fancy was a part of the very atmosphere: so much so that in spite of her farewell letter in his breast-pocket he started every now and then from his reverie, fancying he heard her footstep in the corridor, or her voice in an adjoining room.

His conversation with Bell had brought him little comfort, but it had not convinced him of the evil in which his wife so firmly believed. There was little doubt in his mind that the woman he had married eighteen years ago was identical with Mildred's young companion and John Fausset's *protégée*. But whether that mysterious *protégée* had been John Fausset's daughter was a question open to doubt. The suspicions of a jealous wife, the opinions of the servants' hall, were no conclusive proof.

On the other hand, the weight of evidence leaned to that one solution of the mystery in Mr Fausset's conduct. That a man should charge himself with the care of a child of whose parentage and belongings he could give no satisfactory account – about whom, indeed, he seemed to have given no account at all – was a strange thing. Stranger still was his conduct in bringing that child into his own family, to the hazard of his domestic peace. Stranger even yet that he should have gone down to the grave without giving his daughter any explanation of his conduct from first to last – that he should have left the story of his *protégée* as dark at the end as it had been at the beginning.

Painfully conjuring back to life the phantom forms of a miserable past, George Greswold recalled the few facts which he had ever known of his first wife's history. She was an orphan, without relations or friends. At eighteen years of age she had been transferred from a finishing-school at Brussels to the care of an English artist and his wife, called Mortimer – middle-aged people, the husband with a small talent, the wife with a small income, both of which went further in Brussels than they would have gone in England. They had an apartment on one of the new boulevards at Brussels and a summer retreat in the Ardennes. When the artist and his wife travelled, Vivien went with them, and it was on one of these occasions that George Greswold met her at Florence. Mr Mortimer had let his apartment at Brussels for the winter, and had established himself in the Italian city, where he worked assiduously at a classic style of art which nobody ever seemed to buy, though a good many people pretended to admire.

Vivien Faux. It sounded like a *nom de fantaisie*. She told him that she was nobody, and that she belonged to nobody. She had no home, no people, no surroundings, no history, no associations. She had been educated at an expensive school, and her clothes had been made at a fashionable dressmaker's in the Rue Montagne de la Cour. Everything that a schoolgirl's fancy could desire had been provided for her.

'So far as such things go, I was as well off as the most fortunate of my companions,' she told him; 'but I was a friendless waif all the same, and my schoolfellows despised me. I drank the cup of scorn to the dregs.'

Seeing how painful this idea of her isolation was to her, George Greswold had been careful to avoid all questioning that might gall the open wound. In truth he had no keen curiosity about her past existence. He had taken her for what she was – interesting, clever, and in great need of a disinterested protector. It was enough for him to know that she had been educated as a lady, and that her character was spotless. His marriage had been one of those unions which are of all unions the most fatal – a marriage for pity. A marriage for money, for self-interest, ambition, or family pride may result happily. In a union of mutual interests there is at least a sense of equality, and love may grow with time and custom; but in a marriage for pity the chain galls on both sides, the wife oppressed by a sense of obligation, the husband burdened with a weight of duty.

Of his wife's resources, all George Greswold knew was that she had a life interest in thirty thousand pounds invested in Consols. The dividends were sent her half-yearly by a firm of solicitors, Messrs Pergament & Pergament, of Lincoln's Inn Fields. She had received a letter from the firm a week before her last birthday, which was her twenty-first, informing her of her life interest in this sum, over which she would have no disposing power, nor the power to anticipate any portion of the interest. The half-yearly dividends, she was informed, would in future be sent directly to her at any address she might appoint.

In acknowledging this communication she begged to be informed from whom she had inherited this money, or whether it was the gift of a living benefactor, and whether the benefactor was a relative. The reply from Messrs Pergament & Pergament was cold and formal. They regretted their inability to give her any information as to the source of her income. They were pledged to absolute silence upon this point. In any other matter they would be happy to be of service to her.

George Greswold had married without a settlement. The then state of the law, and the conditions of his wife's income, made her independent of any husband whatever. He could not forestall or rob her of an income of which the capital was in the custody of other people, and over which she had no disposing power. He was a poor man himself at the time, living upon an allowance made him by his mother, eked out by the labour of his pen as a political and philosophical writer; but he had the expectation of the Enderby estate, an expectation which was all but certainty. One fact alone was known to him of his wife's surroundings which might help him to discover her history, and that was the name of the firm in Lincoln's Inn, Messrs Pergament & Pergament, and to them he made up his mind to apply without loss of time.

He went to London on the day after Mildred's journey to Brighton, taking Pamela and her dog with him to an hotel near Hanover Square where he had occasionally stayed. Pamela had been much disturbed by

Mildred's letter, and was full of wonderment, but very submissive, and ready to do anything she was told.

'I don't want to be inquisitive or troublesome, uncle,' she said, as they sat opposite each other in the train, 'but I am sure there is something wrong.'

'Yes, Pamela, there is something wrong; but it is something which will come right again in good time, I hope. All we can do is to be patient.'

His look of quiet pain, and the haggard lines which told of sleepless nights and brooding thoughts, touched Pamela's tender heart; but she was wise enough to know that a sorrow big enough to part husband and wife is not a sorrow to be intruded upon by an outsider.

Mr Greswold drove with his niece to the hotel, established her there with her maid and her terrier in a private sitting-room, and then started for Lincoln's Inn Fields in a hansom.

Messrs Pergament's office had a solid and old-established air, as of an office that had only to do with wealth and respectability. The clerks in the outer room seemed to have grown old on the premises.

'I should like to see the senior member of the firm, if he is at liberty,' said Mr Greswold.

'Mr Champion Pergament is at Wiesbaden. He is a very old gentleman, and seldom comes to the office.'

'The next partner, then——'

'Mr Danvers Pergament is at his place in Yorkshire. If you would like to see his son, Mr Danvers jun——'

'Yes, yes, he will do if there is no one else.'

'There is Mr Maltby. The firm is now Pergament, Pergament, & Maltby.'

'Let me see Mr Danvers Pergament, if you please. I don't want to talk to a new man.'

'Mr Maltby was articled to us seventeen years ago, sir, and has been in the firm ever since, but I believe Mr Pergament is disengaged. Shall I take him your name?'

George Greswold sent in his card. His name would be known to some members of the firm, no doubt – possibly not to others. His married life had been brief.

He was received in a handsome office by a bald-headed gentleman of about five-and-forty, who smiled upon him blandly from a background of oak wainscot and crimson cloth window-curtains, like an old-fashioned portrait.

'Pray be seated, Mr Greswold,' he said, with the visitor's card in his hand, and looking from the card to the visitor.

'Does my name tell you anything about me, Mr Pergament?' asked Greswold gravely.

'George Ransome Greswold,' read the lawyer slowly; 'the name of Greswold is unfamiliar to me.'

'But not that of Ransome. Sixteen years ago my name was George Ransome. I assumed the name of Greswold on my mother's death.'

The solicitor looked at him with renewed attention, as if there were something to startle his professional equanimity in the former name.

'You remember the name of Ransome?' said Greswold interrogatively.

'Yes, it recalls certain events. Very sad circumstances connected with a lady who was our client. You would not wish me to go over that ground, I am sure, Mr Greswold?'

'No, there is no occasion to do that. I hope you believe that I was blameless – or as free from blame as any man can be in his domestic conduct – in the matter to which you have alluded?'

'I have no reason to suppose otherwise. I have never been on the scene of the event. I knew nothing of it until nearly a year after it happened, and then my sources of information were of the slenderest, and my knowledge of painful details never went beyond this office. Pray be assured that I do not wish to say one word that can pain you; I would only ask you to consider me as a totally uninformed person. I have no charge to make – upon anybody's account. I have no questions to ask. The past is forgotten, so far as I and my firm are concerned.'

'Mr Pergament, for me the past is still living, and it is exercising a baneful influence over my present existence. It may blight the rest of my life. You, perhaps, may help to extricate me from a labyrinth of perplexity. I want to know who my first wife was. What was the real name of the young lady who called herself Vivien Faux, and whom I married under that name before the British Consul at Florence? Who were her parents?'

'I cannot tell you.'

'Do you mean that you cannot, or that you will not?'

'I mean both. I do not know that unfortunate lady's parentage. I have no positive knowledge on the subject, though I may have my own theory. I know that certain persons were interested in the young lady's welfare, and that certain funds were placed in our charge for her maintenance. After her death, the capital for which we had been trustees reverted to those persons. *That* is the sum-total of the lady's history so far as it is known to us.'

'Will you tell me the name of the person who gave my wife her income, who placed her at the school at Brussels, by whose instructions she was transferred to the care of Mr and Mrs Mortimer? I want to know that man's name, for that man must have been her father.'

'When my father and I undertook that business for my client, we pledged ourselves to absolute secrecy. The facts of the case are not known even to the other members of the firm. The person in question was our client, and the secret was lodged with us. There is not a priest of the Church of Rome who holds the secrets of the confessional more sacred than we hold that secret.'

'Even if by keeping it you blight and ruin an innocent man's life?'

'I cannot imagine any such consequence of our silence.'

'You cannot? No! Fact is stranger than any man's imagination. Do you happen to know the name of my second wife?'

'I did not even know that you had married again. You were known to our firm as Mr Ransome. We lost sight of you when you changed your name to Greswold.'

'I have been married – happily married – for fourteen years; and the name of my wife was Fausset, Mildred Fausset, daughter of John Fausset, your client.'

Mr Pergament had taken up a penknife in a casual manner, and was trifling with a well-kept thumb-nail, a fine specimen of the filbert tribe, with his eyelids lowered in an imperturbable thoughtfulness, as of a man who was rock. But, cool as he was, George Greswold noticed that at the name of Fausset the penknife gave a little jerk, and the outskirts of the filbert were in momentary danger. Mr Pergament was too wary to look up, however. He sat placid, attentive, with flabby eyelids lowered over washed-out gray eyes. Mr Pergament at five-and-forty was still in the chrysalis or money-making stage, and worked hard nearly all the year round. His father, at sixty-seven, was on the Yorkshire moors, pretending to shoot grouse, and just beginning to enjoy the butterfly career of a man who had made enough to live upon.

'Vivien Faux. Does not that sound to your ear like an assumed name, Mr Pergament?' pursued Greswold. 'Faux: the first three letters are the same as in Fausset.'

And then George Greswold told the solicitor how his second wife had recognised his first wife's photograph, as the likeness of a girl whom she believed to have been her half-sister, and how this act threatened to divide husband and wife for ever.

'Surely Mrs Greswold cannot be one of those bigoted persons who pin their faith upon a prohibition of the Canon Law as if it were the teaching of Christ – a prohibition which the Roman Church was always ready to cancel in favour of its elect?' said the lawyer.

'Unhappily my wife was taught in a very rigid school. She would perish rather than violate a principle.'

'But if your first wife were John Fausset's natural daughter – what then? The law does not recognise such affinities.'

'No, but the Church does. The Roman Church could create a prohibitive affinity in the case of a cast-off mistress; and it is the privilege of our Anglican theology in its highest development to adopt the most recondite theories of Rome. For God's sake be plain with me, Mr Pergament! Was the girl who called herself Vivien Faux, John Fausset's daughter, or was she not?'

'I regret that I cannot answer your question. My promise to my client was of the nature of an oath. I cannot violate that promise upon any consideration whatever. I must ask you, Mr Greswold, as a gentleman, not to urge the matter any farther.'

'I submit,' said Greswold hopelessly. 'If it is a point of honour with you, I can say no more.'

Mr Pergament accompanied him to the threshold of the outer office, and the elderly clerk ushered him to the wide old landing-place beyond. The lawyer had been courteous, but not cordial. There was a shade of distrustfulness in his manner, and he had pretended to no sympathy with Mr Greswold in his difficulties; but George Greswold felt that among those who knew the history of his former marriage there was not much likelihood of friendly feeling towards him. To them he was a man outside the pale.

He left the office sick at heart. This had been his only means of coming at the knowledge of his first wife's parentage, and this means had failed him utterly. The surprise indicated by that slight movement of the lawyer's hand at the first mention of John Fausset's name went far to convince him that Mildred's conviction was based on truth. Yet if John Fausset were Mr Pergament's client, it was very odd that Mr Pergament should be ignorant of the circumstances of Mildred's marriage, and the name and surroundings of her husband. Odd assuredly, but not impossible. On reflection, it seemed by no means unnatural that Mr Fausset should confide his secret to a stranger, and establish a trust with a stranger, rather than admit his family lawyer to his confidence. This provision for an illegitimate daughter would be an isolated transaction in his life. He would select a firm of approved respectability, who were unconcerned in his family affairs, with whom there was no possibility of his wife or daughter being brought into contact.

George Greswold drove from Lincoln's Inn to Queen Anne's Gate, where he spent ten minutes with Mrs Tomkison, and learned all that lady could tell him about his wife's movements: how she had had a long interview with Mr Cancellor before she started for Brighton, and how she was looking very ill and very unhappy. Provided with this small stock of information, he went back to the hotel and dined *tête-à-tête* with Pamela, who had the good sense not to talk to him, and who devoted all her attentions to the scion of Brockenhurst Joe.

When the waiters had left the room for good, and uncle and niece were alone over their coffee, Greswold became more communicative.

'Pamela, you are a good, warm-hearted girl, and I believe you would go some way to serve me,' he said quietly, as he sat looking at Box, who had folded his delicately-pencilled legs in a graceful attitude upon the fender, and was amiably blinking at the fire.

'My dear uncle, I would cut off my head for you——'

'I don't quite want that; but I want your loyal and loving help in this saddest period of my life – yes, the saddest; sadder even than the sorrow of last year; and yet I thought there could be no greater grief than that.'

'Poor Uncle George!' sighed Pamela, bending over the table to take his hand, and clasping it affectionately; 'command me in anything. You know how fond I have always been of you – almost fonder than of my poor father. Perhaps,' she added gravely, 'it is because I always respected you more than I did him.'

'I cannot confide in you wholly, Pamela – not yet; but I may tell you this much. Something has happened to part my wife and me – perhaps for life. It is her wish, not mine, that we should live the rest of our lives apart. There has been no wrong-doing on either side, mark you. There is no blame; there has been no angry feeling; there is no falling off in love. We are both the victims of an intolerable fatality. I would willingly struggle against my doom – defy Fate; but my wife has another way of thinking. She deems it her duty to make her own life desolate and to condemn me to a life-long widowhood.'

'Poor Uncle George!'

'She is now at Brighton with her aunt, Miss Fausset. I am going there to-morrow morning to see her, if she will let me – perhaps for the last time. I want to take you with me; and if Mildred carries out her intention of spending the winter abroad, I want you to go with her. I want you to wind yourself into her confidence and into her heart, to cheer and comfort her, and to shield her from the malice of the world. Her position will be at best a painful one – a wife and no wife – separated from her husband for a reason which she will hardly care to tell the world, perhaps will hardly confide to her dearest friend.'

'I will do anything you wish, uncle – go anywhere, to the end of the world. You know how fond I am of Aunt Mildred. I'm afraid I like her better than I do my sister, who is so wrapped up in that absurd baby that she is sometimes unendurable. But it seems so awfully strange that you and aunt should be parted,' continued Pamela, with a puzzled brow. 'I can't make it out one little bit. I – I don't want to ask questions, Uncle George – at least only just one question: has all this mysterious trouble anything to do with Mr Castellani?'

She turned crimson as she pronounced the name, but Greswold was too absorbed to notice her embarrassment.

'With Castellani? No. How should it concern him?' he exclaimed; and then, remembering the beginning of evil, he added, 'Mr Castellani has nothing to do with our difficulty in a direct manner; but indirectly his presence at Enderby began the mischief.'

'O, uncle, you were not jealous of him, surely?'

'Jealous of him? I jealous of Castellani or any man living? You must know very little of my wife or of me, Pamela, when you can ask such a question.'

'No, no; of course not. It was absurd of me to suggest such a thing, when I know how my aunt adores you,' Pamela said hastily.

In spite of this disavowal, she lay awake half through the night, tormenting herself with all manner of speculations and wild imaginings as to the cause of the separation between George Greswold and his wife and Castellani's connection with that catastrophe.

She went to Brighton with her uncle next day, Box and the maid accompanying them in a second-class compartment. They put up at an hotel upon the East Cliff, which was more domestic and exclusive than the caravansaries towards the setting sun, and conveniently near Lewes Crescent.

'Shall I go with you at once, uncle?' asked Pamela, as Greswold was leaving the house. 'I hope Miss Fausset is not a stern old thing, who will freeze me with a single look.'

'She is not so bad as that, but I will break the ice for you. I am going to see my wife alone before I take you to Lewes Crescent. You can go on the Madeira Walk with Peterson, and give Box an airing.'

George Greswold found his wife sitting alone near the open piano at which Castellani had made such exquisite music the night before. She had been playing a little, trying to find comfort in that grand music of Beethoven, which was to her as the prophecies of Isaiah, or the loftiest passages in the Apocalypse – seeking comfort and hope, but finding none. And now she was gazing sadly at the waste of waters, and thinking that her own future life resembled that barren sea – a wide and sunless waste, with neither haven nor ship in sight.

At the sound of her husband's footsteps entering unannounced at the further door she started up, with her heart beating vehemently, speechless and trembling. She felt as if they were meeting after years of absence – felt as if she must fling herself upon his breast and claim him as her own again, confessing herself too earthly a creature to live without that sweet human love.

She had to steel herself by the thought of obedience to a higher law than that of human passion. She stood before him deathly pale, but firm as a rock.

He came close up to her, laid his hand upon her shoulder, and looked her in the face, earnestly, solemnly even.

'Mildred, is it irrevocable? Can you sacrifice me for a scruple?'

'It is more than a scruple: it is the certainty that there is but one right course, and that I must hold by it to the end.'

'That certainty does not come out of your own heart or your own mind. It is Cancellor who has made this law for you – Cancellor, a fanatic, who knows nothing of domestic love – Cancellor, a man without a wife and without a home. Is he to judge between you and me? Is he, who knows nothing of the sacredness of wedded ties, to be allowed to break them, only because he wears a cassock and has an eloquent tongue?'

'It was he who taught me my duty when I was a child. I accept his teaching now as implicitly as I accepted it then.'

'And you do not mind breaking my heart: that does not hurt you,' said Greswold.

His face was pallid as hers, and his lips trembled, half in anger, half in scorn.

'O, George, you know my own heart is breaking. There can be no greater pain possible to humanity than I have suffered since I left you.'

'And you will inflict this agony, and bear this agony? You will break two hearts because of an anomaly in the marriage law – a rag of Rome – a source of profit to Pope and priest – a prohibition made to be annulled – a trap to fill the coffers of the Church! Do you know how foolish a law it is, child, for which you show this blind reverence? Do you know that it is only a bigoted minority among the nations that still abides by it? Do you know that in that great new world across the seas a woman may be a wife in one colony, and not a wife in another – honourable here, despised there? It is all too foolish. What is it to either of us if my first wife was your half-sister – a fact which neither of us can prove or disprove?'

'God help me! it is proved only too clearly to me. We bear the mark of our birthright in our faces. You must have seen that, George, long before I saw Fay's portrait in your hands. Are we not alike?'

'Not with the likeness of sisters. There is a look which might be a family likeness – a look which puzzled me like the faint memory of a dream when first I knew you. It was long before I discovered what the likeness was, and where it lay. At most it was but a line here and there. The arch of the brow, the form of the eyelid, an expression about the mouth when you smile. Such accidental resemblances are common enough. She was as much like César Castellani as she is like you. I have seen a look in his face that curiously recalls an expression of hers.'

'George, if I were not convinced, do you think I would grieve you, and sacrifice all I have of earthly happiness? I cannot reason upon this question. My conscience has answered it for me.'

'So be it. Let conscience be your guide, and not love. I have done.'

He took both her hands in his, and held them long, looking in her face as he went on with what he had to say to her, gravely, without anger, but with a touch of coldness that placed her very far away from him, and marked the beginning of a life-long strangeness.

'It is settled, then,' he said; 'we part for ever; but we are not going to air our story in the law-courts, or fill latest editions of evening papers with the details of our misery. We don't want the law to annul our marriage upon the ground of a forbidden affinity, and to cast a slur upon our child in her grave.'

'No, no, no!'

'Then, though we are to spend our lives apart henceforward, in the eyes of the world you will still be my wife; and I would not have the lady who was once my wife placed in a false position. You cannot wander about the Continent alone, Mildred – you are too young and too attractive to travel without companionship. I have brought Pamela to be your companion. The presence of my niece at your side will tell the world that you have done no wrong to me or my name. It may be fairly supposed that we part from some incompatibility of temper. You need give no explanations; and you may be assured I shall answer no questions.'

'You are very good,' she faltered. 'I shall be glad to have your niece with me, only I am afraid the life will be a dreary one for her.'

'She does not think that. She is much attached to you. She is a frank warm-hearted girl, with some common sense under a surface of frivolity. She is at my hotel near at hand. If you think your aunt will give her hospitality, she can come to you at once, and you and she can discuss all your plans together. If there is anything in the way of business or money matters that I can arrange for you——'

'No, there is nothing,' she said in a low voice; and then, suddenly, she knelt at his feet, and clasped his hand, and cried over it.

'George, tell me that you forgive me, before we part for ever,' she pleaded; 'pity me, dear; pity and pardon!'

'Yes, I forgive you,' he said, gently raising her in his arms, and leading her to the sofa. 'Yes, child, I pity you. It is not your fault that we are miserable. It may be better that we should part thus. The future might be still darker for us if we did not so part. Good-bye.'

He bent over her as she sat in a drooping attitude, with her forehead leaning against the end of the sofa, her hand and arm hanging lax and motionless at her side. He laid his hand upon her head as if in blessing, and then left her without another word.

'The future might be still darker if we did not part.' She repeated the sentence slowly, pondering it as if it had been an enigma.

Miss Fausset expressed herself pleased to receive Miss Ransome as long as it might suit Mildred's convenience to stay in Lewes Crescent.

'Mr Greswold has acted like a gentleman,' she said, after Mildred had explained that it was her husband's wish his niece should accompany her abroad. 'He is altogether superior to the common run of men. This young lady belongs to the Anglican Church, I conclude?'

'Decidedly.'

'Then she cannot fail to appreciate the services at St Edmund's,' said Miss Fausset; and thereupon gave orders that the second-best spare room should be made ready for Miss Ransome.

Pamela arrived before afternoon tea, bringing Box, who was immediately relegated to the care of the maids in the basement, and the information that her uncle had gone back to Romsey *viâ* Portsmouth, and was likely to arrive at Enderby some time before midnight. Pamela was somewhat embarrassed for the first quarter of an hour, and was evidently afraid of Miss Fausset; but with her usual adaptability she was soon at home in that chilly and colourless drawing-room. She was even reconciled to the banishment of Box, feeling that it was a privilege to have him anywhere in that orderly mansion, and intending to get him clandestinely introduced into her bedroom when the household retired for the night.

She pictured him as pining with grief in his exile, and it would have disillusioned her could she have seen him basking in the glow of the fire in the housekeeper's room, snapping up pieces of muffin thrown him by Franz, and beaming with intelligence upon the company.

A larger tea-table than usual had been set out in the inner drawing-room, with two teapots, and a tempting array of dainty biscuits and tea-cakes, such as the idle mind loveth. It was Miss Fausset's afternoon for receiving her friends, and from four o'clock upwards carriages were heard to draw up below, and loquacious matrons with silent daughters dribbled into the room and talked afternoon tea-talk, chiefly matters connected with the church of St Edmund's and the various charities and institutions associated with that edifice.

It seemed very slow, dull talk to the ears of Pamela, who had been vitiated by sporting society, in which afternoon tea generally smelt of cartridges or pigskin, and where conversation was sometimes enlivened by the handing round of a new gun, or a patent rat-trap, for general inspection. She tried to make talk with one of the youngest ladies present, by asking her if she was fond of tennis: but she felt herself snubbed when the damsel told her she had one of the worst districts in Brighton, and no time for amusements of any kind.

Everybody had taken tea, and it was nearly six o'clock when the feminine assembly became suddenly fluttered and alert at the announcement of two gentlemen of clerical aspect: one tall, bulky, shabby, and clumsy-looking, with a large pallid face, heavy features, heavier brows; the other small and dapper, dressed to perfection in a strictly clerical fashion, with fair complexion and neat auburn beard. The first was Mr Maltravers, Vicar of St Edmund's; the second was his curate, the Honourable and Reverend Percival Cromer, fourth son of Lord Lowestoft. It was considered a grand thing for St Edmund's that it had a man of acknowledged power and eloquence for its vicar, and a peer's son for its curate.

Mr Cromer was at once absorbed by a voluble matron who, with her three daughters, had lingered in the hope of his dropping in after vespers; but he contrived somehow to release himself from the sirens, and to draw Miss Ransome into the conversation. Miss Fausset in the meantime made the Vicar known to Mildred.

'You have often heard me speak of my niece,' she said, when the introduction had been made.

Mildred was sitting apart from the rest, in the bay-window of the inner room. She had withdrawn herself there on pretence of wanting light for her needlework, the same group of azaleas she had been working upon at Enderby, but really in order to be alone with her troubled thoughts; and now Miss Fausset approached her with the tall, ponderous figure of the priest, in his long threadbare coat.

She looked up, and found him scrutinising her intently under his heavy brows. It was a clever face that so looked at her, but it did not engage her sympathy, or convince her of the owner's goodness, as Clement Cancellor's face had always done.

'Yes, I have heard you speak of Mrs Greswold, your only near relative, I think,' he said, addressing Miss Fausset, but never taking his eyes off Mildred.

He dropped into a chair near Mildred, and Miss Fausset went back to her duty at the tea-table, and to join in the conversation started by Mr Cromer, which had more animation than any previous talk that afternoon.

'You find your aunt looking well, I hope, Mrs Greswold?' began the Vicar, not very brilliantly, but what his speech wanted in meaning was made up by the earnestness of his dark gray eyes, under beetling brows, which seemed to penetrate Mildred's inmost thoughts.

'Yes, she looks – as she has always done since I can remember – like a person superior to all mortal feebleness.'

'She is superior to all other women I have ever met, a woman of truly remarkable power and steadfastness; but with natures like hers the sword is sometimes stronger than the scabbard. That slender, upright form has an appearance of physical delicacy, as well as natural refinement. Your aunt's mind is a tower of strength, Mrs Greswold. She has been my strong rock from the beginning of my ministry here; but I tremble for the hour when her health may break down under the task-work she exacts from herself.'

'I know that she has a district, but I do not know the details of her work,' said Mildred. 'Is it very hard?'

'It is very hard, and very continuous. She labours unremittingly among the poor, and she does a great deal of work of a wider and more comprehensive kind. She is deaf to no appeal to her charity. The most distant claims receive her thoughtful attention, even where she does not feel it within the boundary-line of her duty to give substantial aid. She writes more letters than many a private secretary; and, O Mrs Greswold – to you as very near and dear to her – I may say what I would say to no other creature living. It has been my blessed office to be brought face to face with her in the sacrament of confession. I have seen the veil lifted from that white and spotless soul; spotless, yes, in a world of sinners! I know what a woman your aunt is.'

His low searching tones fell distinctly upon Mildred's ear, yet hardly rose above a whisper. The babble, lay and clerical, went on in the other drawing-room, and these two were as much alone in the shadow of the window-curtains and the gray light of the fading day as if they had been priest and penitent in a confessional.

CHAPTER VI

HIGHER VIEWS

After that interview with her husband, which in her own mind meant finality, Mildred Greswold's strength succumbed suddenly, and for more than a week she remained in a state of health for which Miss Fausset's doctor could find no name more specific than low fever. She was not very feverish, he told her aunt. The pulse was rapid and intermittent, but the temperature was not much above the normal limit. She was very weak and low, and she wanted care. He had evidently not quite made up his mind whether she wanted rousing or letting alone – whether he would recommend her to spend the winter at Chamounix and do a little mountaineering, or to vegetate at Nice or Algiers. 'We must watch her,' he said gravely. 'She must not be allowed to go into a decline.'

I have my suspision that Fay is Miss Fausets darghter?

Miss Fausset looked alarmed at this, but her doctor, an acquaintance of fifteen years, assured her that there was no cause for alarm; there was only need of care and watchfulness.

'Her mother died at six-and-thirty,' said Miss Fausset − 'faded away gradually, without any ostensible disease. My brother did everything that care and forethought could do, but he could not save her.'

'Mrs Greswold must not be allowed to fade away,' replied the doctor, with an air of being infallible.

Directly she was well enough to go down to the drawing-room again, Mildred began to talk of starting for Switzerland or Germany. She had inflicted herself and her surroundings upon Lewes Crescent too long already; she told her aunt; and although Miss Fausset expressed herself delighted to have her niece, and reconciled even to Pamela's frivolity and the existence of Box in the lower regions, Mildred felt somehow that her presence interfered with the even tenor of life in that orderly mansion. The only person who made light of Miss Fausset's idiosyncrasies, came to the house at all hours, stayed as late as he chose, disturbed the symmetry of the book-shelves, left Miss Fausset's cherished books lying about on chairs and sofas, and acted in all things after his own fancy, was César Castellani. His manner towards Miss Fausset was unalterably deferential; he never wavered in his respect for her as a superior being; he was full of subtle flatteries and delicate attentions; yet in somewise his ways were the ways of a spoiled child, sure of indulgence and favour. He never stayed in the house, but had his room at an hotel on the cliff, and came to Lewes Crescent whenever fancy prompted, for two or three days at a stretch, then went back to London, and was seen no more for a week or so.

Mildred found that Pamela and Mr Castellani had seen a great deal of each other during her illness. They had sung and played together, they had walked on the cliff − in sight of the drawing-room windows the whole time, Pamela explained, and with Miss Fausset's severe eye upon them. They had devoted themselves together to the education of Box, who had learnt at least three new tricks under their joint instruction, and who, possibly from over-pressure, had acquired a habit of trying to bite Mr Castellani whenever he had an opportunity.

'It is because he is such a horribly unmusical dog,' explained Pamela. 'He managed to creep up to the drawing-room the other day when Miss Fausset was at church, and Mr Castellani came in and began to play, and that dreadful Box planted himself near the piano and howled piteously till I carried him out.'

'My dearest Pamela, I don't think Box's opinion of Mr Castellani or his music matters much,' said Mildred, with gentle gravity, as she lay on the sofa in the back drawing-room, with Pamela's hand clasped in hers; 'but it matters a great deal what you think of him, and I fear you are beginning to think too much about him.'

'Why should I not think of him, aunt, if I like – and he likes? I am my own mistress; there are few girls so independent of all ties; for really nobody cares a straw for me except you and Uncle George. Rosalind is wrapped up in her baby, and Henry is devoted to pigeons, guns, and fishing-tackle. Do you think it can matter to them whom I marry? Why should I be sordid, and say to myself, "I have fifteen hundred a year, and I mustn't marry a man with less than three thousand"? Why should I not marry genius if I like – genius even without a penny?'

'If you could meet with genius, Pamela.'

'You think that Mr Castellani is not a genius?'

'I think not. He is too versatile and too showy. All his gifts are on the surface. Genius is single-minded, aiming at one great thing. Genius is like still water and runs deep. I admit that Mr Castellani is highly gifted as a musician of the lighter sort; not a man who will leave music behind him to live for ever. I admit that he has written a strangely attractive book. But I should be sorry to call him a genius. I should be very sorry to see you throw yourself away, as I believe you would if you were to marry him.'

'That is what a girl's friends always say to her,' exclaimed Pamela. 'To marry the man one loves is to throw oneself away.' And then blushing furiously, she added, 'Pray don't suppose that I am in love with Mr Castellani. There has never been one word of love between us – except in the clouds, by way of philosophical discussion. But, as a fatherless and motherless girl of advanced opinions, I claim the right to marry genius, if I choose.'

'My dear girl, I cannot dispute your independence; but I think the sooner we leave this house the better. The first thing is to make up our minds where we are to go.'

'I don't care a bit, aunt; only you must not leave Brighton till you are much stronger. You will want at least three weeks before you will be able to stand the fatigue of travelling,' said Pamela, surveying the invalid with a critical air.

'We can travel by easy stages. I am not afraid of fatigue. Where shall we go, Pamela – Schwalbach, Wiesbaden, Vevay, Montreux?'

'O, not Schwalbach, aunt. They took me there for iron five years ago, when I had outgrown my strength. Switzerland is always lovely, of course; but I went there with Rosalind after her baby was born, and endured the dreariest six weeks of my existence. Brighton is absolutely delicious at this time of the year. It would be absurd to rush away from the place just when people are beginning to come here.'

Mildred saw that the case was hopeless, and she began to think seriously about her responsibilities in this matter: a frank impetuous girl, her husband's niece, eager to cast in her lot with a man who was obviously an adventurer, living sumptuously with hardly any obvious means, and who might be a scoundrel. She remembered her impression of the face in the church, the Judas face, as she had called it in her own mind: a foolish impression, perhaps, and it might be baseless; yet such first impressions are sometimes warnings not to be lightly set at naught. As yet nothing had come of that warning: no act of Castellani's had shown him a villain; but his advent had begun the misery of her life. Had she never seen him she never might have known this great sorrow. His presence was a constant source of irritation, tempting her to questioning that might lead to further misery. Fay's image had been constantly in her mind of late. She had brooded over that wedded life of which she knew nothing – over that early death which for her was shrouded in mystery.

'And he could tell me so much, perhaps,' she said to herself one evening, sitting by the fire in the inner room, while Castellani played in the distance yonder between the tall windows that let in the gray eastern light.

'Her death was infinitely sad.'

Those were the words which he had spoken of George Greswold's first wife: of Fay, her Fay, the one warm love of her childish years, the love that had stayed with her so long after its object had vanished from her life. That there was something underlying those words, some secret which might add a new bitterness to her sorrow, was the doubt that tortured Mildred as she sat and brooded by the fire, while those lovely strains of Mendelssohn's 'I waited for the Lord' rose in slow solemnity from the distant piano, breathing sounds of peacefulness where there was no peace.

Mr Castellani had behaved admirably since her convalescence. He had asked no questions about her husband, had taken her presence and Pamela's for granted, never hinting a curiosity about this sudden change of quarters. Mildred thought that her aunt had told him something about her separation from her husband. It was hardly possible that she could have withheld all information, seeing the familiar terms upon which those two were; and it might be, therefore, that his discretion was the result of knowledge. He had nothing to learn, and could easily seem incurious.

Mildred now discovered that one source of Castellani's influence with her aunt was the work he had done for the choir of St Edmund's. It was to his exertions that the choral services owed their excellence. The Vicar loved music only as a child or a savage loves it, without knowledge or capacity; and it was Castellani who chose the voices for the choir, and

helped to train the singers. It was Castellani who assisted the organist in
the selection of recondite music, which gave an air of originality to the
services at St Edmund's, and brought the odour of mediaevalism and the
fumes of incense into the Gothic chancel. Castellani's knowledge of
music, ancient and modern, was of the widest. It was his musical
erudition which gave variety to his improvisations. He could delight an
admiring circle with meandering reminiscences of Lully, Corelli, Dussek,
Sphor, Clementi, Cherubini, and Hummel, in which only the
modulations were his own.

In this interval of convalescence Mrs Greswold's life fell into a
mechanical monotony which suited her as well as any other kind of life
would have done. For the greater part of the day she sat in the low
armchair by the fire, a table with books at her side, and her work-basket
at her feet. Those who cared to observe her saw that she neither worked
nor read. She took up a volume now and again, opened it, looked at a
page with dreamy eyes for a little while, and then laid it aside. She took
up the frame with the azaleas, worked half-a-dozen stitches, and put the
frame down again. Her days were given to long and melancholy reveries.
She lived over her married life, with all its happiness, with its one great
pain. She contemplated her husband's character – such a perfect character
it had always seemed to her; and yet his one weak act, his one
suppression of truth, had wrought misery for them both. And then with
ever-recurring persistency she thought of Fay, and Fay's unexplained fate.

'I know him so well, his wife of fourteen years,' she said to herself.
'Can I doubt for an instant that he did his duty to her; that he was loyal
and kind; that whatever sadness there was in her fate it could have been
brought about by no act of his?'

Pamela behaved admirably all this time. She respected Mildred's silence,
and was not overpoweringly gay. She would sit at her aunt's feet working,
wrapped in her own thoughts, or poring over a well-thumbed Shelley,
which seemed to her to express all her emotions for her without any
trouble on her part. She found her feelings about César Castellani made
to measure, as it were, in those mystic pages, and wondered that she and
Shelley could be so exactly alike.

When Mildred was well enough to go out of doors Miss Fausset
suggested a morning with her poor.

'It will brace your nerves,' she said, 'and help you to make up your
mind. If you have really a vocation for the higher life, the life of self-
abnegation and wide usefulness, the sooner you enter upon it the better.
Mind, I say *if*. You know I have given you my advice conscientiously as a
Christian woman, and my advice is that you go back to your husband,
and forget everything but your duty to him.'

'Yes, aunt, I know; but you and I think differently upon that point.'

'Very well,' with an impatient sigh. 'You are obstinate enough there: you have made up your mind so far. You had better make it up a little further. At present you are halting between two opinions.'

Mildred obeyed with meekness and indifference. She was not interested in Miss Fausset's district; she had given no thought yet to the merits of life in a Christian community, among a handful of pious women working diligently for the suffering masses. Her only thought had been of that which she had lost, not of what she might gain.

Miss Fausset came in from the morning service at half-past eight, breakfasted sparingly, and at nine the *ne plus ultra* brougham, the perfection of severity in coach-building, was at the door, and the perfect brown horse was champing his bit and rattling his brazen headgear in over-fed impatience to be off. It seemed to be the one aim of this powerful creature's life to run away with Miss Fausset's brougham, but up to this point his driver had circumvented him. He made very light of the distance between the aristocratic East Cliff and the shabbiest outlying district of Brighton, at the fag end of the London Road, and here Mildred saw her aunt in active work as a ministering angel to the sick and the wretched.

It was only the old, old story of human misery which she saw repeated under various forms; the old, old evidence of the unequal lots that fall from the urn of Fate – Margaret in her sky-blue boudoir, Peggy staggering under her basket of roses – for some only the flowers, for others only the thorns. She saw that changeless background of sordid poverty which makes every other sorrow harder to bear; and she told herself that the troubles of the poor were heavier than the troubles of the rich. Upon her life sorrow had come, like a thunderbolt out of a summer sky; but sorrow was the warp and woof of these lives; joy or good luck of any kind would have been the thunderclap.

She saw that her aunt knew how to deal with these people, and that underneath Miss Fausset's hardness there was a great power of sympathy. Her presence seemed everywhere welcome; and people talked freely to her, unbosoming themselves of every trouble, confident in her power to understand.

'Me and my poor husband calls your aunt our father confessor, ma'am,' said a consumptive tailor's wife to Mildred. 'We're never afraid to tell her anything – even if it seems foolish like – and she always gives us rare good advice – don't she, Joe?'

The invalid nodded approvingly over his basin of beef-tea, Miss Fausset's beef-tea, which was as comforting as strong wine.

In one of the houses they found an Anglican sister, an elderly woman, in a black hood, to whom Miss Fausset introduced her niece. There was an old man dying by inches in the next room; and the Sister had been sitting up with him all night, and was now going home to the performance of other duties. Mildred talked with her for some time about her life, and heard a great many details of that existence which seemed to her still so far off, almost impossible, like a cold pale life beyond the grave. How different from that warm domestic life at Enderby! amidst fairest surroundings, in those fine old rooms, where every detail bore the impress of one's own fancy, one's own pursuits: a selfish life, perhaps, albeit tempered with beneficence to one's immediate surroundings; selfish inasmuch as it was happy and luxurious, while true unselfishness must needs surrender everything, must refuse to wear purple and fine linen and to fare sumptuously, so long as Lazarus lies at the gate shivering and hungry.

Her aunt almost echoed her thoughts presently when she spoke of her goodness to the poor.

'Yes, yes, Mildred, I do some little good,' she said, almost impatiently; 'but not enough – not nearly enough. It is only women like that Sister who do enough. What the rich give must count for very little in the eyes of the Great Auditor. But I do my best to make up for a wasted girlhood. I was as foolish and as frivolous as your young friend Pamela once.'

'That reminds me, aunt, I want so much to talk to you about Pamela.'

'What of her?'

'I am afraid that she admires Mr Castellani.'

'Why should she not admire him?'

'But I suspect she is in danger of falling in love with him.'

'Let her fall in love with him – let her marry him – let her be happy with him if she can.'

There was a recklessness in this counsel which shocked Mildred, coming from such a person as Miss Fausset.

'My dear aunt, it is a very serious matter. George gave Pamela to me for my companion. I feel myself responsible for her happiness.'

'Then don't interfere with her happiness. Let her marry the man she loves.'

'With all my heart, if he were a good man, and if her uncle had no objection. But I know so little about Mr Castellani and his surroundings.'

'He has no surroundings – his mother and father are dead. He has no near relatives.'

'And his character, aunt; his conduct? What do you know of those?'

'Only so much as you can see that I know of them. He comes to my house, and makes himself agreeable to me and my friends. He has given valuable help in the formation and management of the choir. If I am interested in a concert for a charity he sings for me, and works for me like a slave. All his talents are at my service always. I suppose I like him as well as I should like a favourite nephew, if I had nephews from whom to choose a favourite. Of his character – outside my house – I know nothing. I do not believe he has a wife hidden away anywhere; and if Pamela marries him, she can make her intention public in good time to prevent any fiasco of that kind.'

'You speak very scornfully, aunt, as if you had a poor opinion of Mr Castellani.'

'Perhaps I have a poor opinion of mankind in general, Mildred. Your father was a good man, and your husband is another. We ought to think ourselves lucky to have known two such men in our lives. As to César Castellani, I tell you again I know no more of him than you – or very little more – though I have known him so much longer.'

'How long have you known him?'

'About fifteen years.'

'And how was he introduced to you?'

'O, he introduced himself, on the strength of the old connection between the Faussets and the Felixes. It was just before he went to the University. He was very handsome, very elegant, and very much in advance of his years in manners and accomplishments. He amused and interested me, and I allowed him to come to my house as often as he liked.'

'Do you know anything about his means?'

'Nothing definite. He came into a small fortune upon his mother's death, and ran through it. He has earned money by literary work, but I cannot tell you to what extent. If Miss Ransome marry him, I think she may as well make up her mind to keep him. He belongs to the butterfly species.'

'That is rather a humiliating prospect for a wife – rather like buying a husband.'

'That is a point for Miss Ransome to consider. I don't think she is the kind of girl to care much what her whim costs her.'

The brown horse, panting for more work, drew up in front of Miss Fausset's house at this juncture, fidgeted impatiently while the two ladies alighted, and then tore round to his mews.

'You've had a handful with him to-day, I guess, mate,' said a humble hanger-on, as Miss Fausset's coachman stretched his aching arms. 'He's a fine 'oss, but I'd rather you drove 'im than me.'

'I'll tell you what he is,' replied the coachman: 'he's too good for his work. That's his complaint. Dodging in and out of narrer streets, and makin' mornin' calls upon work'ouse paupers, don't suit *him*.'

The time had come when Mildred had to make up her mind where she would go, and having all the world to choose from, and just the same hopeless feeling that Eve may have had on leaving Eden, the choice was a matter of no small difficulty. She sat with a Continental 'Bradshaw' in her hand, turning the leaves and looking at the maps, irresolute and miserable. Pamela, who might have decided for her, clearly hankered after no paradise but Brighton. Her idea of Eden was a house in which Castellani was a frequent visitor.

It was too late for most of the summer places, too early for Algiers or the Riviera. Pamela would not hear of the Rhine or any German watering-place. Montreux might do, perhaps, or the Engadine; but Pamela hated Switzerland.

'Would it not do to spend the winter in Bath?' she said. 'There is very nice society in Bath, I am told.'

'My dear Pamela, I want to get away from society if I can; and I want to be very far from Enderby.'

'Of course. It was thoughtless of me to suggest a society place. Bath, too, within a stone's throw. Dearest aunt, I will offer no more suggestions. I will go anywhere you like.'

'Then let us decide at once. We will go to Pallanza, on Lago Maggiore. I have heard that it is a lovely spot, and later we can go on to Milan or Florence.'

'To Italy! That is like the fulfilment of a dream,' said Pamela with a sigh, feeling that Italy without César Castellani would be like a playhouse when the curtain has gone down and all the lights are out.

She was resigned, however, and not without hope. Castellani might propose before they left Brighton, when he found that parting was inevitable. He had said some very tender things, but of that vaguely tender strain which leaves a man uncommitted. His words had been full of poetry, but they might have applied to some absent mistress, or to love in the abstract. Pamela felt that she had no ground for exultation.

It was in vain that Mildred warned her against the danger of such an alliance.

'Consider what a wretched match it would be for you, Pamela,' she said. 'Think how different from your sister Rosalind's marriage.'

'Different! I should hope so, indeed! Can you imagine, Aunt Mildred, that *I* would marry such a man as Sir Henry Mountford, a man who has hardly a thought outside his stable and his gunroom? Do you know that he spends quite a quarter of every day in the saddle-room, allowing for the wet days, on which he almost lives there? I asked him once why he didn't have his lunch sent over to the stables, instead of keeping us waiting a quarter of an hour, and coming in at last smelling like a saddler's shop.'

'He is a gentleman, notwithstanding, Pamela, and Rosalind seems to get on very well with him.'

'"As the husband is the wife is," don't you know, aunt. You and Uncle George suit each other because you are both intellectual. I should be miserable if I married a man who had done nothing to distinguish himself from the common herd.'

'Perhaps. But do you think you could be very happy married to an accomplished idler who would live upon your fortune – who would have everything to gain, from the most sordid point of view, by marrying you, and of whose fidelity you could never be sure?'

'But I should be sure of him. My instinct would tell me if he were really in love with me. You must think me very silly, Aunt Mildred, if you think I could be deceived in such a matter as that.'

In spite of Pamela's confidence in her own instinct, or, in other words, in her own wisdom, Mildred was full of anxiety about her, and was very eager to place her charge beyond the reach of César Castellani's daily visits and musical talent. She felt responsible to her husband for his niece's peace of mind; doubly responsible in that Pamela's interest had been subordinated to her own comfort and well-being.

She had other reasons for wishing to escape from Mr Castellani's society. That instinctive aversion she had felt at sight of the unknown face in the church was not altogether a sentiment of the past, a prejudice overcome and forgotten. There were occasions when she shrank from the Italian's gentle touch, a delicate white hand hovering for a moment above her own as he offered her a book or a newspaper; there were times when his low sympathetic voice was a horror to her; there were times when she told herself that her self-respect as a wife hardly permitted of her breathing the same air that he breathed.

Innocent and simple-minded as her closely-sheltered life had kept her, in all thoughts, ways, and works unlike the average woman of society, Mildred Greswold was a woman, and she could not but see that César Castellani's feelings for her were of a deeper kind than any sentiment with which Pamela Ransome's charms had inspired him. There were moments when his voice, his face, his manner told his secret only too plainly; but these were but glimpses of the truth, hurried liftings of the curtain, which the man of society let drop again before he had too plainly betrayed himself. He had been careful to keep his secret from Pamela. It was only to the object of his worship that he had revealed those presumptuous dreams of his, and to her only in such wise as she must needs ignore. It would have seemed self-conscious prudery to rebuke indications so subtle and so casual; but Mildred could not ignore them in her own mind, and she waited anxiously for the hour in which she would be well enough to travel. She had all her plans made, had engaged a courier – a friend of Miss Fausset's Franz – and had arranged her route with him: first Northern Italy, and then the South. She wanted to make Pamela's exile as bright

and as profitable to her as she could. The life she was arranging was by
no means the kind of life that Clement Cancellor would have
counselled. It would have seemed to that stern labourer a life of self-
indulgence and frivolity. But the time for the higher ideal would come
by and by, perhaps, when this sense of misery, this benumbed feeling
of indifference to all things, had worn off, and she should be strong
enough to think a little more about other people's sorrows and a little
less about her own.

Mr Maltravers urged upon her the duty of staying in Brighton, and
working as her aunt worked. He had been told that Mrs Greswold was
a woman of independent fortune, and that she had separated herself
from a husband she fondly loved, upon a question of principle. It was
just such a woman as this that Samuel Maltravers liked to see in his
church. Such women were the elect of the earth, predestined to
contribute to the advancement of clerics and the building of chancels
and transepts. The chancel at St Edmund's was a noble one, needing no
extension, its only fault being that it was too big for the church. But
there was room for a transept. The church had been so planned as to
allow of its ultimate cruciform shape, and that transept was the dream
of Mr Maltravers' life. Scarcely had Mrs Greswold's story dropped in
measured syllables from Miss Fausset's lips than Mr Maltravers said to
himself, 'This lady will build my transept.' A woman who could leave a
beloved husband on a question of principle was just the kind of woman
to sink a few superfluous thousands upon the improvement of such a
fane as St Edmund's. Every seat in that fashionable temple was
occupied. More seat-room was a necessity. The hour had come, and
the – woman.

Mr Maltravers endeavoured to convince Mrs Greswold that
Brighton was the one most fitting sphere for an enlightened woman's
labours. Brighton cried aloud for a Christian sister's aid. It had all the
elements in which the heaven-born missionary delights. Phenomenal
wealth on the one side, abject poverty on the other; fashion in the
foreground, sin and misery behind the curtain. Brighton was Pagan
Rome in little. Together with the advanced civilisation, the over-
refinement, the occult pleasures, the art, the luxury, the beauty, the
burning of the Seven-hilled City, Brighton had all the corrupting
influences of her Pagan sister. Brighton was rotten to the core – a
lovely simulacrum – a Dead Sea apple – shining, golden, doomed,
damned.

As he uttered that last terrific word Mr Maltravers sank his voice to
that bass depth some of us can remember in Bishop Wilberforce's climatic
syllables; and so spoken, the word seemed permissible in any serious
drawing-room, awful rather than profane.

It was in vain, however, that the Vicar of St Edmund's strove to convince Mildred that her mission was immediate, and in Brighton; that in his parish, and there alone, could her loftiest dreams find their fulfilment.

'I hope to do some little good to my fellow-creatures by and by,' she said meekly, 'but I do not feel that the time has come yet. I am incapable of anything except just existing. I believe my aunt has told you that I have had a great sorrow——'

'Yes, yes, poor wounded heart, I know, I know.'

'I mean to work by and bye – when I have learned to forget myself a little. Sorrow is so selfish. Just now I feel stupid and helpless. I could do no good to any one.'

'You could build my transept,' thought Mr Maltravers, but he only sighed, and shook his head, and murmured gently, 'Well, well, we must wait; we must hope. There is but one *earthly* consolation for a great grief – I will say nothing of heavenly comfort – and that consolation is to be found in labouring for the good of our sinning, sorrowing fellow-creatures, and for the glory of God – for the glory of God,' repeated Mr Maltravers, harping on his transept. 'There are mourners who have left imperishable monuments of their grief, and of their piety, in some of the finest churches of this land.'

Upon the evening on which Mr Maltravers had pleaded for Brighton, Miss Fausset and her *protégé* were alone together during the half-hour before dinner; the lady resting after a long day in her district: a composed, quiet figure, in fawn-coloured silk gown and point lace kerchief, seated erect in the high-backed chair, with folded hands, and eyes gazing thoughtfully at the fire; the gentleman lounging in a low chair on the other side of the hearth in luxurious self-abandonment, his red-brown eyes shining in the fire-glow, and his red-brown hair throwing off glints of light.

They had been talking, and had lapsed into silence; and it was after a long pause that Miss Fausset said,

'I wonder you have not made the young lady an offer before now.'

'Suppose I am not in love with the young lady?'

'You have been too assiduous for that supposition to occur to me. You have haunted this house ever since Miss Ransome has been here.'

'And yet I am not in love with her.'

'She is a pretty and attractive girl, and disposed to think highly of you.'

'And yet I am not in love with her,' he repeated, with a smile which made Miss Fausset angry. 'To think that you should turn matchmaker, you who have said so many bitter things of the fools who fall in love, and the still greater fools who marry; *you* who stand alone like a granite monolith, like Cleopatra's Needle, or the Matterhorn, or anything grand and solitary and unapproachable; you to counsel the civilised slavery we call marriage!'

'My dear César, I can afford to stand alone; but you cannot afford to surrender your chance of winning an amiable wife with fifteen hundred a year.'

'That for fifteen hundred a year!' exclaimed Castellani, wafting an imaginary fortune from the tips of his fingers with airy insolence. 'Do you think I will sell myself – for so little?'

'That high-flown tone is all very well; but there is one fact you seem to ignore.'

'What is that, my kindest and best?'

'The fact that you are a very expensive person, and that you have to be maintained somehow.'

'That fact shall never force me to marry where I cannot love. At the worst, art shall maintain me. When other and dearer friends prove unkind, I will call upon my maiden aunts the Muses.'

'The Muses hitherto have hardly paid for the gardenias in your buttonhole.'

'O, I know I am not a man of business. I lack the faculty of pounds, shillings, and pence, which is an attribute of some minds. I have scattered my flowers of art upon all the highways instead of nailing the blossoms against a wall and waiting for them to bear fruit. I have been reckless, improvident – granted; and you, out of your abundance, have been kind. Your words imply a threat. You wish to remind me that your kindness cannot go on for ever.'

'There are limits to everything.'

'Hardly to your generosity; certainly not to your wealth. As you garner it, that must be inexhaustible. I cannot think that you would ever turn your back upon me. The link between us is too tender a bond.'

Miss Fausset's face darkened to deepest night.

'Tender do you call it?' she exclaimed. 'If the memory of an unpardonable wrong is tender——' and then, interrupting herself, she cried passionately, 'César Castellani, I have warned you against the slightest reference to the past. As for my generosity, as you call it, you might be wiser if you gave it a lower name – caprice; caprice which may weary at any moment. You have a chance of making an excellent match, and I strongly advise you to take advantage of it.'

'Forgive me if I disregard your advice, much as I respect your judgment upon all other subjects.'

'You have other views, I suppose, then?'

'Yes, I have other views.'

'You look higher?'

'Infinitely higher,' he answered, with his hands locked above his head in a carelessly graceful attitude, and with his eyes gazing at the fire.

He looked like a dreaming fawn: the large, full eyes, the small peaked beard, and close-cut hair upon the arched forehead were all suggestive of the satyr tribe.

The door opened, and Pamela came smiling in, self-conscious, yet happy, delighted at seeing that picturesque figure by the hearth.

CHAPTER VII

THE TIME HAS COME

Three days later Mildred and her young companion started for Italy. The doctor declared that the departure was premature – Mrs Greswold was not strong enough to undertake such a fatiguing journey. But modern civilisation has smoothed the roads that lead over the civilised world, and for a lady who travels with a maid and a courier, journeys are rendered very easy; besides, Mildred had made up her mind to leave Brighton at any hazard.

The hour of parting came for Pamela and Castellani, and although the young lady took care to remind him at least a dozen times a day of that impending severance, not one word of the future, or of any cherished hope on his part, fell from his lips. And yet it had seemed to Pamela that he was devoted to her, that he only waited for the opportunity to speak. It seemed to her also that he felt the pain of parting, for he had an air of deepest melancholy during these farewell days, and talked only of saddest themes. He was in Lewes Crescent nearly all day long – he played the mournfullest strains – he behaved like a man oppressed with a secret sorrow; but never a word of love or marriage did he breathe to Pamela. He pressed her hand gently, with an almost paternal affection, as she leant out of the carriage which was to take her to the station, and bade him a last good-bye.

'Good-bye!' she half sang, half sobbed, in the darkness at the back of the hired landau, as they drove bumping down St James's street. 'Good-bye, summer; good-bye, everything!'

She did not even glance at Hannington's autumn fashions as they drove up the hill. She felt that life was no longer worth dressing for.

'He never could have cared for me,' she thought, as she dropped her silent tears upon Box's thoroughbred neck, 'and yet he seemed – he seemed! Does he seem like that to every girl, I wonder? Is he all seeming?'

After this came a leisurely journey, and then long, slow weeks of a luxurious repose amidst fairest surroundings – a life which to those who have lived and fought the great battle, and come wounded but yet alive out of the fray, is the life paradisaic; but for the fresh, strong soul panting for emotions and excitements, like a young bird that yearns to try the strength of his wings, this kind of languid existence seems like a foretaste of death and nothingness. Mountains and lakes were not enough for Pamela – the azure of an Italian sky, the infinite variety of sunset splendours, the brightness of a morning heralded by a roseate flush on snow-capped hills – all these were futile where the heart was empty. Mildred's maturer grief found some consolation in these exquisite surroundings; but Pamela wanted to live, and those encircling mountains seemed to her as the walls of a gigantic prison.

'It was so nice at Brighton,' she said, looking along the burnished mirror of the lake with despondent eyes, tired of the mystery of those reflected mountains, descending into infinite depths, a world inverted: 'so gay, so cheery – always something going on. Don't you think, aunt, that the air of this place is very relaxing?'

That word relaxing is the keynote of discontent. It is a word that can blight the loveliest spots the sun ever shone upon. It is the speck upon the peach. Be sure that before ever he mentioned the apple, Satan told Eve that Eden was very relaxing.

'I hope you are not unhappy here, my dear Pamela?' said Mildred, evading the question.

'Unhappy? O, no, indeed, dear aunt! I could not be otherwise than happy with you anywhere. There are lots of people who would envy me living on the shore of Lago Maggiore, and seeing those delightful mountains all day long; but I did so enjoy Brighton – the theatre, the Pavilion: always something going on.'

The two ladies had their own suite of apartments in the hotel, and lived in that genteel seclusion which is the privilege of wealth as well as of rank all over the world. Pamela envied the tourists of Cook and Gaze, as she saw them trooping into the *table d'hôte*, or heard their clatter in the public drawing-room. It was all very well to sit in one's own balcony, gazing at the placid lake, while the rabble amused themselves below. One felt one's superior status, and the advantage of being somebody instead of nobody; but when the rabble danced or acted charades, or played dumb crambo, or squabbled over a game at nap, they seemed to have the best of it somehow.

'I almost wish I had been born a vulgarian,' sighed Pamela one evening, when the tourists were revolving to the 'Myosotis Waltz' banged out on a cast-iron grand in the salon below.

Mildred did all she could in the way of excursionising to enliven the dulness of their solitary life; but the beauties of Nature palled upon

Pamela's lively mind. However the day might be occupied in drives to distant scenes of surpassing loveliness, the ever-lengthening evenings had to be spent in the Louis Quatorze salon, where no visitors dropped in to disturb the monotony of books and work, piano and pet-dog.

For Mildred, too, those evening hours seemed unutterably long, and as autumn deepened into winter, her burden seemed heavier to bear. Time brought no consolation, offered no hope. She had lost all that had made life worth living. First, the child who represented all that was brightest and fairest and gayest and most hopeful in her life; next, the husband who was her life itself, the prop and staff, the column around which every tendril of her being was entwined. There was nothing for her in the future but a life of self-abnegation, of working and living for others. The prospect seemed dark and dreary, and she knew now how small a margin of her life had been devoted to God. The idea of devoting herself wholly was too repellent. She knew now that she was very human, wedded to earthly loves and earthly happiness, needing a long purgation before she could attain the saintly attitude.

She thought of Enderby every night as she sat in silent melancholy beside the hearth, where a solitary log crumbled slowly to white ashes on the marble, and where the faint warmth had a perfume of distant pine-woods; she thought of Enderby and its widowed master. Was he living there still, or was he, too, a wanderer? She had heard but little of his movements since she left England. Pamela had written to him, and he had replied, but had said very little about himself. The only news in Rosalind's letters was of the extraordinary development – intellectual and otherwise – of the baby, and the magnitude of Sir Henry's bag. Beyond the baby and the bag, Lady Mountford's pen rarely travelled.

Mildred thought of that absent husband with an aching heart. There were times when she asked herself if she had done well – when she was tempted to total surrender – when the pen was in her hand ready to write a telegram imploring him to come to her – or when she was on the point of giving her orders for an immediate return to England. But pride and principle alike restrained her. She had taken her own course, she had made up her mind deliberately, after long thought and many prayers. She could not tread the backward way, the primrose path of sin. She could but pray for greater strength, for loftier purpose, for that grand power of self-forgetfulness which makes for heaven.

Christmas came and found her in this frame of mind. There were very few tourists now, and the long corridors had a sepulchral air, the snowy mountain-tops were blotted out by mist and rain. For Pamela, Christmastide had been a season of much gaiety hitherto – a season of new frocks and many dances, hunting and hunt-balls, and the change was a severe test of that young lady's temper. She came through the ordeal admirably, never forgot that she had promised her uncle to be his wife's faithful companion, and amused herself as best she could with Italian music and desultory studies. She read Mr Sinnett's books, studied Bohn's edition of Plato's Dialogues, addled her youthful brain with various theories of a far-reaching kind, and fancied herself decidedly mediumistic. That word mediumistic possessed a peculiar fascination for her. She had looked at César Castellani's eyeballs, which were markedly globular – seeming, as it were, reflecting surfaces for the spirit world, a sure indication of the mediumistic temperament. She had seen other signs; and now in this romantic solitude, sauntering by the lake in the misty winter air, just before sundown, she fancied herself almost in communion with that absent genius. Distance could not separate two people when both were eminently mediumistic.

'I believe he is thinking of me at this very moment,' she said to herself one afternoon at the end of the year, 'and I have a kind of feeling that I shall see him – bodily – very soon.'

She forgot to reckon with herself that this kind of feeling could count for very little, since she had experienced it in greater or less degree ever since she had left Brighton. In almost every excursion she had beguiled the tedium of the way with some pleasant day-dream. Castellani would appear in the most unlooked-for manner at the resting-place where they were to lunch. He would have followed them from England at his leisure, and would come upon them unannounced, pleased to startle her by his sudden apparition. In absence she had recalled so many tender speeches, so many indications of regard; and she had taught herself to believe that he really cared for her, and had but been withheld from a declaration by a noble dignity which would not stoop to woo a woman richer than himself.

'He is poor and proud,' she thought.

Poor and proud. How sweet the alliteration sounded!

She had thought of him so incessantly that it was hardly a coincidence, and yet it seemed to her a miracle when his voice sounded behind her in the midst of her reverie.

'You ought not to be out of doors, Miss Ransome, when the sun is so nearly down.'

She turned and faced him, pale first with infinite pleasure, and then rosy to the roots of her flaxen hair.

'When did you come?' she asked eagerly. 'Have you been long in Italy?'

'I only came through the St Gothard last night, breakfasted at Locarno, and came here by road. I have not seen Mrs Greswold yet. She is well, I hope?'

'She is not over-well. She frets dreadfully, I am afraid. It is so sad that she and Uncle George should be living apart for some mysterious reason which nobody knows. They were the most perfect couple.'

'Mrs Greswold is a perfect woman.'

'And Uncle George has the finest character. His first marriage was unhappy, I believe; nobody ever talked about it. I think it was only just known in the family that he had married in Italy when he was a young man, and that his wife had died within a year. It was supposed that she could not have been nice, since nobody knew anything about her.'

'Rather hard upon the dead lady to be condemned by her husband's silence. Will you take me to your aunt?'

'With pleasure. I think she ought to be charmed to see you, for we lead the most solitary existence here. My aunt has set her face against knowing anybody, in the hotel or out of it. And there have been some really charming people staying here; people one would go out of one's way to know. Have you come here for your health?'

'For my pleasure only. I was sick to death of England and of cities. I longed to steep myself in the infinite and the beautiful. Those indigo clouds above the mountains yonder – with that bold splash of orange shining through the gorge – are worth the journey, were there no more than that; and when the wintry stars glass themselves in the lake by and by, ah! then one knows what it is to be the living, acting element in a world of passive beauty. And to think that there are men and women in London groping about in the fog, and fancying themselves alive!'

'Oh, but there are compensations – theatres, concerts, dances.'

'Miss Ransome, I fear you are a Philistine.'

'O, no, no! I adore Nature. I should like to be above those common earthly pleasures – to journey from star to star along the planetary chain, rising at each transition to a higher level, until I came to the spirit world where—— This is the hotel, and we are on the second floor. Would you like the lift?'

'I never walk when I can be carried.'

'Then we will go up in the lift. I used to think it rather good fun at first,' said Pamela with a sigh, remembering how soon that trivial excitement had begun to pall.

Mildred received the unexpected visitor with marked coldness; but it was not easy to remain persistently cold while Pamela was so warm. Castellani was one of those provoking people who refuse to see when they are unwelcome. He was full of talk, gay, bright, and varied. He had all the social events of the past three months to talk about. Society had witnessed the most extraordinary changes – marriages – sudden deaths – everything unlooked for. There had been scandals, too; but these he touched upon lightly, and with a deprecating air, professing himself sorry for everybody.

Mildred allowed him to talk, and was, perhaps, a little more cordial when he took his leave than she had been when he came. He had prevented her from thinking her own thoughts for the space of an hour, and that was something for which to be grateful. He had come there in pursuit of Pamela, no doubt. He could have no other reason. He had been playing his own game, holding back in order to be the more gladly accepted when he should declare himself. It was thus Mildred reasoned with herself; and yet there had been looks and tones which it was difficult for her to forget.

'He is by profession a lady-killer,' she argued; 'no doubt he treats all women in the same way. He cannot help trying to fascinate them; and there are women like Cecilia Tomkison who encourage him to make sentimental speeches.'

She persuaded herself that the looks and tones which had offended meant very little. For Pamela's sake she would like to think well of him.

'You have told me about a great many people,' she said, as he was leaving them, 'but you have told me nothing about my husband. Did you hear if he was still at Enderby – and well?'

'He was still at Enderby up to the end of November, and I believe he was well. I spent three days at Riverdale, and heard of him from Mrs Hillersdon.'

Mildred asked no further question, nor did she invite Mr Castellani to repeat his visit. Happily for his own success in life, he was not the kind of person to wait for invitations.

'I am staying in the hotel,' he said. 'I hope I may drop in sometimes – to-morrow even. Miss Ransome is good enough to say she would like to sing some duets with me.'

'Miss Ransome knows I have not been receiving any visitors,' Mildred answered, with a touch of reproachfulness.

'O, but Mr Castellani is an old friend! The people you avoided were strangers,' said Pamela eagerly.

Mildred made no further protest. Few men would have accepted a permission so grudgingly given; but Castellani stopped at no obstacle when he had a serious purpose to serve: and in this case his purpose was very serious; for life or death, he told himself.

He came next day, and the day after that, and every day for four or five weeks, till the first flush of precocious spring lent beauty to the landscape and softness to the sky. Mildred submitted to his visits as an inevitable consequence of Pamela's folly; submitted, and by and by fell into the habit of being amused by Castellani; interested in his talk of men and women and of books, of which he seemed to have read all of any mark that had ever been written. She allowed herself to be interested; she allowed herself to be soothed by his music; she let him become an

Mr Castellani is a bad man

influence in her life, unawares, caught by a subtlety that had never been surpassed by anybody of lesser gifts than Satan: but never did this presumptuous wooer beguile her into one single thought that wronged her absent husband. Her intellect acknowledged the tempter's intellectual sway, but her heart knew no wavering.

César Castellani had seen a good deal of life, but as he had assiduously cultivated the seamy side, it was hardly strange if he lacked the power of understanding a pure-minded woman. To his mind every woman was a citadel, better or worse defended, but always assailable by treason or strategy, force or art, and never impregnable. Mrs Greswold was his Troy, his Thebes, his ideal of majesty and strength in woman. So far as virtue went upon this earth he believed Mildred Greswold to be virtuous; proud, too; not a woman to lower her crest to the illicit conqueror, or stain her name with the disgrace of a runaway wife. But it had been given to him to disturb a union that had existed happily for fourteen years. It had been given to him to awaken the baneful passion of jealousy, to sow the seeds of suspicion, to part husband and wife. He had gone to work carelessly enough in the first instance, struck with Mildred's beauty and sweetness – full of sentimental recollections of the fair child-face and the bright streaming hair that had passed him like a vision in the sunlight of Hyde Park. He had envied the husband so fair a wife, so luxurious a home, with its air of old-world respectability, that deep-rooted English aristocracy of landed estate, which to the foreign adventurer seemed of all conditions in life the most enviable. He had been impelled by sheer malice when he uttered his careless allusion to George Greswold's past life, and with a word blighted two hearts.

He saw the effect of the speech in the face of the wife, and in the manner of the husband saw that he had launched a thunderbolt. It was with deepest interest he followed up his advantage; watched and waited for further evidence of the evil he had done. He was a close student of the faces of women; above all, when the face was lovely. He saw all the marks of secret care in Mrs Greswold's countenance during the weeks that elapsed between his first visit to Enderby and the charity concert. He saw the deepening shadows, the growing grief, and on the day of the concert he saw the traces of a still keener pain in those pale features and haggard eyes; but for an immediate separation between husband and wife he was not prepared.

He heard at Riverdale of Mrs Greswold's departure from home. The suddenness and strangeness of her journey had set all the servants talking. He found out where she had gone, and hastened at once to call upon his devoted friend Mrs Tomkison, who told him all she had to tell.

'There is some domestic misery – an intrigue on his part, I fear,' said the glib Cecilia. 'Men are such traitors. It would hardly surprise me to-morrow if I was told that Adam was maintaining an expensive *ménage* in St John's Wood. She would tell me nothing, poor darling; but she sent for Mr Cancellor, and was closeted with him for an hour. No doubt she told *him* everything. And then she went off to Brighton.'

Castellani followed to Brighton, and his influence with Miss Fausset enabled him to learn something, but not all. Not one word said Miss Fausset about the supposed identity between George Greswold's first wife and John Fausset's *protégée*; but she told Mr Castellani that she feared her niece's separation from her husband would be permanent.

'Why does she not divorce him,' he said, 'if he has wronged her?'

'He has not wronged her – in the way you mean. And if he had, she could not divorce him, unless he had beaten her. You men made the law, and framed it in your own favour. It is a very sad case, César, and I am not at liberty to say any more about it. You must ask me no more questions.'

Castellani obeyed for the time being; but he did ask further questions upon other occasions, and he exercised all his subtlety in the endeavour to extract information from Miss Fausset. That lady, however, was inflexible; and he had to wait for time to solve the mystery.

'They have parted on account of that first marriage,' he told himself. 'Perhaps she has found out all about the poor lady's fate, and takes the worst view of the catastrophe. That would account for their separation. She would not stay with a husband she suspected; he would not live with a wife who could so suspect. A very pretty quarrel.'

A quarrel – a life-long severance – but not a divorce. There was the difficulty. César Castellani believed himself invincible with women. The weakest, and in some cases the worst, of the sex had educated him into the belief that no woman lived who could resist him. And here was a woman whom he intensely admired, and whose married life it had been his privilege to wreck. She was a rich woman – and it was essential to his success in life that he should marry wealth. With all his various gifts he was not a money-earning man, he would never attain even lasting renown by his talents. For when the good fairies had endowed him with music and poetry, eloquence and grace, the strong-minded, hard-featured fairy called Perseverance came to his christening feast, and seeing no knife and fork laid for her, doomed him to the curse of idleness. He had all the talents which enable a man to shine in society, but he had also the money-spending talent, the elegant tastes and inclinations which require some thousands a year for their sustenance. Hitherto he had lived by his wits – from hand to mouth; but for some years past he had been on the look-out for a rich wife.

He knew that Mildred Greswold was three times richer than Pamela Ransome. The wealth of the Faussets came within the region of his knowledge; and he knew how large a fortune John Fausset had left his daughter, and how entirely that fortune was at her own disposal. He might have had Pamela for the asking; Pamela, with a paltry fifteen hundred a year; Pamela, who sang false and bored him beyond measure. The higher prize seemed impossible; but it was his nature to attempt the impossible. His belief in his own power was boundless.

'She cannot divorce her husband,' he told himself; 'but he may divorce her if she should wrong him, or even seem to wrong him: and the most innocent woman may be compromised if her lover is daring and will risk much for a great *coup*, as I would.'

He thought himself very near success in these lengthening afternoons in the beginning of February, when he was allowed to spend the lovely hour of sundown in Mrs Greswold's *salon*, watching the sunset from the wide plate-glass window, which commanded a panorama of lake and mountain, with every exquisite change from concentrated light to suffused colour, and then to deepening purple that slowly darkened into night. It was the hour in which it was deemed dangerous to be out of doors; but it was the loveliest hour of the day or the night, and Mildred never wearied of that glorious outlook over lake and sky. She was silent for the most part at such a time, sitting in the shadow of the window-curtains, her face hidden from the other two, sitting apart from the world, thinking of the life that had been and could never be again.

Sometimes in the midst of her sad thoughts Castellani would strike a chord on the piano at the other end of the room, and then a tender strain of melody would steal out of the darkness, and that veiled tenor voice would sing some of the saddest lines of Heine, the poet of the broken heart, sadder than Byron, sadder than Musset, sad with the sadness of one who had never known joy. Those words wedded to tenderest melody always moved Mildred Greswold to tears. Castellani saw her tears and thought they were given to him; such tears as yielding virtue gives to the tempter. He knew the power of his voice, the fascination of music for those in whom the love of music is a part of their being. He could not foresee the possibility of failure. He was already admitted to that kind of intimacy which is the first stage of success. He was an almost daily visitor; he came upon the two ladies in their walks and drives, and contrived, unbidden, to make himself their companion; he chose the books that both were to read, and made himself useful in getting library parcels sent from Milan or Paris. He contrived to make himself indispensable, or at least thought himself so. Pamela's eagerness filled up all the gaps; she was so full of talk and vivacity that it was not easy to be sure about the sentiments of her more silent companion; but César Castellani's vanity was the key with which he read Mildred's character and feelings.

'She is a sphinx,' he told himself; 'but I think I can solve her mystery. The magnetic power of such a love as mine must draw her to me sooner or later.'

Mr Castellani had a profound belief in his own magnetism. That word magnetic had a large place in his particular creed. He talked of certain fascinating women – generally a little *passée* – as 'magnetic.' He prided himself upon being a magnetic man.

While César Castellani flattered himself that he was on the threshold of success, Mildred Greswold was deliberating how best to escape from him and his society for ever. Had she been alone there need have been no difficulty; but she saw Pamela's happiness involved in his presence, she saw the fresh young cheek pale at the thought of separation, and she was perplexed how to act for the best. Had Pamela been her daughter she could not have considered her feelings more tenderly. She told herself that Mr Castellani would be a very bad match for Miss Ransome; yet when she saw the girl's face grow radiant at the sound of his footsteps, when she watched her dulness in his absence, that everlasting air of waiting for somebody which marks the girl who is in love, she found herself hoping that the Italian would make a formal proposal, and she was inclined to meet him half-way.

But the new year was six weeks old, and he had not even hinted at matrimonial intentions, so Mildred felt constrained to speak plainly.

'My dearest Pamela, we are drifting into a very uncomfortable position with Mr Castellani,' she began gently. 'He comes here day after day as if he were your *fiancé*, and yet he has said nothing definite.'

Pamela grew crimson at this attack, and her hands began to tremble over her crewel-work, though she tried to go on working.

'I respect him all the more for being in no haste to declare himself, Aunt Mildred,' she said, rather angrily. 'If he were the kind of adventurer you once thought him, he would have made me an offer ages ago. Why should he not come to see us? I'm sure he's very amusing and very useful. Even you seem interested in him and cheered by him. Why should he not come? We have no one's opinion to study in a foreign hotel.'

'I don't know about that, dear. People always hear about things; and it might injure you by and by in society to have your name associated with Mr Castellani.'

'I am sure I should be very proud of it,' retorted Pamela; 'very proud to have my name associated with genius.'

'And you really, honestly believe you could be happy as his wife, Pamela?' asked Mildred gravely.

'I know that I can never be happy with any one else. I don't consider myself particularly clever, aunt, but I believe I have the artistic temperament. Life without art would be a howling wilderness for me.'

'Life means a long time, dear. Think what a difference it must make whether you lead it with a good or a bad man!'

'All the goodness in the world would not make me happy with a husband who was not musical; not John Howard, nor John Wesley, nor John Bunyan, nor any of your model Johns. John Milton *was*,' added Pamela rather vaguely, 'and handsome into the bargain; but I'm afraid he was a little *dry*.'

'Promise me at least this much, Pamela. First, that you will take no step without your uncle's knowledge and advice; and next, that if ever you marry Mr Castellani, you will have your fortune strictly settled upon yourself.'

'O, aunt, how sordid! But perhaps it would be best. If I had the money, I should give it all to him: but if he had the money, with his artistic temperament he would be sure to lavish it all upon other people. He would not be able to pass a picturesque beggar without emptying his pockets. Do you remember how he was impressed by the four old men on the church steps the other day?'

'Yes, but I don't think he gave them anything.'

'Not while we were with him; but you may be sure he did afterwards.'

After this conversation Mrs Greswold made up her mind on two points. She would arrange for a prompt departure to Venice or Naples, whichever might be advised for the spring season; and she would sound Mr Castellani as to his intentions. It was not fair to Pamela that she should be kept in the dark any longer, that the gentleman should be allowed to sing duets with her, and advise her studies, and join her in her walks, and yet give no definite expression to his regard.

Mildred tried to think the best of him as a suitor for her husband's niece. She knew that he was clever; she knew that he was fairly well born. On his mother's side he sprang from the respectable commercial classes; on his father's side he belonged to the art-world. There was nothing debasing in such a lineage. From neither her friend Mrs Tomkison nor from Miss Fausset had she heard anything to his discredit; and both those ladies had known him long. There could therefore be no objection on the score of character. Pamela ought to make a much better marriage in the way of means and position; but those excellent and well-chosen alliances dictated by the wisdom of friends are sometimes known to result in evil; and, in a word, why should not Pamela be happy in her own way?

Having thus reasoned with herself, Mildred watched for an opportunity to speak to Castellani. She had not long to wait. He called rather earlier than usual one afternoon, when Pamela had gone out for a mountain ramble with her dog and her maid, to search for those doubly precious flowers which bloom with the first breath of spring. Castellani had seen the young lady leave the hotel soon after the midday meal, armed with her alpenstock, and accompanied by her attendant carrying a basket. She had fondly hoped that he would offer to join her expedition, to dig out delicate ferns from sheltered recesses, to hunt for mountain hyacinths and many-hued anemones; but he observed her departure *perdu* behind a window-curtain in the reading-room, and half-an-hour afterwards he was ushered into Mrs Greswold's drawing-room.

'I feared you were ill,' he said, 'as I saw Miss Ransome excursionising without you.'

'I have a slight headache, and felt more inclined for a book than for a long walk. Why did you not go with Pamela? I daresay she would have been glad of your company. Peterson is not a lively companion for a mountain ramble.'

'Poor Miss Ransome! How sad to be a young English Mees, and to have to be chaperoned by a person like Peterson!' said Castellani, with a careless shrug. 'No, I had no inclination to join in the anemone hunt. Miss Ransome told me yesterday what she was going to do. I have no passion for wild flowers or romantic walks.'

'But you seem to have a great liking for Miss Ransome's society,' replied Mildred gravely. 'You have cultivated it very assiduously since you came here, and I think I may be excused for fancying that you came to Pallanza on her account.'

'You may be excused for thinking anything wild and improbable, because you are a woman and wilfuly blind,' he answered, drawing his chair a little nearer to hers, and lowering his voice with a touch of tenderness. 'But surely – surely you cannot think that I came to Pallanza on Miss Ransome's account?'

'I might not have thought so had you been a less frequent visitor in this room, where you have come – pardon me for saying so – very much of your own accord. I don't think it was quite delicate or honourable to come here so often, to be so continually in the society of a frank, impressionable girl, unless you had some deeper feeling for her than casual admiration.'

'Mrs Greswold, upon my honour I have never in the whole course of my acquaintance with Miss Ransome by one word or tone implied any warmer feeling than that which you call casual admiration.'

'And you are not attached to her? you do not cherish the hope of winning her for your wife?' asked Mildred seriously, looking at him with earnest eyes.

That calm, grave look chilled him to the core of his heart. His brow flushed, his eyes grew dark and troubled. He felt as if the crisis of his life were approaching, and augury was unfavourable.

'I have never cherished any such hope; I never shall.'

George a madman —
Castellani declares love

'Then why have you come here so continually?'

'For God's sake, do not ask me that question! The time has not come.'

'Yes, Mr Castellani, the time has come. The question should have been asked sooner. You have compromised Miss Ransome by your meaningless assiduities. You have compromised me; for I ought to have taken better care of her than to allow an acquaintance of so ambiguous a character. But I am very glad that I have spoken, and that you have replied plainly. From to-day your visits must cease. We shall go to the south of Italy in a few days. Let me beg that you will not happen to be travelling in the same direction.'

Mildred was deeply indignant. She had cheapened her husband's niece – Randolph Ransome's co-heiress – a girl whom half the young men in London would have considered a prize in the matrimonial market: and this man, who had haunted her at home and abroad for the last seven or eight weeks, dared now to tell her that his attentions were motiveless so far as her niece was concerned.

'O, Mildred, do not banish me!' he cried passionately. 'You must have understood. You must know that it is you, and you only, for whom I care; you whose presence makes life lovely for me, in whose absence I am lost and wretched. You have wrung my secret from me. I did not mean to offend. I would have respected your strange widowhood. I would have waited half a lifetime. Only to see you, to be near you – your slave, your proud, too happy slave. That was all I would have asked. Why may that not be? Why may I not come and go, like the summer wind that breathes round you, like the flowers that look in at your window – faithful as your dog, patient as old Time? Why may it not be, Mildred?'

She stood up suddenly before him, white to the lips, and with cold contempt in those eyes which he had seen so lovely with the light of affection when they had looked at her husband. She looked at him unfalteringly, as she might have looked at a worm. Anger had made her pale, but that was all.

'You must have had a strange experience of women before you would dare to talk to any honest woman in such a strain as this, Mr Castellani,' she said. 'I will not lower myself so far as to tell you what I think of your conduct. Miss Ransome shall know the kind of person whose society she has endured. I must beg that you will consider yourself as much a stranger to her as to me from to-day.'

She moved towards the bell, but he intercepted her.

'You are very cruel,' he said; 'but the day will come when you will be sorry that you rejected the most devoted love that was ever offered to woman, in order to be true to broken bonds.'

'They are not broken. They will hold me to my dying hour.'

'Yes, to a madman and a murderer.'

CHAPTER VIII

NOT PROVEN   Asylum –

Mildred stood speechless for some moments after those words of Castellani's, looking at him with kindling eyes.

'How dare you?' she cried at last. 'How dare you accuse my husband – the noblest of men?'

'The noblest of men do strange things sometimes upon an evil impulse, and when they are not quite right here,' touching his forehead.

'My husband, George Greswold, is too high a mark for your malignity. Do you think you can make me believe evil of him after fourteen years of married life? His intellect is the clearest and the soundest I have ever found in man or woman. You can no more shake my faith in his power of brain than in his goodness of heart.'

'Perhaps not. The George Greswold you know is a gentleman of commanding intellect and unblemished character. But the George Ransome whom I knew seventeen years ago was a gentleman who was shrewdly suspected of having made away with his wife; and who was confined in a public asylum in the environs of Nice as a dangerous lunatic. If you doubt these facts, you have only to go to Nice, or to St Jean, where Mr Ransome and his wife lived for some time in a turtle-dove retirement, which ended tragically. Seventeen years does not obliterate the evidence of such a tragedy as that in which your husband was chief actor.'

'I do not believe one word – and I hope I may never hear your voice again,' said Mildred, with her hand on the electric bell.

She did not remove her hand till her servant, the courier, opened the door. A look told him his duty. Castellani took up his hat without a word; and Albrecht deferentially attended him to the landing, and politely whistled for the lift to convey him to the vestibule below.

Castellani made the descent, feeling like Lucifer when he fell from heaven.

'Too soon!' he muttered to himself. 'She took the cards out of my hands – she forced my play, and spoiled my game. But I have given her something to think about. She will not forget to-day's interview in a hurry.'

Albrecht, the handiest of men, was standing beside him, working the lift.

'Where is your next move to be, Albrecht?' he asked in German.

The noble-born lady had not yet decided, Albrecht told him; but he thought the move would be either to Venice or to Posilippo.

'If I pretended to be a prophet, Albrecht, I should tell thee that the honourable lady will go to neither Venice nor Posilippo; but that thy next move will be to the Riviera, perhaps to Nice.'

Albrecht shrugged his shoulders in polite indifference.

'Look here, my friend, come thou to me when madame gives the order for Nice, and I will give thee a louis for assuring me that I prophesied right,' said Castellani, as he stepped out of the lift.

Mildred walked up and down the room, trying to control the confusion of her thoughts, trying to reason calmly upon that hideous accusation which she had affected to despise, but which yet had struck terror to her soul. Would he dare to bring such a charge – villain and traitor as he was – if there were not some ground for the accusation, some glimmer of truth amidst a cloud of falsehood?

And her husband's manner: his refusal to tell her the history of his first marriage; his reticence, his secrecy – reticence so out of harmony with his boldly truthful nature; the gloom upon his face when she forced him to speak of that past life: all these things came back upon her with appalling force, and even trifles assumed a direful significance.

'O, my beloved! *what* was that dark story, and why did you leave me to hear it from such false lips as those?'

And when with passionate tears she thought how easy it would have been to forgive and pity even a tale of guilt – unpremeditated guilt, doubtless, fatality rather than crime – if her husband had laid his weary head upon her breast and told her all; holding back nothing; confident in the strength of a great love to understand and to pardon. How much easier would it have been to bear the burden of a guilty secret, so shared, in the supreme trustfulness of her husband's love! How light a burden compared with this which was laid upon her! this horror of groping backward into the black night of the past.

'I must know the worst,' she said to herself; 'I will test that scoundrel's accusation. I must know all. I will take no step to injure my dear love. I will seek no help, trust no friend. I must act alone.'

Then came a more agonising thought of the hapless wife – the victim.

'My sister! What was your fate? I *must* know.'

Her thoughts came back always to that point – 'I must know all.'

She recalled the image of that unacknowledged sister, the face bending over her bed when she started up out of a feverish dream, frightened and in tears, to take instant comfort from that loving presence, to fling her arms round Fay's neck, and nestle upon her bosom. Never had that sisterly love failed her. The quiet watcher was always near. A sigh, a faint little murmur, and the volunteer nurse was at her side. Often on waking she had found Fay sitting by her bed, in the dead of the night, motionless and watchful, sleepless from loving care.

Her love for Fay had been one of the strongest feelings of her life. She, who had been ever dutiful to the frivolous, capricious mother, had yet unconsciously given a stronger affection to the companion who had loved her with an unselfish love, which the mother had never shown. Her regard for Fay had been the one romance of her childhood, and had continued the strongest sentiment of her mind until the hour when, for the first time, she knew the deeper love of womanhood, and gave her heart to George Greswold.

And now these two supreme affections rose up before her in dreadful conflict; and in the sister so faithfully loved and so fondly regretted she saw the victim of her still dearer husband.

Pamela's footsteps and Pamela's voice in the corridor startled her in the midst of those dark thoughts. She hurriedly withdrew to her own room, where the maid Louisa was sitting, intent upon one of those infinitesimal repairs which served as an excuse for her existence.

'Go and tell Miss Ransome that I cannot dine with her. My headache is worse than it was when she went out. Ask her to excuse me.'

Louisa obeyed, and Mildred locked the door upon her grief. She sat all through the long evening brooding over the past and the future, impatient to know the worst.

She was on her way to Genoa with Pamela and their attendants before the following noon. Albrecht, the courier, had scarcely time to claim the promised coin from Mr Castellani.

Miss Ransome repined at this sudden departure.

'Just as we were going to be engaged,' she sobbed, when she and Mildred were alone in a railway compartment. 'It is really unkind of you to whisk one off in such a way, aunt.'

'My dear Pamela, you have had a lucky escape; and I hope you will never mention Mr Castellani's name again. He is an utterly bad man.'

'How cruel to say such a thing! – behind his back, too! What has he done that is bad, I should like to know?'

'I cannot enter into details; but I can tell you one thing, Pamela: he has never had any idea of asking you to be his wife. He told me that in the plainest language.'

'Do you mean to say that you questioned him about his feelings – for me?'

'I did what I felt was my duty, Pamela – my duty to you and to your uncle.'

'Duty!' ejaculated Pamela, with such an air that Box began to growl, imagining his mistress in want of protection. 'Duty! It is the most hateful word in the whole of the English language. You asked him when he was going to propose to me – you lowered and humiliated me beyond all that words can say – you – you spoilt everything.'

'Pamela, is this reasonable or just?'

'To be asked when he was going to propose to a girl – with his artistic temperament – the very thing to disgust him,' said Pamela, in a series of gasps. 'If you had WANTED to part us for ever you could not have gone to work better.'

'Whatever I wanted yesterday, I am quite clear about my feelings to-day Pamela. It is my earnest hope that you and Mr Castellani will never meet again.'

'You are very cruel, then – heartless – inhuman. Because *you* have done with love – because you have left my poor Uncle George – Heaven alone knows why – is no one else to be happy?'

'You could not be happy with César Castellani, Pamela. Happiness does not lie that way. I tell you again, he is a bad man.'

'And I tell you again I don't believe you. In what way is he bad? Does he rob, murder, forge, set fire to people's houses? What has he done that is bad?'

'He has traduced your uncle – to me, his wife.'

Pamela's countenance fell.

'You – you may have misunderstood him,' she faltered.

'No, there was no possibility of mistake. He slandered my husband. He let me see in the plainest way that he had no real regard for you, that he did not care how far his frequent visits compromised either you or me. He is utterly base, Pamela – a man without rectitude or conscience. He would have clung to us like some poisonous burr if I had not shaken him off. My dear, dear child,' said Mildred, putting her arm round Pamela's reluctant waist, and drawing the girlish figure nearer to her side, to the relief of Box, who leaped upon their shoulders and licked their faces in a rapture of sympathetic feeling; 'my dear, you have been treated very badly, but I am not to blame. You have had a lucky escape, Pamela. Why be angry about it?'

'It is all very well to talk like that,' sighed the girl, wrinkling her white forehead in painful perplexity. 'He was my day-dream. One cannot renounce one's day-dream at a moment's warning. If you knew the castles I have built – a life spent with him – a life devoted to the cultivation of art! He would have *made* my voice; and we could have had a flat in Queen Anne's Mansions, and a brougham and victoria, and lived within our income,' concluded Pamela, following her own train of thought.

'My dearest, there are so many worthier to share your life. You will have new day-dreams.'

'Perhaps when I am sixty. It will take me a lifetime to forget him. Do you think I could marry a country bumpkin, or any one who was not artistic?'

'You shall not be asked to marry a rustic. The artistic temperament is common enough nowadays. Almost every one is artistic.'

Pamela shrugged her shoulders petulantly, and turned to the window in token that she had said her say. She grieved like a child who has been disappointed of some jaunt looked forward to for long days of expectation. She tried to think herself ill-used by her uncle's wife; and yet that common sense of which she possessed a considerable share told her that she had only herself to blame. She had chosen to fall in love with a showy, versatile adventurer, without waiting for evidence that he cared for her. Proud in the strength of her position as an independent young woman with a handsome fortune and a fairly attractive person, she had imagined that Mr Castellani could look no higher, hope for nothing better than to obtain her hand and heart. She had ascribed his reticence to delicacy. She had accepted his frequent visits as an evidence of his attachment and of his ulterior views.

And now she sat in a sulky attitude, coiled up in a corner of the carriage, with her face to the window, meditating upon her fool's paradise. For seven happy weeks she had seen the man she admired almost daily; and her own intense sympathy with him had made her imagine an equal sympathy on his part. When their hands touched the thrilling vibration seemed mutual; and yet it had been on her side only, poor fool, she told herself now, abased in her own self-consciousness, drinking the cup of humiliation to the dregs.

He had slandered her uncle – yes, that was villany, that was iniquity. She began to think that he was utterly black. She remembered how coldly cruel he had been about the anemone hunt yesterday; how deaf to her girlish hints; never offering his company: colder, crueller than marble. She felt as if she had squandered her love upon Satan. Yet she was not the less angry with Mildred. That kind of interference was unpardonable.

She arrived at Genoa worn out with a fatiguing journey, and in a worse temper than she had ever sustained for so long a period, she whose worst tempers hitherto had been like April showers. Mildred had reciprocated her silence, and Box had been the only animated passenger.

The clever courier had made all his arrangements by telegraph: they spent a night at Genoa; drove round the city next morning; explored churches, palaces, and picture-galleries; and went on to Nice in the afternoon. They arrived at the great bustling station late in the evening, and were driven to one of the hotels on the Promenade des Anglais, where all preparations had been made for their reception: a glowing hearth in a spacious drawing-room opening on to a balcony, lamps and candles lighted, roses on all the tables, maid and man on the alert to receive travellers of distinction. So far as a place which is not home can put on an aspect of homeliness the hotel had succeeded; but Mildred looked round upon the white and gold walls, and the satin fauteuils, with an aching heart, remembering those old rooms at Enderby, and the familiar presence that had first made them dear to her, before the habit of years had made those inanimate things a part of her life.

She was at Nice; she had taken the slanderer's advice, and had gone to the city by the sea, to try and trace out for herself the mystery of the past, to violate her husband's secret, kept so long and so closely, only to rise up after years of happiness, like a murdered corpse exhumed from a forgotten grave.

She was here, on the scene of her husband's first marriage, and for three or four days she walked and drove about the strange busy place aimlessly, hopelessly, no nearer the knowledge of that dark history than she had been at Enderby Manor. Not for worlds would she injure the man she loved. She wanted to know all; but the knowledge must be obtained in such a way as could not harm him. This necessitated diplomacy, which was foreign to her nature, and patience, in which womanly quality she excelled. She had learnt patience in her tender ministrations to a fretful invalid, during those sad slow years in which pretty Mrs Fausset had faded into the grave. Yes, she had learnt to be patient, and to submit to sorrow. She knew how to wait.

The place, delightful as it was in the early spring weather, possessed no charms for her. Its gaiety and movement jarred upon her. The sunsets were as lovely here as at Pallanza, and her only pleasure was to watch that ever-varying splendour of declining day behind the long dark promontory of Antibes; or to see the morning dawn in a flush of colour above the white lighthouse yonder at the point of the peninsula of St Jean. It was in the village of St Jean that George Greswold had lived with his first wife – with Fay. The bright face, pale, yet brilliant, a face in which light took the place of colour; the eager eyes; the small sharp features and thin sarcastic lips, rose up before her with the thought of that union. He must have loved her. She was so bright, so interesting, so full of vivid fancies and changeful emotions. To this hour Mildred remembered her fascination, her power over a child's heart.

Pamela was dull and out of spirits. Not all the Tauchnitz novels in Galignani's shop could interest her. She pronounced Nice distinctly inferior to Brighton; declined even the distraction of the opera.

'Music would only make me miserable,' she exclaimed petulantly. 'I wish I might never hear any again. That hateful band in the gardens tortures me every morning.'

This was not hopeful. Mildred was sorry for her, but too deeply absorbed by her own griefs to be altogether sympathetic.

'She will find some one else to admire before long,' she thought somewhat bitterly. 'Girls who fall in love so easily are easily consoled.'

She had been at Nice more than a week, and had made no effort – yearning to know more – to know all – yet dreading every new revelation. She had to goad herself to action, to struggle against the weight of a great fear – the fear that she might find the slanderer's accusations confirmed instead of being refuted.

Her first step was a very simple one, easy enough from a social point of view. Among old Lady Castle-Connell's intimate friends had been a certain Irish chieftain called The O'Labacolly. The O'Labacolly's daughter had been one of the reigning beauties of Dublin Castle, had appeared for three seasons in London with considerable *éclat*, and in due course had married a Scotch peer, who was lord of an extensive territory in the Highlands, strictly entailed, and of a more profitable estate in the neighbourhood of Glasgow at his own disposal. Lord Lochinvar had been laid at rest in the sepulchre of his forebears, and Lady Lochinvar was a rich widow, still handsome, and still young enough to enjoy all the pleasures of society. She had no children of her own, but she had a favourite nephew, whom she had adopted, and who acted as her escort in her travels, which were extensive, and as her steward in the management of the Glasgow property, which had been settled upon her at her marriage. The Highland territory had gone with the title to a distant cousin of Lady Lochinvar's husband.

Mildred remembered that Castellani had spoken of meeting Mr Ransome and his wife at Lady Lochinvar's palace at Nice. Her first step, therefore, was to make herself known to Lady Lochinvar, who had wintered in this fair white city ever since she came there as a young widow twenty years ago, and had bought for herself a fantastic villa, built early in the century by an Italian prince, on the crest of a hill commanding the harbour.

With this view she wrote to Lady Lochinvar, recalling the old friendship between The O'Labacolly and Lady Castle-Connell, and introducing herself on the strength of that friendship. Lady Lochinvar responded with Hibernian warmth. She called at the Hôtel Westminster that afternoon, and not finding Mrs Greswold at home, left a note inviting her to lunch at the Palais Montano next day.

Mildred promptly accepted the invitation. She was anxious to be alone with Lady Lochinvar, and there seemed a better chance of a *tête-à tête* at the lady's house than at the hotel, where it would have been difficult to exclude Pamela. She drove to that fair hill on the eastward side of the city, turning her back upon the quaint old Italian town, with its narrow streets of tall white houses with red roofs, and its Cathedral dome embedded in the midst, the red and yellow tiles glistening in the sunlight. The two small horses toiled slowly up the height with the great lumbering landau, carrying Mildred nearer and nearer to the bright blue sky and the snow-line glittering on the edge of the distant hills. They went past villas and flower-gardens, hedges of yellow roses and hedges of coral-hued geranium, cactus and agave, palms and orange-trees, shining majolica tubs and white marble balustrades, statues and fountains, oriel windows and Italian cupolas, turrets and towers of every order; while the sapphire sea dropped lower and lower beneath the chalky winding road, as the jutting promontory that shelters Villefranche from the east came nearer and nearer above the blue.

The Italian prince who built the Palais Montano had aspired after Oriental rather than classic beauty. His house was long and low, with two ranges of Moorish windows, and a dome at each end. There was an open loggia on the first floor, with a balustrade of white and coloured marble; there was a gallery above the spacious tesselated hall, screened by carved sandal-wood lattices, behind which the beauties of a harem might be supposed to watch the entrances and exits below. The house was fantastic, but fascinating. The garden was the growth of more than half a century, and was supremely beautiful.

Lady Lochinvar received the stranger with a cordiality which would have set Mildred thoroughly at her ease under happier circumstances. As it was, she was too completely engrossed by the object of her visit to feel any of that shyness which a person of retiring disposition might experience on such an occasion. She was grave and preoccupied, and it was with an effort that she responded to Lady Lochinvar's allusions to the past.

'Your mother and I were girls together,' said the Dowager, 'at dear old Castle-Connell. My father's place was within a drive of the Castle, but away from the river, and one of my first pleasant memories is of your grandfather's gardens and the broad, bright Shannon. What a river! When I look at our stony torrent-beds here, and remember that glorious Shannon!'

'Yet you like Nice better than county Limerick?'

'Of course I do, my dear Mrs Greswold. Ireland is a delicious country – to remember. I saw a good deal of your mother in London before his lordship's death, but after I became a widow, I went very little into English society. I had found English people so narrow-minded. I only endured them for Lochinvar's sake; and after his death I became a rover. I have an apartment in the Champs Elysées and a *pied-à-terre* in Rome; and now and then, when I want to drink a draught of commonplace, when I want to know what the hard-headed, practical British intellect is making of the world in general, I give myself a fortnight at Claridge's. A fortnight is always enough. So, you see, I have had no opportunity of looking up old friends.'

'I never remember seeing you in Upper Parchment Street,' said Mildred.

'My dear, you were a baby at the time I knew your mother. I think you were just able to toddle across the drawing-room the day I bade her good-bye, before I went to Scotland with Lochinvar – our last journey, poor dear man. He died the following winter.'

The butler announced luncheon, and they went into an ideal dining-room, purely Oriental, with hangings of a dull pale pink damask interwoven with lustreless gold, its only ornaments old Rhodes salvers shining with prismatic hues, its furniture of cedar inlaid with ivory.

'I am quite alone to-day,' said Lady Lochinvar. 'My nephew is driving to Monte Carlo by the Cornice, and will not be back till dinner-time.'

'I am very glad to be alone with you, Lady Lochinvar. I feel myself bound to tell you that I had an *arrière-pensée* in seeking your acquaintance, pleasant as it is to me to meet any friend of my mother's youth.'

Lady Lochinvar looked surprised, and even a little suspicious. She began to fear some uncomfortable story. This sad-looking woman – such a beautiful face, but with such unmistakable signs of unhappiness. A runaway wife, perhaps; a poor creature who had fallen into disgrace, and who wanted Lady Lochinvar's help to regain her position, or face her calumniators. Some awkward business, no doubt. Lady Lochinvar was generous to a fault, but she liked showing kindness to happy people, she wanted smiling faces and serenity about her. She had never known any troubles of her own, worse than losing the husband whom she had married for his wealth and position, and saw no reason why she should be plagued with the troubles of other people. Her handsome countenance hardened ever so little as she answered.

'If there is any small matter in which I can be of service to you——' she began.

'It is not a small matter; it is a great matter – to – to a friend of mine,' interrupted Mildred, faltering a little in her first attempt at dissimulation.

Lady Lochinvar breathed more freely.

'I shall be charmed to help your friend if I can.'

The butler came in and out, assisted by another servant, as the conversation went on; but as his mistress spoke to him and to his subordinate only in Italian, Mildred concluded they understood very little English, and did not concern herself about their presence.

'I want you to help me with your recollection of the past, Lady Lochinvar. You were at Nice seventeen years ago, I believe?'

'Between November and April, yes. I have spent those months here for the last twenty years.'

'You remember a Mr Ransome and his wife, seventeen years ago?'

'Yes, I remember them distinctly. I cannot help remembering them.'

'Have you ever met Mr Ransome since that time?'

'Never.'

'And you have not heard anything about him?'

'No, I have never heard of him since he left the asylum on the road to St André. Good heavens, Mrs Greswold, how white you have turned! Pietro, some brandy this moment——'

'No, no! I am quite well – only a little shocked, that is all. I had heard that Mr Ransome was out of his mind at one time, but I did not believe my informant. It is really true, then? He was once mad?'

'Yes, he was mad; unless it was all a sham, a clever assumption.'

'Why should he have assumed madness?'

Lady Lochinvar shrugged her portly shoulders, and lifted her finely-arched eyebrows with a little foreign air which had grown upon her in foreign society.

'To escape from a very awkward dilemma. He was arrested on suspicion of having killed his wife. The evidence against him was weak, but the circumstances of the poor thing's death were very suspicious.'

'How did she die?'

'She threw herself – or she was thrown – from a cliff on the other side of the promontory which you may see from that window.'

Mildred was silent for some moments, while her breath came and went in hurried gasps.

'Might she not have fallen accidentally?' she faltered.

'That would have been hardly possible. It was a place where she had been in the habit of walking for weeks – a path which anybody might walk upon in the daylight without the slightest danger. And the calamity happened in broad day. She could not have fallen accidentally. Either she threw herself over, or he pushed her over in a moment of ungovernable anger. She was a very provoking woman, and had a tongue which might goad a man to fury I saw a good deal of her the winter before her death. She was remarkably clever, and she amused me. I had a kind of liking for her, and I used to let her tell me her troubles.'

'What kind of troubles?'

'O, they all began and ended in one subject. She was jealous, intolerably jealous, of her husband; suspected him of inconstancy to herself if he was commonly civil to a handsome woman. She watched him like a lynx, and did her utmost to make his life a burden to him, yet loved him passionately all the time in her vehement, wrong-headed manner.'

'Poor girl! poor girl!' murmured Mildred, with a stifled sob, and then she asked with intense earnestness, 'but, Lady Lochinvar, you who knew George Ransome, surely *you* never suspected him of murder?'

'I don't know, Mrs Greswold. I believe he was a gentleman, and a man of an open, generous nature; but, upon my word, I should be sorry to pledge myself to a positive belief in his innocence as to his wife's death. Who can tell what a man might do, harassed and tormented as that man may have been by that woman's tongue? I know what pestilential things she could say – what scorpions and adders dropped out of her mouth when she was in her jealous fits – and she may have gone just one step too far – walking by his side upon that narrow path – and he may have turned upon her, exasperated to madness, and – one push – and the thing was done. The edge of a cliff must be an awful temptation under such circumstances,' added Lady Lochinvar solemnly. 'I am sure I would not answer for myself in such a situation.'

'I will answer for *him*,' said Mildred firmly.

'You know him, then?'

'Yes, I know him.'

'Where is he? What is he doing? Has he prospered in life?'

'Yes, and no. He was a happy man – or seemed to be happy – for thirteen years of married life; and then God's hand was stretched out to afflict him, and his only child was snatched away.'

'He married again, then?'

'Yes, he married a second wife fourteen years ago. Forgive me, Lady Lochinvar, for having suppressed the truth till now. I wanted you to answer me more freely than you might have done had you known all. George Ransome is my husband; he assumed the name of Greswold when he succeeded to his mother's property.'

'Then Mr Greswold, your husband, is my old acquaintance. Is he with you here?'

'No. I have left him – perhaps for ever.'

'On account of that past story?'

'No, for another reason, which is my sad secret, and his – a family secret. It involves no blame to him or me. It is a dismal fatality which parts us. You cannot suppose, Lady Lochinvar, that *I* could think my husband a murderer?'

'A murderer? No! I do not believe any one ever thought him guilty of deliberate murder – but that he lost his temper with that unhappy girl, spurned her from him, flung her over the edge of the cliff——'

'O, no, no, no! it is not possible! I know him too well. He is not capable of a brutal act even under the utmost exasperation. No irritation, no sense of injury, could bring about such a change in his nature. Think, Lady Lochinvar. I have been his wife for fourteen years. I must know what his character is like.'

'You know what he is in happy circumstances, with an attached and confiding wife. You cannot imagine him goaded to madness by an unreasonable, hot-headed woman. You remember he was mad for half a year after his wife's death. There must have been some sufficient reason for his madness.'

'His wife's wretched death, and the fact that he was accused of having murdered her, were enough to make him mad.'

And then Mildred remembered how she had tortured her husband by her persistent questions about that terrible past; how, in her jealousy of an unknown rival, she, too, had goaded him almost as that first wife had goaded him. She recalled the look of pain, the mute protest against her cruelty, and she hated herself for the selfishness of her love.

Lady Lochinvar was kind and sympathetic. She was not angry at the trap that had been set for her.

'I can understand,' she said. 'You wanted to know the worst, and you felt that I should be reticent if I knew you were Mr Ransome's wife. Well, I have said all the evil I can say about him. Remember I know nothing except what other people thought and suspected. There was an inquiry about the poor thing's death before the Juge d'Instruction at Villefranche, and Mr Ransome was kept in prison between the first and second inquiry, and then it was discovered that the poor fellow had gone off his head, and he was taken to the asylum. He had no relations in the neighbourhood, nobody interested in looking after him. His acquaintances in Nice knew very little about him or his wife, even when they were living at an hotel on the Promenade des Anglais and going into society. After they left Nice they lived in seclusion at St Jean, and avoided all their acquaintance. Mrs Ransome's health was a reason for retirement; but it may not have been the only reason. There was no one, therefore, to look after the poor man in his misfortunes. He was just hustled away to the madhouse – the inquiry fell through for want of evidence – and for six months George Ransome was buried alive. I was in Paris at the time, and only heard the story when I came back to Nice in the following November. Nobody could tell me what had become of Mr Ransome, and it was only by accident that I heard of his confinement in the asylum some time after he had been released as a sane man.'

'Did his wife ever talk to you of her own history?'

'Never. She was very fond of talking to me about her husband's supposed inconstancy and the mistake she had made in marrying a man who had never cared for her; but about her own people and her own antecedents she was silent as the grave. In a place like Nice, where everybody is idle, there is sure to be a good deal of gossip, and we all had our own ideas about Mrs Ransome. We put her down as the natural daughter of some person of importance, or, at any rate, of good means. She had her own fortune, and was entirely independent of her husband, who was not a rich man at that time.'

'No, it was his mother's death that made him rich. But you did not think he had married for money?'

'No; our theory was that he had been worried into marrying her. We thought the lady had thrown herself at his head, and that all her unhappiness sprang from her knowledge that she had in a measure forced him to marry her.'

'Do you remember the name of the house at St Jean where they lived when they left Nice?'

'Yes, I called there once, but as Mrs Ransome never returned my call, I concluded that they wished to drop their Nice acquaintance, and I heard afterwards that they were living like hermits in a cave. The house is a low white villa, spread out along the edge of a grassy ridge, with a broad stone terrace on one side and a garden and orchard on the other. It is called Le Bout du Monde.'

'I am very grateful to you, Lady Lochinvar, for having been frank with me. I will go and look at the house where they lived. I may find some one, perhaps, who knew them.'

'You want to make further inquiries?'

'I want to find some one who is as convinced of my husband's guiltlessness as I am.'

'That will be difficult. There was very little evidence for or against him. The husband and wife went out to walk together one April afternoon. They left the house in peace and amity, as it seemed to their servants; but some ladies who met and talked to them an hour afterwards thought by Mrs Ransome's manner that she was on bad terms with her husband. When she was next seen she was lying at the foot of a cliff, dead. That is all that is known of the tragedy. You could hardly hang a man or acquit him upon such evidence. It is a case of not proven.'

CHAPTER IX

LOOKING BACK

Lady Lochinvar offered to drive Mrs Greswold to St Jean that afternoon. Her villa was half-way between Nice and Villefranche, and half-an-hour's drive would have taken them to the Bout du Monde; but Mildred preferred to make her explorations alone. There was too much heart-ache in such an investigation to admit of sympathy or companionship.

'You are all goodness to me, dear Lady Lochinvar,' she said, 'and I may come to you again for help before I have done; but I would rather visit the scene of my husband's tragedy alone – quite alone. You cannot tell how sad the story is to me, even apart from my love for him. I may be able to confide in you more fully some day, perhaps.'

Lady Lochinvar kissed her at parting. She did not care for commonplace troubles; she could not sympathise with stupid family quarrels or shortness of money, or any of the vulgar trivialities about which people worry their friends; but a romantic sorrow, a tragedy with a touch of mystery in it, was full of interest for her. And then, Mildred was a graceful sufferer, not hysterical or tiresome in any way.

'I will do anything in the world that I can for you,' she said.

'Will you let me bring my husband's niece to see you?' asked Mildred. 'She has a dull time with me, poor girl, and I think you would like her.'

'She shall come to me this evening, if she has nothing better to do,' said Lady Lochinvar. 'I am fond of young people, and will do my best to amuse her. I will send my carriage for her at half-past seven.'

'That is more than kind. I shall be glad for the poor girl to get a glimpse of something brighter than our perpetual *tête-à-tête*. But there is one thing I ought to speak about before you see her. I think you know something of an Italian called Castellani, a man who is both musical and literary.'

'Yes, I have heard of Mr Castellani's growing fame. He is the author of that delightful story *Nepenthe*, is he not? I knew him years ago – it was in the same winter we have been talking about. He used to come to my parties. Do you know him?'

'He has been a visitor at Enderby – my husband's house – and I have seen something of him in Italy of late. I am sorry to say he has made a very strong impression upon my niece's heart – or upon her imagination – but as I know him to be a worthless person, I am deeply anxious that her liking for him should——'

'Die a natural death. I understand,' interrupted Lady Lochinvar. 'You may be sure I will not encourage the young lady to talk about Mr Castellani.'

Mildred explained her responsibility with regard to Pamela and the young lady's position, with its substantial attraction for the adventurer in search of a wife. She had deemed it her duty to confide thus much in Lady Lochinvar, lest Castellani should change his tactics, and pursue Pamela with addresses which might be only too readily accepted.

She left the Palais Montano at two o'clock, and drove round the bay to St Jean, where the rose-hedges were in flower, and where the gardens were bright with bloom under a sky which suggested an English June.

She left the fly at the little inn where the holiday people go to eat bouillabaisse on Sundays and fête-days, but which was silent and solitary to-day, and then walked slowly along the winding road, looking for the Bout du Monde. The place was prettier and more rustic, after an almost English fashion, than any spot she had seen since she left Enderby. Villas and cottages were scattered in a desultory way upon different levels, under the shelter of precipitous cliffs, and on every bit of rising ground and in every hollow there were orange and lemon groves, with here and there a peach or a cherry in full bloom, and here and there a vivid patch of flowers, and here and there a wall covered with the glowing purple of the Bougainvilliers. Great carouba-trees rose tall and dark amidst all this brightness, and through every opening in the foliage the changeful colour of the Mediterranean shone in the distance, like the jasper sea of the Apocalypse.

Mildred went slowly along the dusty road, looking at all the villas, lingering here and there at a garden gate, and asking any intelligent-looking person who passed to direct her to the Bout de Monde. It was not till she had made the inquiry half-a-dozen times that she obtained any information; but at last she met with a bright-faced market-woman, tramping home with empty baskets after a long morning at Nice, and white with the dust of the hill-side.

'Le Bout du Monde? But that was the villa where the poor young English lady lived whose husband threw her over the cliff,' said the woman cheerily. 'The proprietor changed the name of the house next season, for fear people should fancy it was haunted if the story got about. It is called Montfleuri now.'

'Is there any one living there?' Mildred asked.

No, it was let last year to an English family. O, but an amiable family, rich, ah, but *richissime*, who had bought flowers in heaps of the speaker. But they had left, *malheureusement*. They had returned to their property near London, a great and stupendous property in a district which the flower-woman described as le Crommu-elle Rodd. There had never been such a family in St Jean – five English servants, three English mees who mounted on horseback daily: a benefaction for the whole village. Now, alas! there was no one living at Montfleuri but an old woman in charge.

'Could you take me to the house?' asked Mildred, opening her purse.

The woman would have been all politeness and good-nature without the stimulant offered by that open purse. She had all the southern kindliness and alacrity to oblige, but when the lady dropped half-a-dozen francs into her broad brown hand she almost sank to the earth in a rapture of gratitude.

'Madame shall see the house from garret to cellar if she wishes,' she exclaimed. 'I know the old woman in charge. She is as deaf as one of those stones yonder,' pointing to a block of blue-gray stone lying amidst the long rank grass upon the shelving ground between the road and the sea; 'but if madame will permit *I* will show her the house. Madame is perhaps interested in the story of that poor lady who was murdered.'

'Why do you say that she was murdered?' asked Mildred indignantly. 'You cannot know.'

The woman shrugged her shoulders with a dubious air.

'*Mais*, madame. Nobody but the good God can know: but most of us thought that the Englishman pushed his wife over the cliff. They did not live happily together. Their cook was a cousin of mine, a young woman who went regularly to confession, and would not have spoken falsely for all the world, and she told me there was great unhappiness between them. The wife was often in tears; the husband was often angry.'

'But he was never unkind. Your cousin must know that he was never unkind.'

'Alas! my cousin lies in the same burial-ground yonder with the poor lady,' answered the woman, pointing to the white crest of the hill above Villefranche, where the soldiers were being drilled in the dusty barrack-yard under the cloudless blue. 'She is no more here to tell the story. But no, she did not say the husband was unkind; he was grave and sad; he was not happy. Tears, tears and reproaches, sad words from her, day after day; and from him silence and gloom. Poor people like us, who work for our bread, have no leisure for that kind of unhappiness. "I would rather stand over my *casseroles* than sit in a *salon* and cry," said my cousin.'

'It is cruel to say he caused her death, when you know he was never unkind to her,' said Mildred, as they walked side by side; 'a patient, forbearing husband does not become a murderer all at once.'

'Ah, but continual dropping will wear a stone, madame. She may have tried him too much with her tears. He went out of his mind after her death. Would he have gone mad, do you think, if he had not been guilty?'

'He was all the more likely to go mad, knowing himself innocent, and finding himself accused of a dreadful crime.'

'Well, I cannot tell; I know most of us thought he had pushed her over the cliff. I know the young man who was their gardener said if he had had a wife with that kind of temper he would have thrown her down the well in his garden.'

They were at the Villa Montfleuri by this time, a long, low white house, with a stone terrace over-looking the harbour of Villefranche. The woman opened the gate, and Mildred followed her into the garden and to the terrace upon which the principal rooms opened. There was a latticed verandah in front of the *salon* and dining-room, over which roses and geraniums were trained, and above which the purple Bougainvilliers spread its vivid bloom. The orange-trees grew thick in the orchard, and in their midst stood the stone well down which the gardener said he would have thrown a discontented wife.

The caretaker was not in the house, but all the doors were open. Mildred went from room to room. The furniture was the same as it had been seventeen years ago, the woman told Mildred – furniture of the period of the First Empire, shabby, and with the air of a house that is let to strangers year after year, and in which nobody takes any interest. The clocks on the mantelpieces were all silent, the vases were all empty: everything had a dead look. Only the view from the windows was beautiful with an inexhaustible beauty.

Mildred lingered in the faded *salon*, looking at everything with a melancholy interest. Those two familiar figures were with her in the room. She pictured them sitting there together, yet so far apart in the bitter lack of sympathy – a wife, tormented by jealous suspicions, no less agonising because they were groundless; a husband, long-suffering, weary, with his little stock of marital love worn out under slow torture. She could see them as they might have been in those bygone years. George Greswold's dark, strong face, younger than she had ever known it; for when he first came to her father's house there had been threads of gray in his dark hair and premature lines upon the brow which told of corroding care. She could understand now how those touches of gray had come in the thick wavy hair that clustered close on the broad, strongly-marked brow.

Poor Fay! poor, loving, impulsive Fay!

Child as she had been in those old days in Parchment Street, Mildred had a vivid conception of her young companion's character. She remembered the quick temper, the sensitive self-esteem, which had taken offence of the mere suggestion of slight; she remembered dark hours of brooding melancholy when the girl had felt the sting of her isolated position, had fancied herself a creature apart, neglected and scorned by Mrs Fausset and her butterfly visitors. For Mildred she had been always overflowing with love, and she had never doubted the sincerity of Mildred's affection; but with all the rest of the household, with every visitor who noticed her coldly, or frankly ignored her, she was on the alert for insult and offence. Remembering all this, Mildred could fully realise Lady Lochinvar's account of that unhappy union. A woman so constituted would be satisfied with nothing less than a passionate, all-absorbing love from the man she loved.

The rooms and the garden were haunted by those mournful shades – two faces pale with pain. She, too, had suffered those sharp stings of jealousy; jealousy of a past love, jealousy of the dead; and she knew how keener than all common anguish is that agony of a woman's heart which yearns for sovereign possession over past, present, and future in the life of the man she loves.

The market-woman sat out in the sunshine on the terrace, and waited while Mildred roamed about the garden, picturing that vanished life at every step. There was the *berceau*, the delight of a southern garden, a long, green alley, arched with osiers, over which the brown vine-branches made a network, open to the sunlight and the blue sky now, while the vine was still leafless, but in summer-time a place of coolness and whispering leaves. There was the fountain – or the place where a fountain had once been, and a stone bench beside it. They had sat there perhaps on sunny mornings, sat there and talked of their future, full of hope. They could not have been always unhappy. Fay must have had her bright hours; and then, no doubt, she was dear to him, full of a strange fascination, a creature of quick wit and vivid imagination, light and fire embodied in a fragile earthly tenement.

The sun was nearing the dark edge of the promontory when Mildred left the garden, the woman accompanying her, waiting upon her footsteps, sympathising with her pensive mood, with that instinctive politeness of the southern, which is almost as great a delight to the stranger from the hard, cold, practical north, as the colour of the southern sea, or the ever-varying beauty of the hills.

'Will you show me the place where the English lady fell over the cliff?' Mildred asked; and the woman went with her along the winding road, and then upward to a path along the crest of a cliff, a cliff that seemed low on account of those bolder heights which rose above it, and which screened this eastward-fronting shore of the little peninsula from all the world of the west. The carriage-road wound southward up to the higher ground, but Mildred and her guide followed a footpath which had been trodden on the long rank grass beside the cliff. The rosemary bushes were full of flower: pale, cold gray blossoms, as befitted the herb of death, and a great yellow weed made patches of vivid colour among the blue-gray stones scattered in the long grass on the slope of the hill.

'It was somewhere along this pathway, madame,' said the woman. 'I cannot tell you the exact spot. Some fishermen from Beaulieu picked her up,' pointing across the blue water of the bay to a semicircle of yellow sand, with a few white houses scattered along the curving road, and some boats lying keel upward on the beach. 'She never spoke again. She was dead when they found her there.'

'Did they see her fall?'

'No, madame.'

'And yet people have dared to call her husband a murderer.'

'Ah, but, madame, it was the general opinion. Was it not his guilty conscience that drove him mad? He came here once only after he left the madhouse, wandered about the village for an hour or two, went up to the cemetery and looked once – but once only – at the poor lady's grave, and then drove away as if devils were hunting him. Who can doubt that it was his hand that sent her to her death?'

'No one would believe it who knew him.'

'Everybody at St Jean believed it, even the people who liked him best.'

Mildred turned from her sick at heart. She gave the woman some more money, and then with briefest adieu walked back to the inn where she had left the carriage, and where the horse was dozing with his nose in a bag of dried locust fruit, while his driver sprawled half asleep upon the rough stone parapet between the inn and the bay.

Pamela received her aunt graciously on her return to the hotel, and seemed in better spirits than she had been since she left Pallanza.

'Your Lady Lochinvar has written me the sweetest little note, asking me to dine with her and go to the opera afterwards,' she said. 'I feel sure this must be your doing, aunt.'

'No, dear. I only told her that I had a very nice niece moping at the hotel, and very tired of my dismal company.'

'Tired of you? No, no, aunt. You know better than that. I should no more grow tired of you than I should of Box,' intending to make the most flattering comparison; 'only he had made himself a part of our lives at Pallanza, don't you know, and one could not help missing him.' (The pronoun meant Castellani, and not the dog.) 'I am glad I am going to the opera after all, even if it does remind me of him; and it's awfully kind of Lady Lochinvar to send her carriage for me. I only waited to see you before I began to dress.'

'Go, dearest; and take care to look your prettiest.'

'And you won't mind dining alone?'

'I shall be delighted to know you are enjoying yourself.'

The prospect of an evening's solitude was an infinite relief to Mildred. She breathed more freely when Pamela had gone dancing off to the lift, a fluffy, feathery mass of whiteness, with hooded head and rosy face peeping from a border of white fox. The tall door of the *salon* closed upon her with a solemn reverberation, and Mildred was alone with her own thoughts, alone with the history of her husband's past life, now that she had unravelled the tangled skein and knew all.

She was face to face with the past, and how did it seem in her eyes? Was there no doubt, no agonising fear that the man she had loved as a husband might have slain the girl she had loved as a sister? All those people, those simple and disinterested villagers, who had liked George Ransome well enough for his own sake, had yet believed him guilty: they who had been on the spot, and had had the best opportunities for judging the case rightly.

Could she doubt him, she who had seen honour and fine feeling in every act of his life? She remembered the dream – that terrible dream which had occurred at intervals; sometimes once in a year; sometimes oftener; that awe-inspiring dream which had shaken the dreamer's nerves as nothing but a vision of horror could have shaken them, from which he had awakened more dead than alive, completely unnerved, cold drops upon his pallid brow, his hands convulsed and icy, his eyes glassy as death itself. The horror of that dream even to her, who beheld its effect on the dreamer, was a horror not to be forgotten.

Was it the dream of a murderer, acting his crime over again in that dim world of sleep, living over again the moment of his temptation and his fall? No, no! Another might so interpret the vision, but not his wife.

'I know him,' she repeated to herself passionately; 'I know him. I know his noble heart. He is incapable of one cruel impulse. He could not have done such a deed. There is no possible state of feeling, no moment of frenzy, in which he would have been false to his character and his manhood.'

And then she asked herself if Fay had not been her sister, if there had not been that insurmountable bar to her union with George Greswold, would her knowledge of his first wife's fate, and the suspicion that had darkened his name, have sufficed to part them? Could she, knowing what she now knew, knowing that he had been so suspected, knowing that it was beyond his power ever to *prove* his guiltlessness – could she have gone through the rest of her life with him, honouring him and trusting him as she had done in the years that were gone?

She told herself that she could have so trusted him; that she could have honoured and loved him to the end, pitying him for those dark experiences, but with faith unshaken.

'A murderer and a madman,' she said to herself, repeating Castellani's calumny. 'Murderer I would never believe him; and shall I honour him less because that sensitive mind was plunged in darkness by the horror of his wife's fate?'

Pamela came home before midnight. Lady Lochinvar had driven her to the door. She was in high spirits, and charmed with her ladyship, and thought her ladyship's nephew, Mr Stuart, late of a famous Highland regiment, a rather agreeable person.

'He is decidedly plain,' said Pamela, 'and looks about as intellectual as Sir Henry Mountford, and he evidently doesn't care a jot for music; but he has very pleasant manners, and he told me a lot about Monte Carlo. A brother officer of his, bronchial, with a very nice wife, came to Lady Lochinvar's box in the evening, and she is going to call for me to-morrow afternoon, to take me to the tennis-ground at the Cercle de la Méditerranée, if you don't mind.'

'My dearest, you know I wish only to see you happy and with nice people. I suppose this lady, whose name you have not told me——'

'Mrs Murray. She is very Scotch, but quite charming – nothing fast or rowdy about her – and devoted to her invalid husband. He does not play tennis, poor fellow, but he sits in the sun and looks on, which is very nice for him.'

Mrs Murray made her appearance at two o'clock next day, and Mildred was pleased to find that Pamela had not exaggerated her merits. She was very Scotch, and talked of Lady Lochinvar as 'a purpose woman,' with a Caledonian roll of the *r* in purpose which emphasised the word in its adjectival sense. She had very pretty simple manners, and was altogether the kind of young matron with whom a feather-headed girl might be trusted.

Directly Pamela and her new friend had departed Mildred put on her bonnet, and went out on foot. She had made certain inquiries through Albrecht, and she knew the way she had to go upon the pilgrimage on which she was bent, a pilgrimage of sorrowful memory. There was a relief in being quite alone upon the long parade between the palm-trees and the sea, and to know that she was free from notice and sympathy for the rest of the afternoon.

She walked to the Place Massena, and there accepted the beseeching offers of one of the numerous flymen, and took her seat in a light victoria behind a horse which looked a little better fed than his neighbours. She told the man to drive along the west bank of the Paillon, on the road to St André.

Would not Madame go to St André, and see the wonderful grotto, and the petrifactions?

No, Madame did not wish to go so far as St André. She would tell the drive where to stop.

The horse rattled off at a brisk pace. They are no crawlers, those flys of the South. They drove past the smart shops and hotels on the quay; past the shabby old inn where the diligences put up, a hostelry with suggestions of the past, when the old Italian town was not a winter rendezvous for all the nations, the beaten track of Yankee and Cockney, *calicot* and counter-jumper, Russian prince and Hebrew capitalist, millionaire and adventurer. They drove past the shabby purlieus of the town, workmen's lodging-houses, sordid-looking shops, then an orange-garden here and there within crumbling plaster walls, and here and there a tavern in a shabby garden. To the left of the river, on a sharp pinnacle of hill, stood the Monastery of Cimies, with dome and tower dominating the landscape. Further away, on the other side of the stony torrent-bed, rose the rugged chain of hills stretching away to Mentone and the Italian frontier, and high up against the blue sky glimmered the white domes of the Observatory. They came by and by to a spot where, by the side of the broad high-road, there was a wall enclosing a white dusty yard, and behind it a long white house with many windows, bare and barren, staring blankly at the dry bed of the torrent and the rugged brown hills beyond. At each end of the long white building there was a colonnade with iron bars, open to the sun and the air, and as Mrs Greswold's carriage drew near a man's voice rolled out the opening bars of 'Ah, che la morte!' in a tremendous baritone. A cluster of idlers had congregated about the open gate, to stare and listen; for the great white house was a madhouse, and the grated colonnades right and left of the long façade were the recreation-grounds of the insane – of those worst patients who could not be trusted to wander at their ease in the garden, or to dig and delve upon the breezy hills towards St André.

Mildred visits Madhouse.

The singer was a fine-looking man, dressed in loose garments of some white material, and with long white gloves. He flung himself on to an upper bar of the grating with the air of an athlete, and hung upon the bars with his gloved hands, facing that cluster of loafers as if they had been an audience in a theatre, and singing with all the power of a herculean physique. Mildred told her driver to stop at the gate, and she sat listening while the madman sang, in fitful snatches of a few bars at a time, but with never a false note.

That cage, and the patients pacing up and down, or hanging on to the bars, or standing staring at the little crowd round the gate, moved her to deepest pity, touched her with keenest pain. He had been here, her beloved, in that brief interval of darkest night. She recalled how in one of his awakenings from that torturing dream he had spoken words of strange meaning – or of no meaning, as they had seemed to her then.

'The cage – the cage again!' he had cried in an agonised voice; 'iron bars – like a wild beast!'

These words had been an enigma to her then. She saw the answer to the riddle *here*.

She sat for some time watching that sad spectacle, hearing those broken snatches of song, with intervals of silence, or sometimes a wild peal of laughter.

The loiterers were full of speculations and assertions. The porter at the gate answered some questions, turned a deaf ear to others.

The singer was a Spanish nobleman who had lost a fortune at Monte Carlo the night before, and had been brought here bound hand and foot at early morning. He had tried to kill himself, and now he imagined himself a famous singer, and that the barred colonnade was the stage of the Grand Opéra at Paris.

'He'll soon be all right again,' said the porter with a careless shrug; 'those violent cases mend quickly.'

'But he won't get his money back again, poor devil,' said one of the loiterers, a flyman whose vehicle was standing by the wall, waiting for a customer. 'Hard to recover his senses and find himself without a sou.'

'O, he has rich friends, no doubt. Look at his white kid gloves. He is young and handsome, and he has a splendid voice. Somebody will take care of him. Do you see that old woman sitting over there in the garden? You would not think there was anything amiss with her, would you? No more there is, only she thinks she is the Blessed Virgin. She has been here five-and-thirty years. Nobody pities *her* – nobody inquires about *her*. My father remembers her when she was a handsome young woman at a flower-shop on the Quai Massena, one of the merriest girls in Nice. Somebody told her she was neglecting her soul and going to hell. This set her thinking too much. She used to be at the Cathedral all day, and at confession as often as the priest would hear her. She neglected her shop, and quarrelled with her mother and sisters. She said she had a vocation; and then one fine day she walked to the Cathedral in a white veil, with a bunch of lilies in her hand, and she told all the people she met that they ought to kneel before her and make the sign of the cross, for she was the Mother of God. Three days afterwards her people brought her here. She would neither eat nor drink, and she never closed her eyes, or left off talking about her glorious mission, which was to work the redemption of all the women upon earth.'

'Drive on to the doctor's house,' Mildred said presently; and the fly went on a few hundred yards, and then drew up at the door of a private house, which marked the boundary of the asylum garden.

Mrs Greswold had inquired the name of the doctor of longest experience in the asylum, and she had been referred to Monsieur Leroy, the inhabitant of this house, where the flyman informed her some of the more wealthy patients were lodged. She had come prepared with a little note requesting the favour of an interview, and enclosing her card, with the address of Enderby Manor as well as her hotel in Nice. The English manor and the Hôtel Westminster indicated at least respectability in the applicant; and Monsieur Leroy's reception was both prompt and courteous.

He was a clever-looking man, about sixty years of age, with a fine benevolent head, and an attentive eye, as of one always on the alert. He had spent five-and-thirty of his sixty years in the society of the deranged, and had devoted all his intellectual power to the study of mental disease.

After briefest preliminary courtesies, Mildred explained the purpose of her visit.

'I am anxious to learn anything you can tell me about a patient who was under your care – or, at least, in this establishment – seventeen years ago, and in whom I am deeply interested,' she said.

'Seventeen years is a long time, madame, but I have a good memory, and I keep notes of all my cases. I may be able to satisfy your curiosity in some measure. What was the name of this patient?'

'He was an Englishman called Ransome – George Ransome. He was placed here under peculiar circumstances.'

'*Corpo di Bacco!* I should say they were peculiar, very peculiar circumstances!' exclaimed the doctor. 'Do you know, madame, that Mr Ransome came here as a suspected murderer? He came straight from the gaol at Villefranche, where he had been detained on the suspicion of having killed his wife.'

'There was not one jot of evidence to support such a charge. I know all the circumstances. Surely, sir, you, who must have a wide knowledge of human nature, did not think him guilty?'

'I hardly made up my mind upon that point, even after I had seen him almost every day for six months; but there is one thing I do know about this unhappy gentleman: his lunacy was no assumption, put on to save him from the consequences of a crime. He was a man of noble intellect, large brain-power, and for the time being his reason was totally obscured.'

'To what cause did you attribute the attack?'

'A long period of worry, nerves completely shattered, and finally the shock of that catastrophe on the cliff. Whether his hand pushed her to her death, or the woman flung her life away, the shock was too much for Mr Ransome's weakened and worried brain. All the indications of his malady, from the most violent stages to the gradual progress of recovery, pointed to the same conclusion. The history of the case revealed its cause and its earlier phases: an unhappy marriage, a jealous wife, patience and forebearance on his part, until patience degenerated into despair, the dully apathy of a wearied intellect. All that is easy to understand.'

'You pitied him, then, monsieur?'

'Madame, I pity all my patients; but I found in Mr Ransome a man of exceptional characteristics, and his case interested me deeply.'

'You would not have been interested had you believed him guilty?'

'Pardon me, madame, crime is full of interest for the pathologist. The idea that this gentleman might have spurned his wife from him in a moment of aberration would not have lessened my interest in his mental condition. But although I have never made my mind upon the question of his guilt or innocence, I am bound to tell you, since you seem even painfully interested in his history, that his conduct after his recovery indicated an open and generous nature, a mind of peculiar refinement, and a great deal of chivalrous feeling. I had many conversations with him during the period of returning reason, and I formed a high opinion of his moral character.'

'Did other people think him guilty – the people he had known in Nice, for instance?'

'I fancy there were very few who thought much about him,' answered the doctor. 'Luckily for him and his belongings – whoever they might be – he had dropped out of society for some time before the catastrophe, and he had never been a person of importance in Nice. He had not occupied a villa, or given parties. He lived with his wife at an hotel, and the man who lives at an hotel counts for very little on the Riviera. He is only a casual visitor, who may come and go as he pleases. His movements – unless he has rank or fashion or inordinate wealth to recommend him – excite no interest. He is not a personage. Hence there was very little talk about the lamentable end of Mr Ransome's married life. There were hardly half-a-dozen paragraphs in our local papers, all told; and I doubt if those were quoted in the *Figaro* or *Galignani*. My patient might congratulate himself upon his obscurity.'

'Did no one from England visit him during his confinement here?'

'No one. The local authorities looked after his interest so far as to take care of the ready money which was found in his house, and which sufficed to pay for the poor lady's funeral and for my patient's expenses, leaving a balance to be handed over to him on his recovery. From the hour he left these gates I never heard from him or of him again; but every new year has brought me an anonymous gift from London, such a gift as only a person of refined taste would choose, and I have attributed those annual greetings to Mr George Ransome.'

'It would be only like him to remember past kindness.'

'You know him well, madame?'

'Very well; so well as to be able to answer with my life for his being incapable of the crime of which even you, who saw so much of him, hesitate to acquit him.'

'It is my misfortune, madame, to have seen the darker sides of the human mind, and to know that in the whitest life there may be one black spot – one moment of sin which stultifies a lifetime of virtue. However, it is possible that your judgment is right in this particular case. Be assured I should be glad to think so, and glad to know that Mr Ransome's after days have been all sunshine.'

A sigh was Mildred's only answer. Monsieur Leroy saw tears in her eyes, and asked no more. He was shrewd enough to guess her connection with his former patient – a second wife, no doubt. No one but a wife would be so intensely interested.

'If there is anything I can do for you, or for my old patient——' he began, seeing that his visitor lingered.

'O, no, there is nothing – except if you would let me see the rooms in which he lived.'

'Assuredly. It is a melancholy pleasure, at best, to recall the sorrows we have outlived, but the association will be less painful in your case since the – friend in whom you are interested was so speedily and so thoroughly restored to mental health. I take it that he has never had a relapse?'

'Never, thank God!'

'It was not likely, from the history of the case.'

He led the way across a vestibule and up-stairs to the second floor, where he showed Mrs Greswold two airy rooms, sitting-room and bedroom communicating, overlooking the valley towards Cimies, with the white-walled convent on the crest of the hill, and the white temples of the dead clustering near it; cross and column, Athenian pediment and Italian cupola, dazzling white against the cloudless blue. The rooms were neatly furnished, and there was every appearance of comfort; no suggestion of Bedlam, padded walls, or strait-waistcoats.

'Had he these rooms all the time?' asked Mildred.

'Not all the time. He was somewhat difficult to deal with during the first few weeks, and he was in the main building, under the care of one of my subordinates, till improvement began. By that time I had grown interested in his case, and took him into my own house.'

'Pray let me see the rooms he occupied at first, monsieur; I want to know all. I want to be able to understand what his life was like in that dark dream.'

She knew now what his own dream meant.

Monsieur Leroy indulged her whim. He took her across the dusty garden to the great white house – a house of many windows and long corridors, airy, bare, hopeless-looking, as it seemed to that sad visitor. She saw the two iron-barred enclosures, and the restless creatures roaming about them, clinging to the bars, climbing like monkeys from perch to perch, hanging from the trapeze. The Spaniard had left off singing.

She was shown George Ransome's room, which was empty. The bare whitewashed walls chilled her as if she had gone into an ice-vault. Here on everything there was the stamp of a State prison – iron bars, white walls, a deadly monotony. She was glad to escape into the open air again, but not until she had knelt for some minutes beside the narrow bed upon which George Ransome had lain seventeen years ago, and thanked God for his restoration of reason, and prayed that his declining days might be blessed. She prayed for him, to whom she might nevermore be the source of happiness, she who until so lately had been his nearest and dearest upon earth.

A law which she recognised as duty had risen up between them, and both must go down to the grave in sadness rather than that law should be broken.

BOOK THE THIRD
ATROPOS; OR THAT WHICH MUST BE

CHAPTER I

A WRECKED LIFE

Monsieur Leroy was interested in his visitor, and in nowise hastened her departure. He led her through the garden of the asylum, anxious that she should see that sad life of the shattered mind in its milder aspect. The quieter patients were allowed to amuse themselves at liberty in the garden, and here Mildred saw the woman who fancied herself the Blessed Virgin, and who sat apart from the rest, with a crown of withered anemones upon her iron-gray locks.

The doctor stopped to talk to her in the Niçois language, describing her hallucination to Mildred in his broken English between whiles.

'She is one of my oldest cases, and mild as a lamb,' he said. 'She is what superstition had made her. She might have been a happy wife as a mother but for that fatal influence. Ah, here comes a lady of a very different temper, and not half so easy a subject!'

A woman of about sixty advanced towards them along the dusty gravel path between the trampled grass and the dust-whitened orange-trees, a woman who carried her head and shoulders with the pride of an empress, and who looked about her with defiant eyes, fanning herself with a large Japanese paper fan as she came along, a fan of vivid scarlet and cheap gilt paper, which seemed to intensify the brightness of her great black eyes, as she waved it to and fro before her haggard face: a woman who must once have been beautiful.

'Would you believe that lady was prima donna at La Scala nearly forty years ago?' asked the doctor, as he and Mildred stood beside the path, watching that strange figure, with its theatrical dignity.

The massive plaits of grizzled black hair were wound, coronet-wise, about the woman's head. Her rusty black velvet gown trailed in the dust, threadbare long ago, almost in tatters to-day: a gown of a strange fashion, which had been worn upon the stage – Leonora's or Lucrezia's gown, perhaps, once upon a time.

At sight of the physician she stopped suddenly, and made him a sweeping curtsy, with all the exaggerated grace of the theatre.

'Do you know if they open this month at the Scala?' she asked, in Italian.

'Indeed, my dear, I have heard nothing of their doings.'

'They might have begun their season with the new year,' she said, with a dictatorial air. 'They always did in my time. Of course you know that they have tried to engage me again. They wanted me for Amina, but I had to remind them that I am not a light soprano. When I reappear it shall be as Lucrezia Borgia. There I stand on my own ground. No one can touch me there.'

She sang the opening bars of Lucrezia's first scena. The once glorious voice was rough and discordant, but there was power in the tones even yet, and real dramatic fire in the midst of exaggeration. Suddenly while she was singing she caught the expression of Mildred's face watching her, and she stopped at a breath, and grasped the stranger by both hands with an excited air.

'That moves you, does it not?' she exclaimed. 'You have a soul for music. I can see that in your face. I should like to know more of you. Come and see me whenever you like, and I will sing to you. The doctor lets me use his piano sometimes, when he is in a good humour.'

'Say rather when you are reasonable, my good Maria,' said Monsieur Leroy, laying a fatherly hand upon her shoulder; 'there are days when you are not to be trusted.'

'I am to be trusted to-day. Let me come to your room and sing to her,' pointing to Mildred with her fan. 'I like her face. She has the eyes and lips that console. Her husband is lucky to have such a wife. Let me sing to her. I want her to understand what kind of woman I am.'

'Would it bore you too much to indulge her, madame?' asked the doctor in an undertone. 'She is a strange creature, and it will wound her if you refuse. She does not often take a fancy to any one; but she frequently takes dislikes, and those are violent.'

'I shall be very happy to hear her,' answered Mildred. 'I am in no hurry to return to Nice.'

The doctor led the way back to his house, the singer talking to Mildred with an excited air as they went, talking of the day when she was first soprano at Milan.

'Everybody envied me my success,' she said. 'There were those who said I owed everything to *him*, that he made my voice and my style. Lies, madame, black and bitter lies. I won all the prizes at the Conservatoire. He was one master among many. I owed him nothing – nothing – nothing!'

She reiterated the word with acrid emphasis, and an angry furl of her fan.

'Ah, now you are beginning the old strain!' said the doctor, with a good-humoured shrug of his shoulders. 'If this goes on there shall be no piano for you to-day. I will have no grievances; grievances are the bane of social intercourse. If you come to my *salon* it must be to sing, not to reopen old sores. We all have our wounds as well as you, signorina, but we keep them covered up.'

'I am dumb,' said the singer meekly.

They went into the doctor's private sitting-room. Three sides of the room were lined with books, chiefly of a professional or scientific character. A cottage piano stood in a recess by the fireplace. The woman flew to the instrument with a rapturous eagerness, and began to play. Her hands were faintly tremulous with excitement, but her touch was that of a master as she played the symphony to the finale of 'La Cenerentola.'

'Has she no piano in her own room?' asked Mildred in a whisper.

'No, poor soul. She is one of our pauper patients. The State provides for her, but it does not give her a private room or a piano. I let her come here two or three times a week for an hour or so, when she is reasonable.'

Mildred wondered if it would be possible for her, as a stranger, to provide a room and a piano for this friendless enthusiast. She would have been glad out of her abundance to have lightened a suffering sister's fate, and she determined to make the proposition to the doctor.

The singer played snatches of familiar music – Rossini, Donizetti, Bellini – operatic airs which Mildred knew by heart. She wandered from one scena to another, and her voice, though it had lost its sweetness and sustaining power, was still brilliantly flexible. She sang with a rapturous unconsciousness of her audience, Mildred and the doctor sitting quietly at each side of the hearth, where a single pine log smouldered on the iron dogs above a heap of white ashes.

Presently the music changed to a gayer, lighter strain, and she began an airy cavatina, all coquetry and grace. That joyous melody was curiously familiar to Mildred's ear.

'Where did I hear that music?' she said aloud. 'It seems as if it were only the other day, and yet it is nearly two years since I was at the opera.'

The singer left the cavatina unfinished, and wandered into another melody.

'Ah, I know now!' exclaimed Mildred; 'that is Paolo Castellani's music!'

The woman started up from the piano as if the name had wounded her.

'Paolo Castellani!' she cried. 'What do you know of Paolo Castellani?'

Dr Leroy went over to her, and laid his hand upon her shoulder heavily.

'Now we are in for a scene,' he muttered to Mildred. 'You have mentioned a most unlucky name.'

'What has she to do with Signor Castellani?'

'He was her cousin. He trained her for the stage, and she was the original in several of his operas. She was his slave, his creature, and lived only to please him. I suppose she expected him to marry her, poor soul; but he knew better than that. He contrived to fascinate a French girl, a consumptive, who was travelling in Italy for her health, with a wealthy father. He married the Frenchwoman; and I believe that marriage broke Maria's heart.'

The singer had seated herself at the piano again, and was playing with rapid and brilliant finger, running up and down the keys in wild excitement. Mildred and the physician were standing by the window, talking in lowered voices, unheeded by Maria Castellani.

'Was it that event which wrecked her mind?' asked Mildred, deeply interested.

'No, it was some years afterwards that her brain gave way. She had a brilliant career before her at the time of Castellani's desertion; and she bore the blow with the courage of a Roman. So long as her voice lasted, and the public were constant to her, she contrived to bear up against that burning sense of wrong which has been the distinguishing note of her mind ever since she came here. But the first breath of failure froze her. She felt her voice decaying while she was comparatively a young woman. Her glass told her that she was losing her beauty, that she was beginning to look old and haggard. Her managers told her more. They gave her the cold shoulder, and put newer singers above her head. Then despair took hold of her; she became gloomy and irritable, difficult and capricious in her dealings with her fellow-artists; and then came the end, and she was brought here. She had saved no money. She had been reckless even beyond the habits of her profession. She was friendless. There was nobody interested in her fate——'

'Not even Signor Castellani?'

'Castellani – Paolo Castellani? *Pas si bête*. The man was a compound of selfishness and treachery. She was not likely to get pity from him. The very fact that he had used her badly made her loathsome to him. I doubt if he ever inquired what became of her. If any one had asked him about her, he would have said that she had dropped through – a worn-out voice, a faded beauty – *que voulez-vous?*'

'She had no other friends – no ties?'

'None. She was an orphan at twelve years old, without a sou. Castellani paid for her education, and traded upon her talent. He trained her to sing in his own operas, and in that light, fanciful music she was at her best; though it is her delusion now that she excelled in the grand style. I believe he absorbed the greater part of her earnings, until they quarrelled. Some time after his marriage there was a kind of reconciliation between them. She appeared in a new opera – his last and worst. Her voice was going, his talent had begun to fail. It was the beginning of the end.'

'Has Signor Castellani's son shown no interest in this poor creature's fate?'

'No; the son lives in England, I believe, for the most part. I doubt if he knows anything about Maria.'

The singer had reverted to that familiar music. She sang the first part of an aria, a melody disguised with over-much fioritura, light, graceful, unmeaning.

'That is in his last opera,' she said, rising from the piano, with a more rational air. 'The opera was almost a failure; but I was applauded to the echo. His genius had forsaken him. Follies, follies, falsehoods, crimes. He could not be true to any one or anything. He was as false to his wife as he had been false to me, and to his proud young English signorina; ah, well! who can doubt that he lied to *her*?'

She fell into a meditative mood, standing by the piano, touching a note now and then.

'Young and handsome and rich. Would she have accepted degradation with open eyes? No, no, no. He lied to her as he had lied to me. He was made up of lies.'

Her eyes grew troubled, and her lips worked convulsively. Again the doctor laid his strong broad hand upon her shoulder.

'Come, Maria,' he said in Italian; 'enough for to-day. Madame has been pleased with your singing.'

'Yes, indeed, signora. You have a noble voice. I should be very glad if I could do anything to be of use to you; if I could contribute to your comfort in any way.'

'O, Maria is happy enough with us, I hope,' said the doctor cheerily. 'We are all fond of her when she is reasonable. But it is time she went to her dinner. *A rivederci, signora.*'

Maria accepted her dismissal with a good grace, saluted Mildred and the doctor with her stage curtsy, and withdrew. One side of Monsieur Leroy's house opened into the garden, the other into a courtyard adjoining the high-road.

'Poor soul! I should be so glad to pay for a piano and a private sitting-room for her, if I might be allowed to do so,' said Mildred, when the singer was gone.

'You are too generous, madame; but I doubt if it would be good for her to accept your bounty. She enjoys the occasional use of my piano intensely. If she had one always at her command, she would give up her life to music, which exercises too strong an influence upon her disordered brain to be indulged in *ad libitum*. Nor would a private apartment be an advantage in her case. She is too much given to brooding over past griefs; and the society of her fellow-sufferers, the friction and movement of the public life, are good for her.'

[handwritten: Intrigue with Castellani's dad]

'What did she mean by her talk of an English girl – some story of wrong-doing? Was it all imaginary?'

'I believe there was some scandal at Milan; some flirtation, or possibly an intrigue, between Castellani and one of his English pupils; but I never heard the details. Maria's jealousy would be likely to exaggerate the circumstances; for I believe she adored her cousin to the last, long after she knew that he had never cared for her, except as an element in his success.'

Mildred took leave of the doctor, after thanking him for his politeness. She left a handful of gold for the benefit of the poor patients, and left Dr Leroy under the impression that she was one of the sweetest women he had ever met. Her pensive beauty, her low and musical voice, the clear and resolute purpose of every word and look, were in his mind indications of the perfection of womanhood.

'It is not often that Nature achieves such excellence,' mused the doctor. 'It is a pity that perfection should be short-lived; yet I cannot prognosticate length of years for this lady.'

[handwritten: Will Mildred die early?]

Pamela's spirits were decidedly improving. She talked all dinner-time, and gave a graphic description of her afternoon in the tennis-court behind the Cercle de la Méditerranée.

'I am to see the club-house some morning before the members begin to arrive,' she said. 'It is a perfectly charming club. There is a theatre, which serves as a ballroom on grand occasions. There is to be a dance next week; and Lady Lochinvar will chaperon me, if you don't mind.'

'I shall be most grateful to Lady Lochinvar, dear. Believe me, if I am a hermit, I don't want to keep you in melancholy seclusion. I am very glad for you to have pleasant friends.'

'Mrs Murray is delightful. She begged me to call her Jessie. She is going to take me for a drive before lunch to-morrow, and we are to do some shopping in the afternoon. The shops here are simply lovely.'

'Almost as nice as Brighton?'

'Better. They have more *chic*; and I am told they are twice as dear.'

'Was Mr Stuart at the tennis-court?'

'Yes, he plays there every afternoon when he is not at Monte Carlo.'

'That does not sound like a very useful existence.'

'Perhaps you will say *he* is an adventurer,' exclaimed Pamela, with a flash of temper; and then repenting in a moment, she added: 'I beg your pardon, aunt; but you are really wrong about Mr Stuart. He looks after Lady Lochinvar's estate. He is invaluable to her.'

'But he cannot do much for the estate when he is playing tennis here or gambling at Monte Carlo.'

'O, but he does. He answers no end of letters every morning. Lady Lochinvar says he is a most wonderful young man. He attends to her house accounts here. I am afraid she would be very extravagant if she were not well looked after. She has no idea of business. Mr Stuart has even to manage her dressmakers.'

'Then one may suppose he is really useful – even at Nice. Has he any means of his own, or is he entirely dependent on his aunt?'

'O, he has an income of his own – a modest income, Mrs Murray says, hardly enough for him to get along easily in a cavalry regiment, but quite enough for him as a civilian; and his aunt will leave him everything. His expectations are splendid.'

'Well, Pamela, I will not call *him* an adventurer, and I shall be pleased to make his acquaintance, if he will call upon me.'

'He is dying to know you. May Mrs Murray bring him to tea to-morrow afternoon?'

'With pleasure.'

CHAPTER II

IN THE MORNING OF LIFE

George Greswold succumbed to Fate. He had done all he could do in the way of resistance. He had appealed against his wife's decision; he had set love against principle or prejudice, and principle, as Mildred understood it, had been too strong for love; so there was nothing left for the forsaken husband but submission. He went back to the home in which he had once been happy, and he sat down amidst the ruins of his domestic life; he sat by his desolate hearth through the long dull wintry months, and he made no effort to bring brightness or variety into his existence. He made no stand against unmerited misfortune.

'I am too old to forget,' he told himself; 'that lesson can only be learnt in youth.'

A young man might have gone out as a wanderer – might have sought excitement and distraction amidst strange cities and strange races of men; might have found forgetfulness in danger and hardship, the perils of unexplored deserts, the hazards of untrodden mountains, the hairbreadth escapes of savage life, pestilence, famine, warfare. George Greswold felt no inclination for any such adventure. The mainspring of life had snapped, and he admitted to himself that he was a broken man.

He sat by the hearth in his gloomy library day after day, and night after night, until the small hours. Sometimes he took his gun in the early morning, and went out with a leash of dogs for an hour or two of solitary shooting among his own covers. He tramped his copses in all weathers and at all hours, but he rarely went outside his own domain; nor did he ever visit his cottagers or small tenantry, with whom he had been once so familiar a friend. All interest in his estate had gone from him after his daughter's death. He left everything to the new steward, who was happily both competent and honest.

His books were his only friends. Those studious habits acquired years before, when he was comparatively a poor man, stood by him now. His one distraction, his only solace, was found in the contents of those capacious bookshelves, three-fourths of which were filled with volumes of his own selection, the gradual accumulation of his sixteen years of ownership. His grandfather's library, which constituted the remaining fourth, consisted of those admirable standard works, in the largest possible number of volumes, which formed an item in the furniture of a respectable house during the last century, and which, from the stiffness of their bindings and the unblemished appearance of their paper and print, would seem to have enjoyed an existence of dignified retirement from the day they left the bookseller's shop.

But for those long tramps in the wintry copses, where holly and ivy showed brightly green amidst leafless chestnuts and hazels – but for those communings with the intellect of past and present in the long still winter evenings, George Greswold's brain must have given way under the burden of an undeserved sorrow. As it was, he contrived to live on, peacefully, and even with an air of contentment. His servants surprised him in no paroxysm of grief. He startled them with no strange exclamations. His manner gave no cause for alarm. He accepted his lot in silence and submission. His days were ordered with a simple regularity, so far as the service of the house went. His valet and butler agreed that he was in all things an admirable master.

The idea in the household was that Mrs Greswold had 'taken to religion.' That seemed the only possible explanation for a parting which had been preceded by no domestic storms, for which there was no apparent cause in the conduct of the husband. That idea of the wife having discovered an intrigue of her husband's, which Louisa had discussed in the housekeeper's room at Brighton, was no longer entertained in the servants'-hall at Enderby.

'If there had been anything of that kind, something would have come out by this time,' said the butler, who had a profound belief in the ultimate 'coming out' of all social mysteries.

George Greswold was not kept in ignorance of his wife's movements. Pamela had been shrewd enough to divine that her uncle would be glad to hear from her in order to hear of Mildred, and she had written to him from time to time, giving him a graphic account of her own and her aunt's existence.

There had been only one suppression. The young lady had not once alluded to Castellani's share in their winter life at Pallanza. She had a horror of arousing that dragon of suspicion which she knew to lurk in the minds of all uncles with reference to all agreeable young men. George Greswold had not heard from his niece for more than a fortnight, when there came a letter, written the day after Mildred's visit to the madhouse, and full of praises of Lady Lochinvar and the climate of Nice. That letter was the greatest shock that Greswold had received since his wife had left him, for it told him that she was in a place where she could scarcely fail to discover all the details of his wretched story. He had kept it locked from her, he had shut himself behind a wall of iron, he had kept a silence as of the grave; and now she from whom he had prayed that his fatal story might be for ever hidden was certain to learn the worst.

'Aunt went to lunch with Lady Lochinvar the day after our arrival,' wrote Pamela. 'She spent a long morning with her, and then went for a drive somewhere in the environs, and was out till nearly dinner-time. She looked so white and fagged when she came back, poor dear, and I am sure she had done too much for one day. Lady Lochinvar asked me to dinner, and took me to the new Opera-house, which is lovely. Her nephew was with us – rather plain, and with no taste for music (he said he preferred *Madame Angot* to *Lohengrin*), but enormously clever, I am told, in a solid, practical kind of way.'

Und so weiter, for three more pages.

Mildred had been with Lady Lochinvar – with Lady Lochinvar, who knew all; who had seen him and his wife together; had received them both as her friends; had been confided in, he knew, by that fond, jealous wife; made the recipient of tearful doubts and hysterical accusations. Vivien had owned as much to him.

She had been with Lady Lochinvar, who must know the history of his wife's death and the dreadful charge brought against him; who must know that he had been an inmate of the great white barrack on the road to St André; who in all probability thought him guilty of murder. All the barriers had fallen now; all the floodgates had opened. He saw himself hateful, monstrous, inhuman, in the eyes of the woman he adored.

'She loved her sister with an inextinguishable love,' he thought, 'and she sees me now as her sister's murderer – the cold-blooded, cruel husband, who made his wife's existence miserable, and ended by killing her in a paroxysm of brutal rage: that is the kind of monster I must seem in my Mildred's eyes. She will look back upon my stubborn silence, my gloomy reserve, and she will see all the indications of guilt. My own conduct will condemn me.'

As he sat by his solitary hearth in the cold March evening, the large reading-lamp making a circle of light amidst the gloom, George

Greswold's mind travelled over the days of his youth, and the period of that fatal marriage which had blighted him in the morning of his life, which blighted him now in life's meridian, when, but for this dark influence, all the elements of happiness were in his hand.

He looked back to the morning of life, and saw himself full of ambitious plans and aspiring dreams, well content to be the younger son, to whom it was given to make his own position in the world, scorning the idle days of a fox-hunting squire, resolute to become an influence for good among his fellow-men. He had never envied his brother the inheritance of the soil; he had thought but little of his own promised inheritance of Enderby.

Unhappily that question of the succession to the Enderby estate had been a sore point with Squire Ransome. He adored his elder son, who was like him in character and person, and he cared very little for George, whom he considered a bookish and unsympathetic individual; a young man who hardly cared whether there were few or many foxes in the district, whether the young partridges throve, or perished by foul weather or epidemic disease – a young man who took no interest in the things that filled the lives of other people. In a word, George was not a sportsman; and that deficiency made him an alien to his father's race. There had never been a Ransome who was not 'sporting' to the core of his heart until the appearance of this pragmatical Oxonian.

Without being in any manner scientific or a student of evolution, Mr Ransome had a fixed belief in heredity. It was the duty of the son to resemble the father; and a son who was in all his tastes and inclinations a distinct variety stamped himself as undutiful.

'I don't suppose the fellow can help it,' said Mr Ransome testily; 'but there's hardly a remark he makes which doesn't act upon my nerves like a nutmeg-grater.'

Nobody would have given the Squire credit for possessing very sensitive nerves, but everybody knew he had a temper, and a temper which occasionally showed itself in violent outbreaks – the kind of temper which will dismiss a household at one fell swoop, send a stud of horses to Tattersall's on the spur of the moment, tear up a lease on the point of signature, or turn a son out of doors.

The knowledge that this unsportsmanlike son of his would inherit the fine estate of Enderby was a constant source of vexation to Squire Ransome of Mapledown. The dream of his life was that Mapledown and Enderby should be united in the possession of his son Randolph. The two properties would have made Randolph rich enough to hope for a peerage, and that idea of a possible peerage dazzled the Tory squire. His family had done the State some service; had sat for important boroughs; had squandered much money upon contested elections; had been staunch in times of change and difficulty. There was no reason why a Ransome should not ascend to the Upper House, in these days when peerages are bestowed so much more freely than in the time of Pitt and Fox. The two estates would have made an important property under one ownership; divided, they were only respectable. And what the Squire most keenly felt was the fact that Enderby was by far the finer property, and that his younger son must ultimately be a much richer man than his brother. The Sussex estate had dwindled considerably in those glorious days of contested elections and party feeling; the Hampshire estate was intact. Mr Ransome could not forgive his wife for her determination that the younger son should be her heir. He always shuffled uneasily upon his seat in the old family pew when the 27th chapter of Genesis was read in the Sunday morning service. He compared his wife to Rebecca. He asked the Vicar at luncheon on one of those Sundays what he thought of the conduct of Rebecca and Jacob in that very shady transaction, and the Vicar replied in the orthodox fashion, favouring Jacob just as Rebecca had favoured him.

'I can't understand it,' exclaimed the Squire testily; 'the whole business is against my idea of honour and honesty. I wouldn't have such a fellow as Jacob for my steward if he were the cleverest man in Sussex. And look you here, Vicar. If Jacob was right, and knew he was right, why the deuce was he so frightened the first time he met Esau after that ugly business? Take my word for it, Jacob was a sneak, and Providence punished him rightly with a desolate old age and a quarrelsome family.'

The Vicar looked down at his plate, sighed gently, and held his peace.

The time came when the growing feeling of aversion on the father's part showed itself in outrage and insult which the son could not endure. George remonstrated against certain acts of injustice in the management of the estate. He pleaded the cause of tenant against landlord – a dire offence in the eyes of the Tory Squire. There came an open rupture; and it was impossible for the younger son to remain any longer under the father's roof. His mother loved him devotedly, but she felt that it was better for him to go; and so it was settled, in loving consultation between mother and son, that he should carry out a long-cherished wish of his Oxford days, and explore all that was historical and interesting in Southern Europe, seeing men and cities in a leisurely way, and devoting himself to literature in the meantime. He had already written for some of the high-class magazines; and he felt that it was in him to do well as a writer of the serious order – critic, essayist, and thinker.

His mother gave him three hundred a year, which, for a young man of his simple habits, was ample. He told himself that he should be able to earn as much again by his pen; and so, after a farewell of decent friendliness to his father and his brother Randolph, and tenderest parting with his mother, he set out upon his pilgrimage, a free agent, with the world all before him. He explored Greece – dwelling fondly upon all the old traditions, the old histories. He made the acquaintance of Dr Schliemann, and entered heart and soul into that gentleman's views. This occupied him more than a year, for those scenes exercised a potent fascination upon a mind to which Greek literature was the supreme delight. He spent a month at Constantinople, and a winter in Corfu and Cyprus; he devoted a summer to Switzerland, and did a little mountaineering; and during all his wanderings he contrived to give a considerable portion of his time to literature.

It was after his Swiss travels that he went to Italy, and established himself in Florence for a quiet winter. He hired an apartment on a fourth floor of a palace overlooking the Arno, and here, for the first time since he had left England, he went a little into general society. His mother had sent him letters of introduction to old friends of her own, English and Florentine; he was young, handsome, and a gentleman, and he was received with enthusiasm. Had he been fond of society he might have been at parties every night; but he was fonder of books and of solitude, and he took very little advantage of people's friendliness.

The few houses to which he went were houses famous for good music, and it was in one of these houses that he met Vivien Faux.

It was in the midst of a symphony by Beethoven, while he was standing on the edge of the crowd which surrounded the open space given to the instrumentalists, that he first saw the woman who was to be his wife. She was sitting in the recess of a lofty window, quite apart from the throng – a pale, dark-eyed girl, with roughened hair carelessly heaped above her low, broad forehead. Her slender figure and sloping shoulders showed to advantage in a low-necked black gown, without a vestige of ornament. She wore neither jewels nor flowers, at an assembly where gems were sparkling and flowers breathing sweetness upon every feminine bosom. Her thin, white arms hung loosely in her lap; her back was turned to the performers, and her eyes were averted from the crowd. She looked the image of *ennui* and indifference.

He found his hostess directly the symphony was over, and asked her to introduce him to the young lady in black velvet yonder, sitting alone in the window.

'Have you been struck by Miss Faux's rather singular appearance?' asked Signora Vicenti. 'She is not so handsome as many young ladies who are here to-night.'

'No, she is not handsome, but her face interests me. She looks as if she had suffered some great disappointment.'

'I believe her whole life has been a disappointment. She is an orphan, and, as far as I can ascertain, a friendless orphan. She has good means, but there is a mystery about her position which places her in a manner apart from other girls of her age. She has no relations to whom to refer, no family home to which to return. She is here with some rather foolish people – an English artist and his wife, who cannot do very much for her, and I believe she keenly feels her isolation. It makes her bitter against other girls, and she loses friends as fast as she makes them. People won't put up with her tongue. Well, Mr Ransome, do you change your mind after that?'

'On the contrary, I feel so much the more interested in the young lady.'

'Ah, your interest will not last. However, I shall be charmed to introduce you.'

They went across the room to that distant recess where Miss Faux was still seated, her hair and attitude unchanged since George Ransome first observed her. She started with a little look of surprise when Signora Vicenti and her companion approached; but she accepted the introduction with a nonchalant air, and she replied to Ransome's opening remarks with manifest indifference. Then by degrees she grew more animated, and talked about the people in the room, ridiculing their pretensions, their eccentricities, their costume.

'You are not an *habitué* here?' she asked. 'I don't remember seeing you before to-night.'

'No; it is the first of Signora Vicenti's parties that I have seen.'

'Then I conclude it will be the last.'

'Why?'

'O, no sensible person would come a second time. The music is tolerable if one could hear it anywhere else, but the people are odious.'

'Yet I conclude this is not your first evening here?'

'No; I come every week. I have nothing else to do with myself but to go about to houses I hate, and mix with people who hate me.'

'Why should they hate you?'

'O, we all hate each other, and want to overreach one another. Envy and malice are in the air. Picture to yourself fifty manoeuvring mothers with a hundred marriageable daughters, most of them portionless, and about twenty eligible men. Think how ferocious the competition must be!'

'But you are independent of all that; you are outside the arena.'

'Yes; I have nothing to do with their slave-market, but they hate me all the same; perhaps because I have a little more money than most of them; perhaps because I am nobody – a waif and stray – able to give no account of my existence.'

She spoke of her position with a reckless candour that shocked him.

'There is something to bear in every lot,' he said, trying to be philosophical.

'I suppose so, but I only care about my own burden. Please, don't pretend that you do either. I should despise a man who pretended not to be selfish.'

'Do you think that all men are selfish?'

'I have never seen any evidence to the contrary. The man I thought the noblest and the best did me the greatest wrong it was possible to do me, in order to spare himself trouble.'

Ransome was silent. He would not enter into the discussion of a past history of which he was ignorant, and which was doubtless full of pain.

After this he met her very often, and while other young men avoided her on account of her bitter tongue, he showed a preference for her society, and encouraged her to confide in him. She went everywhere, chaperoned by Mr Mortimer, a dreary twaddler, who was for ever expounding theories of art which he had picked up, parrot-wise, in a London art-school thirty years before. His latest ideas were coeval with Maclise and Mulready. Mrs Mortimer was by way of being an invalid, and sat and nursed her neuralgia at home, while her husband and Miss Faux went into society.

It was at the beginning of spring that an American lady of wealth and standing invited the Mortimers and their *protégée* to a picnic, to which Mr Ransome was also bidden; and it was this picnic which sealed George Ransome's fate. Pity for Vivien's lonely position had grown into a sincere regard. He had discovered warm feelings under that cynical manner, a heart capable of a profound affection. She had talked to him of a child, a kind of adopted sister, whom she had passionately loved, and from whom she had been parted by the selfish cruelty of the little girl's parents.

'My school-life in England had soured me before then,' she said, 'and I was not a very amiable person even at fifteen years old; but *that* cruelty finished me. I have hated my fellow-creatures ever since.'

He pleaded against this wholesale condemnation.

'You were unlucky,' he said, 'in encountering unworthy people.'

'Ah, but one of those people, the child's father, had seemed to me the best of men. I had believed in him as second only to God in benevolence and generosity. When *he* failed I renounced my belief in human goodness.'

Unawares, George Ransome had fallen into the position of her confidant and friend. From friendship to love was an easy transition; and a few words, spoken at random during a ramble on an olive-clad hill, bound him to her for ever. Those unpremeditated words loosed the fountain of tears, and he saw the most scornful of women, the woman who affected an absolute aversion for his sex, and a contempt for those weaker sisters who waste their love upon such vile clay – he saw her abandon herself to a passion of tears at the first word of affection which he had ever addressed to her. He had spoken as a friend rather than as a lover; but those tears bound him to her for life. He put his arm round her, and pillowed the small pale face upon his breast, the dark impassioned eyes looking up at him drowned in tears.

'You should not have said those words,' she sobbed. 'You cannot understand what it is to have lived as I have lived – a creature apart – unloved – unvalued. O, is it true? – do you really care for me?'

'With all my heart,' he answered, and in good faith.

His profound compassion took the place of love; and in that moment he believed that he loved her as a man should love the woman whom he chooses for his wife.

They were married within a month from that March afternoon; and for some time their married life was happy. He wished to take her to England, but she implored him to abandon that idea.

'In England everybody would want to know who I am,' she said. 'I should be tortured by questions about "my people." Abroad, society is less exacting.'

He deferred to her in this, as he would have done in any other matter which involved her happiness. They spent the first half-year of their married life in desultory wanderings in the Oberland and the Engadine, and then settled at Nice for the winter.

Here Mrs Ransome met Lady Lochinvar, whom she had known at Florence, and was at once invited to the Palais Montano; and here for the first time appeared those clouds which were too soon to darken George Ransome's domestic horizon.

There were many beautiful women at Nice that winter: handsome Irish girls, vivacious Americans, Frenchwomen, and Englishwomen; and among so many who were charming there were some whom George Ransome did not scruple to admire, with as much frankness as he would have admired a face by Guido or Raffaelle. He was slow to perceive his wife's distrust, could hardly bring himself to believe that she could be jealous of him; but he was not suffered to remain long in this happy ignorance. A hysterical outburst one night after their return from a ball at the Club-house opened the husband's eyes. The demon of jealousy stood revealed; and from that hour the angel of domestic peace was banished from George Ransome's hearth.

He struggled against that evil influence. He exercised patience, common sense, forbearance; but in vain. There were lulls in the storm sometimes, delusive calms; and he hoped the demon was exorcised. And then came a worse outbreak; more hysterics; despairing self-abandonment; threats of suicide. He bore it as long as he could, and ultimately, his wife's health offering an excuse for such a step, he proposed that they should leave Nice, and take a villa in the environs, in some quiet spot where they might live apart from all society.

Vivien accepted the proposition with rapture; she flung herself at her husband's feet, and covered his hands with tearful kisses.

'O, if I could but believe that you still love me, that you are not weary of me,' she exclaimed, 'I should be the happiest woman in the universe.'

They spent a week of halcyon peace, driving about in quest of their new home. They explored the villages within ten miles of Nice, they breakfasted at village restaurants, in the sunny March noontide, and finally they settled upon a villa at St Jean, within an hour's drive of the great white city, and to this new home they went at the end of the month, after bidding adieu to their friends in Nice.

CHAPTER III

THE RIFT IN THE LUTE

The villa was built on a ledge of ground between the road and the sea. There was a stone terrace in front of the windows of *salon* and dining-room, below which the ground shelved steeply down to the rocks and the blue water. The low irregular-shaped house was screened from the road by a grove of orange and lemon trees, with a peach or a cherry here and there to give variety of colour. In one corner there was a whole cluster of peach-trees, which made a mass of purplish-pinky bloom. The ridges of garden sloping down from the stone terrace were full of white stocks and scarlet anemones. Clusters of red ranunculus made spots of flame in the sun, and the young leaves in the long hedge of Dijon roses wove an interlacing screen of crimson, through which the sun shone as through old ruby glass in a cathedral window. Everywhere there was a feast of perfume and colour and beauty. The little bay, the curving pier, the white-sailed boats, which, seen from the height above, looked no bigger than the gulls skimming across the blue; the quaint old houses of Villefranche on a level with the water, and rising tier above tier to the crest of the hill – pink and blue houses, white and cream-coloured houses, with pea-green shutters and red roofs. Far away to the left, the jutting promontory and the tall white lighthouse; and away southward, the sapphire sea, touched with every changing light and shadow. And this lovely little world at George Ransome's feet, this paradise in miniature, was all the lovelier because of the great rugged mountain-wall behind it, the bare red and yellow hills baked in the sunlight of ages, the strange old-world villages yonder high up on the stony flanks of the hills, the far-away church towers, from which faint sound of bells came now and again as if from fairyland.

It was a delicious spot this little village of St Jean, to which the Niçois came on Sundays and holidays, to eat bouillabaisse at the rustic tavern or to picnic in the shade of century-old olives and old carouba-trees, which made dark masses of foliage between the road and the sea. George Ransome loved the place, and could have been happy there if his wife would only have allowed him; but those halcyon days which marked the beginning of their retirement were too soon ended; and clouds lowered again over the horizon – clouds of doubt and discontent. There are women to whom domestic peace, a calm and rational happiness, is an impossibility, and Vivien was one of these women.

From the beginning her suspicious nature had been on the watch for some hidden evil. She had a fixed idea that the Fates had marked her for misery, and she would not open her heart to the sunlight of happiness.

Was her husband unkind to her? No, he was all kindness; but to her his kindness seemed only a gentleman-like form of toleration. He had married her out of pity; and it was pity that made him kind. Other women were worshipped. It was her fate to be tolerated by a man she adored.

She could never forget her own passionate folly, her own unwomanly forwardness. She had thrown herself into his arms – she who should have waited to be wooed, and should have made herself precious by the difficulty with which she was won.

'How can he help holding me cheap?' she asked herself – 'I who cost him nothing, not even an hour of doubt? From the hour we first met he must have known that I adored him.'

Once when he was rowing her about the bay in the westering sunlight, while the fishermen were laying down their lines, or taking up their baskets here and there by the rocks, she asked him suddenly,

'What did you think of me, George, the first time you saw me – that night at Signora Vicenti's party? Come, be candid. You can afford to tell me the truth now. Your fate is sealed; you have nothing to lose or to gain.'

'Do you think I would tell you less or more than the truth under any circumstances, Viva?' he asked gravely.

'O, you are horribly exact, I know!' she answered, with an impatient movement of her slender sloping shoulders, not looking at him, but with her dark dreamy eyes gazing far off across the bay towards the distant point where the twin towers of Monaco Cathedral showed faint in the distance, 'but perhaps if the truth sounded very rude you might suppress it – out of pity.'

'I don't think the truth need sound rude.'

'Well,' still more impatiently, 'what impression did I make upon you?'

'You must consider that there were at least fifty young ladies in Signora Vicenti's *salons* that evening.'

'And about thirty old women; and I was lost in the crowd.'

'Not quite lost. I remember being attracted by a young lady who sat in a window niche apart——'

'Like "Brunswick's fated chieftain." Pray go on.'

'And who seemed a little out of harmony with the rest of the company. Her manner struck me as unpleasantly ironical, but her small pale face interested me, and I even liked the mass of towzled hair brushed up from her low square forehead. I liked her black velvet gown, without any colour or ornament. It set off the thin white shoulders and long slender throat.'

'Did you think I was rich or poor, somebody or nobody?'

'I thought you were a clever girl, soured by some kind of disappointment.'

'And you felt sorry for me. Say you felt sorry for me!' she cried, her eyes coming back from the distant promontory, and fixing him suddenly, bright, keen, imperious in their eager questioning.

'Yes, I confess to feeling very sorry for you.'

'Did I not know as much? From the very first you pitied me. Pity, pity! What an intolerable burden it is! I have bent under it all my life.'

'My dear Viva, what nonsense you talk! Because I had mistaken ideas about you that first night, when we were strangers——'

'You were not mistaken. I was soured. I had been disappointed. My thoughts were bitter as gall. I had no patience with other girls who had so many blessings that I had never known. I saw them making light of their advantages, peevish, ill-tempered, self-indulgent; and I scorned them. Contempt for others was the only comfort of my barren life. And so my vinegar tongue disgusted you, did it not?'

'I was not disgusted – concerned and interested, rather. Your conversation was original. I wanted to know more of you.'

'Did you think me pretty?'

'I was more impressed by your mental gifts than your physical——'

'That is only a polite way of saying you thought me plain.'

'Viva, you know better than that. If I thought of your appearance at all during that first meeting, be assured I thought you interesting – yes, and pretty. Only prettiness is a poor word to express a face that is full of intellect and originality.'

'You thought me pale, faded, haggard, old for my age,' she said decisively. 'Don't deny it. You must have seen what my glass had been telling me for the last year.'

'I thought your face showed traces of suffering.'

This was one of many such conversations, full of keen questioning on her part, with an assumed lightness of manner which thinly veiled the irritability of her mind. She had changed for the worse since they left

Nice; she had grown more sensitive, more suspicious, more irritable. She was in a condition of health in which many women are despondent or irritable – in which with some women life seems one long disgust, and all things are irksome, even the things that have been pleasantest and most valued before – even the aspect of a lovely landscape, the phrases of a familiar melody, the perfume of a once favourite flower. He tried to cheer her by talking of their future, the time to come when there would be a new bond between them, a new interest in their lives; but she saw all things in a gloomy atmosphere.

'Who knows?' she said. 'I may die, perhaps; or you may love your child better than you have ever loved me, and then I should hate it.'

'Viva, you cannot doubt that my love for our child will strengthen my love for you.'

'Will it?' she asked incredulously. 'God knows it needs strengthening.'

This was hard upon a man whose tenderness and indulgence had been boundless, who had done all that chivalry and a sense of duty can do to atone for the lack of love. He had tried his uttermost to conceal the one bitter truth that love was wanting: but those keen eyes of hers had seen the gap between them, that sensitive ear had discovered the rift in the lute.

One afternoon they climbed the hill to the breezy common on which the lighthouse stands, and dawdled about in the sunshine, gathering the pale gray rosemary bloom and the perfumed thyme which grow among those hollows and hillocks in such wild luxuriance. They were sauntering near the carriage-road, talking very little – she feeble and tired, although it was her own fancy to have walked so far – when they saw a carriage driving towards them – a large landau, with the usual bony horses and shabby jingling harness, and the usual sunburnt good-tempered driver.

Two girls in white gowns and Leghorn hats were in the carriage, with an elderly woman in black. Their laps were full of wild flowers, and branches of wild cherry and pear blossom filled the leather hood at the back of the carriage. They were talking and laughing gaily, all animation and high spirits, as they drew near; and at sight of George Ransome one of them waved her hand in greeting, and called to the driver to stop. They were two handsome Irish girls who had made a sensation at the Battle of Flowers six weeks before. They were spoken of by some people as the belles of Nice. Mr Ransome had pelted them with Parma violets and yellow rosebuds on the Promenade des Anglais, as they drove up and down in a victoria embowered in white stocks and narcissi. He had waltzed with them at the Cercle de la Méditerranée and the Palais Montano; had admired them frankly and openly, not afraid to own even to a jealous wife that he thought them beautiful.

Delia Darcy, the elder and handsomer of the two, leaned over the carriage-door to shake hands with him, while Vivien stood aloof, on a grassy knoll above the road, looking daggers. What right had they to stop their carriage and waylay her husband?

'Who would have thought of finding you in this out-of-the-way spot?' exclaimed Miss Darcy; 'we fancied you had left the Riviera. Are you stopping at Monte Carlo?'

'No, I have taken a villa at St Jean.'

'Is that near here?'

'Very near. You must have skirted the village in driving up here. And has Nice been very gay since we left?'

'No; people have been going away, and we have missed you dreadfully at the opera, and at dances, and at Rumpelmeyer's. What could have induced you to bury yourself alive in a village?' she asked vivaciously, with that sparkling manner which gives an air of flirtation to the most commonplace talk.

'My wife has been out of health, and it has suited us both to live quietly.'

'Poor Mrs Ransome – poor you!' exclaimed Miss Darcy, with a sigh. 'O, there she is! How do you do, Mrs Ransome?' gesticulating with a pretty little hand in a long wrinkled tan glove. 'Do come and talk to us.'

Mrs Ransome bowed stiffly, but did not move an inch. She stood picking a branch of rosemary to shreds with nervous restless fingers, scattering the poor pale blue-gray blossoms as if she were sprinkling them upon a corpse. The two girls took no further notice of her, but both bent forward, talking to Ransome, rattling on about this ball and the other ball, and a breakfast, and sundry afternoon teas, and the goings-on – audacious for the most part – of all the smart people at Nice. They had worlds to tell him, having taken it into their heads that he was a humorist, a cynic, who delighted in hearing of the follies of his fellow-man. He stood with his hat off, waiting for the carriage to drive on, inwardly impatient of delay, knowing with what jealous feelings Vivien had always regarded Delia Darcy, dreading a fit of ill-temper when the Irish girls should have vanished by and by below the sandy edge of the common. He listened almost in silence, giving their loquacity no more encouragement than good manners obliged.

'Why don't you come to the next dance at the Cercle de la Méditerranée?' said Delia coaxingly; 'there are so few good dancers left, and your step is just the one that suits me best. There are to be amateur theatricals to begin with – scenes from *Much Ado*; and I am to be Beatrice. Won't that tempt you?' she asked, with the insolence of an acknowledged beauty, spoiled by the laxer manners of a foreign settlement, lolling back in the carriage, and smiling at him with brilliant

Irish gray eyes, under the shadow of her Leghorn hat, with a great cluster of daffodils just above her forehead, the yellow bloom showing vividly against her dark hair.

The other sister was only a paler reflection of this one, and echoed her speeches, laughing when she laughed.

'Surely you will come to see Delia act Beatrice?' she said. 'I can't tell you how well she does it. Sir Randall Spofforth is the Benedict.'

'My dears, we shall have no time to dress for dinner!' expostulated the duenna, feeling that this kind of thing had lasted long enough. *'En avant, cocher.'*

'Won't you come?' pleaded the pertinacious Delia; 'it is on the twenty-ninth, remember – next Thursday week.'

The carriage rolled slowly onward.

'I regret that I shall not be there,' said Ransome decisively.

Delia shook her parasol at him in pretended anger.

He rejoined his wife. She stood surrounded by the shreds of rosemary and thyme which she had plucked and scattered while he was talking. She was very pale; and he knew only too well that she was very angry.

'Come, Viva, it is time we turned homeward,' he said.

'Yes, the sun has gone down, has it not?' she exclaimed mockingly, as she looked after the carriage, which sank below the ragged edge of heather and thyme yonder, as if it had dropped over the cliff.

'Why, my love, the sun is above our heads!'

'Is it? *Your* sun is gone down, anyhow. She is very lovely, is she not?'

The question was asked with sudden eagerness, as if her life depended upon the reply. She was walking quickly in her agitation, going down the hill much faster than she had mounted it.

'Yes, they are both handsome girls, feather-headed, but remarkably handsome,' her husband answered carelessly.

'But Delia is the lovelier. *She* is your divinity.'

'Yes, she is the lovelier. The other seems a copy by an inferior hand.'

'And she is so fond of you. It was cruel to refuse her request, when she pleaded so hard.'

'How can you be so foolish or so petty, Vivien? Is it impossible for me to talk for five minutes with a handsome girl without unreasonable anger on your part?'

'Do you expect me to be pleased or happy when I see your admiration of another woman – admiration you do not even take the trouble to conceal? Do you suppose I can ever forget last winter – how I have seen you dancing with that girl night after night? Yes, I have had to sit and watch you. I was not popular, I had few partners; and it is bad form to dance more than once with one's husband. I have seen her in your arms, with her head almost lying on your shoulder, again and again, as if it were her natural place. "What a handsome couple!" I have heard people say; "are they engaged?" Do you think *that* was pleasant for me?'

'You had but to say one word, and I would have left off dancing for ever.'

'Another sacrifice – like your marriage.'

'Vivien, you would provoke a saint.'

'Yes, it is provoking to be chained to one woman when you are dying for another.'

'How much oftener am I to swear to you that I don't care a straw for Miss Darcy?'

'Never again,' she answered. 'I love you too well to wish you to swear a lie.'

They had come down from the common by this time, and were now upon a pathway nearer home – a narrow footpath on the edge of the cliff opposite Beaulieu; the gently-curving bay below them, and behind and above them orchards and gardens, hill and lighthouse. It was one of their chosen walks. They had paced the narrow path many an afternoon when the twin towers of Monaco showed dark in the shadow of sundown.

'Vivien, I think you are the most difficult creature to live with that ever a man had for his wife,' said Ransome, stung to the quick by her persistent perversity.

'I am difficult to live with, am I?' she cried. 'Why don't you go a step further – why don't you say at once that you wish I were dead?' she cried, with a wild burst of passion. 'Say that you wish me dead.'

'I own that when you torment me, as you are doing to-day, I have sometimes thought of death – yours or mine – as the only escape from mutual misery,' he answered gloomily.

He had been sauntering a few paces in front of her along the narrow path between the olive-garden and the edge of the cliff, she following slowly – both in a desultory way, and talking to each other without seeing each other's face. The cliff sank sheer below the pathway, with only a narrow margin of rushy grass between the footpath and the brink of the precipice. It was no stupendous depth, no giddy height from which the eye glanced downward, sickening at the horror of the gulf. One looked down at the jewel-bright waves and the many-hued rocks, the fir-trees growing out of the crags, without a thought of danger; and yet a false step upon those sunburnt rushes might mean instant death.

He came to a sudden standstill after that last speech, and stood leaning with both hands upon his stick, angry, full of gloom, feeling that he had said a cruel thing, yet not repenting of his cruelty. He stood there expectant of her angry answer; but there was only silence.

Silence, and then a swift rushing sound, like the flight of a great bird. He looked round, and saw that he was alone!

CHAPTER IV

DARKNESS

She had flung herself over the cliff. That rustling noise was the sound of her gown as it brushed against the rushes and seedling firs that clothed the precipice with verdure. He looked over the cliff, and saw her lying among the rocks, a white motionless figure, mangled and crushed, dumb and dead, his victim and his accuser.

His first impulse was to fling himself over the edge where she had cast away her life a minute ago; but common sense overcame that movement of despair. A few yards further towards the point the side of the cliff was less precipitous. There were jutting ledges of rock and straggling bushes by which a good climber might let himself down to the beach, not without hazard, but with a fair chance of safety. As he scrambled downward he saw a fisherman's boat shooting across the bay, and he thought that his wife's fall had been seen from the narrow strip of sandy shore yonder towards Beaulieu.

She was lying on her side among the low wet slabs of rock, the blue water lapping round her. There was blood upon her face, and on one mangled arm, from which the muslin sleeve was ripped. Her gown had caught in the bushes, and was torn to shreds; and the water flowing so gently in and out among her loosened hair was tinged with blood.

Her eyes were wide open, staring wildly, and they had a glassy look already. He knew that she was dead.

'Did you see her fall?' he asked the men in the boat, as they came near.

'No,' said one. 'I heard the gulls scream, and I knew there was something. And then I looked about and saw something white lying there, under the cliff.'

They lifted her gently into the boat, and laid her on a folded sail at the bottom, as gently and as tenderly as if she were still capable of feeling, as if she were not past cure. George Ransome asked no question, invited no opinion. He sat in the stern of the boat, dumb and quiet. The horror of this sudden doom had paralysed him. What had he done that this thing should happen, this wild revenge of a woman's passionate heart which made him a murderer? What had he done? Had he not been patient and forbearing, indulgent beyond the common indulgence of husbands to fretful wives? Had he not blunted the edge of wrath with soft answers? Had he not been affectionate and considerate even when love was dead? And yet because of one hard speech, wrung from his irritated nerves, this wild creature had slain herself.

The two fishermen looked at him curiously. He saw the dark southern eyes watching him; saw gravity and restraint upon those fine olive faces which had been wont to beam with friendly smiles. He knew that they suspected evil, but he was in no mood to undeceive them. He sat in an apathetic silence, motionless, stupefied almost, while the men rowed slowly round the point in the golden light of sundown. He scarcely looked at that white still figure lying at the bottom of the boat, the face hidden under a scarlet kerchief which one of the men had taken from his neck. He sat staring at the rocky shore, the white gleaming lighthouse, the long ridge of heathy ground on the crest of the hill, the villas, the gardens with their glow of light and colour, the dark masses of foliage clustering here and there amidst the bright-hued rocks. He looked at everything except his dead wife, lying almost at his feet.

There was an inquiry that evening before the Juge d'Instruction at Villefranche, and he was made to give an account of his wife's death. He proved a very bad witness. The minute and seemingly frivolous questions addled his brain. He told the magistrate how he had looked round and found the path empty: but he could not say how his wife had fallen – whether she had flung herself over the edge or had fallen accidentally, whether her foot had slipped unawares, whether she had fallen face forward, or whether she had dropped backwards from the edge of the cliff.

'I tell you again that I did not see her fall,' he protested impatiently.

'Did you usually walk in advance of your wife?' asked the Frenchman. 'It was not very polite to turn your back upon a lady.'

'I was worried, and out of temper.'

'For what reason?'

'My wife's unhappy jealousy created reasons where there were none. The people who know me know that I was not habitually unkind to her.'

'Yet you gave her an answer which so maddened her that she flung herself over the cliff in her despair?'

'I fear that it was so,' he answered, with the deepest distress depicted in his haggard face. 'She was in a nervous and irritable condition. I had always borne that fact in mind until that moment. She stung me past endurance by her groundless jealousies. I had been a true and loyal husband to her from the hour of our marriage. I had never wronged her by so much as a thought; and yet I could not talk to a pretty peasant-girl, or confess my admiration for any woman I met in society, without causing an outbreak of temper that was almost madness. I bore with her long and patiently. I remembered that the circumstances of her childhood and youth had been adverse, that her nature had been warped and perverted; I forgave all faults of temper in a wife who loved me; but this afternoon – almost for the first time since our marriage – I spoke unkindly, cruelly perhaps. I have no wish to avoid interrogation, or to conceal any portion of the truth.'

'You did not push her over the cliff?'

'I did not. Do I look like a murderer, or bear the character of a man likely to commit murder?'

The examination went on, with cruel reiteration of almost the same questions. The Judge d'Instruction was a hard-headed legal machine, who believed that the truth might be wrung out of any criminal by persistent questioning. He suspected Ransome, or deemed it his duty to suspect him, and he ordered him to be arrested on leaving the court; so George Ransome passed the night after his wife's death in the lock-up at Villefranche.

What a night that was for a man to live through! He sat on a stone bench, listening to the level plish-plash of that tideless sea ever so far beneath him. He heard the footsteps going up and down the steep stony street of that wonderful old seaport; he heard the scream of the gulls and the striking of the clock on the crest of the hill as he sat motionless, with his elbows on his knees, and his head in his hands, brooding over that swift, sudden horror of yesterday.

Could it have been an accident? Did she step backwards unawares and slip over the edge? No; he remembered where she was standing when he last looked at her, some distance from the side of the cliff, standing among the heather and wild thyme which grew down to the edge of the little path. She must have made a rapid rush to the brink after that fatal speech of his. She had flung her life away in a single impulse of blind, mad anger – or despair. She had not paused for an instant to take thought. Alas! he knew her so well; he had so often seen those sudden gusts of passion; the rush of crimson to the pale small face; the quivering lips striving impotently for speech; the fury in the dark eyes, and the small nervous hands clenched convulsively. He had seen her struggle with the demon of anger, and had seen the storm pass swifter than a tempest-driven cloud across the moon. Another moment and she would burst into tears, fling her arms round his neck, and implore him to forgive her.

'I love you too well ever to know happiness,' she said.

That was her favourite apology.

'It is only people without passions who can be happy,' she told him once. 'I sometimes think that you belong to that family.'

And she was dead; she whose undisciplined love had so plagued and tried him, she was dead; and he felt himself her murderer.

Alas! doubly a murderer, since she had perished just at that time when her life should have been most precious to him, when he should have made any sacrifice to secure her peace. He who had seen all the evils of a fretful temper exhibited in her character had yet been weak enough to yield to a moment of anger, and to insult the woman whom he ought to have cherished.

A long-familiar line of Byron's haunted his brain all through the night, and mixed itself with that sound of footsteps on the street of stairs, and the scream of the gulls, and the flapping of the waves against the stone quay.

> 'She died, but not alone——'

She who was to have been the mother of his first-born child was lying dead in the white-walled villa where they had once been happy.

Hush! In the soft clear light of an April morning he heard the tolling of the church bell, solemn, slow, measured, at agonising intervals, which left an age of expectancy between the heavy strokes of the clapper.

Vivos voco, mortuos plango.

They bury their dead at daybreak in that fair land of orange and lemon groves. In the early morning of the first day after death, the hastily-fashioned coffin was carried out into the sunshine, and the funeral procession wound slowly up the hill towards the graveyard near the church of Villefranche. George Ransome knew how brief is the interval between death and burial on that southern shore, and he had little doubt that the bell was tolling for her whose heart was beating passionately when the sun began to sink.

So soon! Her grave would be filled in and trodden down before they let him out of prison.

It had never seemed to him that he was to stay long in captivity, or that there could be any difficulty in proving his innocence of any part in the catastrophe, except that fatal part of having upset the balance of a weak mind, and provoked a passionate woman to suicide. As for the confinement of the past night, he had scarcely thought about it. He had a curious semi-consciousness of time and place which was a new experience to him. He found himself forgetting where he was and what had happened. There were strange gaps in his mind – intervals of oblivion – and then there were periods in which he sat looking at the slanting shaft of sunlight between the window and the ground, and trying to count the motes that danced in that golden haze.

The day passed strangely, too – sometimes at railroad pace, sometimes with a ghastly slowness. Then came a night in which sleep never visited his eyelids – a night of bodily and mental restlessness, the greater part of which he spent in futile efforts to open the heavily-bolted door, or to drag the window-bars from their stone sockets. His prison was a relic of the Middle Ages, and Hercules himself could not have got out of it.

In all those endeavours he was actuated by a blind impulse – a feverish desire to be at large again. Not once during that night did he think of his dead wife in her new-made grave on the side of the hill. He had forgotten why they had shut him up in that stony chamber – or rather had imagined another reason for his imprisonment.

He was a political offender – had been deeply concerned in a plot to overthrow Victor Emanuel, and to create a Republic for Italy. He himself was to be President of that Republic. He felt all the power to rule and legislate for a great nation. He compared himself with Solon and with Pericles, to the disadvantage of both. There was a greatness in him which neither of those had ever attained.

'I should rule them as God Himself,' he thought. 'It would be a golden age of truth and justice – a millennium of peace and plenty. And while the nations are waiting for me I am shut up here by the treachery of France.'

Next morning he was taken before the Juge d'Instruction for the second time. The two fishermen who picked up his wife's corpse were present as witnesses; also his wife's maid, and the three other servants; also his wife's doctor.

He was again questioned severely, but this time nothing could induce him to give a direct answer to any question. He raved about the Italian Republic, of which he was to be chief. He told the French magistrate that France had conspired with the Italian tyrant to imprison and suppress him.

'Every other pretence is a subterfuge,' he said. 'My popularity in Italy is at the root of this monstrous charge. There will be a rising of the whole nation if you do not instantly release me. For your own sake, sir, I warn you to be prompt.'

'This man is pretending to be mad,' said the magistrate.

'I fear there is more reality than pretence about the business,' said the doctor.

He took Ransome to the window, and looked at his eyes in the strong white light of noon. Then he went over to the magistrate, and they whispered together for some minutes, while the prisoner sat staring at the floor and muttering to himself.

After that there came a long dark interval in George Ransome's life – a waking dream of intolerable length, but not unalloyed misery; for the hallucinations which made his madness buoyed him up and sustained him during some part of that dark period. He talked with princes and statesmen; he was not alone in the madhouse chamber, or in the madhouse garden, or in that great iron cage where even the most desperate maniacs were allowed to disport themselves in the air and the sunlight as in a gymnasium. He was surrounded by invisible friends and flatterers, by public functionaries who quailed before his glance and were eager to obey his commands. Sometimes he wrote letters and telegrams all day long upon any scraps of paper which his keepers would give him;

sometimes he passed whole days in a dreamy silence with arms folded, and abstracted gaze fixed on the distant hill-tops, like Napoleon at St Helena, brooding over the future of nations.

By and by there came a period of improvement, or what was called improvement by the doctors, but which to the patient seemed a time of strange blankness and disappointment. All those busy shadows which had peopled his life, his senators and flatterers, had abandoned him; he was alone in that strange place amidst a strange people, most of whom seemed to be somewhat wrong in their heads. He was able to read the newspapers now, and was vexed to find that his speeches were unreported, his letters and manifestoes unpublished; disappointed to find that Victor Emanuel was still King of Italy and the new Republic still a web of dreams.

His temper was very fitful at this time, and he had intervals of violence. One morning he found himself upon the hills, digging with half-a-dozen other men, young and old, dressed pretty much like himself. It was in the early summer morning, before the sun had made the world too hot for labour. It was rapture to him to be there, digging and running about on the dewy hillside, in an amphitheatre of mountains, high above the stony bed of the Paillon. The air was full of sweet odours, orange and lemon bloom, roses and lilies, from the gardens and orchards below. He felt that earth and sky were rapturously lovely, that life was a blessing and a privilege beyond all words. He had not the consciousness of a single care, or even a troubled memory. His quarrel with his father, his self-imposed exile, his marriage and its bitter disillusions, his wife's tragical fate: all were forgotten. He felt as a sylph might feel – a creature without earthly obligations, revelling in the glory of Nature.

This new phase of being lasted so long as the hills and the sky wore their aspect of novelty. It was succeeded by a period of deepest depression, a melancholy which weighed him down like a leaden burden. He sat in the madhouse garden apart from the rest, brooding over the darkness of life. He had no hopes, no desires.

Gradually memory began to return. He asked why his wife did not come to see him. 'She used to be so fond of me,' he said, 'foolishly fond of me; and now she deserts me.'

Then he talked of going home again. The image of his latest dwelling-place had gradually shaped itself in his mind. He saw the hedges of pale amber roses, the carouba-trees, dark against the glittering blue of the sea, which shone through every opening in the branches like a background of lapis lazuli, and the rugged mountains rising above the low curving shore steeply towards the sky, with patches of olive here and there on their stony flanks, but for the most part bare and barren, reddish-yellow, steeped in sunlight.

Yes, he remembered every feature of that lovely and varied scene. The village of Eza yonder on the mountain-road – a cluster of stony dwellings perched upon rocky foundations, hardly to be distinguished from the rough crags upon which they were built – and higher still, in a cleft of those yellow hills, Turbia, and its cloven towers, the birthplace of Roman Emperors. How lovely it all was, and how pleasant it had been to lounge in his garden, where the light looked dazzling on beds of white gilly-flowers, and where the blue summer sea smiled in the far distance, with a faint purple cloud yonder on the horizon which represented Corsica!

Why had he ever left that familiar home? Why could he not return to it?

'Get me a carriage,' he said to one of the attendants; 'I want to go home immediately. My wife is waiting for me.'

It is not customary to make explanations to patients even in the best-regulated asylums. Nobody answered him; nobody explained anything to him. He found himself confronted with a dogged silence. He wore himself out in an agony of impatience, like a bird beating itself to death against its bars. He languished in a miserable ignorance, piecing his past life together bit by bit, with a strange interweaving of fancies and realities, until by slow degrees the fancies dropped out of the web and left him face to face with the truth.

At last the record of the past was complete. He knew that his wife was dead, and remembered how she had died. He knew that he had been a prisoner, first in gaol and then in a lunatic asylum; but he did not acknowledge to himself that he had been mad. He remembered the bell tolling in the saffron light of dawn; he remembered the magistrate's exasperating questions; he remembered everything.

After this he sank into a state of sullen despair, and silence and apathy were accepted as the indications of cure. He was told by the head physician that he could leave the institution whenever he pleased. There was an account against him as a private patient, which had been guaranteed by his landlord, who knew him to be a man of some means. His German man-servant had been to the asylum many times to inquire about him. The doctor recommended him to travel – in Switzerland – until the end of the autumn, and to take his servant as his attendant and courier. 'Change of air and scene will be of inestimable advantage to you,' said the doctor; 'but it would not be wise for you to travel alone.'

'What month is it?'

'August – the twenty-second.'

'And my wife died early in April,' he said. 'Only a few months; and I feel as if I had been in this place a century.'

He took the doctor's advice. He cared very little where he went or what became of him. Life and the world, his own individuality, and the beautiful earth around and about him were alike indifferent to him. He went back to the villa at St Jean, and to the garden he had loved so well in the bright fresh spring-time. All things had an overgrown and neglected look in the ripeness of expiring summer; too many flowers, a rank luxuriance of large leaves and vivid blossoms – fruit rotting in the long grass – an odour of decaying oranges, the waste of the last harvest. He went up to the graveyard on the hill above the harbour. It was not a picturesque burial-place. The cemetery at Cimies was far more beautiful. The cemetery at Nice was in a grander position.

He felt sorry that she should lie here, amidst the graves of sailors and fishermen – as even if after death she were slighted and hardly used.

He was summoned back to England early in the following year to his mother's death-bed. Neither she nor any of his family had known the miserable end of his married life. They knew only that he had married, and had lost his wife after a year of marriage. Hazard had not brought any one belonging to him in contact with any of those few people who knew the details of that tragical story.

His mother's death made him rich and independent, but until the hour he met Mildred Fausset his life was a blank.

CHAPTER V

THE GRAVE ON THE HILL

After that visit to the great white barrack on the road to St André, Mildred felt that her business at Nice was finished, there was nothing more for her to learn. She knew all the sad story now – all, except those lights and shadows of the picture which only the unhappy actor in that domestic tragedy could have told her. The mystery of the past had unfolded itself, stage by stage, from that Sunday afternoon when César Castellani came to Enderby Manor, and out of trivial-seeming talk launched a thunderbolt. The curtain was lifted. There was no more to be done. And yet Mildred lingered at Nice, loving the place and its environs a little for their own beauty, and feeling a strange and sorrowful interest in the scene of her husband's misfortunes.

There was another reason for remaining in the gay white city in the fact that Lady Lochinvar had taken a fancy to Miss Ransome, and that the young lady seemed to be achieving a remarkably rapid cure of her infatuation for the Italian. It may have been because at the Palais Montano she met a good many Italians, and that the charm of that nationality became less potent with familiarity. There was music, too, at the Palais, and to spare, according to Mr Stuart, who was not an enthusiast, and was wont to shirk his aunt's musical reunions.

Mildred was delighted to see her husband's niece entering society under such agreeable auspices. She went out with her occasionally, just enough to make people understand that she was not indifferent to her niece's happiness; and for the rest, Lady Lochinvar and Mrs Murray were always ready to chaperon the frank, bright girl, who was much admired by the best people, and was never at a loss for partners at dances, whoever else might play wallflower.

Mrs Greswold invited Mr and Mrs Murray and Malcolm Stuart to a quiet little dinner at the Westminster, and the impression the young man made upon Mildred's mind was altogether favourable. He was certainly not handsome, but his plainness was of an honest Scottish type, and his freckled complexion and blue eyes, sandy hair and moustache, were altogether different from the traditional Judas colouring of Castellani's auburn beard and hazel eyes. Truth and honesty beamed in the Scotchman's open countenance. He looked every inch a soldier and a gentleman.

That he admired Pamela was obvious to the most unobservant eye; that she affected to look down upon him was equally obvious; but it might be that her good-humoured scorn of him was more pretence than reality. She made light of him openly as one of that inferior race of men whose minds never soar above the stable, the gunroom, or the homefarm, and whose utmost intellectual ingenuity culminates in the invention of a salmon-fly or the discovery of a new fertiliser for turnip-fields.

'You are just like my brother-in-law, Henry Mountford,' she told him.

'From the air with which you say that, I conclude Sir Henry Mountford must be a very inferior person.'

'Not at all. He is the kind of man whom all other men seem to respect. I believe he is one of the best shots in England. His bags are written about in the newspapers; and I wonder there are any pigeons left in the world, considering the way he has slaughtered them.'

'I saw him shoot at Monte Carlo the year before last.'

'Yes; he went there and back in a week on purpose to shoot. Imagine any man coming to this divine Riviera, this land of lemon-groves and palms, and roses and violets, just to slaughter pigeons!'

'He won the Grand Prix. It was a pretty big feather in his cap,' said Mr Stuart. 'Am I to conclude that you dislike sporting men?'

'I prefer men who cultivate their minds.'

'Ah, but a man who shoots well and rides straight, and can play a big salmon, and knows how to manage a farm, cannot be altogether an imbecile. I never knew a really fine rider yet who was a fool. Good horsemanship needs so many qualities that fools don't possess; and to be a crack shot, I assure you that a man must have some brains and a good deal of perseverance; and perseverance is not a bad thing in its way, Miss Ransome.'

He looked at her with a certain significance in his frank blue eyes, looked at her resolutely, as some bold young Vandal or Visigoth might have looked at a Roman maiden whom he meant to subjugate.

'I did not say that sportsmen were fools,' she answered sharply. 'I only say that the kind of man I respect is the man whose pleasures are those of the intellect – who is in the front rank among the thinkers of his age – who——'

'Reads Darwin and the German metaphysicians, I suppose. I tried Darwin to see if he would help me in my farming, but I can't say I got very much out of him in that line. There's more in old Virgil for an agriculturist. I'm not a reading man, you see, Miss Ransome. I find by the time I've read the daily papers my thirst for knowledge is pretty well satisfied. There's such a lot of information in the London papers, and when you add the *Figaro* and the *New York Herald*, there's not much left for a man to learn. I generally read the Quarterlies – as a duty – to discover how many dull books have enriched the world during the previous three months.'

'That's a great deal more reading than my brother-in-law gets through. He makes a great fuss about his *Times* every morning; but I believe he seldom goes beyond the births, marriages, and deaths, or a report of a billiard match. He reads the *Field*, as a kind of religion, and *Baily's Magazine*; and I think that's all.'

'Do you like men who write books, Miss Ransome, as well as men who read them?'

Pamela crimsoned to the roots of her hair at this most innocent question. Malcolm Stuart marked that blush with much perplexity.

'When one is interested in a book one likes to know the author,' she replied, with cautious vagueness.

'Do you know many writers?'

'Not many – in fact, only one.'

'Who is he?'

'Mr Castellani, the author of *Nepenthe*.'

'*Nepenthe?* – ah, that's a novel people were talking about some time ago. My aunt was full of it, because she fancied it embodied some of her own ideas. She wanted me to read it. I tried a few chapters,' said Malcolm, making a wry face. 'Sickly stuff.'

'People who are not in the habit of reading the literature of imagination can hardly understand such a book as *Nepenthe*,' replied Pamela severely. 'They are out of touch with the spirit and the atmosphere of the book.'

'One has to be trained up to that kind of thing, I suppose. One must forget that two and two make four, in order to get into the proper frame of mind, eh? Is the author of *Nepenthe* an interesting man?'

He was shrewd enough to interpret the blush aright. The author of *Nepenthe* was a person to be dreaded by any aspirant to Miss Ransome's favour.

'He is like his book,' answered Pamela briefly.

'Is he a young man?'

'I don't know your idea of youth. He is older than my aunt – about five-and-thirty.'

Stuart was just thirty. One point in his favour, anyhow, he told himself, not knowing that to a romantic girl years may be interesting.

'Handsome?'

'*That* is always a matter of opinion. He is just the kind of man who ought to have written *Nepenthe*. That is really all I can tell you,' said Pamela, with some irritation. 'I believe Lady Lochinvar knew Mr Castellani when he was a very young man. She can satisfy your curiosity about him.'

'I am not curious. Castellani? An Italian, I suppose, one of my aunt's innumerable geniuses. She has a genius for discovering geniuses. When I see her with a new one, I am always reminded of a child with a little coloured balloon. So pretty – till it bursts!'

Pamela turned her back upon him in a rage, and went over to the piano to talk to Mrs Murray, who was preparing to sing one of her *répertoire* of five Scotch ballads.

'Shall it be "Gin a body" or "Huntingtower"?' she asked meekly; and nobody volunteering a decisive opinion, she chirruped the former coquettish little ballad, and put a stop to social intercourse for exactly four minutes and a half.

After that evening Mr Stuart knew who his rival was, and with what kind of influence he had to contend. An author, a musical man, a genius! Well, he had very few weapons with which to fight such an antagonist, he who was neither musical, nor literary, nor gifted with any of the graces which recommend a lover to a sentimental girl. But he was a man, and he meant to win her. He admired her for her frank young prettiness, so unsophisticated and girlish, and for that perfect freshness and truthfulness of mind which made all her thoughts transparent. He was too much a man of the world to ignore the fact that Miss Ransome of Mapledown would be a very good match for him, or that such a marriage would strengthen his position in his aunt's esteem. Women bow down to success. Encouraged by these considerations, Mr Stuart pursued the even tenor of his way, and was not disheartened by the idea of the author of *Nepenthe*, more especially as that attractive personage was not on the ground. He had one accomplishment over and above the usual outdoor exercises of a country gentleman. He could dance, and he was Pamela's favourite partner wherever she went. No one else waltzed as well. Not even the most gifted of her German acquaintance; not even the noble Spaniards who were presented to her.

He had another and still greater advantage in the fact that he was often in the young lady's society. She was fond of Lady Lochinvar, and spent a good deal of her life at the Palais Montano, where, with Mrs Murray's indefatigable assistance, there were tennis-parties twice a week. That charming garden, with its numerous summer-houses, made a kind of club for the privileged few who were permitted *les petites entrées*.

While Pamela was enjoying the lovely springtide amongst people whose only thought was of making the best of life, and getting the maximum of sunshine, Mildred Greswold spent her days in sad musings upon an irrevocable past. It was her melancholy pleasure to revisit again and again the place in which her husband had lived, the picturesque little village under the shadow of the tall cliff, every pathway which he must have trodden, every point from which he must have gazed across the bay, seaward or landward in his troubled reveries.

She dwelt with morbid persistence on the thought of those two lives, both dear to her, yet in their union how terrible a curse! She revisited the villa until the old caretaker grew to look upon her as a heaven-sent benefactress, and until the village children christened her the English Madonna, that pensive look recalling the face of the statue in the church yonder, so mildly sad, a look of ineffable sweetness tinged with pain. She sat for hours at a stretch in the sunlit garden, amongst such flowers as must have been blooming there in those closing hours of Fay's wedded life, when the shadow of her cruel fate was darkening round her, though she knew it not. She talked to people who had known the English lady. Alas! they were all dubious in their opinions. None would answer boldly for the husband's innocence. They shrugged their shoulders – they shook their heads. Who could say? Only the good God would ever know the truth about that story.

The place to which she went oftenest in those balmy afternoons was the burial-ground on the hill, where Fay's grave, with its white marble cross, occupied one of the highest points in the enclosure, and stood out sharp and clear against the cloudless sapphire.

The inscription on that marble was of the briefest:

'VIVIEN RANSOME.
Died April 24th, 1868.
Eternally lamented.'

Below the cross stretched the grass mound, without shrub or flower. It was Mildred's task to beautify this neglected grave. She brought a florist from the neighbourhood to carry out her own idea, and on her instruction he removed the long, rank grass from the mound, and planted a cross of roses, eight feet long, dwarf bush-roses closely planted, Gloire de Dijon and Maréchal Niel.

She remembered how Fay had revelled in the rose-garden at The Hook, where midsummer was a kind of carnival of roses. Here the roses would bloom all the year round, and there would be perpetual perfume and blossom and colour above poor Fay's cold dust.

CHAPTER VI

PAMELA CHANGES HER MIND

Lucifer himself, after his fall, could not have felt worse than César Castellani when he followed Mildred Greswold to Nice, as he did within a week after she left Pallanza.

He went to Nice partly because he was an idle man, and had no desire to go back to English east winds just when the glory of the southern springtide was beginning. He was tolerably well furnished with money, and Nice was as good to him as any other place, while the neighbourhood of Monte Carlo was always an attraction. He followed in Mildred's footsteps, therefore; but he had no idea of forcing himself upon her presence for some time to come. He knew that his chances were ruined in that quarter for the time being, if not for ever.

This was his first signal overthrow. Easy conquests had so demoralised him that he had grown to consider all conquests easy. He had unlimited faith in the charm of his own personality – his magnetic power, as he called it: and, behold! his magnetic power had failed utterly with this lovely, lonely woman, who should have turned to him in her desolation as the flowers turn to the sun.

For once in his life he had overrated himself and his influence; and in so doing he had lost the chance of a very respectable alliance.

'Fifteen hundred a year would be at least bread and cheese,' he reflected, 'and to marry an English heiress of a good old family would solidify my position in society. The girl is pretty enough, and I could twist her round my finger. She would bore me frightfully; but every man must suffer something. There is always a discord somewhere amidst the harmony of life; and if one's teeth are not too often set on edge by that false note, one should be content.'

He remembered how contemptuously he had rejected the idea of such a marriage in his talk with Miss Fausset, and how she had been set upon it.

'I should stand ever so much better with her if I married well, and solidified myself into British respectability. I might naturalise myself, and go into Parliament perhaps, if that would please the good soul at Brighton. What will she leave me when she dies, I wonder? She is muter than the Sphinx upon that point. And will she ever die? Brighton is famous for pauper females of ninety and upwards. A woman like Miss Fausset, who lives in cotton-wool, and who has long done with the cares and passions of life, might go well into a second century. I don't see any brilliancy in the prospect *there*; but so long as I please her and do well in the world she will no doubt be generous.'

He told himself that it was essential he should make some concession to Miss Fausset's prejudices now that he had failed with Mildred. So long as he had hoped to win that nobler prize he had been careless how he jeopardised the favour of his elderly patroness. But now he felt that her favour was all in all to him, and that the time for trifling was past.

She had been very generous to him during the years that had gone by since she first came to his aid almost unasked, and helped him to pay his college debts. She had come to the rescue many times since that juvenile entanglement, and her patience had been great. Yet she had not failed to remonstrate with him at every fresh instance of folly and self-indulgent extravagance. She had talked to him with an unflinching directness; she had refused further help; but somehow she had always given way, and the cheque had been written.

Again and again she had warned him that there were limits even to her forbearance.

'If I saw you working earnestly and industriously, I should not mind, even if you were a failure,' said his benefactress severely.

'I have worked, and I have produced a book which was *not* a failure,' replied César, with his silkiest air.

'One book in a decade of so-called literary life! Did the success of that book result in the payment of one single debt?'

'Dearest lady, would you have a man waste his own earnings – the first-fruits of his pen – the grains of fairy gold that filtered through the mystic web of his fancy – would you have him fritter away that sacred product upon importunate hosiers or vindictive bootmakers? *That* money was altogether precious to me. I kept it in my waistcoat pocket as long as ever I could. The very touch of the coin thrilled me. I believe cabmen and crossing-sweepers had most of it in the long-run,' he concluded, with a remorseful sigh.

Miss Fausset had borne with his idleness and his vanity, as indulgent mothers bear with their sons; but he felt that she was beginning to tire of him. There were reasons why she should always continue forbearing; but he wanted to insure himself something better than reluctant subsidies.

These considerations being taken into account, Mr Castellani was fain to own to himself that he had been a fool in rejecting the substance for the shadow, however alluring the lovely shade might be.

'But I loved her,' he sighed; 'I loved her as I had never loved until I saw her fair Madonna face amidst the century-old peace of her home. She filled my life with a new element. She purified and exalted my whole being. And she is thrice as rich as that prattling girl!'

He ground his teeth at the remembrance of his failure. There had been no room for doubt. Those soft violet eyes had been transformed by indignation, and had flashed upon him with angry fire. That fair Madonna face had whitened to marble with suppressed passion. Not by one glance, not by one tremor in the contemptuous voice, had the woman he loved acknowledged his influence.

He put up at the Cosmopolitan, got in half-a-dozen French novels of the most advanced school from Galignani's Library, and kept himself very close for a week or two; but he contrived to find out what the ladies at the Westminster were doing through Albrecht the courier, who believed him to be Miss Ransome's suitor, and was inclined to be communicative, after being copiously treated to bocks, or *petits verres*, as the case might be.

From Albrecht, Castellani heard how Miss Ransome spent most of her time at the Palais Montano, or gadding about with her ladyship and Mrs Murray; how, in Albrecht's private opinion, the balls and other dissipations of Nice were turning that young lady's head; how Mrs Greswold went for lonely drives day after day, and would not allow Albrecht to show her the beauties of the neighbourhood, which it would have been alike his duty and pleasure to have done. He had ascertained that her favourite, and, indeed, habitual, drive was to St Jean, where she was in the habit of leaving the fly at the little inn while she strolled about the village in a purposeless manner. All this appeared to Albrecht as eccentric and absurd, and beneath a lady of Mrs Greswold's position. She would have employed her time to more advantage in going on distant excursions in a carriage and pair, and in lunching at remote hotels, where Albrecht would have been sure of a *bonne main* from a gratified landlord, as well as his commission from the livery-stable.

Castellani heard with displeasure of Pamela's dancings and junketings, and he told himself that it was time to throw himself across her pathway. He had not been prepared to find that she could enjoy life without him. Her admiration of him had been so transparent, her sentimental fancy so naïvely revealed, that he had believed himself the sultan of her heart, having only to throw the handkerchief whenever it might suit him to claim his prey. Much as he prided himself upon his knowledge of human

nature, as exemplified in the softer sex, he had never estimated the
fickleness of a shallow sentimental character like Pamela's. No man with a
due regard to the value and dignity of his sex could conceive the ruthless
rapidity with which a young lady of this temperament will transfer her
affections and her large assortment of day-dreams and romantic fancies
from one man to another. No man could conceive her capacity for
admiring in Number Two all those qualities which were lacking in
Number One. No man could imagine the exquisite adaptability of
girlhood to surrounding circumstances.

Had Castellani taken Miss Ransome when she was in the humour, he
would have found her the most amiable and yielding of wives; a model
English wife, ready to adapt herself in all things to the will and the
pleasure of her husband; unselfish, devoted, unassailable in her belief in
her husband as the first and best of men. But he had not seized his
opportunity. He had allowed nearly a month to go by since his defeat at
Pallanza, and he had allowed Pamela to discover that life might be
endurable, nay, even pleasant, without him.

And now, hearing that the young lady was gadding about, and divining
that such gadding was the high-road to forgetfulness, Mr Castellani made
up his mind to resume his sway over Miss Ransome's fancy without loss
of time. He called upon a dashing American matron whom he had
visited in London and Paris, and who was now the occupant of a villa on
the Promenade des Anglais, and in her drawing-room he fell in with
several of his London acquaintances. He found, however, that his
American friend, Mrs Montagu W. Brown, had not yet succeeded in
being invited to the Palais Montano, and only knew Lady Lochinvar and
Miss Ransome by sight.

'Her ladyship is too stand-offish for my taste,' said Mrs Montagu
Brown, 'but the girl seems friendly enough – no style – not as we
Americans understand style. I am told she ranks as an heiress on this side,
but at the last ball at the Cercle she wore a frock that I should call dear at
forty dollars. That young Stuart is after her, evidently. I hope you are
going to the dance next Tuesday, Mr Castellani? I want some one nice to
talk to now my waltzing days are over.'

Castellani protested that Mrs Montagu Brown was in the very heyday
of a dancer's age, and would be guilty of gross cruelty to terpsichorean
society in abandoning that delightful art.

'You make me tired,' said Mrs Montagu Brown, with perfect good-
humour. 'There are plenty of women who don't know when they're old,
but I calculate every woman knows when she weighs a hundred and sixty
pounds. When my waist came to twenty-six inches I knew it was time to
leave off waltzing; and I was pretty good at it, too, in my day, I can tell
you.'

'With that carriage you must have been divine,' replied César; 'and I believe the cestus of the Venus de Milo must measure over twenty-six inches.'

'The Venus de Milo has no more figure than the peasant-women one sees on the promenade, women who seem as if they set their faces against the very idea of a waist. Be sure you get a card for Tuesday. I hate a dude; but I love to have some smart men about me wherever I go.'

'I shall be there,' said Castellani, bending over his hostess and imparting a confidential pressure to her fat white hand by way of leave-taking, before he slipped silently from the room.

He had studied the art of departure as if it were a science: never lingered, never hummed and hawed; never said he must go and didn't; never apologised for going so soon while everybody was pining to get rid of him.

The next day there was a battle of flowers; not the great floral fête before the sugar-plum carnival, but an altogether secondary affair, pleasant enough in the balmy weather of advancing spring.

Every one of any importance was on the promenade, and among the best carriages appeared Lady Lochinvar's barouche, decorated with white camellias and carmine carnations. She had carefully eschewed that favourite mixture of camellias and Parma violets which has always a half-mourning or funereal air. Malcolm Stuart and Miss Ransome sat side by side on the front seat with a great basket of carnations on their knees, with which they pelted their acquaintance, while Lady Lochinvar, in brown velvet and ostrich plumage, reposed at her ease in the back of the spacious carriage, and enjoyed the fun without any active participation.

It was Pamela's first experience in flower-fights, and to her the scene seemed enchanting. The afternoon was peerless. She wore a white gown, as if it had been midsummer, and white gowns were the rule in most of the carriages. The sea was at its bluest, the pink walls and green shutters, white walls and red roofs, the orange-trees, cactus and palm, made up a picture of a city in fairyland, taken as a background to a triple procession of carriages all smothered in Parma violets, Dijon roses, camellias, and narcissus, with here and there some picturesque coach festooned with oranges and lemons amidst tropical foliage.

The carriages moved at a foot-pace; the pavements were crowded with smart people, who joined in the contest. Pamela's lap was full of bouquets, which fell from her in showers as she stood up every now and then to fling a handful of carnations into a passing carriage.

Presently, while she was standing thus, flushed and sparkling, she saw a familiar figure on the foot-path by the sea, and paled suddenly at the sight.

It was César Castellani, sauntering slowly along, in a short coat of light-coloured cloth, and a felt hat of exactly the same delicate shade. He came to the carriage-door. There was a block at the moment, and he had time to talk to the occupants.

'How do you do, Lady Lochinvar? You have not forgotten me, I hope – César Castellani – though it is such ages since we met?'

He only lifted his hat to Lady Lochinvar, waiting for her recognition, but he held out his hand to Pamela.

'How do you like Nice, Miss Ransome? As well as Pallanza, I hope?'

'Ever so much better than Pallanza.'

There was a time when that coat and hat, the *soupçon* of dark blue velvet waistcoat just showing underneath the pale buff collar, the loose China silk handkerchief carelessly fastened with a priceless intaglio, the gardenia and pearl-gray gloves, would have ensnared Pamela's fancy: but that time was past. She thought that César's costume looked effeminate and underbred beside the stern simplicity of Mr Stuart's heather-mixture *complet*. The scales had fallen from her eyes; and she recognised the bad taste and the vanity involved in that studied carelessness, that artistic combination of colour.

She remembered what Mildred had said of Mr Castellani, and she was deliberately cold. Lady Lochinvar was gracious, knowing nothing to the Italian's discredit.

'I remember you perfectly,' she said. 'You have changed very little in all these years. Be sure you come and see me. I am at home at five almost every afternoon.'

The carriage moved on, and Pamela sat in an idle reverie for the next ten minutes, although the basket of carnations was only half empty.

She was thinking how strange it was that her heart beat no faster. Could it be that she was cured – and so soon? It was even worse than a cure; it was a positive revulsion of feeling. She was vexed with herself for ever having exalted that over-dressed foreigner into a hero. She felt she had been un-English, unwomanly even, in her exaggerated admiration of an exotic. And then she glanced at Malcolm Stuart, and averted her eyes with a conscious blush on seeing him earnestly observant of her.

He was plain, certainly. His features had been moulded roughly, but they were not bad features. The lines were rather good, in fact, and it was a fine manly countenance. He was fair and slightly freckled, as became a Scotchman; his eyes were clear and blue, but could be compared to neither sapphires nor violets, and his eyelashes were lighter than any cultivated young lady could approve. The general tone of his hair and complexion was ginger; and ginger, taken in connection with masculine beauty, is not all one would wish. But then ginger is not uncommon in the service, and it is a hue which harmonises agreeably with Highland bonnets and tartan. No doubt Mr

Stuart had looked really nice in his uniform. He had certainly appeared to advantage in a Highland costume at the fancy ball the other night. Some people had pronounced him the finest-looking man in the room.

And, again, good looks are of little importance in a man. A plainish man, possessed of all the manly accomplishments, a dead shot and a crack rider, can always appear to advantage in English society. Pamela was beginning to think more kindly of sporting men, and even of Sir Henry Mountford.

'I'm sure Mr Stuart would get on with him,' she thought, dimly foreseeing a day when Sir Henry and her new acquaintance would be brought together somehow.

César Castellani took immediate advantage of Lady Lochinvar's invitation. He presented himself at the Palais Montano on the following afternoon, and he found Pamela established there as if she belonged to the house. It was she who poured out the tea, and dispensed those airy little hot cakes, which were a kind of idealised galette, served in the daintiest of doyleys, embroidered with Lady Lochinvar's cipher and coronet.

Mr and Mrs Murray were there, and Malcolm Stuart, the chief charm of whose society seemed to consist in his exhibition of an accomplished Dandie Dinmont which usurped the conversation, and which Castellani would have liked to inocculate then and there with the most virulent form of rabies. Pamela squatted on a little stool at the creature's feet, and assisted in showing him off. She had acquired a power over him which indicated an acquaintance of some standing.

'What fools girls are!' thought Castellani.

His conquests among women of maturer years had been built upon rock as compared with the shifting quicksand of a girl's fancy. He began to think the genus girl utterly contemptible.

'He has but one fault,' said Pamela, when the terrier had gone through various clumsy evolutions in which the bandiness of his legs and the length of his body had been shown off to the uttermost. 'He cannot endure Box, and Box detests him. They never meet without trying to murder each other, and I'm very much afraid,' bending down to kiss the broad hairy head, 'that Dandie is the stronger.'

'Of course he is. Box is splendid for muscle, but weight must tell in the long-run,' replied Mr Stuart.

'My grandmother had a Dandie whose father belonged to Sir Walter Scott,' began Mrs Murray: 'he was simply a per-r-r-fect dog, and my mamma——'

Castellani fled from this inanity. He went to the other end of the room, where Lady Lochinvar was listening listlessly to Mr Murray, laid himself out to amuse her ladyship for the next ten minutes, and then departed without so much as a look at Pamela.

'The spell is broken,' he said to himself, as he drove away. 'The girl is next door to an idiot. No doubt she will marry that sandy Scotchman. Lady Lochinvar means it, and a silly-pated miss like that can be led with a thread of floss silk. *Moi je m'en fiche.*'

About a week after Mr Castellani's reappearance Mildred Greswold received a letter from Brighton, which made a sudden change in her plans.

It was from Mr Maltravers the Incumbent of St Edmund's:

'St Edmund's Vicarage.

'Dear Mrs Greswold, – After our thoroughly confidential conversations last autumn I feel justified in addressing you upon a subject which I know is very near to your heart, namely, the health and welfare, spiritual as well as bodily, of your dear aunt and my most valued parishioner, Miss Fausset. The condition of that dear lady has given me considerable uneasiness during the last few months. She had refused to take her hand from the plough; she labours as faithfully as ever in the Lord's vineyard; but I see with deepest regret that she is no longer the woman she was, even a year ago. The decay has been sudden, and it has been rapid. Her strength begins to fail her, though she will hardly admit as much, even to her medical attendant, and her spirits are less equable than of old. She has intervals of extreme depression, against which the efforts of friendship, the power of spiritual consolation, are unavailing.

'I feel it my duty to inform you, as one who has a right to be interested in the disposal of Miss Fausset's wealth, that my benfactress has consummated the generosity of past years by a magnificent gift. She has endowed her beloved Church of St Edmund with an income which, taken in conjunction with the pew-rents, an institution which I hope hereafter to abolish, raises the priest of the temple from penury to comfort, and affords him the means of helping the poor of his parish with his alms as well as with his prayers and ministrations. This munificent gift closes the long account of beneficence betwixt your dear aunt and me. I have nothing further to expect from her for my church or for myself. It is fully understood between us that this gift is final. You will understand, therefore, that I am disinterested in my anxiety for this precious life.

'You, dear Mrs Greswold, are your aunt's only near relative, and it is but right you should be the companion and comforter of her declining days. That the shadow of the grave is upon her I can but fear, although medical science sees but slight cause for alarm. A year ago she was a vigorous woman, spare of habit certainly, but with a hardness of bearing and manner which promised a long life. To-day she is a broken woman, nervous, fitful, and, I fear, unhappy, though I can conceive no cause for sadness in the closing years of such a noble life as hers has been, unselfish, devoted to good works and exalted thoughts. If you can find it compatible with your other ties to come to Brighton, I would strongly recommend you to come without loss of time, and I believe that the change which you will yourself perceive in my valued friend will fully justify the course I take in thus addressing you. – I am ever, dear Mrs Greswold, your friend and servant,

'SAMUEL MALTRAVERS.'

Mildred gave immediate orders to courier and maid, her trunks were to be packed that afternoon, a *coupé* was to be taken in the Rapide for the following day, and the travellers were to go straight through to Paris. But when she announced this fact to Pamela the damsel's countenance expressed utmost despondency.

'Upon my word, aunt, you have a genius for taking one away from a place just when one is beginning to be happy!' she exclaimed in irrepressible vexation.

She apologised directly after upon hearing of Miss Fausset's illness.

'I am a horrid ill-tempered creature,' she said; 'but I really am beginning to adore Nice. It is a place that grows upon one.'

'What if I were to leave you with Lady Lochinvar? She told me the other day that she would like very much to have you to stay with her. You might stay till she leaves Nice, which will be in about three weeks' time, and you could travel with her to Paris. You could go from Paris to Brighton very comfortably, with Peterson to take care of you. Perhaps you would not mind leaving Nice when Lady Lochinvar goes?'

Pamela sparkled and blushed at the suggestion.

'I should like it very much, if Lady Lochinvar is in earnest in asking to have me.'

'I am sure she is in earnest. There is only one stipulation I must make, Pamela. You must promise me not to renew your intimacy with Mr Castellani.'

'With all my heart, aunt. My eyes have been opened. He is thoroughly bad style.'

CHAPTER VII

AS THE SANDS RUN DOWN

Mildred was in Brighton upon the third day after she left Nice. She had sent no intimation of her coming to her aunt, lest her visit should be forbidden. A nervous invalid is apt to have fancies, and to resent anything that looks like being taken care of. She arrived, therefore, unannounced, left her luggage at the station, and drove straight to Lewes Crescent, where the butler received her with every appearance of surprise.

It was early in the afternoon, and Miss Fausset was sitting in her accustomed chair in the back drawing-room, near the fire, with her book-table on her right hand. The balmy spring-time which Mildred had left at Nice had not yet visited Brighton, where the season had been exceptionally cold, and where a jovial north-easter was holding his revels all over Kemp Town, and enlivening the cold gray sea. A pleasant bracing day for robust health and animal spirits; but not altogether the kind of atmosphere to suit an elderly spinster suffering from nervous depression.

Miss Fausset started up, flushed with surprise, at Mildred's entrance. Her niece had kept her acquainted with her movements, but had told her nothing of the drama of her existence since she left Brighton.

'My dear child, I am very glad to see you back,' she said gently. 'You are come to stay with me for a little while, I hope, before——'

She hesitated, and looked at Mildred earnestly.

'Are you reconciled to your husband?' she asked abruptly, as if with irrepressible anxiety.

'Reconciled?' echoed Mildred; 'we have never quarrelled. He is as dear to me to-day as he was the day I married him – dearer for all the years we spent together. But we are parted for ever. You know that it must be so, and you know why.'

'I hoped that time would have taught you common sense.'

'Time has only confirmed my resolution. Do not let us argue the point, aunt. I know that you mean kindly, but I know that you are false to your own principles – to all the teaching of your life – when you argue on the side of wrong.'

Miss Fausset turned her head aside impatiently. She had sunk back into her chair after greeting Mildred, and her niece perceived that she, who used to sit erect as a dart, in the most uncompromising attitude, was now propped up with cushions, against which her wasted figure leaned heavily.

'How have you got through the winter, aunt?' Mildred asked presently.

'Not very well. It has tried me more than any other winter I can remember. It has been a long weary winter. I have been obliged to give up the greater part of my district work. I held on as long as ever I could, till my strength failed me. And now I have to trust the work to others. I have my lieutenants – Emily Newton and her sister – who work for me. You remember them, perhaps. Earnest good girls. They keep me *en rapport* with my poor people; but it is not like personal intercourse. I begin to feel what it is to be useless – to cumber the ground.'

'My dear aunt, how can you talk so? Your life has been so full of usefulness that you may well afford to take rest now that your health is not quite so good as it has been. Even in your drawing-room here you are doing good. It is only right that young people should carry out your instructions, and work for you. I have heard, too, of your munificent gift to St Edmund's.'

'It is nothing, my dear. When all is counted, it is nothing. I have tried to lead a righteous life. I have tried to do good; but now sitting alone by this fire day after day, night after night, it all seems vain and empty. There is no comfort in the thought of it all, Mildred. I have had the praise of men, but never the approval of my own conscience.'

There was a brief silence, Mildred feeling it vain to argue against her aunt's tone of self-upbraiding, unable to fathom the mind which prompted the words.

'Then you are not going back to your husband?' Miss Fausset asked abruptly, as if in utter forgetfulness of all that had been said; and then suddenly recollecting herself, 'you have made up your mind, you say. Well, in that case you can stay with me – make this your home. You may take up my work, perhaps – by and by.'

'Yes, aunt, I hope I may be able to do so. My life has been idle and useless since my great sorrow. I want to learn to be of more use in the world; and you can teach me, if you will.'

'I will, Mildred. I want you to be happy. I have made my will. You will inherit the greater part of my fortune.'

'My dear aunt, I don't want——'

'No, you are rich enough already, I know; but I should like you to have still larger means, to profit by my death. You will use your wealth for the good of others, as I have tried – feebly tried – to use mine. You will be rich enough to found a sisterhood, if you like – the Sisters of St Edmund. I have done all I mean to do for the Church. Mr Maltravers knows that.'

'Dear aunt, why should we talk of these things? You have many years of life before you, I hope.'

'No, Mildred, the end is not far off. I feel worn out and broken. I am a doomed woman.'

'But you have had no serious illness since I was here?'

'No, no, nothing specific; only languor and shattered nerves, want of appetite, want of sleep: the sure indications of decay. My doctor can find no name for my malady. He tries one remedy after another, until I weary of his experiments. I am glad you have come to me, Mildred; but I should be gladder if you were going back to your husband.'

'O, aunt, why do you say things which you know must torture me?'

'Because I am worried by your folly. Well, I will say no more. You will stay with me and comfort me, if you can. What have you done with Pamela?'

Mildred told her aunt about Lady Lochinvar's invitation.

'Ah! she is with Lady Lochinvar. A very frivolous person, I suppose. Your husband's niece is a well-meaning silly girl; sure to get into mischief of some kind. Is she still in love with César Castellani?'

'I think not – I hope not. I believe she is cured of that folly.'

'You call it a folly? Well, perhaps you are right. It may be foolishness for a girl to follow the blind instinct of her heart.'

'For an impulsive girl like Pamela.'

'Yes, no doubt she is impulsive, generous, and uncalculating; a girl hardly to be trusted with her own fate,' said Miss Fausset, with a sigh, and then she lapsed into silence.

Mr Maltravers had not exaggerated the change in her. It was only too painfully evident. Her manner and bearing had altered since Mildred had seen her last. Physically and mentally her nature seemed to have relaxed and broken down. It was as if the springs that sustained the human machine had snapped. The whole mechanism was out of gear. She who had been so firm of speech and meaning, who had been wont to express herself with a cold and cutting decisiveness, was now feeble and wailing, repeating herself, harping upon the same old string, obviously forgetful of that which had gone before.

Mildred felt that she would be only doing her duty in taking up her abode in the great dull house, and trying to soothe the tedium of decay. She could do very little, perhaps, but the fact of near kindred would be in itself a solace, and for her own part she would have the sense of duty done.

'I will stay with you as long as you will have me, aunt,' she said gently. 'Albrecht is below. May I send to the station for my luggage?'

'Of course, and your rooms shall be got ready immediately. The house will be yours before very long, perhaps. It would be strange if you could not make it your home!'

She touched a spring on her book-table, which communicated with the electric-bell, and Franz appeared promptly.

'Tell them to get Mrs Greswold's old rooms ready at once, and send Albrecht to the station for the luggage,' ordered Miss Fausset, with something of her old decisiveness. 'Louisa is with you, I suppose?' she added to her niece.

'Louisa is at the station, looking after my things. Albrecht leaves me to-day. He has been a good servant, and I think he has had an easy place. I have not been an eager traveller.'

'No; you seem to have taken life at a slow pace. What took you to Nice? It is not a place I should have chosen if I wanted quiet.'

Mildred hesitated for some moments before she replied to this question.

'You know one part of my sorrow, aunt; and I think I might trust you with the whole of that sad story. I went to Nice because it was the place where my husband lived with his first wife – where my unhappy sister died.'

'She died at Nice?' repeated Miss Fausset, with an abstracted air, as if her power of attention, which had revived for a little just now, were beginning to flag.

'She died there, under the saddest circumstances. I am heart-broken when I think of her and that sad fate. My own dear Fay, how hard that your loving heart should be an instrument of self-torture! She was jealous of her husband – causelessly, unreasonably jealous – and she killed herself in a paroxysm of despair!'

The awfulness of this fact roused Miss Fausset from her apathy. She started up from amongst her cushions, staring at Mildred in mute horror, and her wasted hands trembled as they grasped the arm of her chair.

'Surely, surely that can't be true!' she faltered. 'It is too dreadful! People tell such lies – an accident, perhaps, exaggerated into a suicide. An overdose of an opiate!'

'No, no; it was nothing like that. There is no doubt. I heard it from those who knew. She flung herself over the edge of the cliff; she was walking with her husband – my husband, George Greswold – then George Ransome; they were walking together; they quarrelled; he said something that stung her to the quick, and she threw herself over the cliff. It was the wild impulse of a moment, for which an all-merciful God would not hold her accountable. She was in very delicate health, nervous, hysterical, and she fancied herself unloved, betrayed, perhaps. Ah, aunt, think how hardly she had been used – cast off, disowned, sent out alone into the world – by those who should have loved and protected her. Poor, poor Fay! My mother sent her away from The Hook where she was so happy. My mother's jealousy drove her out – a young girl, so friendless, so lonely, so much in need of love. It was my mother's doing; but my father ought not to have allowed it. If she was weak he was strong, and Fay was his daughter. It was his duty to protect her against all the world. You know how I loved my father; you know that I reverence his memory; but he played a coward's part when he sent Fay out of his house to please my mother.'

She was carried away by her passionate regret for that ill-used girl whose image had never lost its hold upon her heart.

'Not a word against your father, Mildred. He was a good man. He never failed in affection or in duty. He acted for the best according to his lights in relation to that unhappy girl – unhappy – ill-used – yes, yes, yes. He did his best, Mildred. He must not be blamed. But it is dreadful to think that she killed himself.'

'Had you heard nothing of her fate, aunt? My father must have been told, surely. There must have been some means of communication. He must have kept himself informed about her fate, although she was banished, given over to the care of strangers. If he had owned a dog which other people took care of for him he would have been told when the dog died.'

Miss Fausset felt the unspeakable bitterness of this comparison.

'You must not speak like that of your father, Mildred. You ought to know that he was a good man. Yes, he knew, of course, when that poor girl died, but it was not his business to tell other people. I only heard incidentally that she had married, and that she died within a year of her marriage. I heard no more. It was the end of a sad story.'

Again there was an interval of silence. It was six o'clock; the sun was going down over the sea beyond the West Pier, and the lawn, and the fashionable garden where the gay world congregates; and this eastern end of the long white seafront was lapsing into grayness, through which a star shone dimly here and there. It looked a cold, dull world after the pink hotel and the green shutters, the dusty palms and the turquoise sea of the Promenade des Anglais; but Mildred was glad to be in England, glad to be so much nearer him whose life companion she could never be again.

Franz brought her some tea presently, and informed her that her rooms were ready, and that Louisa had arrived with the luggage. Albrecht had left his humble duty for his honoured mistress, and was gone.

'When your father died, you looked through his papers and letters, no doubt?' said Miss Fausset presently, after a pause in the conversation.

'Yes, aunt, I looked through my dear father's letters, and arranged everything with our old family solicitor, Mr Cresswell,' answered Mildred, surprised at a question which seemed to have no bearing upon anything that had gone before.

'And you found no documents relating to – that unhappy girl?'

'Not a line – not a word. But I had not expected to find anything. The history of her birth was the one dark secret of my father's life – he would naturally leave no trace of the story.'

'Naturally, if he were wiser than most people. But I have observed that men of business have a passion for preserving documents, even when they are worthless. People keep compromising papers with the idea of destroying them on their deathbeds, or when they feel the end is near; and then death comes without warning, and the papers remain. Your father's end was somewhat sudden.'

'Sadly sudden. When he left Enderby in the autumn he was in excellent health. The shooting had been better than usual that year, and I think he had enjoyed it as much as the youngest of our party. And then he went back to London, and the London fogs – caught cold, neglected himself, and we were summoned to Parchment Street to find him dying of inflammation of the lungs. It was terrible – such a brief farewell, such an irreparable loss.'

'I was not sent for,' said Miss Fausset severely. 'And yet I loved your father dearly.'

'It was wrong, aunt; but we hoped against hope almost to the last. It was only within a few hours of the end that we knew the case was hopeless, and to summon you would have been to give him the idea that he was dying. George and I pretended that our going to him was accidental. We were so fearful of alarming him.'

'Well, I daresay you acted for the best; but it was a heavy blow for me to be told that he was gone – my only brother – almost my only friend.'

'Pray don't say that, aunt. I hope you know that I love you.'

'My dear, you love me because I am your father's sister. You consider it your duty to love me. My brother loved me for my own sake. He was a noble-hearted man.'

Miss Fausset and her niece dined together *tête-à-tête*, and spent the evening quietly on each side of the hearth, with their books and work, the kind of work which encourages pensive brooding, as the needle travels slowly over the fabric.

'I wonder you have no pets, aunt – no favourite dog.'

'I have never cared for that kind of affection, Mildred. I am of too hard a nature, perhaps. My heart does not open itself to dogs and cats, and parrots are my abomination. I am not like the typical spinster. My only solace in the long weary years has been in going among people who are more unhappy than myself. I have put myself face to face with sordid miseries, with heavy life-long burdens; and I have asked myself, What is *your* trouble compared with these?'

'Dear aunt, it seems to me that your life must have been particularly free from trouble and care.'

'Perhaps, in its outward aspect. I am rich, and I have been looked up to. But do you think those long years of loneliness – the aimless, monotonous pilgrimage through life – have not been a burden? Do you think I have not – sometimes, at any rate – envied other women their children and their husbands – the atmosphere of domestic love, even with its attendant cares and sorrows? Do you suppose that I could live for a quarter of a century as I have lived, and not feel the burden of my isolation? I have made people care for me through their self-interest. I have made people honour me, because I have the means of helping them. But who is there who cares for me, Gertrude Fausset?'

'You cannot have done so much for others without being sincerely loved in return.'

'With a kind of love, perhaps – a love that has been bought.'

'Why did you never marry, aunt?'

'Because I was an heiress and a good match, and distrusted every man who wanted to marry me. I made a vow to myself, before my twentieth birthday, that I would never listen to words of love or give encouragement to a lover; and I most scrupulously kept that vow. I was called a handsome woman in those days; but I was not an attractive woman at any time. Nature had made me of too hard a clay.'

'It was a pity that you should keep love at arm's length.'

'Far better than to have been fooled by shams, as I might have been. Don't say any more about it, Mildred. I made my vow, and I kept it.'

Mildred resigned herself quietly to the idea of the dull slow life in Lewes Crescent. This duty of solacing her aunt's declining days was the only duty that remained to her, except that wider duty of caring for the helpless and the wretched. And she told herself that there could be no better school in which to learn how to help others than the house of Miss Fausset, who had given so much of her life to the poor.

She had been told to consider her aunt's house as her own, and that she was at liberty to receive Pamela there as much and as often as she liked. She did not think that Pamela would be long without a settled home. Mr Stuart's admiration and Lady Lochinvar's wishes had been obvious; and Mildred daily expected a gushing letter from the fickle damsel, announcing her engagement to the Scotchman.

At four o'clock on the day after Mildred's arrival, Miss Fausset's friends began to drop in for afternoon tea and talk, and Mildred was surprised to see how her aunt rallied in that long-familiar society. It seemed as if the praises and flatteries of these people acted upon her like strong wine. The languid attitude, the weary expression of the pale drawn face, were put aside. She sat erect again; her eyes brightened, her ear was alert to follow three or four conversations at a time; nothing escaped her. Mildred began to think that she had lived upon the praises of men rather than upon the approval of conscience — that these assiduities and flatteries of a very commonplace circle were essential to her happiness.

Mr Maltravers came after the vesper service, full of life and conversation, vigorous, self-satisfied, with an air of Papal dominion and Papal infallibility, so implicitly believed in by his flock that he had learned to believe as implicitly in himself. The flock was chiefly feminine, and worshipped without limit or reservation. There were husbands and sons, brothers and nephews, who went to church with their womenkind on Sunday; but these were for the most part without enthusiasm for Mr Maltravers. Their idea of public worship went scarcely beyond considering Sunday morning service a respectable institution, not to be dispensed with lightly.

Mr Maltravers welcomed Mildred with touching friendliness.

'I knew you would not fail your aunt in the hour of need,' he said; 'and now I hope you are going to stay with her, and to take up her work when she lays it down, so that the golden thread of womanly charity may be unbroken.

'I hope I may be able to take up her work. I shall stay with her as long as she needs me.'

'That is well. You found her sadly changed, did you not?'

'Yes, she is much changed. Yet how bright she looks this afternoon! what interest she takes in the conversation!'

'The flash of the falchion in the worn-out scabbard,' said Mr Maltravers.

A layman might have said sword, but Mr Maltravers preferred falchion, as a more picturesque word. Half the success of his preaching had lain in the choice of picturesque words. There were sceptics among his masculine congregation who said there were no ideas in his sermons; only fine words, romantic similes – a perpetual recurrence of fountains and groves, sunset splendours and roseate dawns, golden gates and starry canopies, seas of glass, harps of gold. But if his female worshippers felt better and holier after listening to him, what could one ask more? – and they all declared that it was so. They came out of church spiritualised, overflowing with Christian love, and gave their pence eagerly to the crossing-sweepers on their way home.

The dropping in and the tea-drinking went on for nearly two hours. Mr Maltravers took four cups of tea, and consumed a good deal of bread-and-butter, abstaining from the chocolate biscuits and the pound-cake which the ladies of the party affected; abstaining on principle, as saints and eremites of old abstained from high living. He allowed himself to enjoy the delicate aroma of the tea and the delicately-cut bread-and-butter. He was a bachelor, and lived poorly upon badly-cooked food at his vicarage. His only personal indulgence was in the accumulation of a theological library, in which all the books were of a High Church cast.

When the visitors were all gone Miss Fausset sank back into her chair, white and weary-looking, and Mildred left her to take a little nap while she went up to her own room, half boudoir, half dressing-room, a spacious apartment, with a fine sea-view. Here she sat in a reverie, and watched the fading sky and the slow dim stars creeping out one by one.

Was she really to take up her aunt's work, to live in a luxurious home, a lonely loveless woman, and to go out in a methodical, almost mechanical way so many times a week, to visit among the poor? Would such a life as that satisfy her in all the long slow years?

The time would come, perhaps, when she would find peace in such a life – when her heart would know no grief except the griefs of others; when she would have cast off the fetters of selfish cares and selfish yearnings, and would stand alone, as saints and martyrs and holy women of old had stood – alone with God and His poor. There were women she knew, even in these degenerate days, who so lived and so worked, seeking no guerdon but the knowledge of good done in this world, and the hope of the crown immortal. Her day of sacrifice had not yet come. She had not been able to dissever her soul from the hopes and sorrows of earth. She had not been able to forget the husband she had forsaken – even for a single hour. When she knelt down to pray at night, when she awoke in the morning, her thoughts were with him. 'How does he bear his solitude? Has he learnt to forget me and to be happy?' Those questions were ever present to her mind.

And now at Brighton, knowing herself so near him, her heart yearned more than ever for the sight of the familiar face, for the sound of the beloved voice. She pored over the time-table, and calculated the length of the journey – the time lost at Portsmouth and Bishopstoke – every minute until the arrival at Romsey; and then the drive to Enderby. She pictured the lanes in the early May – the hedgerows bursting into leaf, the banks where the primroses were opening, the tender young ferns just beginning to uncurl their feathery fronds, the spear-points of the hartstongue shooting up amidst rank broad docks, and lords and ladies, and the flower on the leafless blackthorn making patches of white amongst the green.

How easy it was to reach him! how natural it would seem to hasten to him after half a year of exile! and yet she must not. She had pledged herself to honour the law; to obey the letter and the spirit of that harsh law which decreed that her sister's husband could not be hers.

She knew that he was at Enderby, and she had some ground for supposing that he was well, and even contented. She had seen the letters which he had written to his niece. He had written about the shooting, his horses, his dogs; and there had been no word to indicate that he was out of health, or in low spirits. Mildred had pored over those brief letters, forgetting to return them to their rightful owner, cherishing them as if they made a kind of link between her and the love she had resigned.

How firm the hand was! – that fine and individual penmanship which she had so admired in the past – the hand in which her first love-letter had been written. It was but little altered in fifteen years. She recalled the happy hour when she received that first letter from her affianced husband. He had gone to London a day or two after their betrothal, eager to make all arrangements for their marriage, impatient for settlements and legal machinery which should make their union irrevocable, full of plans for immediate improvements at Enderby.

She remembered how she ran out into the garden to read that first letter – a long letter, though they had been parted less than a day when it was written. She had gone to the remotest nook in that picturesque riverside garden, a rustic bower by the water's edge, an osier arbour over which her own hands had trained the Céline Forestieri roses. They were in flower on that happy day – clusters of pale yellow bloom, breathing perfume round her as she sat beneath the blossoming arch and devoured her lover's fond words. O, how bright life had been then for both of them! – for her without a cloud.

He was well – that was something to know; but it was not enough. Her heart yearned for fuller knowledge of his life than those letters gave. Wounded pride might have prompted that cheerful tone. He might wish her to think him happy and at ease without her. He thought that she had used him ill. It was natural, perhaps, that he should think so, since he could not see things as she saw them. He had not her deep-rooted convictions. She thought of him and wondered about him till the desire for further knowledge grew into an aching pain. She must write to some one; she must do something to quiet this gnawing anxiety. In her trouble she thought of all her friends in the neighbourhood of Enderby; but there was none in whom she could bring herself to confide except Rollinson, the curate. She had thought first of writing to the doctor, but he was something of a gossip, and would be likely to prattle to his patients about her letter, and her folly in forsaking so good a husband. Rollinson she felt she might trust. He was a thoughtful young man, despite his cheery manners and some inclination to facetiousness of a strictly clerical order. He was one of a large family, and had known trouble, and Mildred had been especially kind to him and to the sisters who from time to time had shared his apartments at the carpenter's, and had revelled in the gaieties of Enderby parish, the penny-reading at the schoolhouse, the sale of work for the benefit of the choir, and an occasional afternoon for tea and tennis at the Manor. Those maiden sisters of the curate's had known and admired Lola, and Mr Rollinson had been devoted to her from his first coming to the parish, when she was a lovely child of seven.

Mildred wrote fully and frankly to the curate.

'I cannot enter upon the motive of our separation,' she wrote, 'except so far as to tell you that it is a question of principle which has parted us. My husband has been blameless in all his domestic relations, the best of husbands, the noblest of men. Loving him with all my heart, trusting and honouring him as much as on my wedding-day, I yet felt it my duty to leave him. I should not make this explanation to any one else at Enderby, but I wish you to know the truth. If people ever question you about my reasons you can tell them that it is my intention ultimately to enter an Anglican Sisterhood, or it may be to found a Sisterhood, and to devote my declining years to my sorrowing fellow-creatures. This is my fixed intention, but my vocation is yet weak. My heart cleaves to the old home and all that I lost in leaving it.

'And now, my kind friend, I want you to tell me how my husband fares in his solitude. If he were ill and unhappy he would be too generous to complain to me. Tell me how he is in health and spirits. Tell me of his daily life, his amusements, occupations. There is not the smallest detail which will not interest me. You see him, I hope, often; certainly you are likely to see him oftener than any one else in the parish. Tell me all you can, and be assured of my undying gratitude. – Ever sincerely yours,

'MILDRED GRESWOLD.'

Mr Rollinson's reply came by return of post:

'I am very glad you have written to me, dear Mrs Greswold. Had I known your address, I think I should have taken the initiative, and written to you. Believe me, I respect your motive for the act which has, I fear, cast a blight upon a good man's life; and I will venture to say no more than that the motive should be a very strong one which forces you to persevere in a course that has wrecked your husband's happiness, and desolated one of the most delightful and most thoroughly Christian homes I had ever the privilege of entering. I look back and recall what Enderby Manor was, and I think what it is now, and I can hardly compare those two pictures without tears.

'You ask me to tell you frankly all I can tell about your husband's mode of life, his health and spirits. All I can tell is summed up in four words: his heart is broken. In my deep concern about his desolate position, in my heartfelt regard for him, I have ventured to force my society upon him sometimes when I could not doubt it was unwelcome. He received me with all his old kindness of manner; but I am sympathetic enough to know when a man only endures my company, and I know that his feeling was at best endurance. But I believe that he trusts me, and that he was less upon his guard with me than he is with other acquaintances. I have seen him put on an appearance of cheerfulness with other people. I have heard him talk to other people as if life had in nowise lost its interest for him. With me he dropped the mask. I saw him brooding by his hearth, as he broods when he is alone. I heard his involuntary sighs. I saw the image of a shipwrecked existence. Indeed, Mrs Greswold, there is nothing else that I can tell you if you would have me truthful. You have broken his heart. You have sacrificed your love to a principle, you say. You should be very sure of your principle. You ask me as to his habits and occupations. I believe they are about as monotonous as those of a galley-slave. He walks a great deal – in all weathers and at all hours – but rarely beyond his own land. I don't think he often rides; and he has not hunted once during the season. He did a little shooting in October and November, quite alone. He has had no staying visitor within his doors since you left him.

'I have reason to know that he goes to the churchyard every evening at dusk, and spends some time beside your daughter's grave. I have seen him there several times when it was nearly dark, and he had no apprehension of being observed. You know how rarely any one enters our quiet little burial-ground, and how complete a solitude it is at that twilight hour. I am about the only passer-by, and even I do not pass within sight of the old yew-tree above your darling's resting-place, unless I go a little out of my way between the vestry-door and the lych-gate. I have often gone out of my way to note that lonely figure by the grave. Be assured, dear Mrs Greswold, that in sending you this gloomy picture of a widowed life I have had no wish to distress you. I have exaggerated nothing. I wish you to know the truth; and if it lies within your power – without going against your conscience – to undo that which you have done, I entreat you to do so without delay. There may not be much time to be lost. – Believe me, devotedly and gratefully your friend,

'FREDERICK ROLLINSON.'

Mildred shed bitter tears over the curate's letter. How different the picture it offered from that afforded by George Greswold's own letters, in which he had written cheerily of the shooting, the dogs and horses, the changes in the seasons, and the events of the outer world! That frank easy tone had been part of his armour of pride. He would not abase himself by the admission of his misery. He had guessed, no doubt, that his wife would read those letters, and he would not have her know the extent of the ruin she had wrought.

She thought of him in his solitude, pictured him beside their child's grave, and the longing to look upon him once more – unseen by him, if it could be so – became irresistible. She determined to see with her own eyes if he were as unhappy as Mr Rollinson supposed. She, who knew him so well, would be better able to judge by his manner and bearing – better able to divine the inner workings of his heart and mind. It had been a habit of her life to read his face, to guess his thoughts before they found expression in words. He had never been able to keep a secret from her, except that one long-hidden story of the past; and even there she had known that there was something. She had seen the shadow of that abiding remorse.

'I am going to leave you for two days, aunt,' she said rather abruptly, on the morning after she received Rollinson's letter. 'I want to look at Lola's grave. I shall go from here to Enderby as fast as the train will take me; spend an hour in the churchyard; go on to Salisbury for the night; and come back to you to-morrow afternoon.'

'You mean that you are going back to your husband?'

'No, no. I may see him, perhaps, by accident. I shall not enter the Manor House. I am going to the churchyard – nowhere else.'

'You would be wiser if you went straight home. Remember, years hence, when I am dead and gone, that I told you as much. You must do as you like – stay at an inn at Salisbury, while your own beautiful home is empty, or anything else that is foolish and wrong-headed. You had better let Franz go with you.'

'Thanks, aunt; I would not take him away on any account. I can get on quite well by myself.'

She left Brighton at midday, lost a good deal of time at the two junctions, and drove to within a few hundred yards of Enderby Church just as the bright May day was melting into evening. There was a path across some meadows at the back of the village that led to the churchyard. She stopped the fly by the meadow-gate, and told the man to drive round to Mr Rollinson's lodgings, and wait for her there; and then she walked slowly along the narrow footpath, between the long grass, golden with buttercups in the golden evening.

It was a lovely evening. There was a little wood of oaks and chestnuts on her left hand as she approached the churchyard, and the shrubberies of Enderby Manor were on her right. The trees she knew so well – her own trees – the tall mountain-ash and the clump of beeches, rose above the lower level of lilacs and laburnums, acacia and rose maple. There was a nightingale singing in the thick foliage yonder – there was always a nightingale at this season somewhere in the shrubbery. She had lingered many a time with her husband to listen to that unmistakable melody.

The dark foliage of the churchyard made an inky blot midst all that vernal greenery. Those immemorial yews, which knew no change with the changing years, spread their broad shadows over the lowly graves, and made night in God's acre while it was yet day in the world outside. Mildred went into the churchyard as if into the realm of death. The shadows closed round her on every side, and the change from light to gloom chilled her as she walked slowly towards the place where her child was lying.

Yes, he was there, just as the curate had told her. He stood leaning against the long horizontal branch of the old yew, looking down at the marble which bore his daughter's name. He was very pale, and his sunken eyes and hollow cheeks told of failing health. He stood motionless, in a gloomy reverie. His wife watched him from a little way off; she stood motionless as himself – stood and watched him till the beating of her heart sounded so loud in her own ears that she thought he too must hear that passionate throbbing.

She had thought when she set out on her journey that it would be sufficient for her just to see him, and that having seen him she would go away and leave him without his ever knowing that she had looked upon him. But now the time had come it was not enough. The impulse to draw nearer and to speak to him was too strong to be denied: she went with tottering footsteps to the side of the grave, and called him by his name:

'George! George!' holding out her hands to him piteously.

CHAPTER VIII

'HOW SHOULD I GREET THEE?'

The marble countenance scarcely changed as he looked up at her. He took no notice of the out-stretched hands.

'What brings you here, Mildred?' he asked coldly.

'I heard that you were ill; I wanted to see for myself,' she faltered.

'I am not ill, and I have not been ill. You were misinformed.'

'I was told you were unhappy.'

'Did you require to be told that? You did not expect to hear that I was particularly happy, I suppose? At my age men have forgotten how to forget.'

'It would be such a relief to my mind if you could find new occupations, new interests, as I hope to do by and by – a wider horizon. You are so clever. You have so many gifts, and it is a pity to bury them all here.'

'My heart is buried here,' he answered, looking down at the grave.

'Your heart, yes; but you might find work for your mind – a noble career before you – in politics, in philanthropy.'

'I am not ambitious, and I am too old to adapt myself to a new life. I prefer to live as I am living. Enderby is my hermitage. It suits me well enough.'

There was a silence after this – a silence of despair. Mildred knelt on the dewy grass, and bent herself over the marble cross, and kissed the cold stone. She could reach no nearer than that marble to the child she loved. Her lips lingered there. Her heart ached with a dull pain, and she felt the utter hopelessness of her life more keenly than she had felt it yet. If she could but die there, at his feet, and make an end!

She rose after some minutes. Her husband's attitude was unchanged; but he looked at her now, for the first time, with a direct and earnest gaze.

'What took you to Nice?' he asked.

'I wanted to know – all about my unhappy sister.'

'And you are satisfied – you know all; and you think as some of my neighbours thought of me. You believe that I killed my wife.'

'George, can you think so meanly of me – your wife of fourteen years?'

'You spare me, then, so far, in spite of circumstantial evidence. You do not think of me as a murderer?'

'I have never for a moment doubted your goodness to that unhappy girl,' she answered, with a stifled sob. 'I am sorry for her with all my heart; but I cannot blame you.'

'There you are wrong. I was to blame. You know that I do not easily lose my temper – to a woman, least of all; but that day I lost control over myself – lost patience with her just when she was in greatest need of my forbearance. She was nervous and hysterical. I forgot her weakness. I spoke to her cruelly – lashed and goaded by her causeless jealousies – so persistent, so irritating – like the continual dropping of water. How I have suffered for that moment of anger God alone can know. If remorse can be expiation, I have expiated that unpremeditated sin!'

'Yes, yes, I know how you have suffered. Your dreams have told me.'

'Ah, those dreams! You can never imagine the agony of them. To fancy her walking by my side, bright and happy, as she so seldom was upon this earth, and to tell myself that I had never been unkind to her, that her suicide was a dream and a delusion, and then to feel the dull cold reality creep back into my brain, and to know that I was guilty of her death. Yes, I have held myself guilty. I have never paltered with my conscience. Had I been patient to the end, she might have lived to be the happy mother of my child. Her whole life might have been changed. I never loved her, Mildred. Fate and her own impulsive nature flung her into my arms; but I accepted the charge; I made myself responsible to God and my own conscience for her well-being.'

Mildred's only answer was a sob. She stretched out her hand, and laid it falteringly upon the hand that hung loose across the branch of the yew, as if in token of trustfulness.

'Did you find out anything more in your retrospective gropings – at Nice?' he asked, with a touch of bitterness.

She was silent.

'Did you hear that I was out of my mind after my wife's death?'

'Yes.'

'Did that shock you? Did it horrify you to know you had lived fourteen years with a *ci-devant* lunatic?'

'George, how can you say such things! I could perfectly understand how your mind was affected by that dreadful event – how the strongest brain might be unhinged by such a sorrow. I can sympathise with you, and understand you in the past as I can in the present. How can you forget that I am your wife, a part of yourself, able to read all your thoughts?'

'I cannot forget that you have been my wife; but your sympathy and your affection seem very far off now – as remote almost as that tragedy which darkened my youth. It is all past and done with – the sorrow and pain, the hope and gladness. I have done with everything – except my regret for my child.'

'Can you believe that I feel the parting less than you, George?' she asked piteously.

'I don't know. The parting is your work. You have the satisfaction of self-sacrifice – the pride which women who go to church twice a day have in renouncing earthly happiness. They school themselves first in trifles – giving up this and that – theatres, fiction, cheerful society – and then their ambition widens. These petty sacrifices are not enough, and they renounce a husband and a home. If the husband cannot see the necessity, and cannot kiss the rod, so much the worse for him. His wife has the perverted pride of an Indian widow who flings her young life upon the funeral pile, jubilant at the thought of her own exalted virtue.'

'Would you not sacrifice your happiness to your conscience, George, if conscience spoke plainly?' Mildred asked reproachfully.

'I don't know. Human love might be too strong for conscience. God knows I would not have sacrificed you to a scruple – to a law made by man. God's laws are different. There is no doubt about them.'

The evening was darkening. The nightingale burst out suddenly into loud melody, more joyous than her reputation. Mildred could see the lights in the house that had been her home. The lamp-light in the drawing-room shone across the intervening space of lawn and shrubberies; the broad window shone vividly at the end of a vista, like a star. O lovely room, O happy life; so far off, so impossible for evermore!

'Good-night and good-bye,' Mildred sighed, holding out her hand.

'Good-bye,' he answered, taking the small cold hand, only to let it drop again.

He made no inquiry as to how she had come there, or whither she was going. She had appeared to him suddenly as a spirit in the soft eventide, and he let her go from him unquestioned, as if she had been a spirit. She felt the coldness of her dismissal, and yet felt that it could be no otherwise. She must be all to him or nothing. After love so perfect as theirs had been there could be no middle course.

She went across the meadow by the way she had come, and through the village street, where all the doors were closed at this hour, and paraffin-lamps glowed brightly in parlour-windows. Dear little humble street, how her heart yearned over it as she went silently by like a ghost, closely veiled, a slender figure dressed in black! She had been very fond of her villagers, had entered into their lives and been a brightening influence for most of them, she and her child. Lola had been familiar with every creature in the place, from the humpbacked cobbler at the corner to the gray-haired postmaster in the white half-timbered cottage yonder, where the letter-boxes were approached by a narrow path across a neat little garden. Lola had entered into all their lives, and had been glad and sorry with them with a power of sympathy which was the only precocious element in her nature. She had been a child in all things except charity; there she had been a woman.

There was a train for Salisbury in half-an-hour, and there was a later train at ten o'clock. Mildred had intended to travel at the earlier hour, but she felt an irresistible inclination to linger in the beloved place where her happiness was buried. She wanted to see some one who would talk to her of her husband, and she knew that the curate could be trusted; so she determined upon waiting for the later train, in the event of her finding Mr Rollinson at home.

The paraffin-lamp in the parlour over the carpenter's shop was brighter than any other in the village, and Mr Rollinson's shadow was reflected on the blind, with the usual tendency towards caricature. The carpenter's wife, who opened the door, was an old friend of Mrs Greswold's, and was not importunate in her expressions of surprise and pleasure.

'Please do not mention to any one that I have been at Enderby, Mrs Mason,' Mildred said quietly. 'I am only here for an hour or two on my way to Salisbury. I should like to see Mr Rollinson, if he is disengaged.'

'Of course he is, ma'am, for you. He'll be overjoyed to see you, I'm sure.'

Mrs Mason bustled up the steep little staircase, followed closely by Mildred. She flung open the door with a flourish, and discovered Mr Rollinson enjoying a tea-dinner, with the *Times* propped up between his plate and the teapot.

He started to his feet at sight of his visitor like a man distraught, darted forward and shook hands with Mildred, then glanced despairingly at the table. For such a guest he would have liked to have had turtle and ortolans; but a tea-dinner, a vulgar tea-dinner – a dish of pig's trotters, a couple of new-laid eggs, and a pile of buttered toast! He had thought it a luxurious meal when he sat down to it, five minutes ago, very sharp set.

'My dear Mrs Greswold, I am enchanted. You have been travelling? Yes. If – if you would share my humble collation – but you are going to dine at the Manor, no doubt.'

'No; I am not going to the Manor. I should be very glad of a cup of tea, if I may have one with you.'

'Mrs Mason, a fresh teapot, directly, if you please.'

'Yes, sir.'

'And could you not get some dinner for Mrs Greswold? A sole and a chicken, a little asparagus. I saw a bundle in the village the day before yesterday,' suggested the curate feebly.

'On no account. I could not eat any dinner. I will have an egg and a little toast, if you please,' said Mildred, seeing the curate's distressed look, and not wishing to reject his hospitality.

'Will you really, now? Mrs Mason's eggs are excellent; and she makes toast better than any one else in the world, I think,' replied Rollinson, flinging his napkin artfully over the trotters, and with a side glance at Mrs Mason which implored their removal.

That admirable woman grasped the situation. She whisked off the dish, and the curate's plate with its litter of bones and mustard. She swept away crumbs, tidied the tea-tray, brought a vase of spring flowers from a cheffonier to adorn the table, lighted a pair of wax candles on the mantelpiece, and gave a touch of elegance to the humble sitting-room, while Mildred was taking off her mantle and bonnet, and sinking wearily into Mr Rollinson's easy-chair by the hearth, where a basket of fir-cones replaced the winter fire.

She felt glad to be with this old familiar friend – glad to breathe the very air of Enderby after her six months' exile.

'Your letter frightened me,' she said, when she was alone with the curate. 'I came to look at my husband. I could not help coming.'

'Ah, dear Mrs Greswold, if you could only come back for good – nothing else is of any use. Have you seen him?'

'Yes,' she sighed.

'And you find him sadly changed?'

'Sadly changed. I wish you would try to rouse him – to interest him in farming – building – politics – anything. He is so clever; he ought to have so many resources.'

'For his mind, perhaps; but not for his heart. You are doing all you can to break that.'

Mildred turned her head aside with a weary movement, as of a creature at bay.

'Don't talk about it. You cannot understand. You look up to Clement Cancellor, I think. You would respect his opinion.'

'Yes; he is a good man.'

'He is – and he approves the course I have taken. He is my confidant and my counsellor.'

'You could have no better adviser in a case of conscience – yet I can but regret my friend's ruined life, all the same. But I will say no more, Mrs Greswold. I will respect your reserve.'

Mrs Mason came bustling in with a tea-tray, on which her family teapot – the silver teapot that had been handed down from generation to generation since the days of King George the Third – and her very best pink and gold china sparkled and glittered in the lamp-light. The toast and eggs might have tempted an anchorite, and Mildred had eaten nothing since her nine-o'clock breakfast. The strong tea revived her like good old wine, and she sat resting and listening with interest to Mr Rollinson's account of his parishioners, and the village chronicle of the last six months. How sweet it was to hear the old familiar names, to be in the old place, if only for a brief hour!

'I wonder if they miss me?' she speculated. 'They never seemed quite the same – after – after the fever.'

'Ah, but they know your value now. They have missed you sadly, and they have missed your husband's old friendly interest in their affairs. He has given me *carte blanche*, and there has been no one neglected, nothing left undone; but they miss the old personal relations, the friendship of past days. You must not think that the poor care only for creature comforts and substantial benefits.'

'I have never thought so. And now tell me all you can about my husband. Does he receive no one?'

'No one. People used to call upon him for a month or two after you left, but he never returned their visits, he declined all invitations, and he made his friends understand pretty clearly that he had done with the outside world. He rarely comes to the eleven-o'clock service on Sundays, but he comes to the early services, and I believe he walks into Romsey sometimes for the evening service. He has not hardened his heart against his God.'

'Do you see him often?'

'About once a week. I take him my report of the sick and poor. I believe he is as much interested in that as he can be in anything; but I always feel that my society is a burden to him, in spite of his courteousness. I borrow a book from him sometimes, so as to have an excuse for spending a few minutes with him when I return it.'

'You are a good man, Mr Rollinson, a true friend,' said Mildred, in a low voice.

'Would to God that my friendship could do more for him! Unhappily it can do so little.'

The fly came back for Mildred at nine o'clock. She had telegraphed from Brighton to the inn at Salisbury where she was to spend the night, and her room was ready for her when she arrived there at half-past ten: a spacious bedroom with a four-post bed, in which she lay broad awake all night, living over and over again that scene beside the grave, and seeing her husband's gloomy face, and its mute reproach. She knew that she had done wrong in breaking in upon his solitude, she who renounced the tie that bound her to him; and yet there had been something gained. He knew now that under no stress of evidence could she ever believe him guilty of his wife's death. He knew that his last and saddest secret was revealed to her, and that she was loyal to him still – loyal although divided.

She went to the morning service at the Cathedral. She lingered about the grave old Close, looking dreamily in at the gardens which had such an air of old-world peace. She was reluctant to leave Salisbury. It was near all that she had loved and lost. The place had the familiar air of the district in which she had lived so long – different in somewise from all other places, or seeming different by fond association.

She telegraphed to her aunt that she might be late in returning, and lingered on till three o'clock in the afternoon, and then took the train, which dawdled at three or four stations before it came to Bishopstoke – the familiar junction where the station-master and the superintendents knew her, and asked after her husband's health, giving her a pain at her heart with each inquiry. She would have been glad to pass to the Portsmouth train unrecognised, but it was not to be.

'You have been in the South all the winter, I hear, ma'am. I hope it was not on account of your health?'

'Yes,' she faltered, 'partly on that account,' as she hurried on to the carriage which the station-master opened for her with his own hand.

His face was among her home faces. She had travelled up and down the line very often in the good days that were gone – with her husband and Lola, and their comfort had been cared for almost as if they had been royal personages.

It was night when she reached Brighton, and Franz was on the platform waiting for her, and the irreproachable brougham was drawn up close by, the brown horse snorting, and with eyes of fire, not brooking the vicinity of the engine, though too grand a creature to know fear.

She found Miss Fausset in low spirits.

'I have missed you terribly,' she said. 'I am a poor creature. I used to think myself independent of sympathy or companionship – but that is all over now. When I am alone for two days at a stretch I feel like a child in the dark.'

'You have lived too long in this house, aunt, I think,' Mildred answered gently. 'Forgive me if I say that it is a dull house.'

'A dull house? Nonsense, Mildred! It is one of the best houses in Brighton.'

'Yes, yes, aunt, but it is dull, all the same. The sun does not shine into it; the colouring of the furniture is gray and cold——'

'I hate gaudy colours.'

'Yes, but there are beautiful colours that are not gaudy – beautiful things that warm and gladden one. The next room,' glancing back at the front drawing-room and its single lamp, 'is full of ghosts. Those long white curtains, those faint gray walls, are enough to kill you.'

'I am not so fanciful as that.'

'Ah, but you are fanciful, perhaps without knowing it. The influence of this dull gray house may have crept into your veins and depressed you unawares. Will you go to the Italian Lakes with me next September, aunt? Or, better, will you go to the West of England with me next week – to the north coast of Cornwall, which will be lovely at this season? I am sure you want change. This monotonous life is killing you.'

'No, no, Mildred. There is nothing amiss with my life. It suits me well enough, and I am able to do good.'

'Your lieutenants could carry on all that while you were away.'

'No; I like to be here; I like to organise, to arrange. I can feel that my life is not useless, that my talent is placed at interest.'

'It could all go on, aunt; it could indeed. The change to new scenes would revive you.'

'No. I am satisfied where I am. I am among people whom I like, and who like and respect me.'

She dwelt upon the last words with unction, as if there were tangible comfort in them.

Mildred sighed and was silent. She had felt it her duty to try and rouse her aunt from the dull apathy into which she seemed gradually sinking, and she thought that the only chance of revival was to remove her from the monotony of her present existence.

Later on in the evening the fire had been lighted in the inner drawing-room, Miss Fausset feeling chilly, in spite of the approach of summer, and aunt and niece drew near the hearth for cheerfulness and comfort. The low reading-lamp spread its light only over Miss Fausset's book-table and the circle in which it stood. The faces of both women were in shadow, and the lofty room with its walls of books was full of shadows.

'You talk so despondently of life sometimes, aunt, as if it had been all disappointment,' said Mildred, after a long silence, in which they had both sat watching the fire, each absorbed by her own thoughts; 'yet your girlhood must have been bright. I have heard my dear father say how indulgent *his* father was, how he gave way to his children in everything.'

'Yes, he was very indulgent; too indulgent perhaps. I had my own way in everything; only – one's own way does not always lead to happiness. Mine did not. I might have been a happier woman if my father had been a tyrant.'

'You would have married, perhaps, in that case, to escape from an unhappy home. I wish you would tell me more about your girlish years, aunt. You must have had many admirers when you were young, and amongst them all there must have been some one for whom you cared – just a little. Would it hurt you to talk to me about that old time?'

'Yes, Mildred. There are some women who can talk about such things – women who can prose for hours to their granddaughters or their nieces – simpering over the silliness of the past – boasting of conquests which nobody believes in; for it is very difficult to realise the fact that an old woman was ever young and lovely. I am not of that temper, Mildred. The memory of my girlhood is hateful to me.'

'Ah, then there was some sad story – some unhappy attachment. I was sure it must have been so,' said Mildred, in a low voice. 'But tell me of that happier time before you went into society – the time when you were in Italy with your governess, studying at the Conservatoire at Milan. I thought of you so much when I was at Milan the other day.'

'I have nothing to tell about that time. I was a foreigner in a strange city, with an elderly woman who was paid to take care of me, and whose chief occupation was to take care of herself: a solicitor's widow, whose health required that she should winter in the South, and who contrived to make my father pay handsomely for her benefit.'

'And you were not happy at Milan?'

'Happy! no. I got on with my musical education – that was all I cared for.'

'Had you no friends – no introductions to nice people?'

'No. My chaperon made my father believe that she knew all the best families in Milan, but her circle resolved itself into a few third-rate musical people who gave shabby little evening-parties. You bore me to death, Mildred, when you force me to talk of that time, and of that woman, whom I hated.'

'Forgive me, aunt, I will ask no more questions,' said Mildred, with a sigh.

She had been trying to get nearer to her kinswoman, to familiarise herself with that dim past when this fading life was fresh and full of hope. It seemed to her as if there was a dead wall between her and Miss Fausset – a barrier of reserve which should not exist between those who were so near in blood. She had made up her mind to stay with her aunt to the end, to do all that duty and affection could suggest, and it troubled her that they should still be strangers. After this severe repulse she could make no further attempt. There was evidently no softening influence in the memory of the past. Miss Fausset's character, as revealed by that which she concealed rather than by that which she told, was not beautiful. Mildred could but think that she had been a proud, cold-hearted young woman, valuing herself too highly to inspire love or sympathy in others; electing to be alone and unloved.

After this, time went by in a dull monotony. The same people came to
see Miss Fausset day after day, and she absorbed the same flatteries,
accepted the same adulation, always with an air of deepest humility. She
organised her charities, she listened to every detail about the
circumstances, and even the mental condition and spiritual views of her
poor. Mildred discovered before long that there was a leaven of hardness
in her benevolence. She could not tolerate sin, she weighed every life in
the same balance, she expected exceptional purity amidst foulest
surroundings. She was liberal of her wordly goods; but her mind was as
narrow as if she had lived in a remote village a hundred years ago.
Mildred found herself continually pleading for wrong-doers.

The only event or excitement which the bright June days brought with
them was the arrival of Pamela Ransome, who was escorted to Brighton
by Lady Lochinvar herself, and who had been engaged for the space of
three weeks to Malcolm Stuart, with everybody's consent and approval.

'I wrote to Uncle George the very day I was engaged, aunt, as well as
to you; and he answered my letter in the sweetest way, and he is going to
give me a grand piano,' said Pamela, all in a breath.

Lady Lochinvar explained that, much as she detested London, she
had felt it her solemn duty to establish herself there during her
nephew's engagement, in order that she might become acquainted with
Pamela's people, and assist her dear boy in all his arrangements for the
future. When a young man marries a nice girl with an estate worth
fifteen hundred a year – allowing for the poor return made by land
nowadays – everything ought to go upon velvet. Lady Lochinvar was
prepared to make sacrifices, or, in other words, to contribute a
handsome portion of that fortune which she intended to bequeath to
her nephew. She could afford to be generous, having a surplus far
beyond her possible needs, and she was very fond of Malcolm Stuart,
who had been to her as a son.

'I was quite alone in the world when my husband died,' she told
Mildred. 'My father and my own people were all gone, and I should have
been a wretched creature without Malcolm. He was the only son of
Lochinvar's favourite sister, who went off in a decline when he was eight
years old, and he had been brought up at the Castle. So it is natural, you
see, that I should be fond of him and interested in his welfare.'

Pamela kissed her, by way of commentary.

'I think you are quite the dearest thing in the world,' she said, 'except
Aunt Mildred.'

It may be seen from this remark that the elder and younger lady were
now on very easy terms. Mildred had stayed in Paris with Lady
Lochinvar, and a considerable part of her trousseau, the outward and
visible part, had been chosen in the *ateliers* of fashionable Parisian

dressmakers and man milliners. The more humdrum portion of the bride's raiment was to be obtained at Brighton, where Pamela was to spend a week or two with her aunt before she went to London to stay with the Mountfords, who had taken a house in Grosvenor Gardens, from which Pamela was to be married.

'And where do you think we are to be married, aunt?' exclaimed Pamela excitedly.

'At St George's?'

'Nothing so humdrum. We are going to be married in the Abbey – in Westminster Abbey – the burial-place of heroes and poets. I happened to say one day when Malcolm and I were almost strangers – it was at Rumpelmeyer's, sitting outside in the sun, eating ices – that I had never seen a wedding in the Abbey, and that I should love to see one; and Malcolm said we must try and manage it some day – meaning anybody's wedding, of course, though he pretends now that he always meant to marry me there himself.'

'Presumptious on his part,' said Mildred, smiling.

'O, young men are horribly presumptious; they know they are in a minority – there is so little competition – and a plain young man, too, like Malcolm. But I suppose he knows he is nice,' added Pamela conclusively.

'Don't you think it will be lovely for me to be married in the Abbey?' she asked presently.

'I think, dear, in your case I would rather have been married from my own house, and in a village church.'

'What, in that poky little church at Mapledown? I believe it is one of the oldest in England, and it is certainly one of the ugliest. Sir Henry Mountford suggested making a family business of it; but Rosalind and I were both in favour of the Abbey. We shall get much better notices in the society papers,' added Pamela, with a business-like air, as if she had been talking about the production of a new play.

'Well, dear, as I hope you are only to be married once in your life, you have a right to choose your church.'

Pamela was bitterly disappointed presently when her aunt refused to be present at her wedding.

'I will spend an hour with you on your wedding morning, and see you in your wedding-gown, if you like, Pamela; but I cannot go among a crowd of gay people, or share in any festivity. I have done with all those things, dear, for ever and ever.'

Pamela's candid eyes filled with tears. She felt all the more sorry for her aunt, because her own cup of happiness was overflowing. She looked round the silver-gray drawing-room, and her eyes fixed themselves on the piano which *he* had played, so often, so often, in the tender twilight, in the shadowy evening when that larger room was left almost without any light save that which came through the undraped archway yonder. But Castellani was no longer a person to be thought of in italics. From the moment Pamela's eyes had opened to the excellence of Mr Stuart's manly and straightforward character, they had also become aware of the Italian's deficiencies. She had realised the fact that he was a charlatan; and now she looked wonderingly at the piano, at a loss to understand the intensity of bygone emotions, and inclined to excuse herself upon the ground of youthful foolishness.

'What a silly romantic wretch I must have been!' she thought; 'a regular Rosa Matilda! As if the happiness of life depended upon one's husband having an ear for music!'

Mildred was by no means unsympathetic about the trousseau, although she herself had done with all interest in fashion and finery. She drove about to the pretty Brighton shops with Pamela, and exercised a restraining influence upon that young lady's taste, which inclined to the florid. She sympathised with the young lady's anxiety about her wedding-gown, which was to be made by a certain Mr Smithson, a *faiseur* who held potent sway over the ladies of fashionable London, and who gave himself more airs than a Prime Minister. Mr Smithson had consented to make Miss Ransome a wedding-gown – despite her social insignificance and the pressure of the season – provided that he were not worried about the affair.

'If I have too many people calling upon me, or am pestered with letters, I shall throw the thing up,' he told Lady Mountford one morning, when she took him some fine old rose-point for the petticoat. 'Yes, this lace is pretty good. I suppose you got it in Venice. I have seen Miss Ransome, and I know what kind of gown she can wear. It will be sent home the day before the wedding.'

With this assurance, haughtily given, Lady Mountford and her sister had to be contented.

'If I were your sister I would let a woman in Tottenham Court Road make my gowns rather than I would stand such treatment,' said Sir Henry; at which his wife shrugged her shoulders and told him he knew nothing about it.

'The cut is everything,' she said. 'It is worth putting up with Smithson's insolence to know that one is the best-dressed woman in the room.'

'But if Smithson dresses all the other women——'

'He doesn't. There are very few who have the courage to go to him. His manners are so humiliating – he as good as told me I had a hump – and his prices are enormous.'

'And yet you call me extravagant for giving seventy pounds for a barb!' cried Sir Henry; 'a bird that might bring me a pot of money in prizes.'

The grand question of trousseau and wedding-gown being settled, there remained only a point of minor importance – the honeymoon. Pamela was in favour of that silly season being spent in some rustic spot, far from the madding crowd, and Pamela's lover was of her opinion in everything.

'We have both seen the best part of the Continent,' said Pamela, taking tea in Mildred's upstairs sitting-room, which had assumed a brighter and more home-like aspect in her occupation than any other room in Miss Fausset's home; 'we don't want to rush off to Switzerland or the Pyrenees; we want just to enjoy each other's society and to make our plans for the future. Besides, travelling is so hideously unbecoming. I have seen brides with dusty hats and smuts on their faces who would have been miserable if they had only known what objects they were.'

'I think you and Mr Stuart are very wise in your choice, dear,' answered Mildred. 'England in July is delicious. Have you decided where to go?'

'No, we can't make up our minds. We want to find a place that is exquisitely pretty – yet not too far from London, so that we may run up to town occasionally and see about our furnishing. Sir Henry offered us Rainham, but as it is both ugly and inconvenient I unhesitatingly refused. I don't want to spend my honeymoon in a place pervaded by prize pigeons.'

'What do you think of the neighbourhood of the Thames, Pamela?' asked Mildred thoughtfully. 'Are you fond of boating?'

'Fond! I adore it. I could live all my life upon the river.'

'Really! I have been thinking that if you and Mr Stuart would like to spend your honeymoon at The Hook it is just the kind of place to suit you. The house is bright and pretty, and the gardens are exquisite.'

Pamela's face kindled with pleasure.

'But, dear aunt, you would never think——' she began.

'The place is at your service, my dear girl. It will be a pleasure for me to prepare everything for you. I cannot tell you how dearly I love that house, or how full of memories it is for me. The lease of my father's house in Parchment Street was sold after his death, and I only kept a few special things out of the furniture, but at The Hook nothing has been altered since I was a child.'

Pamela accepted the offer with rapture, and wrote an eight-page letter to her lover upon the subject, although he was coming to Brighton next day, and was to dine in Lewes Crescent. Mildred was pleased at being able to give so much pleasure to her husband's niece. It may be also that she snatched at an excuse for revisiting a spot she fondly loved.

She offered to take Pamela with her, to explore the house and gardens, and discuss any small arrangements for the bride's comfort, but against this Miss Ransome protested.

'I want everything to be new to us,' she said, 'all untrodden ground, a delicious surprise. I am sure the place is lovely; and I want to know no more about it than I know of fairyland. I haven't the faintest notion what a Hook can be in connection with the Thames. It may be a mountain or a glacier, for anything I know to the contrary; but I am assured it is delightful. Please let me know nothing more, dearest aunt, till I go there with Malcolm. It is adorable of you to hit upon such a splendid idea. And it will look very well in the society papers,' added Pamela, waxing business-like. '"Mr and Mrs Malcolm Stuart!" (O, how queer that sounds!) "are to spend their honeymoon at The Hook, the riverside residence of the bride's aunt." I wonder whether they will say "the well-known residence"?' mused Pamela.

Mildred went up to town with Miss Ransome and her betrothed at the end of the young lady's visit. Miss Fausset had been coldly gracious, after her manner, had allowed Mr Stuart to come to her house whenever he pleased, and had given up the rarely-used front drawing-room to the lovers, who sat and whispered and tittered over their own little witticisms, by the distant piano, and behaved altogether like those proverbial children of whom we are told in our childhood, who are seen but not heard. Mildred lunched in Grosvenor Gardens, and went to Chertsey by an afternoon train. The housekeeper who had once ruled over both Mr Fausset's houses, subject to interference from Bell, was now caretaker at The Hook, with a housemaid under her. She was an elderly woman, but considerably Bell's junior, and she was an admirable cook and manager. A telegram two days before had told her to expect her mistress, and the house was in perfect order when Mrs Greswold arrived in the summer twilight. All things had been made to look as if the place were in family occupation, though no one but the two servants had been living there since Mr Fausset's death. The familiar aspect of the rooms smote Mildred with a sudden unexpected pain. There were the old lamps burning on the tables, the well-remembered vases – her mother's choice, and always artistic in form and colour – filled with the old June flowers from garden and hothouse. Her father's chair stood in its old place in the bay-window in front of the table at which he used to write his letters sometimes, looking out at the river between whiles. Mrs Dawson had put a lamp in his study, a small room opening out of the drawing-room, and with windows on two sides, and both looking towards the river, which he had loved so well. The windows were open in the twilight, and the rose-garden was like a sea of bloom.

In her father's room nothing was altered. As it had been in the last days he had lived there, so it was now.

'I haven't moved so much as a penholder, ma'am,' said Dawson tearfully.

CHAPTER IX

LITERA SCRIPTA MANET

The house and grounds were in such perfect order that there was very
little to be done in the way of preparation for the honeymoon visitors.
Even the pianos had been periodically tuned, and the clocks had been
regularly wound. Two or three servants would have to be engaged for the
period, and that was all; and even this want Mrs Dawson proposed to
supply without going off the premises.

The housemaid had a sister, who was an accomplished parlourmaid
and carver; the under-gardener's eldest daughter was pining for a
preliminary canter in the kitchen, and the gardener's wife was a retired
cook, and would be delighted to take all the rougher part of the cooking,
while Mrs Dawson devoted her art to those pretty tiny kickshaws in
which she excelled. There were peaches ripening in the peach-house,
and the apricots were going to be a show. There was wine in the cellar
that would have satisfied an alderman on his honeymoon. Mildred's
business at The Hook might have been completed in a day, yet she
lingered there for a week, and still lingered on, loving the place with a
love which was mingled with pain, yet happier there than she could have
been anywhere else in the world, she thought.

The chief gardener rowed her about the river, never going very far
from home, but meandering about the summer stream, by flowery
meadows, and reedy eyots, and sometimes diverging into a tributary
stream, where the shallow water seemed only an excuse for wild flowers.
He had rowed her up and down those same streams when she was a child
with streaming hair and he was the under-gardener. He had rowed her
about in that brief summer season when Fay was her companion.

She revisited all those spots in which she had wandered with her lover.
She would land here or there along the island, and as she remembered
each particular object in the landscape, her feet seemed to grow light
again, with the lightness of joyous youth, as they touched the familiar
shore. It was almost as if her youth came back to her.

Thus it was that she lingered from day to day, loth to leave the beloved
place. She wrote frankly to her aunt, saying how much good the change
of air and scene had done her, and promising to return to Brighton in a
few days. She felt that it was her duty to resume her place beside that
fading existence; and yet it was an infinite relief to her to escape from
that dull gray house, and the dull gray life. She acknowledged to herself
that her aunt's life was a good life, full of unselfish work and large charity,
and yet there was something that repelled her, even while she admired. It
was too much like a life lived up to a certain model, adjusted line by line

to a carefully-studied plan. There was a lack of spontaneity, a sense of
perpetual effort. The benevolence which had made Enderby village like
one family in the sweet time that was gone had been of a very different
character. There had been the warmth of love and sympathy in every
kindness of George Greswold's, and there had been infinite pity for
wrong-doers. Miss Fausset's almsgiving was after the fashion of the
Pharisee of old, and it was upon the amount given that she held herself
justified before God, not upon the manner of giving.

In those quiet days, spent alone in her old home, Mildred had chosen
to occupy Mr Fausset's study rather than the large bright drawing-room.
The smaller room was more completely associated with her father. It was
here – seated in the chair before the writing-table, where she was sitting
now – that he had first talked to her of George Greswold, and had
discussed her future life, questioning his motherless girl with more than a
father's tenderness about the promptings of her own heart. She loved the
room and all that it contained for the sake of the cherished hands that
had touched these things, and the gentle life that had been lived here.
There had been but one error in his life, she thought – his treatment of
Fay.

'He ought not to have sent her away,' she thought; 'he saw us happy
together, his two daughters, and he ought not to have divided us, and
sent her away to a loveless life among strangers. If he had only been frank
and straightforward with my mother she might have forgiven all.'

Might, perhaps. Mildred was not sure upon that point; but she felt very
sure that it was her father's duty to have braved all consequences rather
than to have sent his unacknowledged child into exile. That fact of not
acknowledging her seemed in itself such a tremendous cruelty that it
intensified every lesser wrong.

Mrs Dawson understood her mistress's fancy for her father's room, and
Mildred's meals were served here, at a Sunderland-table in the bay-
window, from which she could see the boats go by, Mrs Dawson having a
profound belief in the efficacy of the boats as a cure for low spirits.

'People sometimes tell me it must be dull at The Hook,' she said; 'but,
lor! they don't know how many boats go by in summer-time. It's almost
as gay as Bond Street.'

Mildred lived alone with old memories in the flower-scented room,
where the Spanish blinds made a cool and shadowy atmosphere, while
the roses outside were steeped in sunshine. Those few days were just the
most perfect summer days of the year. She felt sorry that they had not
been reserved for Pamela's honeymoon. Such sunshine was almost wasted
on her, whose heart was so full of sadness.

It was her last afternoon at The Hook, or the afternoon which she
meant to be her last, having made up her mind to go back to Brighton

and duty on the following day, and she had a task before her, a task which she had delayed from day to day, just as she had delayed her return to her aunt.

She had to put away those special and particular objects which had belonged to her father and mother, and had been a part of their lives. These were too sacred to be left about now that strangers were to occupy the rooms of the dead. Hitherto no stranger had entered those rooms since John Fausset's death, nothing had been removed or altered. No documents relating to property or business of any kind had been kept at The Hook. Mr Fausset's affairs had all been put in perfect order after his wife's death, and there had been no ransacking for missing title-deeds or papers of any kind. It had been understood that all papers and letters of importance were either with Mr Fausset's solicitors or at the house in Parchment Street, and thus the household gods had been undisturbed in the summer retreat by the river.

Mildred had spent the morning in her mother's rooms, putting away all those dainty trifles and prettinesses which had gathered round the frivolous, luxurious life, as shells and bright-coloured weeds gather among the low rocks on the edge of the sea. She had placed everything carefully in a large closet in her mother's dressing-room, covered with much tissue-paper, secure from dust and moth; and now she began the same kind of work in her father's room, the work of removing all those objects which had been especially his: the old-fashioned silver inkstand, the well-worn scarlet morocco blotting-book, with his crest on the cover, and many inkspots on the leather lining inside, his penholders and penknives, and a little velvet pen-wiper which she had made for him when she was ten years old, and which he had kept on his table ever afterwards.

She looked round the room thoughtfully for a place of security for these treasures. She had spent a good deal of time in rearranging her father's books, which careful and conscientious dusting had reduced to a chaotic condition. Now every volume was in its place, just as *he* had kept them in the old days when it had been her delight to examine the shelves and to carry away a book of her father's choosing.

The bookcases were by Chippendale, with fretwork cornices and mahogany panelling. The lower part was devoted to cupboards, which her father had always kept under lock and key, but which she supposed to contain only old magazines, pamphlets, and newspapers, part of that vast mass of literature which is kept with a view to being looked at some day, and which finally drifts unread to the bourne of all waste paper, and is ground into pulp again, and rolls over the endless web again, and comes back upon the world printed with more intellectual food for the million of skippers and skimmers.

Yes, one of those mahogany panelled cupboards would serve Mildred's purpose admirably. She selected a key from one of the bunches in her key-box, and opened the cupboard nearest the door.

It was packed tight with *Army Lists, New Monthly Magazines*, and *Edinburgh Reviews* – packed so well that there was scarcely an interstice that would hold a pin. She opened the next cupboard. *Sporting Magazine, Blackwood, Ainsworth*, and a pile of pamphlets. No room there.

She opened the third, and found it much more loosely packed, with odd newspapers, and old Prayer Books and Bibles: shabby, old-fashioned books, which had served for the religious exercises of several generations of Faussets, and had been piously preserved by the owner of The Hook. There was room here perhaps for the things in the writing-table, if all these books and papers were rearranged and closely packed.

Mildred began her work patiently. She was in no hurry to have done with her task; it brought her nearer to her beloved dead. She worked slowly, dreamily almost, her thoughts dwelling on the days that were gone.

She took out the Prayer Books and Bibles one by one, looking at a fly-leaf now and then. John Fausset, from his loving mother, on the day of his confirmation, June 17, 1835; Lucy Jane Fausset, with her sister Maria's love, April 3, 1804; Mark Fausset, in memory of little Charlie, December 1, 1807. Such inscriptions as these touched her, with their reminiscences of vanished affection, of hearts long mingled with the dust.

She put the books on one side in a little pile on the carpet, as she knelt before the open cupboard, and then she began to move the loose litter of newspapers. The *Morning Herald,* the *Morning Chronicle*, the *Sun*. Even *these* were of the dead.

The cupboard held much more than she had expected. Behind the newspapers there were two rows of pigeons-holes, twenty-six in all, filled – choke-full, some of them – with letters, folded longwise, in a thoroughly business-like manner.

Old letters, old histories of the family heart and mind, how much they hold to stir the chords of love and pain! Mildred's hand trembled as she stretched it out to take one of those letters, idly, full of morbid curiosity about those relics of a past life.

She never knew whether it had been deliberation or hazard which guided her hand to the sixth pigeon-hole, but she thought afterwards that her eye must have been caught by a bit of red ribbon – a spot of bright colour – and that her hand followed her eye mechanically. However this may have been, the first thing that she took from the mass of divers correspondence in the twenty-six pigeon-holes was a packet of about twenty letters tied with a red ribbon.

Each letter was carefully indorsed 'M F' and a date. Some were on foreign paper, others on thick gilt-edged note. A glance at the uppermost letter showed her a familiar handwriting – her aunt's, but very different from Miss Fausset's present precise penmanship. The writing here was more hurried and irregular, bolder, larger, and more indicative of impulse and emotion.

No thought of possible wrong to her aunt entered Mildred's mind as she untied the ribbon and seated herself in a low chair in front of the bookcase, with the letters loose in her lap. What secrets could there be in a girl's letters to her elder brother which the brother's daughter might not read, nearly forty years after they were written? What could there be in that yellow paper, in that faded ink, except the pale dim ghosts of vanished fancies, and thoughts which the thinker had long outlived?

'I wonder whether my aunt would care to read these old letters?' mused Mildred. 'It would be like calling up her own ghost. She must have almost forgotten what she was like when she wrote them.'

The first letter was from Milan, full of enthusiasm about the Cathedral and the Conservatoire, full of schemes for work. She was practising six hours a day, and taking nine lessons a week – four for piano, two for singing, three for harmony. She was in high spirits, and delighted with her life.

'I should practise eight hours a day if Mrs Holmby would let me,' she wrote, 'but she won't. She says it would be too much for my health. I believe it is only because my piano annoys her. I get up at five on these summer mornings, and practise from six to half-past eight; then coffee and rolls, and off to the Conservatoire; then a drive with Mrs Holmby, who is too lazy to walk much; and then lunch. After lunch vespers at the Cathedral, and then two hours at the piano before dinner. An hour and a half between dinner and tea, which we take at nine. Sometimes one of Mrs Holmby's friends drops in to tea. You needn't be afraid: the men are all elderly, and not particularly clean. They take snuff, and their complexions are like mahogany; but there is one old man, with bristly gray hair standing out all over his head like a brush, who plays the 'cello divinely, and who reminds me of Beethoven. I am learning the "Sonate Pathétique," and I play Bach's preludes and fugues two hours a day. We went to La Scala the night before last; but I was disappointed to find they were playing a trumpery modern opera by a Milanese composer, who is all the rage here.'

Two or three letters followed, all in the same strain, and then came signs of discontent.

'I have no doubt Mrs Holmby is a highly respectable person, and I am sure you acted for the best when you chose her for my chaperon, but she is a lump of prejudice. She objects to the Cathedral. "We are fully justified in making ourselves familiar with its architectural beauties," she said, in her pedantic way, "but to attend the services of that benighted church is to worship in the groves of Baal." I told her that I had found neither groves nor idols in that magnificent church, and that the music I heard there was the only pleasure which reconciled me to the utter dulness of my life at Milan – I was going to say my life with her, but thought it better to be polite, as I am quite in her power till you come to fetch me.

'Don't think that I am tired of the Conservatoire, after teasing you so to let me come here, or even that I am home-sick. I am only tired of Mrs Holmby; and I daresay, after all, she is no worse than any other chaperon would be. As for the Conservatoire, I adore it, and I feel that I am making rapid strides in my musical education. My master is pleased with my playing of the "Pathétique," and I am to take the "Eroica" next. What a privilege it is to know Beethoven! He seems to me now like a familiar friend. I have been reading a memoir of him. What a sad life – what a glorious legacy he leaves the world which treated him so badly!

'I play Diabelli's exercises for an hour and a half every morning, before I look at any other music.'

In the next letter Mildred started at the appearance of a familiar name.

'Your kind suggestion about the Opera House has been followed, and we have taken seats at La Scala for two nights a week. Signor Castellani's opera is really very charming. I have heard it now three times, and liked it better each time. There is not much learning in the orchestration; but there is a great deal of melody all through the opera. The Milanese are mad about it. Signor Castellani came to see Mrs Holmby one evening last week, introduced by our gray-haired 'cello-player. He is a clever-looking man, about five-and-thirty, with a rather melancholy air. He writes his librettos, and is something of a poet.

'We have made a compromise about the Cathedral. I am to go to vespers if I like, as my theological opinions are not in Mrs Holmby's keeping. She will walk with me to the Cathedral, leave me at the bottom of the steps, do her shopping or take a gentle walk, and return for me when the service is over. It only lasts three-quarters of an hour, and Mrs Holmby always has shopping of some kind on her hands, as she does all her own marketing, and buys everything in the smallest quantities. I suppose by this means she makes more out of your handsome allowance for my board – or fancies she does.'

There were more letters in the same strain, and Castellani's name appeared often in relation to his operas; but there was no further mention of social intercourse. The letters grew somewhat fretful in tone, and there were repeated complaints of Mrs Holmby. There were indications of fitful spirits – now enthusiasm, now depression.

'I have at least discovered that I am no genius,' she wrote. 'When I attempt to improvise, the poverty of my ideas freezes me; and yet music with me is a passion. Those vesper services in the Cathedral are my only consolation in this great dull town.

'No, dear Jack, I am not home-sick. I have to finish my musical education. I am tired of nothing, except Mrs Holmby.'

After this there was an interval. The next letter was dated six months later. It was on a different kind of paper, and it was written from Evian, on the Lake of Geneva. Even the character of the penmanship had altered. It had lost its girlish dash, and something of its firmness. The strokes were heavier, but yet bore traces of hesitation. It was altogether a feebler style of writing.

The letter began abruptly:

'I know that you have been kind to me, John – kinder, more merciful than many brothers would have been under the same miserable circumstances; but nothing you can do can make me anything else than what I have made myself – the most wretched of creatures. When I walk about in this quiet place, alone, and see the beggars holding out their hands to me, maimed, blind, dumb perhaps, the very refuse of humanity, I feel that their misery is less than mine. *They* were not brought up to think highly of themselves, and to look down upon other people, as I was. *They* were never petted and admired as I was. They were not brought up to think honour the one thing that makes life worth living – to feel the sting of shame worse than the sting of death. They fall into raptures if I give them a franc – and all the wealth of the world would not give me one hour of happiness. You tell me to forget my misery. Forget – now! No, I have no wish to leave this place. I should be neither better nor happier anywhere else. It is very quiet here. There are no visitors left now in the neighbourhood. There is no one to wonder who I am, or why I am living alone here in my tiny villa. The days go by like a long weary dream, and there are days when the gray lake and the gray mountains are half hidden in mist, and when all Nature seems of the same colour as my own life.

'I received the books you kindly chose for me, a large parcel. There is a novel among them which tells almost my own story. It made me shed tears for the first time since you left me at Lausanne. Some people say they find a relief in tears, but my tears are not of that kind. I was ill for nearly a week after reading that story. Please don't send me any more novels. If they are about happy people they irritate me; if they are sorrowful stories they make me just a shade more wretched than I am always. If you send me books again let them be the hardest kind of reading you can get. I hear there is a good book on natural history by a man called Darwin. I should like to read that. – Gratefully and affectionately your sister.

'M F'

This letter was dated October. The next was written in November from the same address.

'No, my dear John, your fears were unfounded, I have not been ill. I wish I had been – sick unto death! I have been too wretched to write, that was all. Why should I distress you with a reiteration of my misery – and I *cannot* write, or think about anything else? I have no doubt Darwin's book is good, but I could not interest myself in it. The thought of my own misery comes between me and every page I read.

'You ask me what I mean to do with my life when my dark days are over. To that question there can but be one answer. I mean, so far as it is possible, to forget. I shall go down to my grave burdened with my dismal secret; but I shall exercise every faculty I possess to keep that secret to the end. *He* is not likely to betray me. The knowledge of his own baseness will seal his lips.

'Your suggestion of a future home in some quiet village, either in England or abroad, is kindly meant, I know, but I shudder at the mere idea of such a life. To pass as a widow; to have to answer every prying acquaintance – the doctor, the clergyman – people who would force themselves upon me, however secluded my life might be; to devote myself to a duty which in every hour of my existence would remind me of my folly and of my degradation: I should live like the galley-slave who drags his chain at every step.

'You tell me that the tie which would be a sorrow in the beginning might grow into a blessing. That could never be. You know very little of a woman's nature when you suggest such a possibility. What *can* your sex know of a woman's agony under such circumstances as mine? *You* are never made to feel the sting of dishonour.'

A light began to dawn on Mildred as she read this second letter from Evian. The first might mean anything – an engagement broken off, a proud girl jilted by a worthless lover, the sense of degradation that a woman feels in having loved unwisely – in having wasted confidence and affection upon an unworthy object: Mildred had so interpreted that despairing letter. But the second revealed a deeper wound, a darker misery.

There were sentences that stood out from the context with unmistakable meaning. 'When my dark days are over' – 'to pass as a widow' – 'to devote myself to a duty which would remind me of my folly and my degradation.'

That suggestion of a secluded life – of a care which should grow into a blessing – could mean only one thing. The wretched girl who wrote that letter was about to become a mother, under conditions which meant life-long dishonour.

White as marble, and with hands that trembled convulsively as they held the letter, Mildred Greswold read on, hurriedly, eagerly, breathlessly, to the last line of the last letter. She had no scruples, no sense of wrong-doing. The secret hidden in that little packet of letters was a secret which she had a right to know – she above all other people, she who had been cheated and fooled by false imaginings.

The third letter from Evian was dated late in January:

'I have been very ill – dangerously, I believe – but my doctor took unnecessary trouble to cure me. I am now able to go out of doors again, and I walk by the lake for half-an-hour every day in the morning sun. The child thrives wonderfully, I am told; but if there is to be a change of nurses, as there must be – for this woman here must lose sight of her charge and of me when I leave this place – the change cannot be made too soon. If Boulogne is really the best place you can think of, your plan would be to meet me with the nurse at Dijon, where we can take the rail. We shall post from here to that town. I am very sorry to inflict so much trouble upon you, but it is a part of my misery to be a burden to you as well as to myself. When once this incubus is safely disposed of, I shall be less troublesome to you.

'No, my dear John, there is no relenting, no awakening of maternal love. For me that must remain for ever a meaningless phrase. For me there can be nothing now or ever more, except a sense of aversion and horror – a shrinking from the very image of the child that must never call me mother, or know the link between us. All that can possibly be done to sever that link I shall do; and I entreat you, by the love of past years, to help me in so doing. My only chance of peace in the future is in total severance. Remember that I am prepared to make any sacrifice that can secure the happiness of this wretched being, that can make up to her——'

'That can make up to *her!*'

Mildred's clutch tightened upon the letter. This was the first mention of the infant's sex.

'——For the dishonour to which she is born. I will gladly devote half my fortune to her maintenance and her future establishment in life, if she should grow up and marry. Remember also that I have sworn to myself never to entertain any proposal of marriage, never to listen to words of love from any man upon earth. You need have no fear of future embarrassment on my account. I shall never give a man the right to interrogate my past life. I resign myself to a solitary existence – but not to a life clouded with shame. When I go back to England and resume my place in society, I shall try to think of this last year of agony as if it were a bad dream. You alone know my secret, and you can help me if you will. My prayer is that from the hour I see the child transferred to the new nurse at Dijon, I shall never look upon its face again. The nurse can go back to her home as fast as the train will carry her, and I can go back to London with you.'

The next letter was written seven years later, and addressed from Kensington Gore:

'I suppose I ought to answer your long letter by saying that I am glad the child has good health, that I rejoice in her welfare, and so on. But I cannot be such a hypocrite. It hurts me to write about her; it hurts me to think of her. My heart hardens itself against her at every suggestion of her quickness, or her prettiness, or any other merit. To me she can be nothing except – disgrace. I burnt your letter the instant it was read. I felt as if some one was looking over my shoulder as I read it. I dared not go down to lunch for fear Mrs Winstanley's searching eyes should read my secret in my face. I pretended a headache, and stayed in my room till our eight-o'clock dinner, when I knew I should be safe in the dim religious light which my chaperon affects as the most flattering to wrinkles and pearl-powder.

'But I am not ungrateful, my dear John. I am touched even by your kindly interest in that unfortunate waif. I have no doubt you have done wisely in placing her with the good old lady at Barnes, and that she is very happy running about the Common. I am glad I know where she is, so that I may never drive that way, if I can possibly help it. Your old lady must be rather a foolish woman, I should think, to change Fanny into Fay, on the strength of the child's airy movements and elfin appearance; but as long as this person knows nothing of her charge's history her silliness cannot matter.'

A letter of a later date was addressed from Lewes Crescent.

'I am horrified at what you have done. O, John, how could you be so reckless, so forgetful of my reiterated entreaties to keep that girl's existence wide apart from mine or yours? And you have actually introduced her into your own house as a relation; and you actually allow her to be called by your name! Was ever such madness? You stultify all that has been done in the past. You open the door to questionings and conjectures of the most dreadful kind. No, I will not see her. You must be mad to suggest such a thing. My feeling about her to-day is exactly the same as my feeling on the day she was born – disgust, horror, dread. I will never – willingly – look upon her face.

'Do you remember those words in *Bleak House?* "Your mother, Esther, is your disgrace, and you were hers." So it is with that girl and me. Can love be possible where there is this mutual disgrace?

'For God's sake, get the girl out of your house as soon as you can! Send her to some good school abroad – France, Germany, where you like, and save me from the possibility of discovery. My secret has been kept – my friends look up to me. I have outlived the worst part of my misery, and have learnt to take some interest in life. I could not survive the discovery of my wretched story.'

A later letter was briefer and more business-like.

'I fully concur in the settlement you propose, and would as willingly make the sum 40,000*l.* as 30,000*l.* Remember that, so far as money can go, I am anxious to do the *uttermost.* I hope she will marry soon, and marry well, and that she may lead a happy and honourable life under a new name – a name that she can bear without a blush. I should be much relieved if she could continue to live abroad.'

This was the last letter in the bundle tied with red ribbon. In the same pigeon-hole Mildred found the draft of a deed of gift, transferring 30,000*l.* India Stock to Fanny Fausset, otherwise Vivien Faux, on her twenty-first birthday, and with the draft there were several letters from a firm of solicitors in Lincoln's Inn Fields relating to the same deed of gift.

The last of the letters fell from Mildred's lap as she sat with her hands clasped before her face, dazed by this sudden light which altered the aspect of her life.

'Fool, fool, fool!' she cried.

The thought of all she had suffered, and of the suffering she had inflicted on the man she loved, almost maddened her. She had condemned her father – her generous, noble-hearted father – upon evidence that had seemed to her incontrovertible. She had believed in a stain upon that honourable life – had believed him a sinner and a coward. And Miss Fausset knew all that she had forfeited by that fatal misapprehension, and yet kept her shameful secret, caring for her own reputation more than for two blighted lives.

She remembered how she had appealed to her aunt to solve the mystery of Fay's parentage, and how deliberately Miss Fausset had declared her ignorance. She had advised her niece to go back to her husband, but that was all.

Mildred gathered the letters together, tied them with the faded ribbon, and then went to her father's writing-table and wrote these lines, in a hand that trembled with indignation:

'I know all the enclosed letters can tell me. You have kept your secret at the hazard of breaking two hearts. I know not if the wrong you have done me can ever be set right; but this I know, that I shall never again enter your house, or look upon your face, if I can help it. I am going back to my husband, never again to leave him, if he will let me stay.

'MILDRED GRESWOLD.'

She packed the letters securely in one of the large banker's envelopes out of her father's desk. She sealed the packet with her father's crest, intending to register and post it with her own hands on her way to Romsey; and then, with a heart that beat with almost suffocating force, she consulted the time-table, and tried to match trains between Reading and Basingstoke.

There was a train from Chertsey to Reading at five. She might catch that and be home – home – home – how the word thrilled her! some time before midnight. She would have gone back if it had been to arrive in the dead of night.

CHAPTER X

MARKED BY FATE

It was nearly ten o'clock when Mildred drove through the village of Enderby, and saw the lights burning in the familiar cottage windows, the post-office, and the little fancy shop where Lola had been so constant a purchaser in the days gone by. Her eyes were full of tears as she looked at the humble street: happy tears, for her heart thrilled with hope as she drew near home.

'He cannot withhold his forgiveness,' she told herself. 'He knows that I acted for conscience' sake.'

Five minutes more and she was standing in the hall, questioning the footman, who stared at her with a bewildered air, as the most unexpected of visitors.

'Is your master at home?' she asked.

'Yes, ma'am, master's in the library. Shall I announce you?'

'No, no – I can find him. Help my maid to take my things to my room.'

'Yes, ma'am. Have you dined, or shall I tell cook to get something ready?'

'No, no. I have dined,' she answered hurriedly, and went on to the library, to that very room in which she had made the fatal discovery of Fay's identity with her husband's first wife.

He was sitting in the lamp-light, just as he was sitting that night when she fell fainting at his feet. The windows were open to the summer night, books were scattered about on the table, and heaped on the floor by his side. Whatever comfort there may be in such company, he had surrounded himself with that comfort. He took no notice of the opening of the door, and she was kneeling at his feet before he knew that she was in the room.

'Mildred, what does this mean? Have we not parted often enough?'

'There was no reason for our parting – except my mistaken belief. I am here to stay with you till my death, if you will have me, George. Be merciful to me, my dearest! I have acted for conscience' sake. I have been fooled, deluded by appearances which might have deceived any one, however wise. Forgive me, George; forgive me for the sake of all I have suffered in doing what I thought to be my duty!'

He lifted her from her knees, took her to his heart without a word, and kissed her. There was a silence of some moments, in which each could hear the throbbing of the other's heart.

'You were wrong after all, then,' he said at last; 'Vivien was not your half-sister?'

'She was not.'

'Whose child was she?'

'You must not ask me that, George. It is a secret which I ought not to tell even to you. She was cruelly used, poor girl, more cruelly even than I thought she had been when I believed she was my father's daughter. I have undeniable evidence as to her parentage. She was my blood-relation, but she was not my sister.'

'How did you make the discovery?'

'By accident – this afternoon at The Hook. I found some papers and letters of my father's in a cupboard below the bookcase. I knew nothing of their existence – should never have thought of searching for private papers there, for I had heard my father often say that he kept only magazines and pamphlets – things he called rubbish – in those cupboards. I wanted to put away some things, and I stumbled on a packet of letters which revealed the secret of Fay's birth. I can come back to my duty with a clear conscience. May I stay with you, George?'

'May you? Well, yes; I suppose so,' with another kiss and a tender little laugh. 'One cannot make a broken vase new again, but we may pick up the pieces and stick them together again somehow. You have taken a good many years out of my life, Mildred, and I doubt if you can give them back to me. I feel twenty years older than I felt before the beginning of this trouble; but now all is known, and you are my wife again – well, there may be a few years of gladness for us yet. We will make the most of them.'

All things dropped back into the old grooves at Enderby Manor. Mrs Greswold and her husband were seen together at church on the Sunday morning after Mildred's return, much to the astonishment of the congregation, who immediately began to disbelieve in all their own convictions and assertions of the past half-year, and to opine that the lady had only been in the South for her health, more especially as it was known that Miss Ransome had been her travelling companion.

'If she had quarrelled with her husband, she would hardly have had her husband's niece with her all the time,' said Mrs Porter, the doctor's wife.

'But if there was no quarrel, why did he shut himself up like a hermit, and look so wretched if one happened to meet him?' asked somebody else.

'Well, there she is, anyhow, and she looks out of health, so you may depend some London physician ordered her abroad. They might as well have consulted Porter, who ought to know her constitution by this time. He'd have ordered her to Ventnor for the winter, and saved them both a good deal of trouble; but there, people never think they can be cured without going to Cavendish Square.'

Mildred's strength seemed to fail her more in the happiness of that unhoped-for reunion than it had ever done during her banishment. She wanted to do so much at Enderby: to visit about among her shabby-genteel old ladies and her cottagers as in the cloudless time before Lola's death; to superintend her garden; to visit old friends whose faces were endeared by fond association with the past; to be everywhere with her husband: walking with him in the copses, riding about the farms, and on the edge of the forest, in the dewy summer mornings. She wanted to do all these things, and she found that her strength would not let her.

'I hope that my health is not going to give way, just when I am so happy,' she said to her husband one day, when she felt almost fainting after their morning ride.

He took alarm instantly, and sent off for Mr Porter, though Mildred made light of her feelings next moment. The family practitioner sounded her with the usual professional gravity, but his face grew more serious as he listened to the beating of her heart. He affected, however, to think very little of her ailments, talked of nerves, and suggested bromide of something, as if it were infallible; but when George Greswold went out into the hall with him he owned that all was not right.

'The heart is weak,' he said. 'I hope there may be no organic mischief, but——'

'You mean that I shall lose her,' interrupted Greswold, in a husky whisper.

His own heart was beating like the tolling of a church bell – beating with the dull, heavy stroke of despair.

'No, no. I don't think there's any immediate danger, but I should like you to take higher advice – Clark or Jenner, perhaps?'

'Of course. I will send for some one at once.'

'The very thing to alarm her. She ought to be kept free from all possible anxiety or excitement. Don't let her ride – except in the quietest way – or walk far enough to fatigue herself. You might take her up to town for a few days on the pretence of seeing picture-galleries or something, and then coax her to consult a physician, just for *your* satisfaction. Make as light as you can of her complaint.'

'Yes, yes. I understand. O, God, that it should be so, after all; when I thought I had come to the end of sorrow!' This in an undertone. 'For pity's sake, Porter, tell me the worst! You think it a bad case?'

Porter shook his head, tried to speak, grasped George Greswold's hand, and made for the door. Mr and Mrs Greswold had been his patients and friends for the last fifteen years, and in his rough way he was devoted to them.

'See Jenner as soon as you can,' he said. 'It is a very delicate case. I would rather not hazard an opinion.'

George Greswold went out to the lawn where he had sat on the Sunday evening before Lola's death. It had been summer then, and it was summer now – the time of roses, before the song of the nightingale had ceased amidst the seclusion of twilit branches. He sat down upon the bench under the cedar, and gave himself up to his despair. He had tasted again the sweet cup of domestic peace – he had been gladdened again by the only companionship that had ever filled his heart, and now in the near future he saw the prospect of another parting, and this time without hope on earth. Once again he told himself that he was marked out by Fate.

'I suppose it must always be so,' he thought; 'in the lots that fall from the urn there must be some that are all of one colour – black – black as night.'

Mildred came out to the lawn with him, followed by Kassandra, who had deserted the master for the mistress since her return, as if in a delight mixed with fear lest she should again depart.

'What has become of you, George? I thought you were coming back to the morning-room directly, and it is nearly an hour since Mr Porter went away.'

'I came into the garden – to – to see your new shrubbery.'

'Did you really? how good of you! It is hardly to be called a new shrubbery – only a little addition to the old one. It will give an idea of distance when the shrubs are good enough to grow tall and thick. Will you come with me and tell me what you think of it?'

'Gladly, dear, if it will not tire you.'

'Tire me to walk to the shubbery! No, I am not quite so bad as that, though I find I am a bad walker compared with what I used to be. I daresay I am out of training. I could walk any distance at Brighton last autumn. A long walk on the road to Rottingdean was my only distraction; but at Pallanza I began to flag, and the hotel people were always suggesting drives, so I got out of the habit of walking.'

He had his hand through her arm, and drew her near him as they sauntered across the lawn, with a hopeless wonder at the thought that she was here at his side, close to his heart, all in all to him to-day, and that the time might soon come when she would have melted out of his life as that fair daughter had done, when the grave under the tree should mean a double desolation, an everlasting despair.

'Is there *any* world where we shall be together again?' he asked himself. 'What is immortality worth to me if it does not mean reunion? To go round upon the endless wheel of eternity, to be fixed into the universal life, to be a part of the Creator Himself! Nothing in a life to come can be gain to me if it do not give me back what I have lost.'

They dawdled about the shrubbery, man and wife, arm linked with arm, looking at the new plantings one by one; she speculating how many years each tree would take to come to perfection.

'They will make a very good effect in three or four years, George. Don't you think so? That *Picea nobilis* will fill the open space yonder. We have allowed ten feet clear on every side. The golden brooms grow only too quickly. How serious you look! Are you thinking of anything that makes you anxious?'

'I am thinking of Pamela and her sweetheart. I should like to make Lady Lochinvar's acquaintance before the marriage.'

'Shall I ask her here?'

'She could hardly come, I fancy, while the wedding is on the *tapis*. I propose that you and I should go up to London to-morrow, put up at our old hotel – we shall be more independent there than at Grosvenor Gardens – and spend a few days quietly, seeing a good deal of the picture-galleries, and a little of our new connections – and of Rosalind and her husband, whom we don't often see. Would you like to do that, Mildred?'

'I like anything you like. I delight in seeing pictures with you, and I shall be glad to see Rosalind; and if Pamela really wishes us to be present at her wedding, I think we ought to be there, don't you, George?'

'If you would like it dearest; if——'

He left the sentence unfinished, fearing to betray his apprehension. Till he had consulted the highest authorities in the land he felt that he could know but little of that hidden malady which paled her cheek and gave heaviness to the pathetic eyes.

They were in Cavendish Square, husband and wife, on the morning after their arrival in town, by special appointment with the physician. Mildred submitted meekly to a careful consultation – only for his own satisfaction, her husband told her, making light of his anxiety.

'I want you to be governed by the best possible advice, dearest, in the care of your health.'

'You don't think there is danger, George; that I am to be taken away from you, just when all our secrets and sorrows are over?'

'Indeed, no, dearest! God grant you may be spared to me for many happy years to come!'

'There is no reason, I think, that it should not be so. Mr Porter said my complaint was chiefly nervous. He would not wonder at my nerves being in a poor way if he knew how I suffered in those bitter days of banishment.'

The examination was long and serious, yet conducted by the physician with such gentle *bonhomie* as not to alarm the patient. When it was over, he dismissed her with a kindly smile, after advice given upon very broad lines.

'After the question of diet, which I have written for you here,' he said, handing her half a sheet of paper, 'the only other treatment I can counsel is self-indulgence. Never walk far enough to feel tired, or fast enough to be out of breath. Live as much as possible in the open air, but let your life out of doors be the sweet idleness of the sunny South, rather than our ideal bustling, hurrying British existence. Court repose – tranquillity for body and mind in all things.'

'You mean that I am to be an invalid for the rest of my life, as my poor mother was for five years before her death?'

'At what age did your mother die?'

'Thirty-four. For a long time the doctors would hardly say what was the matter with her. She suffered terribly from palpitation of the heart, as I have done for the last six months; but the doctors made light of it, and told my father there was very little amiss. Towards the end they changed their opinion, and owned that there was organic disease. Nothing they could do for her seemed of much use.'

Mildred went back to the waiting-room while her husband had an interview with the doctor; an interview which left him but the faintest hope – only the hope of prolonging a fading life.

'She may last for years, perhaps,' said the physician, pitying the husband's silent agony, 'but it would be idle to disguise her state. She will never be strong again. She must not ride, or drive, or occupy herself in any way that can involve violent exertion, or a shock to the nerves. Cherish her as a hothouse flower, and she may be with you for some time yet.'

'God bless you, even for that hope,' said Greswold, and then he spoke of his niece's wedding, and the wish for Mildred's presence.

'No harm in a wedding, I think, if you are careful of her: no over-exertion, no agitating scenes. The wedding may cheer her, and prevent her brooding on her own state. Good-day. I shall be glad to know the effect of my prescription, and to see Mrs Greswold again in a month or two, if she is strong enough to come to London. If you want me at any time in the country——'

'You will come, will you not? Remember she is all that is precious to me upon this earth. If I lose her I lose everything.'

'Send for me at any time. If it is possible for me to go to you I will go.'

CHAPTER XI

LIKE A TALE THAT IS TOLD

Pamela's wedding was one of the most successful functions of the London season; and the society papers described the ceremony with a fulness of detail which satisfied even the bride's avidity for social fame. Mr Smithson sent her gown just an hour before it had to make its reverence before the altar in the Abbey; and Pamela, who had been in an almost hysterical agony for an hour-and-a-half, lest she should have no gown in which to be married, owned, as she pirouetted before the cheval-glass, that the fit was worth the suspense.

The ladies who write fashion articles in the two social arbiters were rapturous about Mr Smithson's *chef-d'oeuvre*, and gave glowing accounts of certain trousseau gowns which they had been privileged to review at an afternoon tea in Grosvenor Gardens a week before the event. Pamela's delight in these paragraphs was intensified by the idea that César Castellani would read them, though it is hardly likely that listless skimmer of modern literature went so deep as fashion articles.

'He will see at least that if he had married me he would not have married quite a nobody,' said Pamela, in a summer reverie upon the blue water in front of The Hook, where she and her husband dawdled about in a punt nearly all day, expatiating upon each other's merits. And so floats this light bark gaily into a safe and placid haven, out of reach of privateer or pirate such as the incomparable Castellani.

It was not until after Pamela's wedding, and nearly a month after Mildred's discovery of the letters in the bookcase, that Miss Fausset made any sign; but one August morning her reply came in the shape of a letter, entreating Mildred to go to her, as an act of charity to one whose sands had nearly run out.

'I will not sue to you *in formâ pauperis*,' she wrote, 'so I do not pretend that I am a dying woman; but I believe I have not very long to live, and before my voice is mute upon earth I want to tell you the history of one year of my girlhood. I want you to know that I am not altogether the kind of sinner you may think me. I will not write that history, and if you refuse to come to me, I must die and leave it untold, and in that case my death-bed will be miserable.'

Mildred's gentle heart could not harden itself against such an appeal as this. She told her husband only that her aunt was very ill and ardently desired to see her; and after some discussion it was arranged that she should travel quietly to Brighton, he going with her. He suggested that they should stop in Miss Fausset's house for a night or two, but Mildred told him she would much prefer to stay at an hotel; so it was decided that they should put up at the quiet hotel on the East Cliff, where Mr Greswold had taken Pamela nearly a year before.

Mildred's health had improved under the physician's *régime*; and her husband felt hopeful as they travelled together through the summer landscape, by that line which she had travelled in her desolation – the level landscape with glimpses of blue sea and stretches of gray beach or yellow sand, bright in the August noontide.

George Greswold had respected Mildred's reserve, and had never urged her to enlighten him as to the secret of his first wife's parentage; but he had his ideas upon the subject, and, remembering his interview with the solicitor and that gentleman's perturbation at the name of Fausset, he was inclined to think that the pious lady of Lewes Crescent might not be unconcerned in the mystery. And now this summons to Brighton seemed to confirm his suspicions.

He went no further than Miss Fausset's threshold, and allowed his wife to go to her aunt alone.

'I shall walk up and down and wait till you come out again,' he said, 'so I hope that you won't stay too long.'

He was anxious to limit an interview which might involve agitation for Mildred. He parted from her almost reluctantly at the doorway of the gloomy house, with its entrance-hall of the pattern of forty years ago, furnished with barometer, umbrella-stand, and tall chairs, all in Spanish mahogany, and with never a picture or a bust, bronze or porcelain, to give light and colour to the scene.

Miss Fausset had changed for the worse even in the brief interval since Mildred had last seen her. She was sitting in the back drawing-room as usual, but her table and chair had been wheeled into the bay-window, which commanded a garden with a single tree and a variety of house-tops and dead walls.

'So you have come,' she said, without any form of greeting. 'I hardly expected so much from you. Sit down there, if you please. I have a good deal to tell you.'

'I had intended never to enter your house again, aunt. But I could not refuse to hear anything you have to say in your own justification. Only there is one act of yours which you can never justify – either to me or to God.'

'What is that, pray?'

'Your refusal to tell me the secret of Fay's birth, when my happiness and my husband's depended upon my knowing it.'

'To tell you that would have been to betray my own secret. Do you think, after keeping it for nine-and-thirty years, I was likely to surrender it lightly? I would sooner have cut my tongue out. I did what I could for you. I told you to ignore idle prejudice and go back to your husband. I told you what was due from you to him, over and above all sanctimonious scruples. You would not listen to me, and whatever misery you have suffered has been misery of your own creation.'

'Do not let us talk any more about it, aunt. I can never think differently about the wrong you have done me. Had I not found those letters — by the merest accident, remember — I might have gone down to my grave a desolate woman. I might have died in a foreign land, far away from the only voice that could comfort me in my last hours. No; my opinion of your guilty silence can never change. You were willing to break two hearts rather than hazard your own reputation; and yet you must have known that I would keep your secret, that I should sympathise with the sorrow of your girlhood,' added Mildred, in softened tones.

Miss Fausset was slow in replying. Mildred's reproaches fell almost unheeded upon her ear. It was of herself she was thinking, with all the egotism engendered by a lonely old age, without ties of kindred or friendship, with no society but that of flatterers and parasites.

'I asked you if you had found any letters of your father's relating to that unhappy girl,' she said. 'I always feared his habit of keeping letters — a habit he learnt from my father. Yet I hoped that he would have burnt mine, knowing, as he did, that the one desire of my life was to obliterate that hideous past. Vain hope. I was like the ostrich. If I hid my secret in England, it was known in Italy. The man who destroyed my life was a traitor to the core of his heart, and he betrayed me to his son. He told César how he had fascinated a rich English girl, and fooled her with a mock marriage; and fifteen years ago the young man presented himself to me with the full knowledge of that dark blot upon my life — to me, here, where I had held my head so high. He let me know the full extent of his knowledge in his own subtle fashion; but he always treated me with profound respect — he pretended to be fond of me; and, God help me, there was a charm for me in the very sound of his voice. The man who cheated me out of my life's happiness was lying in his grave: death lessens the bitterness of hatred, and I could not forget that I had once loved him.'

The tears gathered slowly in the cold gray eyes, and rolled slowly down the hollow cheeks.

'Yes, I loved him, Mildred — loved him with a foolish, inexperienced girl's romantic love. I asked no questions. I believed all he told me. I flung myself blindfold into the net. His genius, his grace, his fire — ah, you can never imagine the charm of *his* manner, the variety of his talent, compared with which his son's accomplishments are paltry. You see me now a hard, elderly woman. As a girl I was warm-hearted and impetuous, full of enthusiasm and imagination, while I loved and

believed in my lover. My whole nature changed after that great wrong –
my heart was frozen.'

There was a silence of some moments, and then Miss Fausset
continued in short agitated sentences, her fingers fidgeting nervously
with the double eye-glass which she wore on a slender gold chain:

'It was his genius I worshipped. He was at the height of his success. The
Milanese raved about him as a rival to Donizetti; his operas were the rage.
Can you wonder that I, a girl passionately fond of music, was carried away
by the excitement which was in the very air I breathed? I went to the
opera night after night. I heard that fascinating music till its melodies
seemed interwoven with my being. I suppose I was weak enough to let
the composer see how much I admired him. He had quarrelled with his
wife; and the quarrel – caused by his own misconduct – had resulted in a
separation which was supposed to be permanent. There may have been
people in Milan who knew that he was a married man, but my chaperon
did not; and he was careful to suppress the fact from the beginning of our
acquaintance.

'Yes, no doubt he found out that I was madly in love with him. He
pretended to be interested in my musical studies. He advised and taught
me. He played the violin divinely, and we used to play *concertante* duets
during the long evenings, while my chaperon dozed by the fire, caring
very little how I amused myself, so long as I did not interfere with her
comfort. She was a sensual, selfish creature, given over to self-indulgence,
and she let me have my own way in everything. He used to join me at
the Cathedral at vespers. How my heart thrilled when I found him there,
sitting in the shadowy chancel in the gray November light! for I knew it
was for my sake he went there, not from any religious feeling. Our hands
used to meet and clasp each other almost unconsciously when the music
moved us as it went soaring up to the gorgeous roof, in the dim light of
the hanging lamps before the altar. I have found myself kneeling with my
hand in his when I came out of a dream of Paradise to which that
exquisite music had lifted me. Yes, I loved him, Mildred; I loved him as
well as ever you loved your husband – as passionately and unselfishly as
woman ever loved. I rejoiced in the thought that I was rich, for his sake. I
planned the life that we were to live together; a life in which I was to be
subordinate to him in all things – his adoring slave. I suppose most girls
have some such dream. God help them, when it ends as mine did!'

Again there was a silence – a chilling muteness upon Mildred's part.
How could she be sorry for this woman who had never been sorry for
others; who had let her child travel from the cradle to the grave without
one ray of maternal love to light her dismal journey! She remembered
Fay's desolate life and blighted nature – Fay, who had a heart large
enough for a great unselfish love. She remembered her aunt's

impenetrable silence when a word would have restored happiness to a ruined home; she remembered, and her heart was hardened against this proud, selfish woman, whose life had been one long sacrifice to the world's opinion.

'I loved him, Mildred, and I trusted him as I would have trusted any man who had the right to call himself a gentleman,' pursued Miss Fausset, eager to justify herself in the face of that implacable silence. 'I had been brought up, after the fashion of those days, in a state of primeval innocence. I had never, even in fiction, been allowed to come face to face with the cruel realities of life. I was educated in an age which thought *Jane Eyre* an improper novel, and which restricted a young woman's education to music and modern languages; the latter taught so badly, for the most part, as to be useless when she travelled. My knowledge of Italian would just enable me to translate a libretto when I had it before me in print, or to ask my way in the streets; but it was hardly enough to make me understand the answer. It never entered into my mind to doubt Paolo Castellani when he told me that, although we could not, as Papist and Protestant, be married in any church in Milan, we could be united by a civil marriage before a Milanese authority, and that such a marriage would be binding all the world over. Had I been a poor girl I might of my own instinct have suspected treachery; but I was rich and he was poor, and he would be a gainer by our marriage. Servants and governesses had impressed me with the sense of my own importance, and I knew that I was what is called a good match. So I fell into the trap, Mildred, as foolishly as a snared bird. I crept out of the house one morning after my music-lesson, found my lover waiting for me with a carriage close by, went with him to a dingy office in a dingy street, but which had a sufficient official air to satisfy my ignorance, and went through a certain formula, hearing something read over by an elderly man of grave appearance, and signing my name to a document after Paolo had signed his.

'It was all a sham and a cheat, Mildred. The old man was a Milanese attorney, with no more power to marry us than he had to make us immortal. The paper was a deed-of-gift by which Paolo Castellani transferred some imaginary property to me. The whole thing was a farce; but it was so cleverly planned that the cheat was effected without the aid of an accomplice. The old man acted in all good faith, and my blind confidence and ignorance of Italian accepted a common legal formality as a marriage. I went from that dark little office into the spring sunshine happy as ever bride went out of church, kissed and complimented by a throng of approving friends. I cared very little as to what my brother might think of this clandestine marriage. He would have refused his consent beforehand, no doubt, but he would reconcile himself to the inevitable by and by. In any event, I should be independent of his control. My fortune would be at my own disposal after my one-and-twentieth birthday – mine, to throw into my husband's lap.

'That is nearly the end of my story, Mildred. We went from Milan to Como, and after a few days at Bellagio crossed to St Gothard, and sauntered from one lovely scene to another till we stopped at Vevay. For just six weeks I lived in a fool's paradise; but by that time my brother had traced us to Vevay – having learnt all that could be learnt about Castellani at Milan before he started in pursuit of us. He came, and my dream ended. I knew that I was a dishonoured woman, and that all my education, my innate pride in myself, and my fortune had done for me, was to place me as low as the lowest creature in the land. I left Vevay within an hour of that revelation a broken-hearted woman. I never saw my destroyer's face again. You know all, Mildred, now. Can you wonder that I shrank with abhorrence from the offspring of my disgrace – that I refused ever to see her after I had once released myself from the hateful tie?'

'Yes, I do wonder; I must always wonder that you were merciless to her – that you had no pity for that innocent life.'

'Ah, you are your father's daughter. He wished me to hide myself in some remote village so that I might taste the sweets of maternal affection, enjoy the blessed privilege of rearing a child who at every instant of her life would remind me of the miserable infatuation that had blighted my own. No, Mildred, I was not made for such an existence as that. I have tried to do good to others; I have laboured for God's Church and God's poor. That has been my atonement.'

'It would have been a better atonement to have cared for your own flesh and blood; but with your means and opportunities you might have done both. I loved Fay, remember, aunt. I cannot forget how bright and happy she might have been. I cannot forget the wrongs that warped her nature.'

'You are very hard, Mildred, hard to a woman whose days are numbered.'

'Are not my days numbered, aunt?' cried Mildred, with a sudden burst of passion. 'Was not my heart broken when I left this house last year to go into loneliness and exile, abandoning a husband I adored? That parting was my death-blow. In all the long dreary days that have gone by since then my hold upon life has been loosening. You might have saved me that agony. You might have sent me back to my home rejoicing – and you would not. You cared more for your own pride than for my happiness. You might have made your daughter's life happy – and you would not. You cared more for the world's esteem than for her welfare. As you sacrificed her, your daughter, you have sacrificed me, your niece.

I know that I am doomed. Just when God has given me back the love that makes life precious, I feel the hand of death upon me, and know that the hour of parting is near.'

'I have been a sinner, Mildred; but I have suffered – I have suffered. You ought not to judge me. You have never known shame.'

That last appeal softened Mildred's heart. She went over to her aunt's chair, and leant over her and kissed her.

'Let the past be forgotten,' she said, 'and let us part in love.'

And so, a quarter of an hour later, they parted, never to meet again on earth.

Miss Fausset died in the early winter, cut off by the first frost, like a delicate flower. She had made no change in the disposal of her property, and her death made Mildred Greswold a very rich woman.

'My aunt loved the poor,' said Mildred, when she and her husband spoke of this increase of wealth. 'We are both so much richer than our needs, George. We have lived in sunshine for the most part. When I am gone I should like you to do some great thing for those who live in shadow.'

'My beloved, I shall remain upon this earth only to obey your will.'

He lived just long enough to keep his promise. The Greswold Hospital remains, a monument of thoughtful beneficence, in one of the most wretched neighbourhoods south of the Thames; but George Greswold and his race are ended like a tale that is told.

César Castellani, enriched by a legacy from Miss Fausset, contrives still to flourish, and still to wear a gardenia in the button-hole of an artistic coat; but fashions change quickly in the realm of light literature, and the star of the author of *Nepenthe* is sunk in the oblivion that engulfs ephemeral reputations. Castellani is still received in certain drawing-rooms; but it is in the silly circles alone that he is believed in as a man who has only missed greatness because he is too much of an artist to be a steadfast worker.

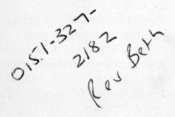